A Quick Overview of Book Chapters

Chapter 1 Microsoft Windows Vista Operating System..........................19-72

Chapter 2 Microsoft Windows Vista New Features...............................74-134

Chapter 3 Microsoft Internet Explorer 7.0...136-161

Chapter 4 Microsoft Control Panel Applets..163-224

Chapter 5 Group Policy Object Editor...226-247

Chapter 6 Microsoft Windows Vista Administrative Tools.......................249-285

Chapter 7 Keyboard Shortcuts...287-296

Glossary..297-301

Copyrights

BookSurge Publishing

7290 B Investment Drive

North Charleston, SC 29418

Dedication Page

This book is dedicated to my family members, father - Mohammad Mahroof-Tahir, mother - Hanif Jan, sisters - Bilquees Mahroof, Taqdees Mahroof, and Tahseen Mahroof, brother - Nasir Khan, brother-in-law, Masood Sabir, and grandmother - Karam Jan. Also, many thanks to my friends and beloved family members who contributed a lot to publish this book.

About Author

The author has been working in the field of information technology in different universities of United States of America. He has been involved in computer imaging processes, deploying security patches for servers, troubleshooting network (LAN, WAN, Wireless) technologies, fixing hardware and software related issues and documenting them on daily basis, and offering information technology related workshops at different educational institutions. The author holds A+ certification, Network+ certification, and MCTS (Microsoft Certified Technology Specialist) certification in addition to his degree in information technology and minor in Statistics.

Introduction

This book is written to understand Microsoft Windows Vista operating system in depth. This book is consisting of 7 chapters. Each chapter is consisting of necessary topics to cover all aspects of Windows Vista.

Chapter 1 provides step by step instructions to install an upgrade/fresh copy of Windows Vista, comparison of Windows Vista versions, and steps to downgrade your system from Windows Vista to Windows XP, if necessary.

Chapter 2 guides you through to measure the performance of hardware components, steps to install Parental Controls for your family members to keep track of computer usage while you are at work, steps to install and configure Windows Defender to protect your system against spywares, and unwanted software that can be installed on your computer without your consent, steps to encrypt system drive to enhance overall system security, manage and monitor computer resources with adding gadgets to the Windows Sidebar, increase system performance with adding non-volatile flash memory, view list of pre-installed hidden Windows programs, invite users to work online using Windows Meeting Space, diagnose memory errors using memory diagnostics tool, perform complete PC backup and restore backup if system crashes unexpectedly, customize power settings, adjust power button, manage all e-mail accounts using Windows Mail, manage contact list using Windows Contact, report an application issue to Microsoft to see the existing solution of the problem, participate in Microsoft Improvement program to improve the efficiency of Windows Vista, and steps to check your system requirements to run Windows Aero.

Chapter 3 describes the Internet Explorer browser homepage settings, browser history settings, language pack settings, steps to customize web font, configure pop-up blocker settings to stop unnecessary pop-ups, steps to configure web browser to stop phishing website attacks, monitor and manage add-ons, block objectionable content of a website, configure auto complete and feed contents settings.

Chapter 4 explains the control panel applets to change hardware configurations e.g. enabling a device, installing a local or a network printer, and so on.

Chapter 5 describes Group Policy Objects to configure hardware and software settings for user's profile to minimize the security risk for your system.

Chapter 6 explains the steps connecting to a remote machine to perform administrative tasks or regular maintenance, and troubleshoot or fix computer problems remotely by asking a co-worker or a friend. This chapter also explains the network types, user account types and boot settings.

Chapter 7 combines useful command lines to open a program using keyboard shortcuts. At the end of the each chapter, author compiled a list of frequently asked questions and answers that may help you to pass Microsoft exam, if you are using this book to prepare for MCTS (Microsoft Certified Technology Specialist) certification.

Table of Contents

Topics **Page #**

A Quick Overview of Book Chapters.. 01

Copyrights...02

Dedication Page..03

About Author...04

Introduction...05

Chapter 1 Microsoft Windows Vista Operating System

Windows Vista Start Menu...19

Windows Vista Explorer...20

Comparison of Microsoft Windows Vista Versions.........................21-22

Vista Clean Installation Verses Vista Upgrade.............................22-23

Recommended Minimum Windows Vista Hardware Requirements......23-24

Microsoft Upgrade License Eligibility..24

32-bit Upgrade Path Verses 64-bit Upgrade Path.............................24

Windows Vista Versions Upgrade Path...25

32-bit Operating System Upgrade Path...25

64-bit Operating System Upgrade Path...26

Unsupported Microsoft Operating Systems.......................................26

Windows Vista Upgrade Advisor...27-31

Windows Vista Clean Installation..32-38

Windows Vista Upgrade Process..39-43

Windows Vista Service Pack 1..44

Load Hard Disk Driver...44-46

Create Hard Disk Partition..47

Format Hard Disk Partition..48

Extend Hard Disk Partition..48-49

Delete Hard Disk Partition..49

Windows XP Clean Installation...49-62

Frequently Asked Questions and Answers.......................................63-72

Chapter 2 Microsoft Windows Vista New Features

Welcome Center...74-75

Open Welcome Center..74

Disable Welcome Center...75

Windows Experience Index (WEI) Score.......................................75-65

Navigate WEI Base Score Table......................................75-76

Parental Controls..76-79

Open Parental Controls..76

Configuring Parental Controls..76-79

Windows Defender..79-85

Windows Defender Configurations...................................80

Windows Defender Updates...80

System Scanning Options..81

Join Microsoft SpyNet Community...................................81

Windows Defender Options..82

Automatic Scanning..82

Default Actions Options...83

Real-time Protection Options...83

Administrator Options..84

Manage Start-up Programs...84

Manage Currently Running Programs...............................84

Manage Network Connected Programs............................84-85

Manage Winsock Service Providers..................................85

Windows Defender Advanced Options.............................85

Table of Contents

BitLocker Drive Encryption..86-89

BitLocker Drive Preparation Tool....................................86-87

Setup BitLocker Drive Encryption....................................87-89

Windows Sidebar..89-92

Open Windows Sidebar..89-90

Add Gadgets on Windows Sidebar....................................90

Remove Gadgets from Windows Sidebar...........................90-91

Windows Sidebar Startup Options....................................91-92

Windows Sidebar Display Settings....................................92

Ready Boost..92-93

Hidden Windows Features..93-94

Open Hidden Windows Features..94

Windows Meeting Space..94-98

Windows Meeting Space Setup..95-98

Memory Diagnostics Tool..98-99

Memory Diagnostics Scan..98

Real-time Monitoring Report..98-99

Backup Files...99-101

Restore Files...101-103

Complete PC Backup..103-105

Power Management..105-107

Adjust Power Settings..105

Power Play Settings...106

Define Power Button...106-107

System Wakeup Password..107

Windows Mail..108

Add Windows Mail Account..108-111

Windows Mail Options..111-116

Send/Receive Email from Server.................................116

Mail Message Rules...117

Newsgroup Message Rules..117

View Windows Contacts..118

Junk Mail Options...118

Adding User to Safe Senders List................................119

Adding User to Blocked Senders List............................119

Blocking Top-level Domains......................................120

Adding Blocked Encoding List...................................120

Customizing Phishing Filter Options...........................120-121

Requesting/Sending Secure Receipts............................121

Set/Change International Settings..............................121-122

Add Signature..122

Windows Contacts...122-123

Create Windows Contacts.......................................123

Problem Reports and Solutions Tool...................................123-127

Open Problem Reports and Solutions............................124

Check for New Solutions.. 124

Check Existing Solutions.. 125

View Problem History...125

Customize Problem Reports and Solutions Settings............ .126

Clear Problem and Solution History.............................126

Customer Experience Improvement Settings.................. 126-127

Snipping Tool... 127

Windows Aero...128

Frequently Asked Questions and Answers.............................129-134

Chapter 3 Microsoft Internet Explorer 7.0

Internet Explorer..136

Internet Explorer General Options.......................................136-140

Change Internet Explorer Browser Homepage...................136

Delete Browsing History..137

Customize Browsing History Settings.............................138

Add/Remove Language Pack...................................138-139

Customize Web Site Fonts.......................................139-140

Internet Explorer Privacy Options.......................................140-143

Internet Privacy Settings...140-141

Per Site Privacy..142

Remove Managed Websites...143

Internet Explorer Security Options.......................................143-150

Protected Mode..143

Reset Internet Explorer Settings..................................144

Pop-up Blocker Settings...145-146

Turn on Pop-up Blocker.. 146

Turn off Pop-up Blocker...146

Phishing Filter Settings... .146-147

Download Internet Explorer Updates 147

Manage Add-ons...147-149

Enable/Disable Add-on Manager Window.......................150

Disable all Add-ons Temporarily.................................150

Content Advisor...150-154

ICRA3 Content Level Rating...................................150-151

Content Advisor Approved Websites..........................151-152

Change Content Advisor Supervisor Password...............152-153

Website Contents Permission..153
Remove Content Advisor Password...............................154
Auto Complete.. ..154-155
Feed Contents..155-156
Configure Feed Contents Settings...............................155-156
Frequently Asked Questions and Answers..............................157-161

Chapter 4 Microsoft Control Panel Applets

Device Manager..163-170
Open Device Manager.. 163
Enable Hardware Device.. 164
Disable Hardware Device.. 164
Wakeup Network Adaptor.......................................164-165
Update Device Driver..165-166
Rolling Back Device Driver......................................167
Add Legacy Hardware...167-170
Tablet PC Input Panel..171-173
Open Tablet PC Input Panel......................................171-173
Tablet PC Input Panel on the Taskbar.........................171-172
Tablet PC Settings...172-173
Task Manager...174
Taskbar...174-176
USB Drive Toolbar on Taskbar.................................175-176
Start Menu...176-177
Start Menu Customization..177
Classics Start Menu...178
Enable Classic Start Menu...178

Table of Contents

Run Command...179-180

Open Run Command..179

Add Run Command in Start Menu..............................179-180

Windows Calendar...180-186

Open Windows Calendar..180

Add an Appointment...181

Add Recurrence to the Appointment..............................181

Add Reminder for an Appointment..............................182

Add Location of the Meeting......................................182

Delete an Appointment...182

Create New Task...182

Delete a Task...183

Print Appointments...183

Publish Calendar...184-185

View Published Calendar Details.................................185

Stop Publishing Calendar...185-186

Subscribe to a Calendar...186

Windows DVD Maker..186-187

Open Windows DVD Maker.......................................186

Burn DVD...187

DVD Options..187

Hardware and Sound Control Panel Applet........................... 188-190

Open Hardware and Sound Applet...............................188

Adjust Sound Volume..188

Setup Sound System...188-190

Phone and Modem Setup.. 191

Table of Contents

Local and Network Printers……………………………………...191-197

Install Local Printer……………………………………....191-194

Remove a Printer……………………………………………195

Rename Printer……………………………………………….. 195

Configure Printer Ports…………………………………...195-196

Limit Printing Time…………………………………………196

Permission to Maintain Printers……………………………...197

Appearance and Personalization Control Panel Applet……………….197

Display Configuration……………………………………………197-201

Change Desktop Background………………………………… 197

Adjust Screen Resolution……………………………………...198

Refresh Screen Rate………………………………………...198-199

Computer Themes………………………………………………...199

Screen Saver Customization………………………………...200

Adjust Font Size (DPI) ……………………………………..200-201

Mouse Configuration……………………………………………201-203

Mouse Button Configuration……………………………… 201

Mouse Clicklock Configuration…………………………….202

Mouse Pointer Configuration…………………………………202

Visibility of Mouse Cursor…………………………………203

Keyboard Configuration………………………………………………203

Scanners and Cameras Configuration………………………………..204-205

Security Center……………………………………………………...206-209

Check Windows Updates……………………………………...206

Windows Updates Configuration……………………………...207

Windows Firewall Configuration…………………………...208-209

Programs and Features..209-213

View Windows Installed Updates.................................210

Compatibility Wizard..210-213

Clock, Language, and Region Settings................................213-215

Time and Date Settings Configuration..........................215-216

Daylight Saving Time Configuration............................216-217

Additional Clocks Configuration...................................217

Ease of Access Center..218-219

Windows Magnifier Configuration.............................. 218

Windows Vista Narrator Configuration..........................219

Windows Vista On-Screen Keyboard Configuration............219

Frequently Asked Questions and Answers..............................220-224

Chapter 5 Group Policy Object Editor

User Account Control Policy..226

Open Local Security Setting Editor...............................226

Local Security Account Policy.....................................226-229

Enforce Password Policy...227

Maximum Password Age Policy..................................227-228

Minimum Password Length Policy...............................228

Password Must Meet Complexity Requirements Policy......228-229

Store Passwords Using Reversible Encryption Policy...........229

Local Security Account Lockout Policy...............................230-234

Account Lockout Threshold..230

Audit a User..231-232

View Audit Log.. 233-234

Registry Editor... 234-246

Open Registry Editor.. 234

HKEY_CLASSES_ROOT Registry Key..........................235

HKEY_CURRENT_USER Registry Key..........................235

HKEY_LOCAL_MACHINE Registry Key.......................235

HKEY_USERS Registry Key.. 236

HKEY_CURRENT_CONFIG Registry Key 236

Add User Permissions..236-238

Auditing for System Registry.................................238-239

Registry Key Owner...240-241

Ownership Effective Permissions..............................241-242

Add Registry Key.. 242

Find Registry Key..242

Print Registry Key..243

Copy key Name...243

Registry Favorites...243-244

Edit Registry Key Value Data....................................245

Modify Registry Key Binary Data............................245-246

Registry Editor Help Topics.......................................246

About Registry Editor..246

Frequently Asked Questions and Answers................................ 247

Chapter 6 Microsoft Windows Vista Administrative Tools

Remote Desktop...249-256

Open Remote Desktop Connection.................................249

Establish Remote Desktop Connection......................... 249-250

Remote Desktop Options... 250-254

Remote Desktop Connection Settings.............................254

Add Remote Desktop Local User.....255

Configure Remote Desktop Connection Port.....256

Windows Remote Assistance..... 256-257

Open Windows Remote Assistance..... 256-257

Remote Assistance Settings.....257

User Accounts..... 258-262

Open User Accounts Window.....258

Setup User Accounts..... 258-259

Change User Account Type.....259

Change User Account Password..... 259-260

Remove User Account Password.....260

Remove User Account.....261

User Account Control.....261-262

Advanced User Account Properties..... 262

Local Area Network.....263-268

Open Network Sharing Center..... 263

Local Area Network Status.....263-264

Disable Local Area Network Connection.....264

Enable Local Area Network Connection.....265

Change Network Location Type.....265-266

IP Address and DNS Server Configuration.....266-267

Diagnose and Repair Network Connection.....268

Shared Resource.....268-272

Share Folder with a Local User.....268-269

Printer Sharing.....269-270

File Sharing.....270

Password Protected Sharing.....270

Network Discovery....271

Media Sharing.... 271-272

System Configuration Settings....272-276

Open System Configuration Window....272

Configure Startup Options.... 273

Diagnostic Startup Mode.... 273

Selective Startup Mode.... 273

Normal Startup Mode....273

Boot System Configuration Settings....273-274

Application Services Configuration....275

Startup Services....275

System Tools... 276

Frequently Asked Questions and Answers....277-285

Chapter 7 Keyboard Shortcuts

General Windows Logo Key Shortcuts....287

Control Key (CTRL), Alternative Key (ALT), Shift key, and Function Key Shortcuts.... 288

Windows General Microsoft Office Shortcuts....289-290

Control Panel Shortcuts....291-294

Command Prompt....295

System File Utility.... 296

Glossary.... 297-301

Chapter 1- Microsoft Windows Vista Operating System

Topics covered in this chapter:

- Windows Vista Start Menu
- Windows Vista Explorer
- Comparison of Microsoft Windows Vista Versions
- Vista Clean Installation Verses Vista Upgrade
- Recommended Minimum Windows Vista Hardware Requirements
- Windows Vista Versions Upgrade Path
- Unsupported Microsoft Operating Systems
- Microsoft Operating Systems Upgrade License Eligibility
- 32-bit Upgrade Path Verses 64-bit Upgrade Path
- 32-bit Operating System Upgrade Path
- 64-bit Operating System Upgrade Path
- Windows Vista Upgrade Advisor
- Windows Vista Clean Installation
- Windows Vista Upgrade Process
- Windows Vista Service Pack 1
- Load Hard Disk Driver
- Format Hard Disk Partition
- Create Hard Disk Partition
- Delete Hard Disk Partition
- Extend Hard Disk Partition
- Windows XP Clean Installation

Windows Vista Start Menu

Windows Start Menu is a user interface for Microsoft operating systems to launch programs. It also allows Microsoft users to have access to their personal folders, control panel applets and network utilities. *Start Menu* can be accessed by clicking on *Start button* (located at the left-bottom of the desktop), or pressing *Windows Logo Key* from the keyboard.

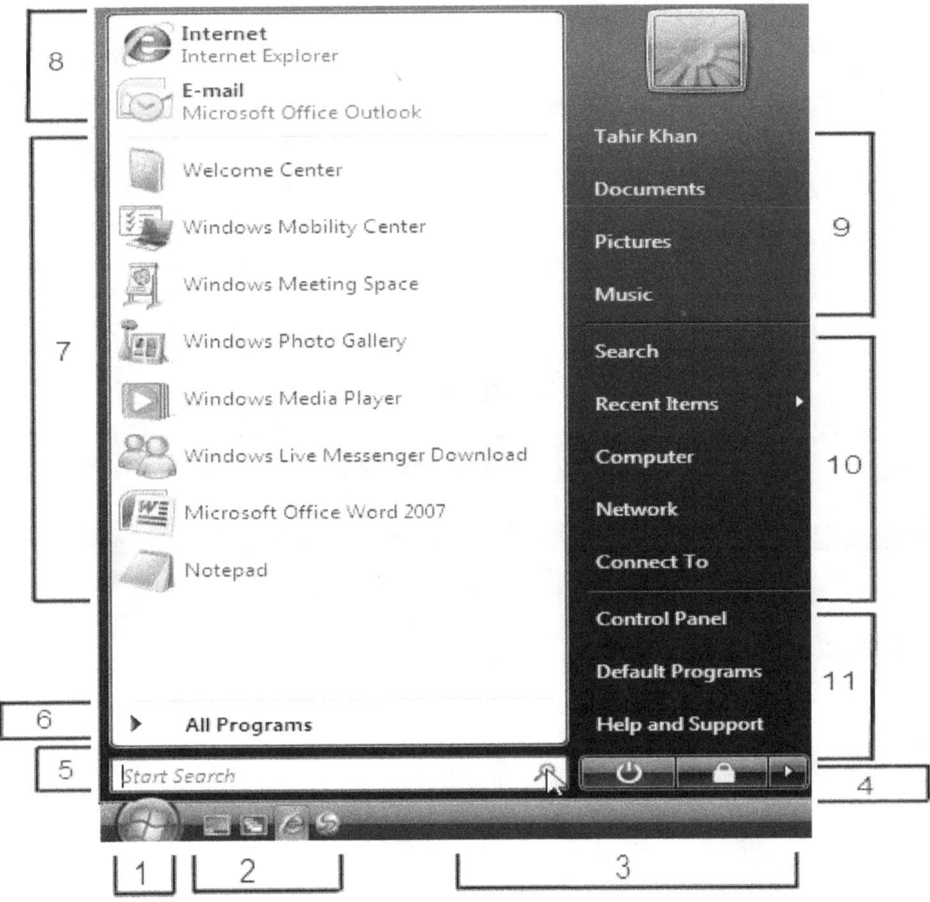

1. Start button
2. Quick access toolbar
3. Taskbar
4. Computer shutdown options
5. Search bar
6. Display all programs
7. Last frequently used programs list
8. Pinned programs
9. User's personal folders
10. Network, recent items, computer, connect to, and search folders
11. Access to control panel, help and support, and default programs

Windows Vista Explorer

Windows Explorer is a part of the Microsoft Windows Vista operating system. It provides detailed information about the files, folders, and system drives. It can be accessed by holding down *Windows Logo Key* and *E* (letter E) simultaneously.

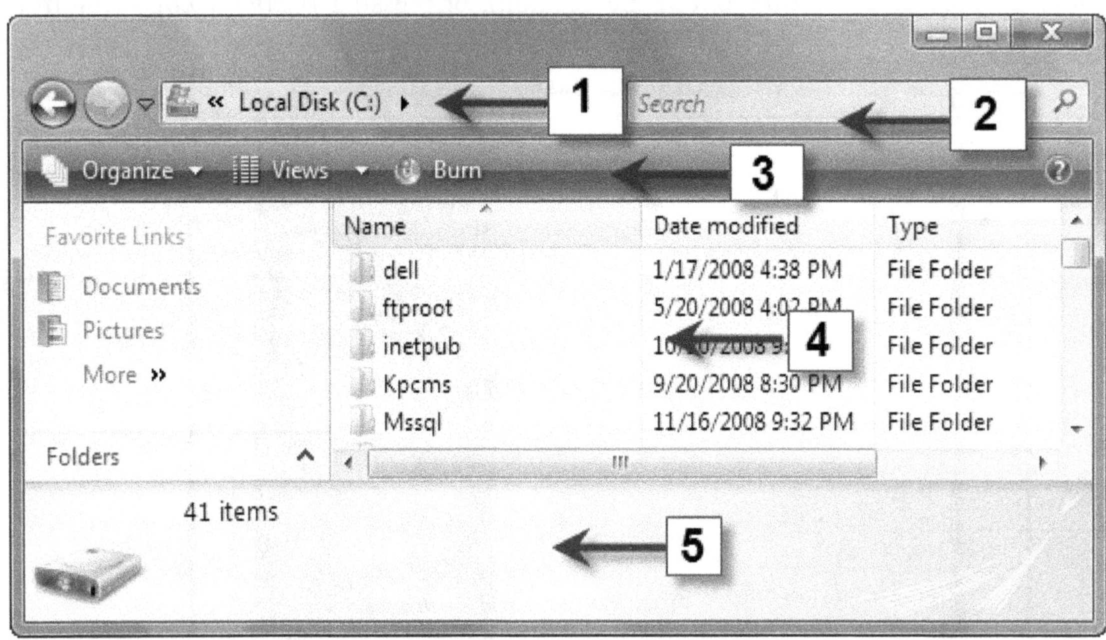

1. Local drive/folder path
2. Search bar
3. Command bar
4. List pane
5. Detail pane

Comparison of Microsoft Windows Vista Versions

Microsoft Corporation has released eight versions of Windows Vista edition all over the world. The five versions of Windows Vista are available in the United States, and rest of the Windows Vista versions are coded for the international market. It is recommended to compare and contrast Windows Vista version features to make a better decision to buy a particular version of Microsoft operating system. The following table shows the comparison of Microsoft Windows Vista versions.

	Home Basic	Home Premium	Business	Ultimate	Enterprise
Parental Controls	Yes	Yes	No	Yes	No
Windows Photo Gallery	Yes	Yes	Yes	Yes	Yes
Windows Defender	Yes	Yes	Yes	Yes	Yes
Windows Aero	No	Yes	Yes	Yes	Yes
Windows Media Center	No	Yes	No	Yes	No
Windows Tablet PC Support	No	Yes	Yes	Yes	Yes
PC Backup	No	Yes	Yes	Yes	Yes
Windows Meeting Space	No	Yes	Yes	Yes	Yes
Windows Fax and Scan	No	No	Yes	Yes	Yes
Windows BitLocker Drive Encryption	No	No	No	Yes	Yes
Group Policy Support	No	No	Yes	Yes	Yes
Windows DVD Maker	No	Yes	No	Yes	No
Remote Desktop	Client only	Client only	Host & client	Host & client	Host & client
Encrypting File System	No	No	Yes	Yes	Yes
Domain Support	No	No	Yes	Yes	Yes
Small Business Resources	No	No	Yes	Yes	No

	Home Basic	Home Premium	Business	Ultimate	Enterprise
Windows Anytime Upgrade	Yes	Yes	Yes	No	No
Windows Shadow Copies	No	No	Yes	Yes	Yes
Internet Information Server	No	No	Yes	Yes	Yes
Two-Processor Support	No	No	Yes	Yes	Yes
Offline Files and Folder	No	No	Yes	Yes	Yes

Vista Clean Installation Verses Vista Upgrade

Microsoft provides an upgrade path from Windows XP to Windows Vista if your system meets upgrade hardware requirements. Both the ***Windows Vista Capable PC*** hardware and the ***Windows Vista Premium Ready PC*** hardware are available in the market to meet the upgrade requirements.

The minimum hardware requirements for the ***Windows Vista Capable PC*** are:

- Must have a minimum of 512 MB of RAM (Random Access Memory)
- Must have at-least 800 MHz of 32-bit or 64-bit CPU (Central Processing Unit)
- A DirectX 9 graphics processor
- Windows Display Driver Module (WDDM) with minimum of 64 MB RAM or preferable 128 MB RAM
- 20 GB hard-disk with at-least 15 GB free space

The minimum hardware requirements for the ***Windows Vista Premium Ready PC*** are following:

- 1 GHz of 32-bit or 64-bit processor
- 1 GB of system memory
- 40 GB of hard-drive with 15 GB free space
- DVD-ROM drive
- Audio output capable
- Windows Aero capable
- 128 MB of video card memory
- DirectX 9 graphics support with WDDM driver

The following table shows an upgrade path from Microsoft Windows XP and Windows 2000 to Microsoft Windows Vista. There is no upgrade path available from 32-bit version to 64-bit version of the Windows operating systems.

	Vista Home Basic	**Vista Home Premium**	**Vista Business**	**Vista Ultimate**	**Vista Enterprise**
XP Home	Upgrade	Upgrade	Upgrade	Upgrade	Clean
XP Professional	Clean	Clean	Upgrade	Upgrade	Clean
XP Media Center	Clean	Upgrade	Clean	Upgrade	Clean
XP Tablet PC	Clean	Clean	Upgrade	Upgrade	Clean
XP Pro. X64	Clean	Clean	Clean	Clean	Clean
Windows 2000	Clean	Clean	Clean	Clean	Clean

Recommended Minimum Windows Vista Hardware Requirements

A Windows Vista hardware requirement varies depending on system configuration and the programs that will be installed on the system. The Windows Vista Home Basic requires minimum hardware requirements as compared to the rest of the Windows Vista editions. A comparison of Windows Vista hardware requirement is given in below table.

Windows Vista Home Basic	**Windows Vista Premium/Business/Ultimate/Enterprise**
800 Megahertz (MHz) 32-bit (x86) Processor	1 GHz 32-bit (X86) Processor
800 MHz 64-bit (X64) Processor	1 GHz 64-bit (X64) Processor
512 Megabytes (MB) System Memory (RAM)	1 GB System Memory (RAM)
DirectX-9 Graphics Card	DirectX-9 Graphics Card with WDDM driver
32 MB Graphics Card Memory	128 MB Graphics Card Memory
20 Gigabyte (GB) Hard Disk (Minimum)	40 Gigabyte (GB) Hard Disk (Minimum)

15 GB of Free Hard Disk Space	15 GB of Free Hard Disk Space
Internal or External DVD Drive	Internal or External DVD Drive
Internet Access Capability	Internet Access Capability
Audio Output Capability	Audio Output Capability

Microsoft Upgrade License Eligibility

The following operating systems are eligible to get an upgrade license. An upgrade license enables Microsoft users to perform an upgrade installation from any of the following version of Microsoft to one of the Microsoft Windows Vista editions.

- Windows XP Home
- Windows XP Professional
- Windows XP Professional x64
- Windows XP Media Center
- Windows XP Tablet PC
- Windows 2000
- Windows Vista Home Basic (32-bit or 64-bit)
- Windows Vista Home Premium (32-bit and 64-bit)
- Windows Vista Business (32-bit and 64-bit)
- Windows Vista Ultimate (32-bit and 64-bit)

32-bit Upgrade Path Verses 64-bit Upgrade Path

It is recommended to know which upgrade path is available for your system before starting an upgrade process. To check the system configuration of your machine, click ***Start***, and type ***System*** in the search field (located at the left-bottom of the desktop), and then select ***System*** from programs list. In the ***System*** window, check the system type of your machine under ***System*** section. In most cases, 32-bit and 64-bit operating systems can be installed on 86-bit CPU, and 64-bit CPU, respectively. However, a 32-bit operating system can be installed on a computer that has a 64-bit processor, but you cannot install a 64-bit operating system on a computer that has a 32-bit processor.

Windows Vista Versions Upgrade Path

The following table shows an upgrade path from one version of Windows Vista edition to another version of Windows Vista.

Upgrade From	**Vista Home Basic**	**Vista Home Premium**	**Vista Business**	**Vista Ultimate**
Vista Home Basic	Upgrade	Upgrade	Upgrade	Upgrade
Vista Home Premium	Clean	Upgrade	Clean	Upgrade
Vista Business	Clean	Clean	Upgrade	Upgrade
Vista Ultimate	Clean	Clean	Clean	Clean

32-bit Operating System Upgrade Path

The following table shows an upgrade path of a 32-bit operating system.

Upgrade From	**Vista Home Basic**	**Vista Home Premium**	**Vista Business**	**Vista Ultimate**
Windows XP Home (SP2+)	Yes	Yes	Yes	Yes
Windows XP Pro. (SP2+)	No	No	Yes	Yes
Windows XP Tablet (SP2+)	No	No	Yes	Yes
Windows XP Media Center 2002 (SP2+)	No	No	No	No
Windows XP Media Center 2004 (SP2+)	No	Yes	No	Yes
Windows XP Media Center 2005 (SP2+)	No	Yes	No	Yes
Windows Vista Home Basic	Yes	Yes	Yes	Yes
Windows Vista Home Premium	No	Yes	No	Yes
Windows Vista Business	No	No	Yes	Yes
Windows Vista Ultimate	No	No	No	Yes

64-bit Operating System Upgrade Path

The following table shows an upgrade path of a 64-bit operating system.

Upgrade From	**Vista Home Basic**	**Vista Home Premium**	**Vista Business**	**Vista Ultimate**
Windows XP Home (SP2+)	No	No	No	No
Windows XP Professional (SP2+)	No	No	No	No
Windows XP Professional (SP2+) x64	No	No	No	No
Windows XP Tablet (SP2+)	No	No	No	No
Windows XP Media Center 2002 (SP2+)	No	No	No	No
Windows XP Media Center 2004 (SP2+)	No	No	No	No
Windows XP Media Center 2005 (SP2+)	No	No	No	No
Windows Vista Home Basic	Yes	Yes	Yes	Yes
Windows Vista Home Premium	No	No	No	No
Windows Vista Business	No	No	Yes	Yes
Windows Vista Ultimate	No	No	No	Yes
Windows Vista Enterprise	No	No	Yes	Yes

Unsupported Microsoft Operating Systems

Microsoft Corporation does not provide either an upgrade path or a custom installation for Microsoft users who are still using one of the following legacy systems.

- Microsoft Windows 95
- Microsoft Windows 98
- Microsoft Windows Millennium, Microsoft Windows NT 4.0 or Earlier Versions

Windows Vista Upgrade Advisor

Windows Vista Upgrade Advisor is a free utility available to download from Microsoft website to identify the current system configuration to check, if your system is ready to be upgraded to one of the Windows Vista editions. To download the *Upgrade Advisor* utility, type the following URL (*Universal Resource Locator*) in Internet Explorer browser, http://www.microsoft.com/downloads/details.aspx?FamilyId=42B5AC83-C24F-4863-A389-3FFC194924F8&displaylang=en and then click on ***Download*** to install a copy of *Windows Vista Upgrade Advisor* for your system to verify hardware and software requirements.

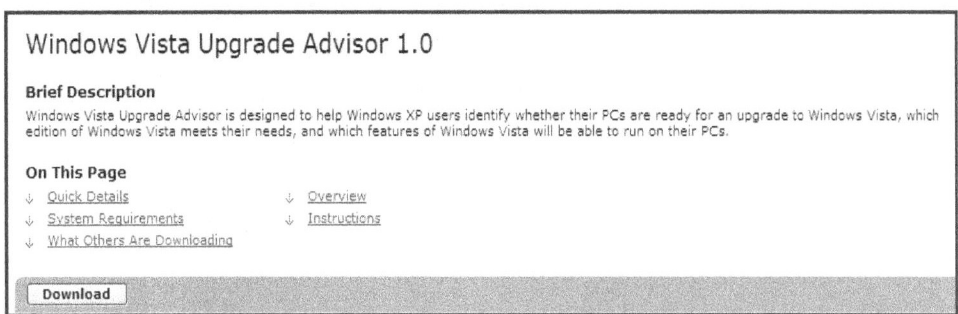

Click on ***Save***, if you would like to save *Windows Vista Upgrade Advisor* file in your system, otherwise click on ***Run*** if you would like to run the program now.

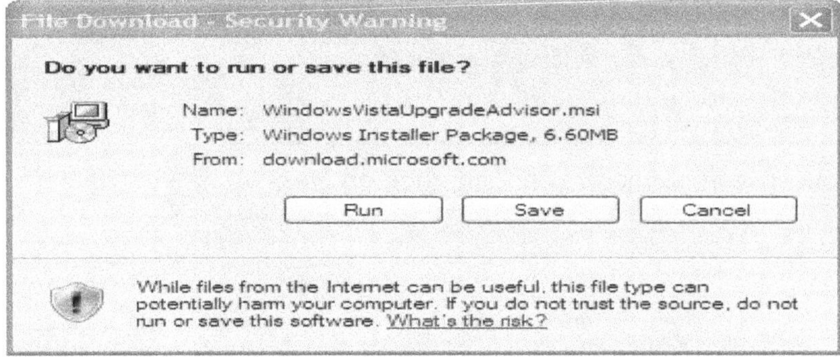

This process may take few minutes preparing your system to run this program.

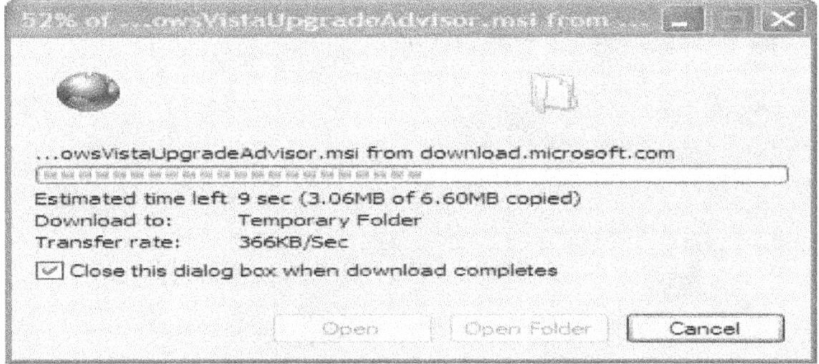

Click on ***Run*** to extract the content of the program.

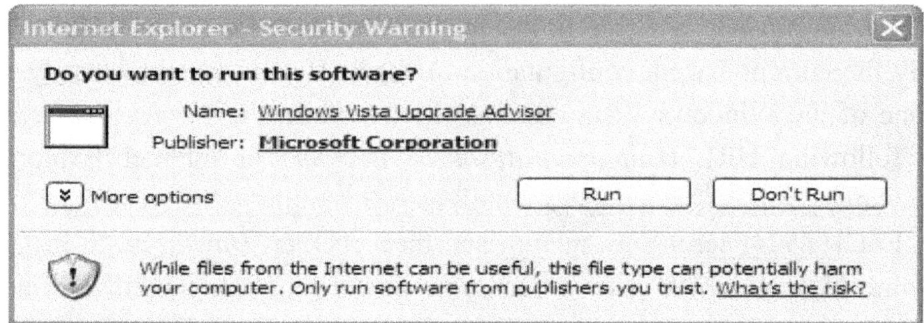

From the *Windows Vista Upgrade Advisor* wizard, click on ***Next*** to install *Upgrade Advisor*.

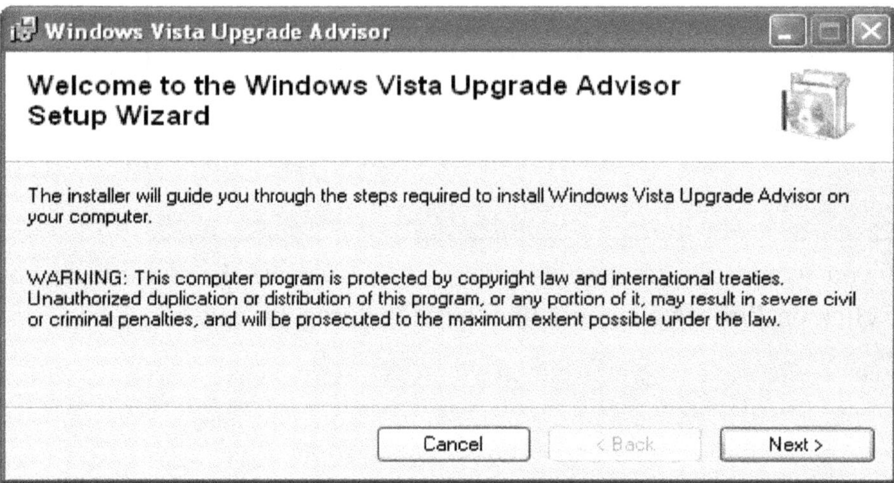

Read and accept Microsoft license agreement, and then click on ***Next***.

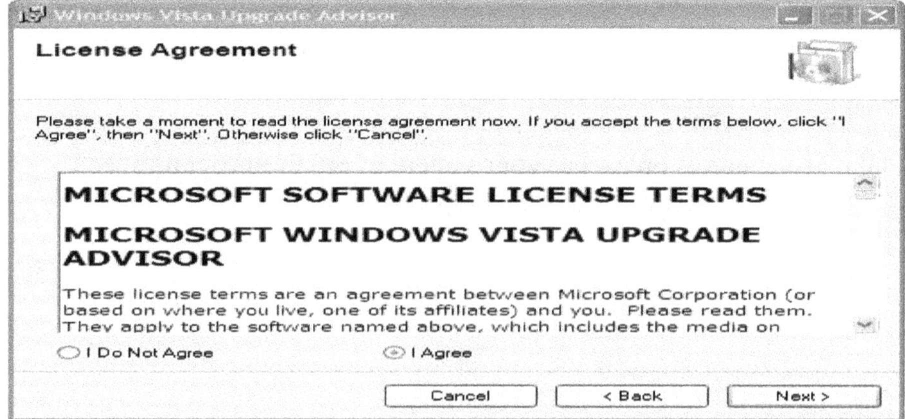

Click on ***Next*** after verifying the location of the folder in which Windows Vista upgrade Advisor files will be saved.

By default, system creates a desktop shortcut for this program. Select ***Don't Create Desktop Shortcut*** option if you do not want to create a desktop shortcut and then click on **Next**.

Installation process may take several minutes depending on your system performance.

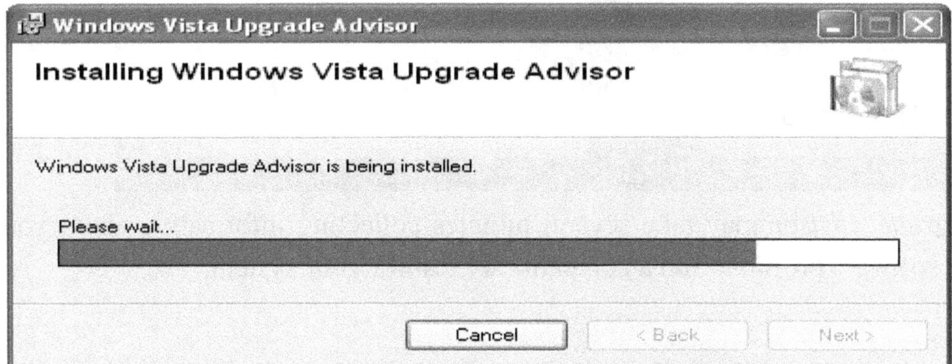

The *Windows Vista Upgrade Advisor* program will be launched by default after clicking on ***Close*** button. If you would like to launch the program later, clear the ***Launch Windows Vista Upgrade Advisor*** checkbox.

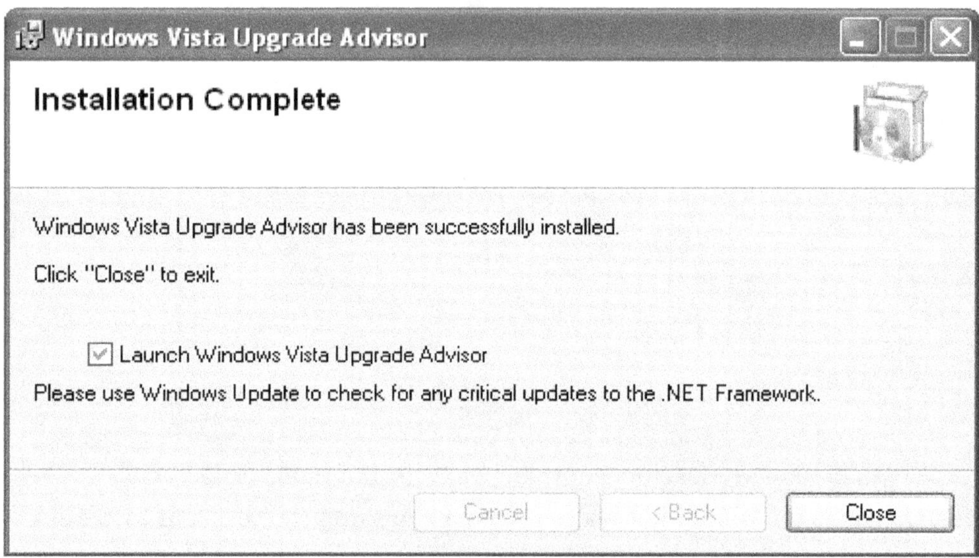

From the *Windows Vista Upgrade Advisor 1.0* window, click on ***Start Scan***.

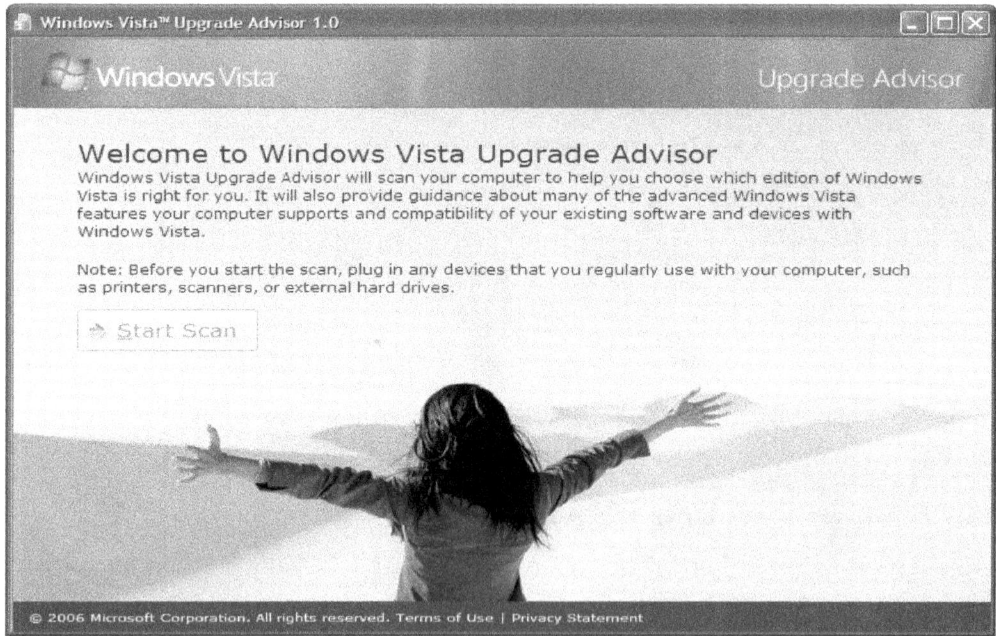

Windows Upgrade Advisor may take several minutes collecting information about your hardware and software profile to run a compatibility test for your system.

To compare Windows Vista editions, click on ***Compare Editions*** to see different features that Windows Vista offers for different versions of Windows. To view the report in detail, click on ***See Details***.

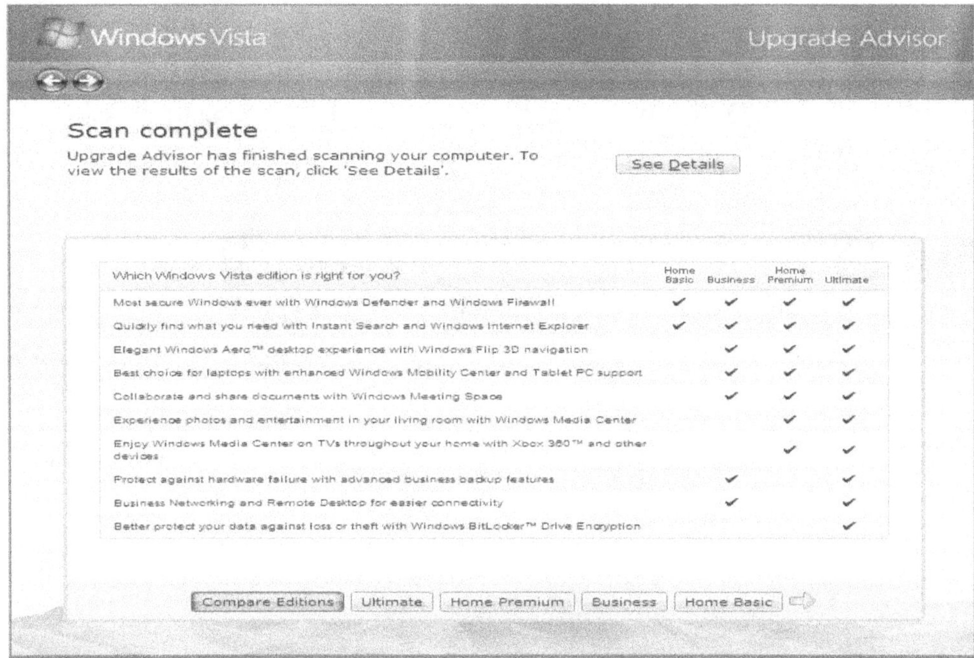

Analyze the report carefully and then take suggested action(s) before upgrading your system to one of the available Microsoft Vista editions from one of the older version of Microsoft operating systems.

Windows Vista Clean Installation

To install a clean copy of Windows Vista on your machine, insert the Windows Vista DVD disk into the DVD ROM and then reboot/restart the system. Computer will detect the DVD disk by itself and will start downloading Windows files from the DVD disk. This process may take several minutes downloading Windows system files. If your system did not detect the DVD disk by itself, reboot the computer and start pressing ***F12*** key from keyboard as soon as computer starts, until you see the option of making boot orders or allow you to boot your system from the DVD ROM.

Adjust the ***language to install***, ***time and currency format***, and ***keyboard or input method*** preferences and then click on ***Next*** to continue.

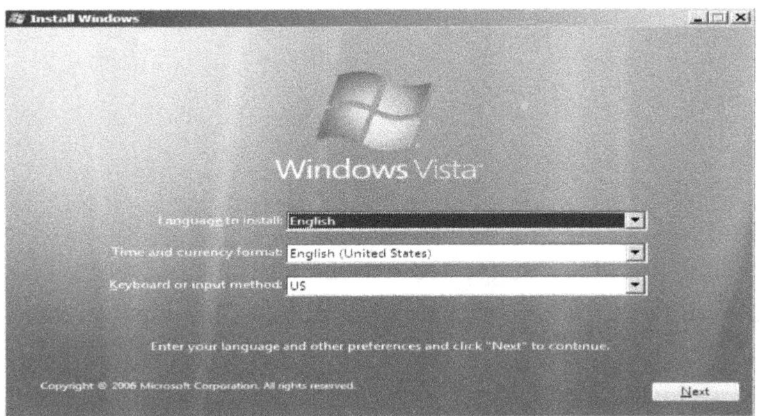

If you would like to review information about your hardware specifications and operating system before installing *Windows Vista* version of Microsoft, click on ***What to know before installing Windows***. Click on ***Install now*** to continue installing Windows.

You may need to wait for several minutes as Windows gathers necessary information before continuing to the next level of Windows installation.

Enter the product key that came with your system and then click on ***Next*** to continue installing operating system.

If you would like to read privacy statement before installing Windows Vista on your machine, click on ***Read our privacy statement***.

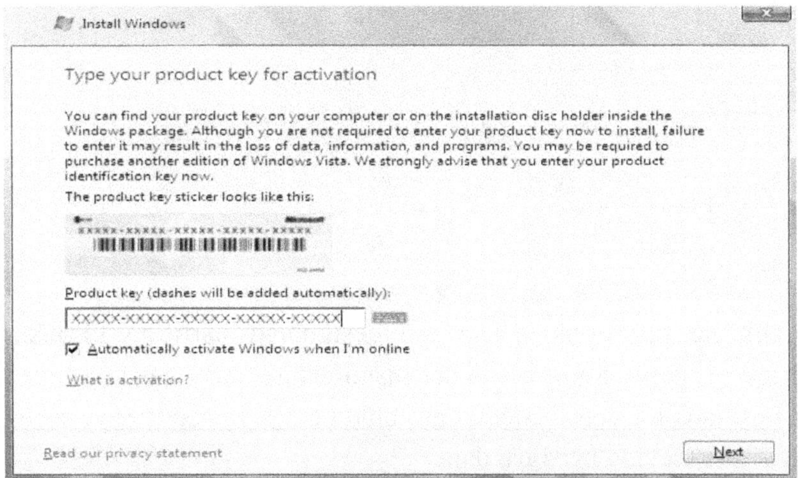

Read and accept the license terms and conditions, and then click on ***Next***.

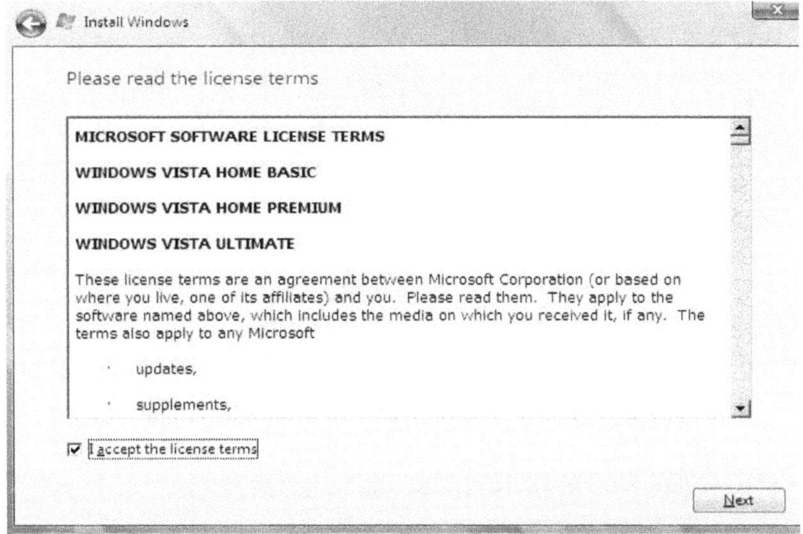

If you decided to choose ***Custom (advanced)*** option to install Windows Vista, you are installing a clean copy of Windows. This option does not keep your personal data, files, folders, and program settings that are currently installed on your machine. Make sure you have a complete backup of your files before performing a clean Windows installation. A complete backup procedure is explained in detail in chapter # 2.

Select ***Custom (advanced)*** option to continue installing a clean copy of Windows Vista.

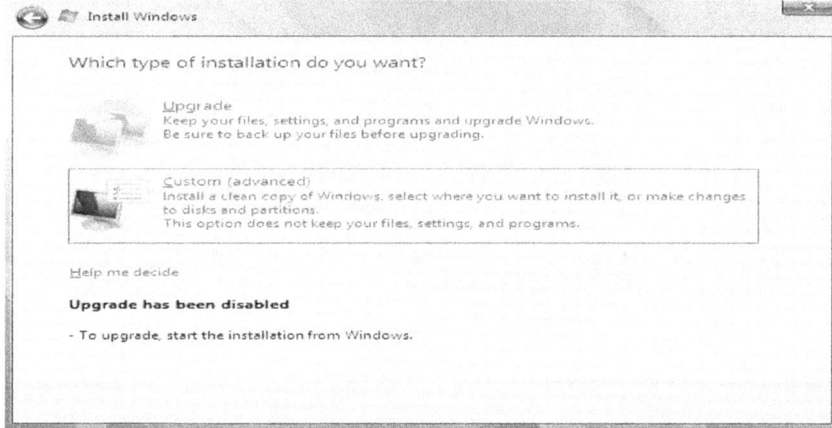

If your hard-drive has multiple partitions, select the designated partition to install Windows in it and then click on ***Next***. Some computer manufactures may have more than one pre-installed hard-disk partitions for your system, one could be designated to save system files, and others can be reserved for saving personal data.

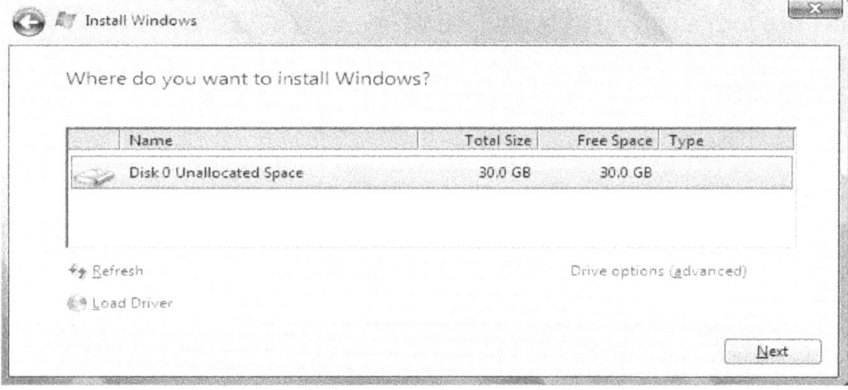

Windows will install necessary files to run the operating system. This process may take several minutes and your computer may restart several times by itself during the installation process.

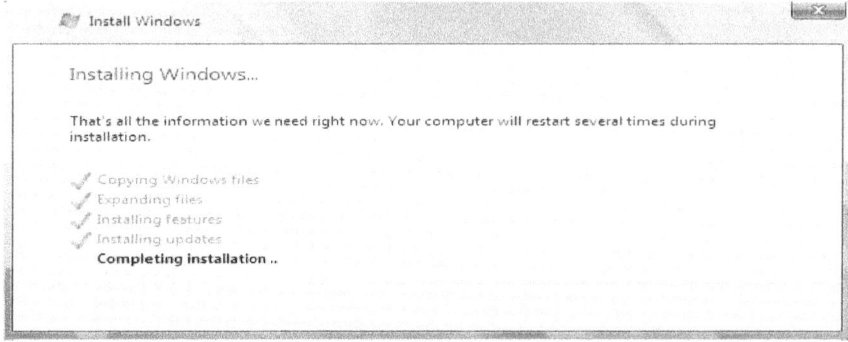

You will be asked to provide a username and password that you would like to use for Windows Vista account. Create username and password that must meet the complexity requirements as given below, and then click on ***Next*** to continue.

a. Should not use user's account name.
b. Should not use two consecutive characters that is part of the user's full name.
c. Should have at-least six characters length password.
d. Should contain at-least one uppercase character (A through Z), at-least one lowercase character (a through z), at-least one digit (0 through 9) or at-least one non-alphabetic character (!, @, #. $, %, ^, &, *, etc).

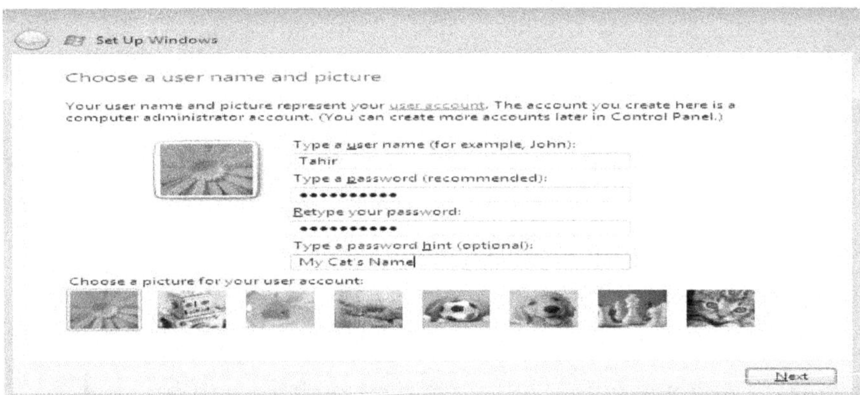

The system will suggest a computer name, either keep the computer name which is created by the system or re-name it according to your preferences. To continue installation process to the next level, click on ***Next***.

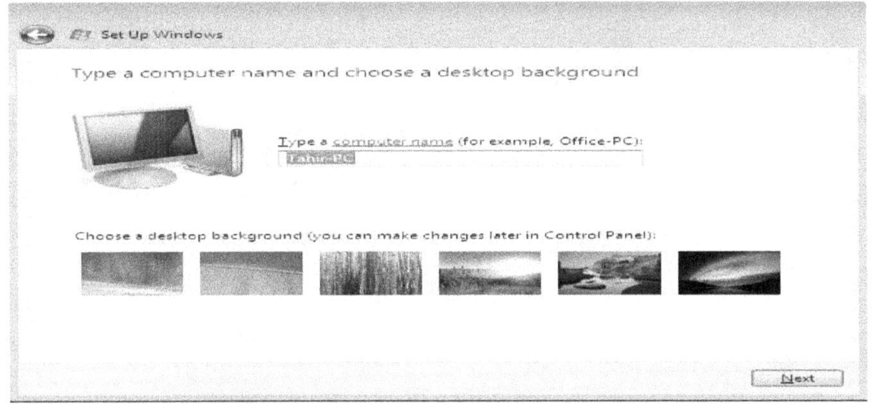

Choose one of the following Windows update options to continue.

a. ***Use recommended settings***: The system will install important and recommended updates for your system. If you decided to choose this option, then following features will turn on automatically:

    a. **Windows automatic updating**: The important and recommended updates for your system will be installed on release of new Microsoft updates.
    b. **Enhanced spyware protection**: Windows Vista provides a spyware program, *Windows Defender*, to protect your computer against spywares. The system downloads and installs *Windows Defender* updates to enhance the security of your system against malicious spywares.
    c. **Windows problem reporting**: The Windows Vista has *Microsoft Error Reporting* tool that sends necessary information to Microsoft to identify the cause of the problem. If the solution of the problem already exists, the solution will be presented to you to fix the issue that you are having with your system.
    d. **Driver from Windows updates**: Windows Vista is capable of downloading and installing device drivers. If the device drivers are available online, it will be downloaded and installed for your system.
    e. **Internet Explorer Phishing Filter**: Phishing filter for Internet Explorer will automatically turn on to check against spam websites.

b. ***Install important updates only***: Only important updates will be installed for your system, but not recommended updates. You must turn on recommended updates features to receive spyware protection updates, solutions to problems updates, and device driver updates.

c. ***Ask me later***: If you decided to choose this option, your computer might not be protected against security threats.

It is recommended to choose ***Use recommended settings*** option to protect your system against any security threads in computing industry. Continuing Windows installation to the next level, choose one of the above mentioned Windows updates options and then click on ***Next***.

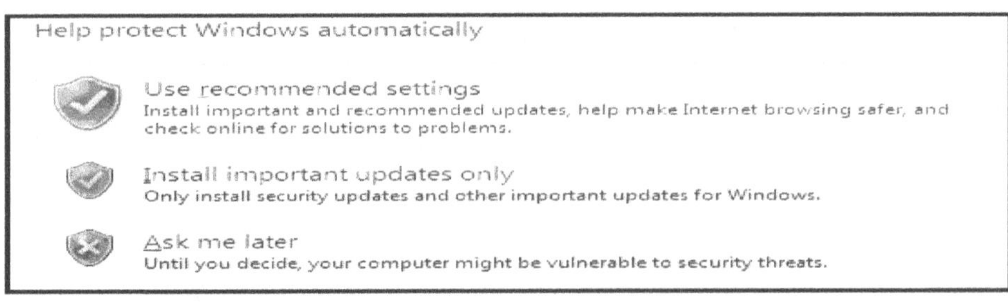

Review time and date settings and then click on ***Next***.

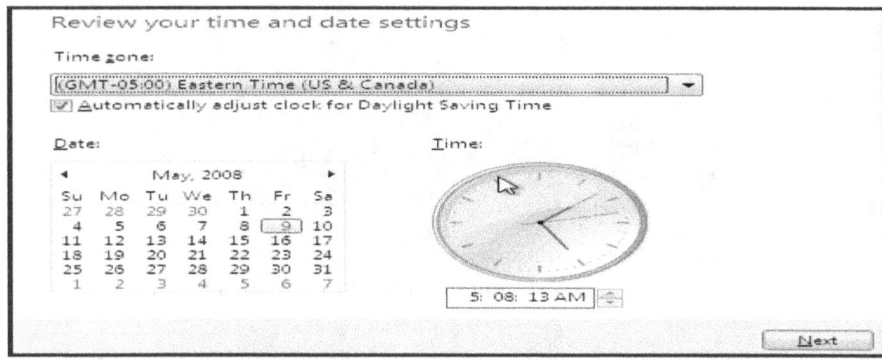

Select computer's network location for your system. A public network is designated to work in public areas, such as an airport, coffee shop, and unsecure places where a security key is not required to connect to the Internet. A private network is known to be more secure network which must be selected, if the security is the main concern for your system. Select one of the available network locations to continue.

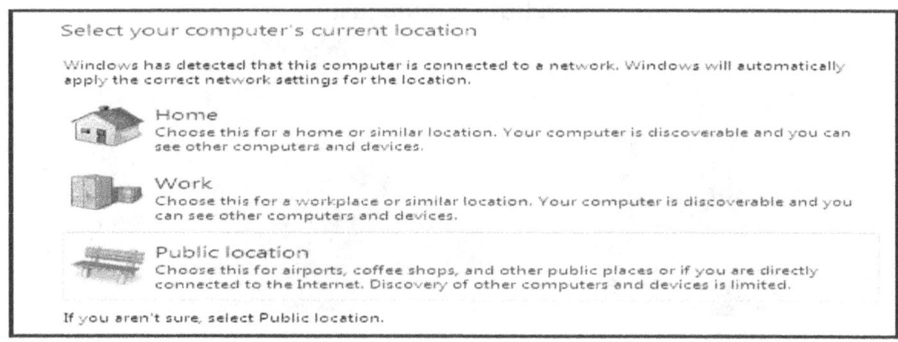

Click on ***Start*** to set up Windows.

This process may take several minutes to perform necessary operations to complete Windows installation process. You may see some or all of the following screens.

Windows checks computer….

Getting it done just….

Connect and communicate….

Connect play, have fun

A more secure environment

Connect and communicate….

Turn everyday moments…

The power to find everything

Getting it done just….

Enter the ***Password*** to get into the system. It may take several minutes before you log-in to the system.

Windows Vista Upgrade Process

To upgrade your system, follow step by step instructions to upgrade your system from older version of Microsoft Windows to newer version of Microsoft Windows Vista operating system.

Insert the Windows Vista DVD disk into the DVD ROM drive, and then click ***Run Setup.exe*** from the dialog box to run Windows Vista setup.

If your system did not prompt you to choose setup.exe file from the ***AutoPlay*** dialog box, open ***C*** drive (system volume drive) by double-clicking on ***Computer*** icon and then navigating to the DVD-drive. Right-click on the DVD-drive, and then choose ***Install or run program*** option from the menu.

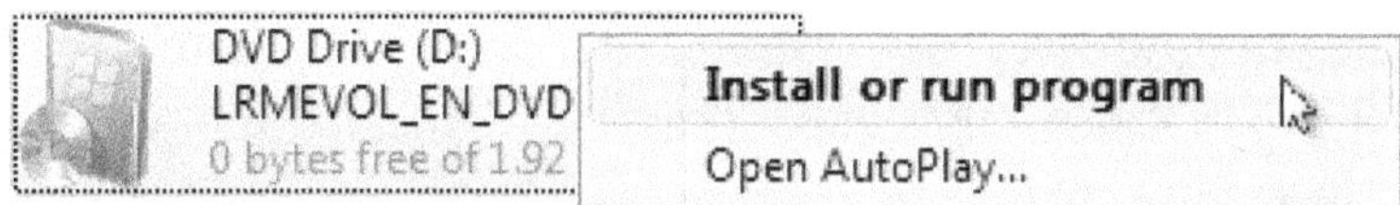

Provide administrative credentials, if asked. Depending on your computer security settings, you may be warned for an unidentified program that wants access to your computer, click on ***Allow*** to continue the process.

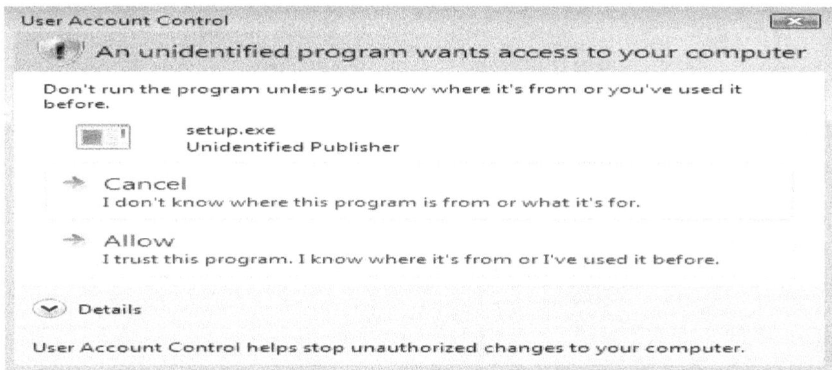

If you would like to check the compatibility of your system before installing the *Windows Vista* on your machine, click on ***Check Compatibility Online*** link.

This link takes you to the website to download *Windows Vista Upgrade Advisor* program. From that website, download ***Windows Vista Upgrade Advisor 1.0*** program and then run the wizard to install *Windows Upgrade Advisor.* For detailed information, see the page number 27 of chapter 1.

Click on ***Install now*** to start installing Windows Vista. If you would like to review information related to your upgraded hardware specification and upgraded operating system, click on ***What to know before installing Windows*** link.

Windows may take several minutes to gathers necessary information before you are prompt to the next level of Windows installation.

It is recommended to download critical updates for your system before you start upgrading your system. If you want to download the important updates for your system, click the ***Go online to get the latest updates for installation (recommended)*** option. But you must remain connected with the Internet while downloading Windows updates. Your system may need several minutes to download important updates for your system. If your system was not successful to get latest *Windows Updates*, cancel the Windows installation process and then perform a Windows updates scan by going to Microsoft website, *update.microsoft.com.*

If you decided not to get the latest updates for your system now, click on ***Do not get the latest updates for installation*** option. The Windows installation process may not be successful if your system does not have the latest Windows updates installed.

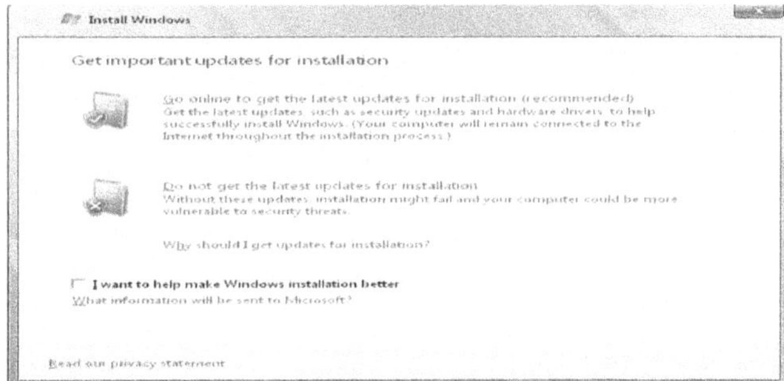

If you would like to help Microsoft Corporation to improve the installation process for Microsoft users, check the ***I want to help make Windows installation better*** option to participate in this program. Click on ***What information will be sent to Microsoft*** link to read about, how to help Microsoft to make Windows installation process better.

Enter the product key that came with your system and then click on ***Next*** to continue installing operating system. If you decided to activate Windows manually, you must clear the ***Automatically activate Windows when I'm online*** checkbox. If you would like to read privacy statement before installing Windows Vista on your machine, click on ***Read our privacy statement***.

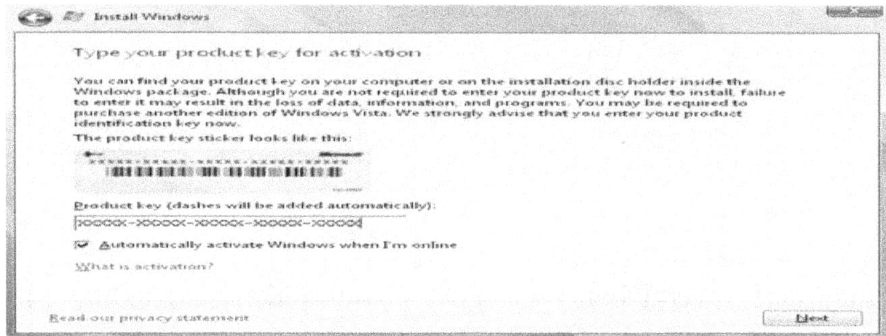

Read and accept the license terms and conditions, and then click on ***Next***.

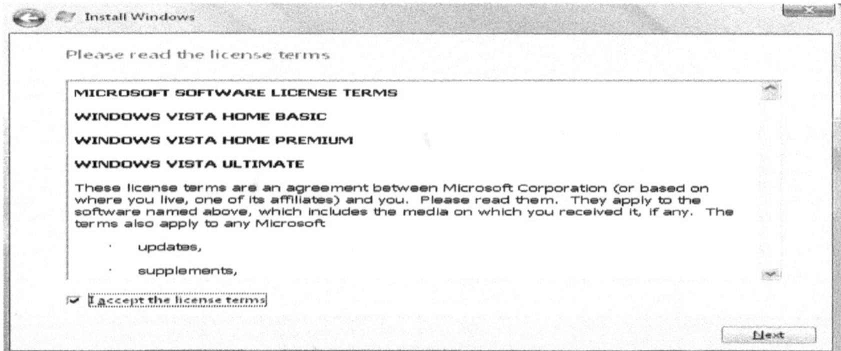

Select the ***Upgrade*** option to continue upgrading your system to the Microsoft Windows Vista from an older version of *Microsoft Windows XP* edition. An upgrade process keeps your computer files, settings, and programs but it is recommended to have a complete back up of your PC, in case your system crashes during an upgrade process.

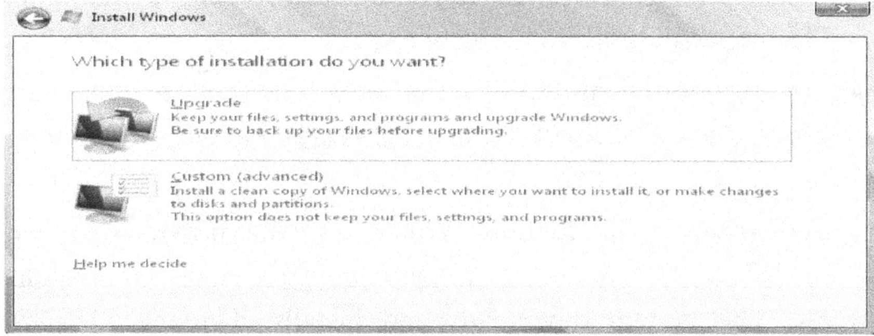

Your system may take several minutes to detect and generate potential issues report that may cause for your operating system to run inconsistently. Review the compatibility report carefully before continuing Windows installation process. Click on ***Next*** to continue installation of Windows.

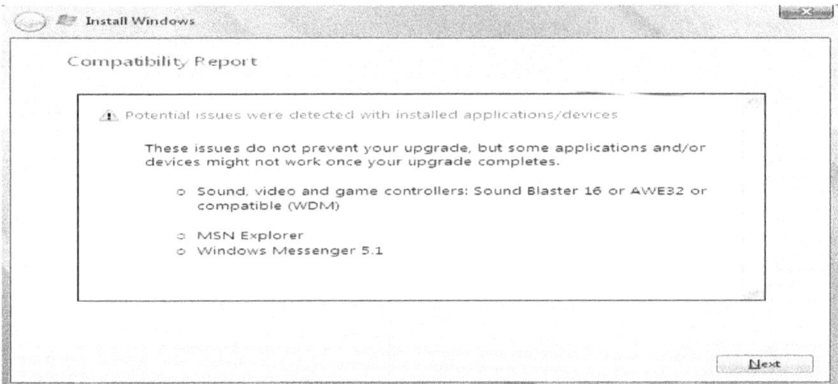

The upgrade process may take several hours to copy windows files, expanding files, installing features, installing updates, and completing upgrade installation. Your computer may restart several times by itself during an upgrade process.

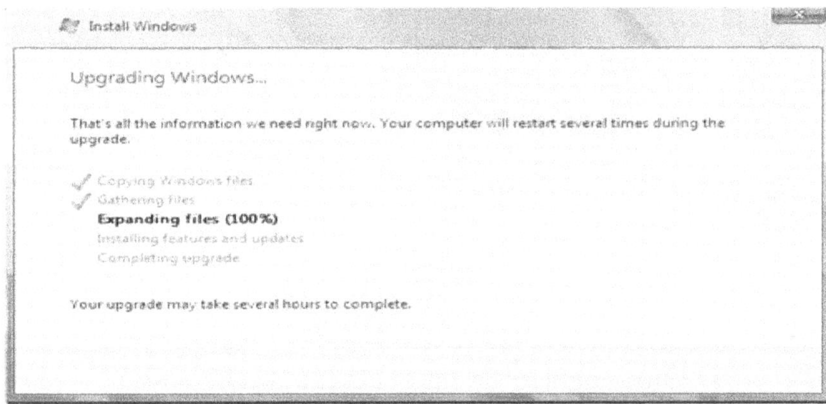

Choose one of the following Windows update options to continue.

a. ***Use recommended settings***: The system will install important and recommended updates for your system. If you decided to choose this option, then following features will turn on automatically:

   a. **Windows automatic updating**: The important and recommended updates for your system will be installed on release of new Microsoft updates.

   b. **Enhanced spyware protection**: Windows Vista provides spyware program, *Windows Defender*, to protect your computer against spywares. The system downloads and installs *Windows Defender* updates to enhance the security of your system against malicious spywares.

c. **Windows problem reporting**: The Windows Vista has *Microsoft Error Reporting* tool that sends necessary information to Microsoft to identify the cause of the problem. If the solution of the problem already exists, the solution will be presented to you to fix the issue that you are having with your system.

d. **Driver from Windows updates**: Windows Vista is capable of downloading and installing device drivers. If the device drivers are available online, it will be downloaded and installed for your system.

e. **Internet Explorer Phishing Filter**: Phishing filter for Internet Explorer will be automatically turned on to check against spam websites. Phishing filter provides you a safe zone to browse web through Internet Explorer.

b. ***Install important updates only***: Only important updates will be installed for your system, but not recommended updates. You must turn on recommended updates features to receive spyware protection updates, solutions to problems updates, and device driver updates.

c. ***Ask me later***: If you decided to choose this option, your computer might not be protected against security threats.

It is recommended to choose ***Use recommended settings*** option to protect your system against any security threads in computing industry. Continuing Windows installation to the next level, choose one of the above mentioned Windows updates options and then click on ***Next***.

Review time and date settings and then click on ***Next***. After reviewing time and date settings, select computer's network location. A public network is designated to work in public areas, such as an airport, coffee shop, and unsecure places where a security key is not required connecting to the Internet. A private network is designed to provide you more secure network. Select the available network location to continue. It may take few minutes to start up the Windows. If you were able to logon to the system, it means you were successful to upgrade Windows Vista operating system from older version to a new version of Microsoft operating system.

Windows Vista Service Pack 1

Microsoft Corporation released Windows Vista Service Pack 1 (SP1) for public with improved performance of operating system on February 4, 2008. SP1 is available to current Windows Vista users through Windows Update if ***Recommended Updates*** option is configured properly for your system. The 32-bit and 64-bit stand-alone installers can be downloaded by going to the Microsoft website at http://www.microsoft.com/downloads/Results.aspx?displaylang=en&nr=50. Initially, the service pack 1 was released in 5 languages, English, French, Spanish, German and Japanese. However, a support package for other 31 languages was released on 14th April 2008.

Before installing SP1 for your system, perform a spyware and virus scan against malicious software. If your system does not have an anti-virus program installed, you can perform a free full scan for your system by going to the safety.live.com. If your system did not find any spyware and virus then you can install SP1 for your system. It is recommended to disable spyware and ant-virus programs while installing SP1.

Load Hard Disk Driver

Insert the Windows Vista DVD disk into the DVD ROM and then reboot/restart the system. Computer will detect the DVD disk by itself and will start downloading Windows files from the DVD disk. This process may take several minutes downloading Windows system files. If your system did not detect the DVD disk by itself, reboot the computer and start pressing ***F12*** key from keyboard as soon as computer starts, until you see the option of making boot orders or allow you to boot your system from the DVD ROM.

You will be prompted to adjust the ***language to install***, ***time and currency format***, and ***keyboard or input method*** preferences and then click on ***Next*** to continue.

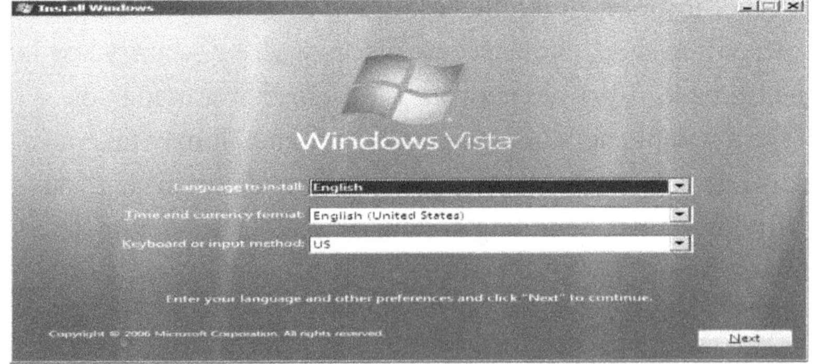

If you would like to review information about your hardware specifications and operating system before installing *Windows Vista* version of Microsoft, click on ***What to know before installing Windows***. Click on ***Install now*** to continue installing Windows.

Enter the product key that came with your system and then click on ***Next*** to continue installing operating system. If you would like to read privacy statement before installing Windows Vista on your machine, click on ***Read our privacy statement***.

Read and accept the license terms and conditions, and then click on ***Next***.

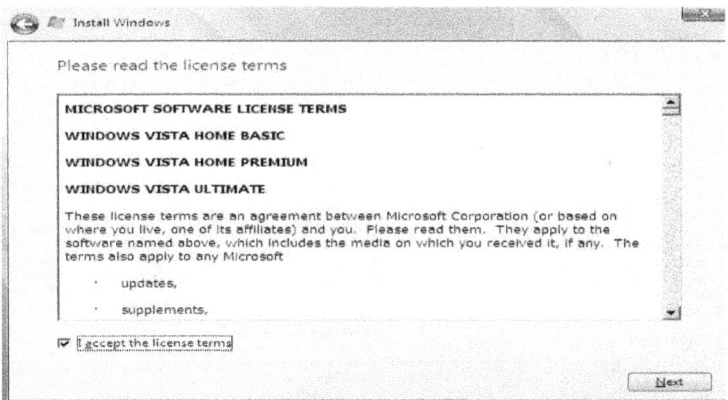

Choose ***Custom (advanced)*** option.

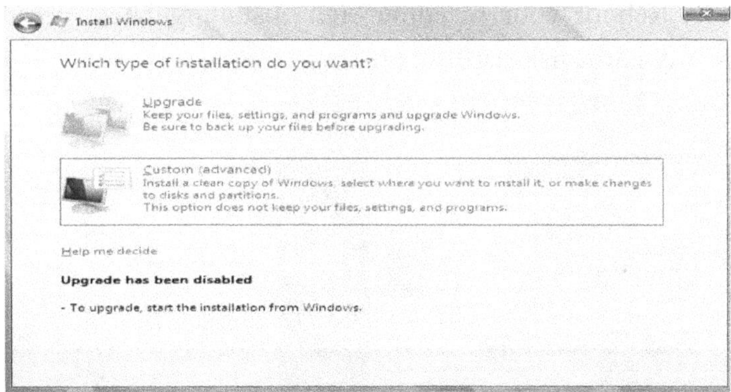

Click on desired disk partition, and then click on the ***Drive options (advanced)*** to have access to options such as *delete*, *format*, *load driver*, *extend the size of hard-drive partition*, and *refresh*.

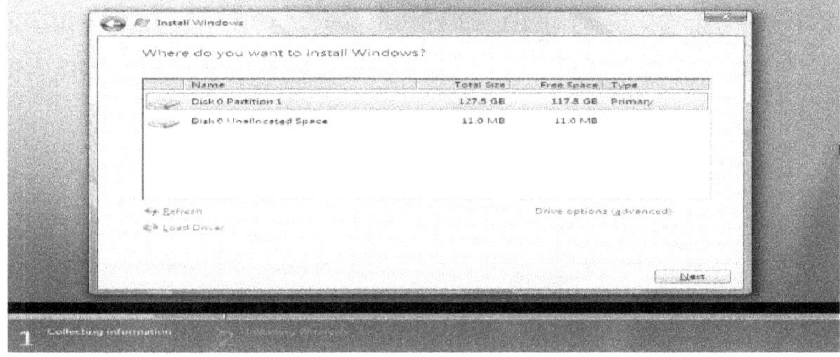

If the hard-drive partition(s) are not visible while installing *Microsoft Windows Vista* operating system. You need to install hard-drive drivers so system can recognize the hard-drive partitions during the Windows installation process. To load driver for hard-drive, click on ***Load Driver*** option.

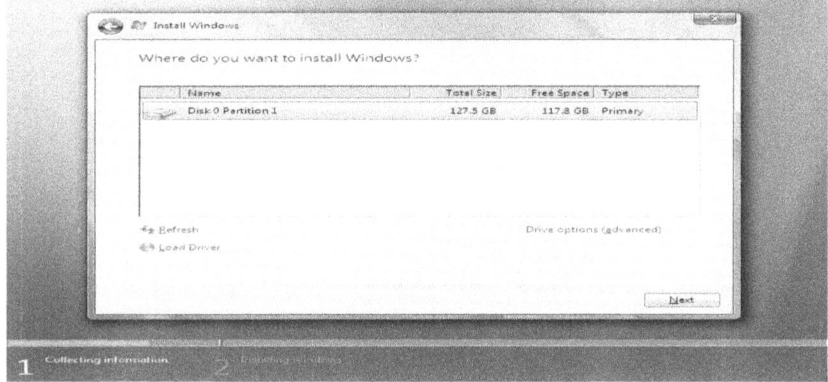

Click on ***Browse*** button, from the dialog box, select the drive volume that has device driver in it and then click on ***OK***. Reboot your machine after installing latest device driver, if you are still unable to see any hard-disk partition(s).

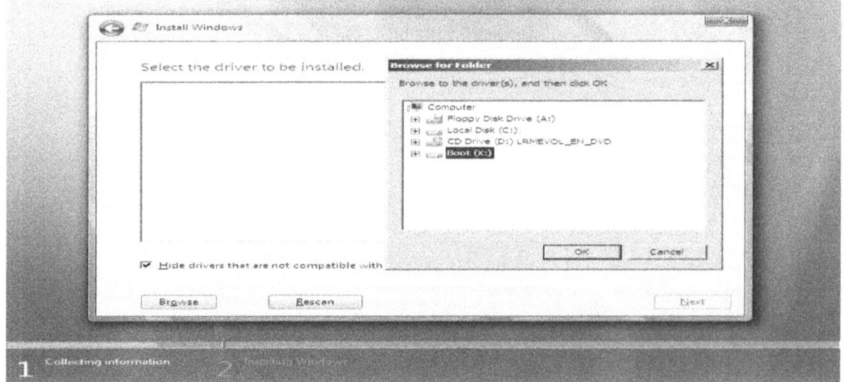

Create Hard Disk Volume/Partition

To create a new volume/partition in hard-disk, you must have unallocated space available. Click on designated unallocated space disk that you wish to use to create a new volume/partition, and then click on ***New***. Type the size of hard-disk volume and then click on ***Apply*** to create a new disk volume for your system. This process may take few minutes to complete.

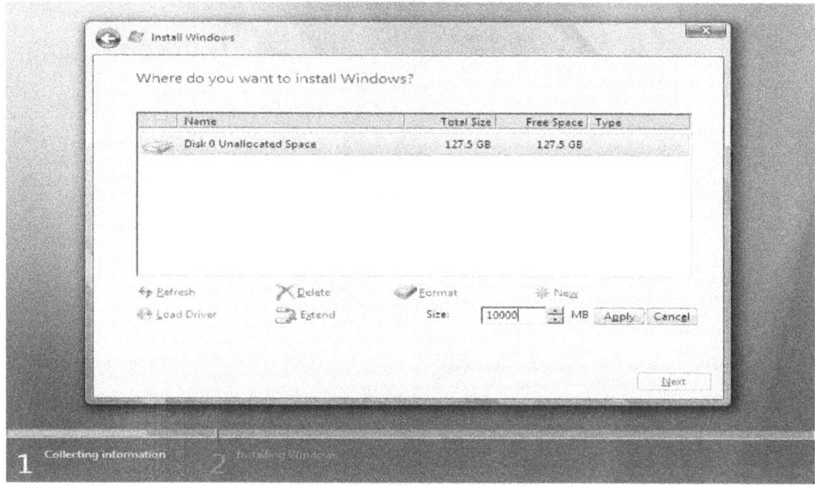

A new hard-disk partition is being created and it is ready to use to store data or install Windows Vista operating system on it.

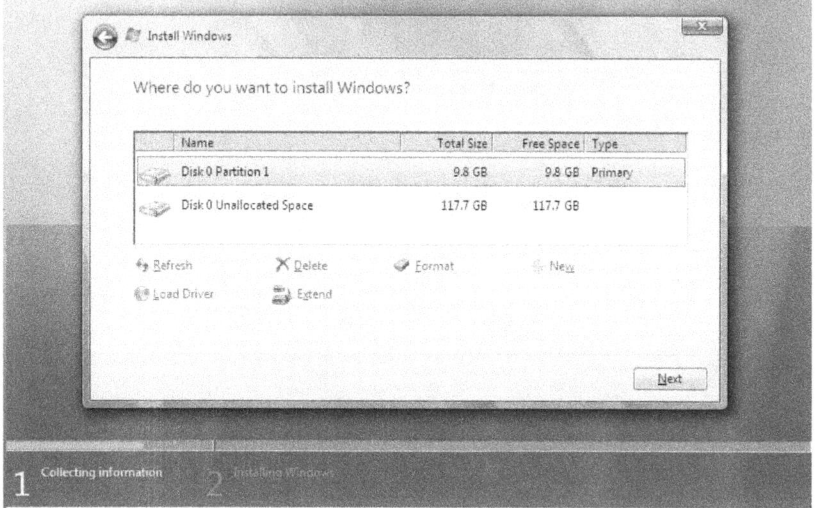

Format Hard Disk Partition

Click the designated partition that you want to format, and then click on ***Format***. This process may take several minutes to complete the process. You cannot format an unallocated space disk.

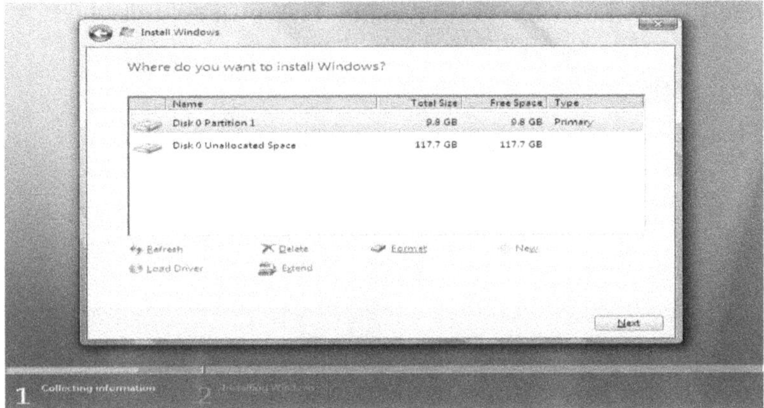

Click on ***OK*** to allow disk partition to be formatted. It is recommended to back up important data before performing a format on a hard-drive partition. The stored data in hard-disk partition will be deleted permanently after it is formatted.

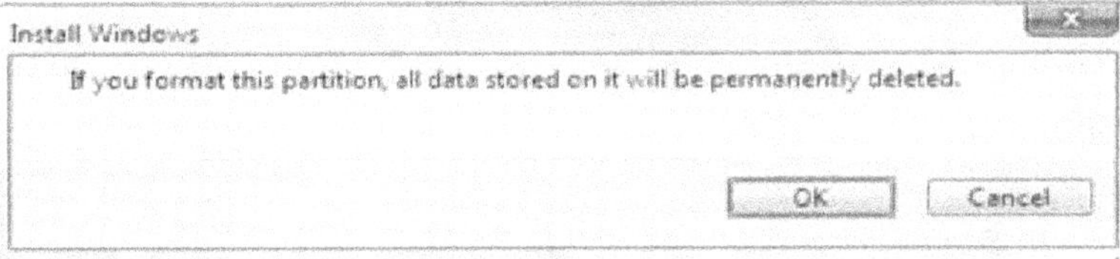

Extend Hard Disk Partition

To extend a partition, select the designated partition and then click on ***Extend***. Type the size for new extended volume and then click on ***Apply*** to create a new extended volume for your system.

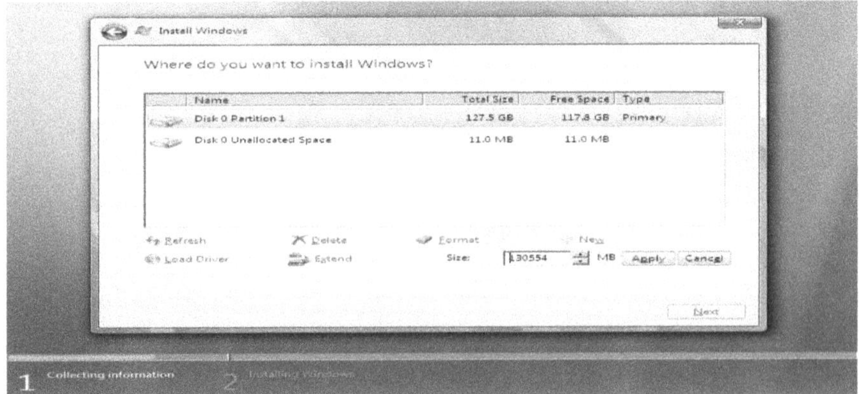

Click ***OK*** to continue the process of extending hard-disk partition. Extending a partition is not a reversible process.

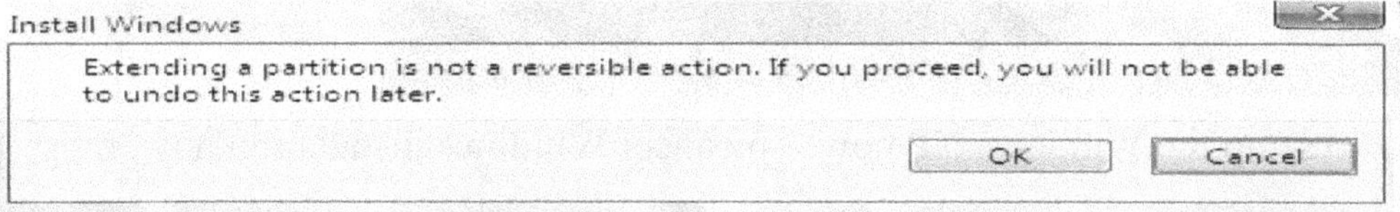

Delete Hard Disk Volume/Partition

Select the hard-disk partition that you want to delete, and then click on ***Delete*** option. Click on ***OK*** to continue the process of deleting hard-disk partition. It is recommended to have a complete backup of your partition before deleting it.

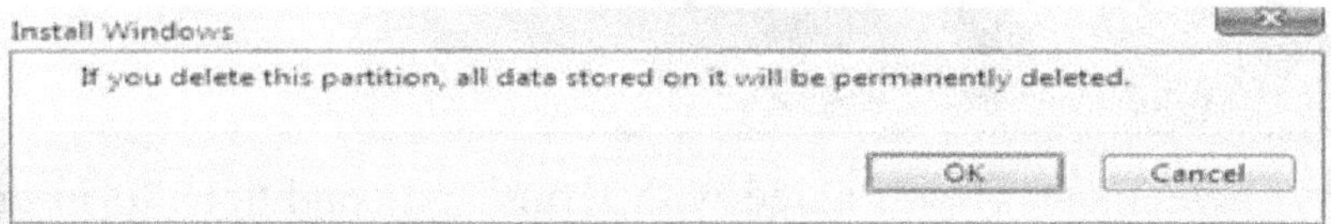

Windows XP Clean Installation

Windows XP was released on October 25, 2001, and it is succeeded by Windows Vista operating system which was released worldwide to the general public on January 30, 2007. The Microsoft operating systems performance can be tested for free of charge for 30 days, and afterward activation is required to use product according to Microsoft terms and conditions. If your system needs to be downgraded from Windows Vista to Windows XP, the steps are explained below.

Insert the Windows XP Professional CD into your CD/DVD-ROM drive and reboot/restart the system. Computer will boot with the CD-ROM and will ask you to ***Press any key to boot from CD*** to continue installing *Windows XP*, press ***Enter***.

```
Press any key to boot from CD..
```

If you do not see above the screen, reboot the computer and start pressing ***F12*** key *from keyboard* as soon as computer starts, until you see the option of making boot orders or allow you to boot your system from the DVD/CD ROM.

Your system will load a blue screen and the ***Setup*** will start copying files. This process may take several minutes depending on your computer speed and performance.

This step does not apply to all Windows XP users. Advanced Windows XP users may install SCSI or RAID drivers. If you decided to install a third party or RAID driver for your hard-drive, press ***F6*** and then follow on-screen instructions to install hard-disk drivers.

```
Setup is inspecting your computer's hardware configuration...
```

Press ***Enter*** to setup the Windows XP now. To cancel Windows installation now, press ***F3***.

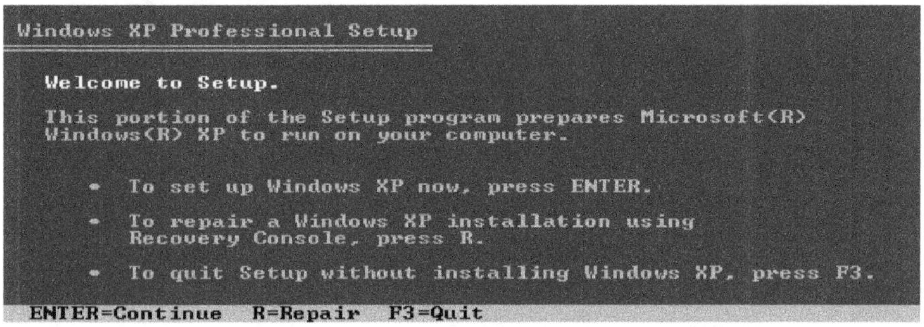

```
Windows XP Professional Setup

  Welcome to Setup.

  This portion of the Setup program prepares Microsoft(R)
  Windows(R) XP to run on your computer.

      •  To set up Windows XP now, press ENTER.

      •  To repair a Windows XP installation using
         Recovery Console, press R.

      •  To quit Setup without installing Windows XP, press F3.

ENTER=Continue  R=Repair  F3=Quit
```

Read Windows XP license agreement. If you agree with terms and conditions to install *Windows XP*, then press ***F8*** to accept and continue installation process. If you do not agree with Microsoft terms and conditions, press ***F3*** to cancel the *Windows XP* installation process.

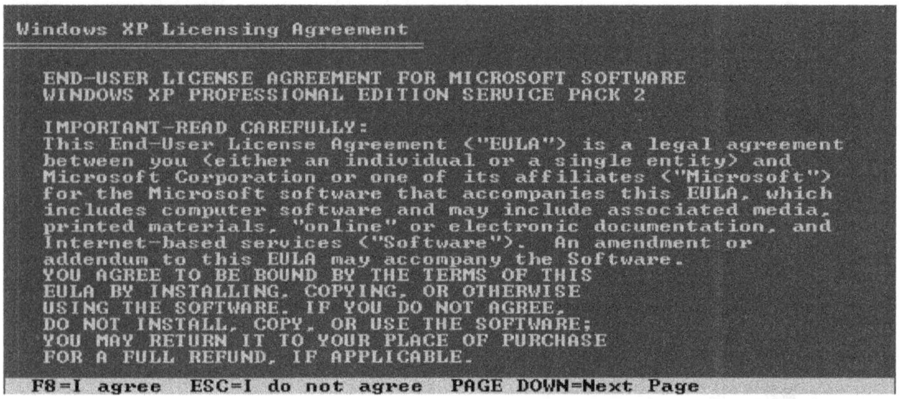

```
Windows XP Licensing Agreement

  END-USER LICENSE AGREEMENT FOR MICROSOFT SOFTWARE
  WINDOWS XP PROFESSIONAL EDITION SERVICE PACK 2

  IMPORTANT-READ CAREFULLY:
  This End-User License Agreement ("EULA") is a legal agreement
  between you (either an individual or a single entity) and
  Microsoft Corporation or one of its affiliates ("Microsoft")
  for the Microsoft software that accompanies this EULA, which
  includes computer software and may include associated media,
  printed materials, "online" or electronic documentation, and
  Internet-based services ("Software").  An amendment or
  addendum to this EULA may accompany the Software.
  YOU AGREE TO BE BOUND BY THE TERMS OF THIS
  EULA BY INSTALLING, COPYING, OR OTHERWISE
  USING THE SOFTWARE. IF YOU DO NOT AGREE,
  DO NOT INSTALL, COPY, OR USE THE SOFTWARE;
  YOU MAY RETURN IT TO YOUR PLACE OF PURCHASE
  FOR A FULL REFUND, IF APPLICABLE.
F8=I agree  ESC=I do not agree  PAGE DOWN=Next Page
```

Setup may scan for previous Windows installation, press ***ENTER*** if prompted.

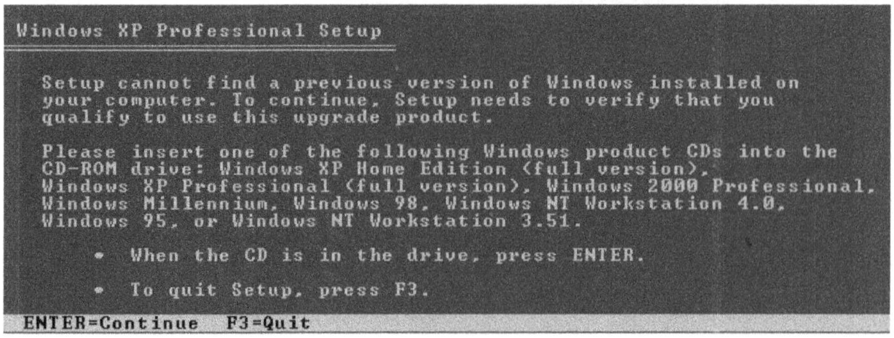

```
Windows XP Professional Setup

  Setup cannot find a previous version of Windows installed on
  your computer. To continue, Setup needs to verify that you
  qualify to use this upgrade product.

  Please insert one of the following Windows product CDs into the
  CD-ROM drive: Windows XP Home Edition (full version),
  Windows XP Professional (full version), Windows 2000 Professional,
  Windows Millennium, Windows 98, Windows NT Workstation 4.0,
  Windows 95, or Windows NT Workstation 3.51.

      •  When the CD is in the drive, press ENTER.

      •  To quit Setup, press F3.

ENTER=Continue  F3=Quit
```

If Windows XP operating system has been installed on your machine previously, the Windows will allow you to repair the operating system by pressing letter ***R*** from keyboard, otherwise press ***Esc*** to install fresh copy of Windows XP. To quit the installation process, press ***F3***.

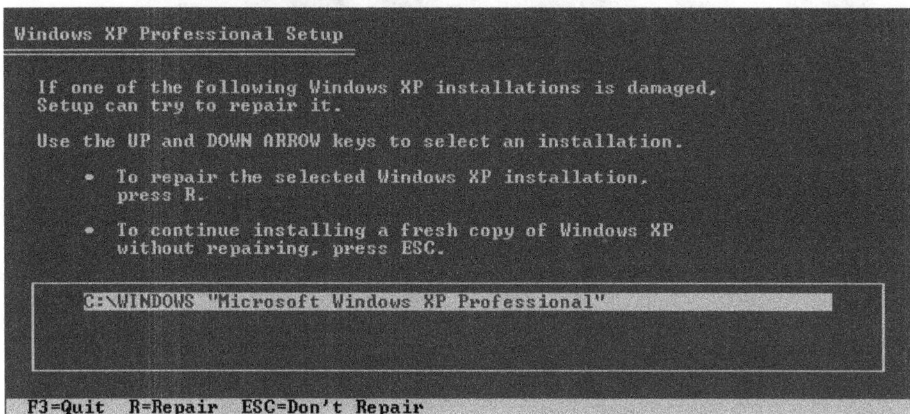

If you want to create a new partition or delete a selected partition of the hard-disk, press the letter ***C***, or the letter ***D*** from the keyboard, respectively and then follow on-screen instructions to perform the task. If not, hit ***Enter*** to install the Windows into the selected hard-drive partition. If you hard-drive has more than one partition for your system, make sure you are formatting designated partition of the hard-drive.

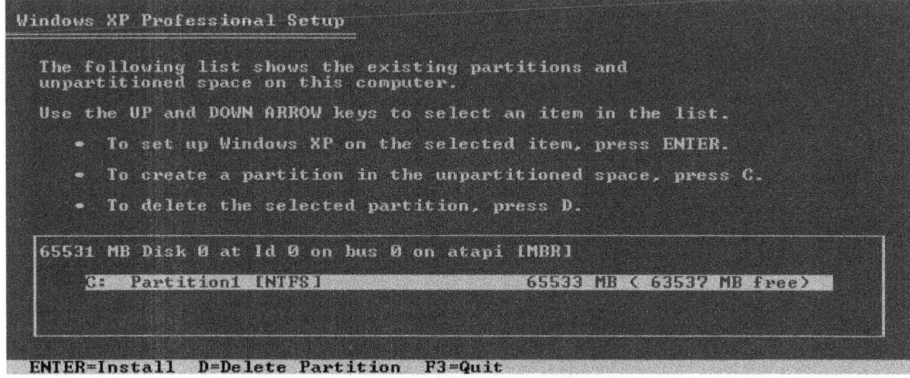

If the hard-drive partition contains system files of another operating system, you will be warned not to install new operating system in the same partition. If you would like to select different partition to install *Microsoft Windows XP*, press ***ESC*** key from keyboard to create a new partition to install Windows on it, otherwise press letter ***C*** from keyboard to install Windows in the selected partition.

Choose one of the available file systems to format the hard-drive of the computer. It is recommended to choose NTFS (New Technology File System) option to format the hard-drive, if this option is available for your system. NTFS has better security system over FAT (Encrypting File System).

Windows XP Professional Setup

Setup will install Windows XP on partition

C: Partition1 [NTFS] 65533 MB (63537 MB free)

on 65531 MB Disk 0 at Id 0 on bus 0 on atapi [MBR].

Use the UP and DOWN ARROW keys to select the file system you want, and then press ENTER. If you want to select a different partition for Windows XP, press ESC.

Format the partition using the NTFS file system (Quick)
Format the partition using the NTFS file system
Leave the current file system intact (no changes)

ENTER=Continue ESC=Cancel

To format the drive, press letter ***F*** from keyboard, otherwise press ***ESC*** to select a different partition of the hard-drive to install Windows XP on it.

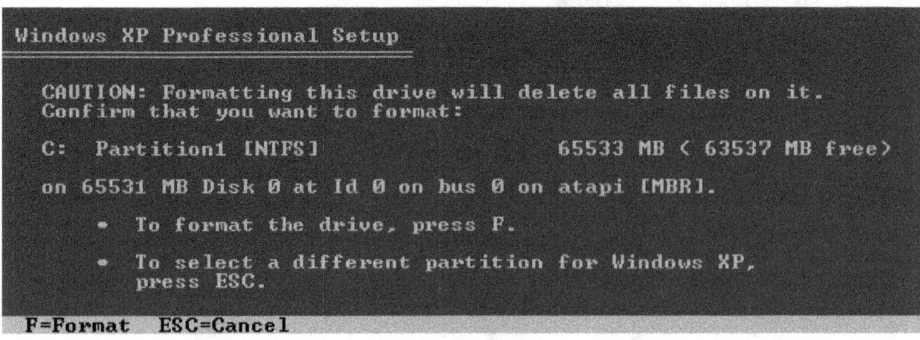

This process may take several minutes.

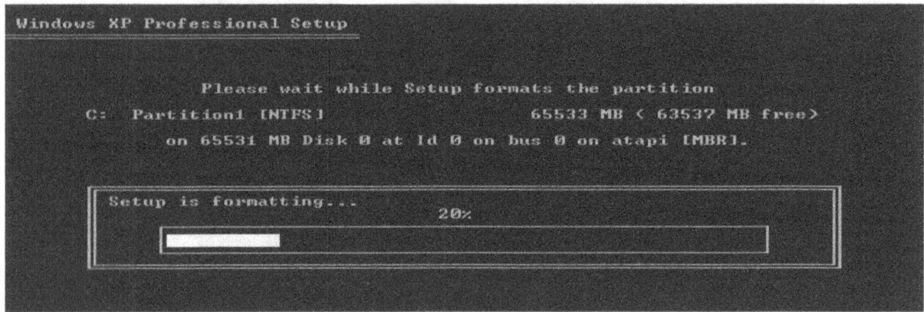

Setup will start copying new files for your system. This process may take several minutes depending on your computer performance.

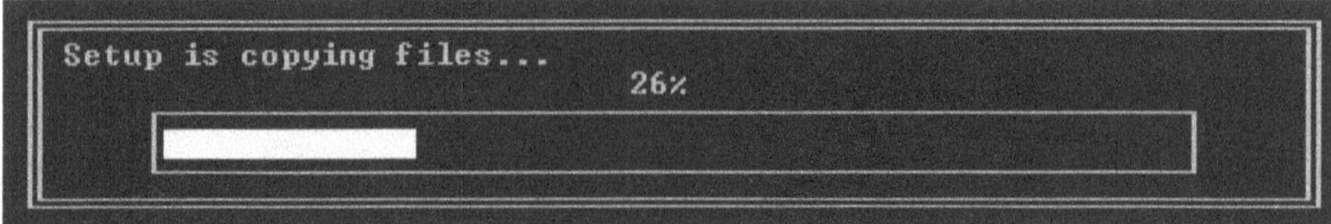

System may take few minutes to initializes Windows configuration.

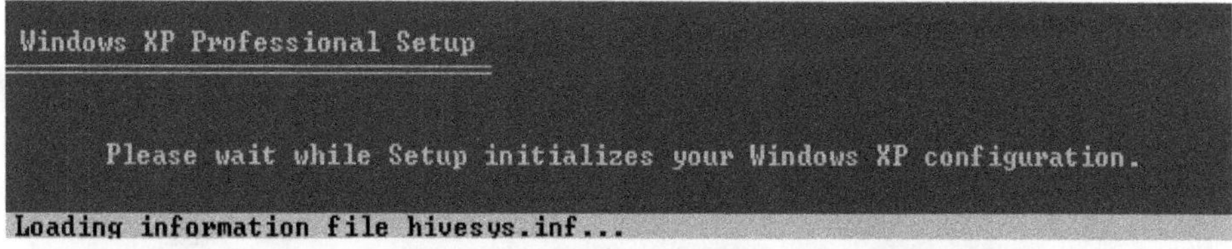

Press ***Enter*** to reboot the system or wait until it reboots itself.

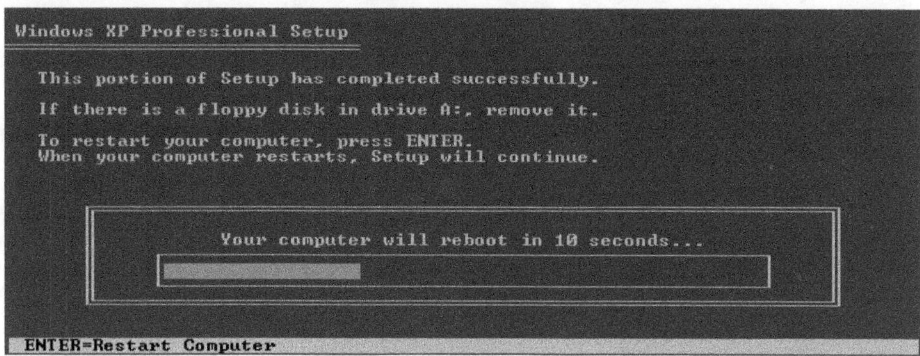

Ignore, if ***Press any key to boot from CD*** screen window is prompted.

This process may take several minutes to perform necessary operations to complete Windows installation process. You may see some or all of the following screens.

An exciting new look

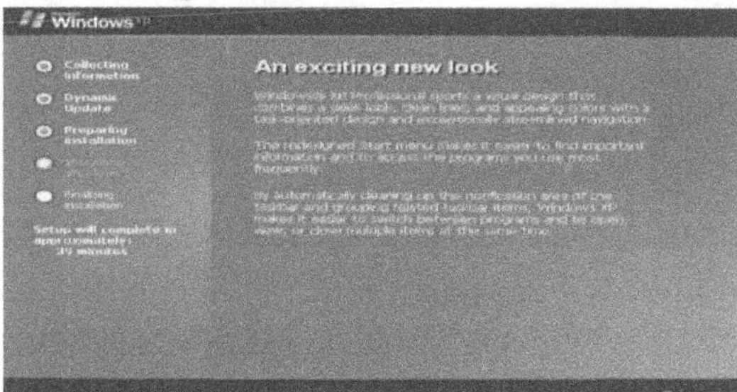

Try the easiest Windows® yet

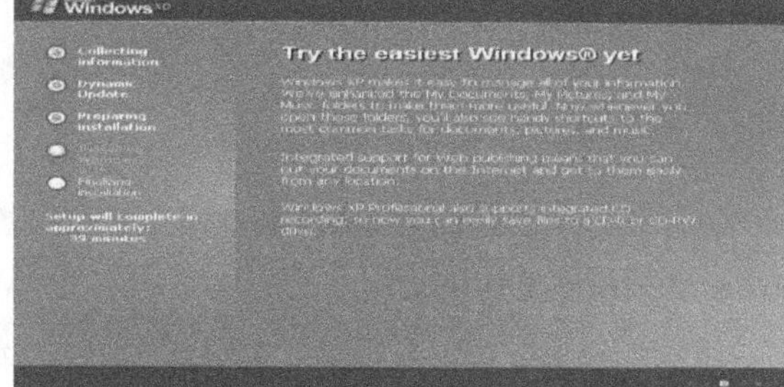

Stay up to date

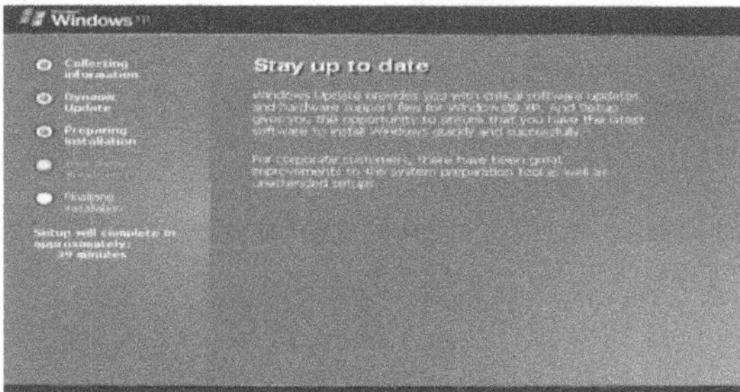

Your computer will be faster….

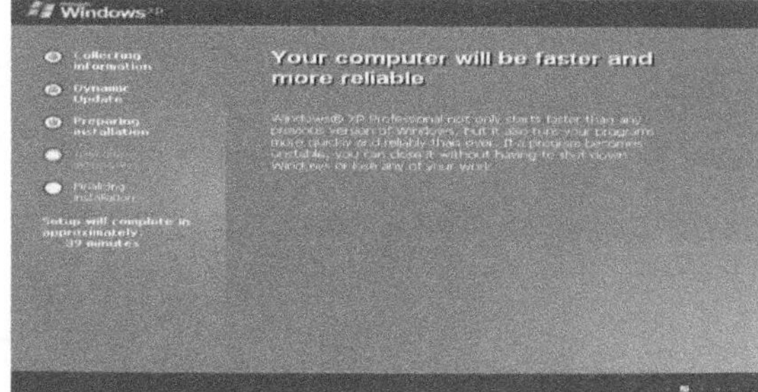

Get support for the latest hardware ….

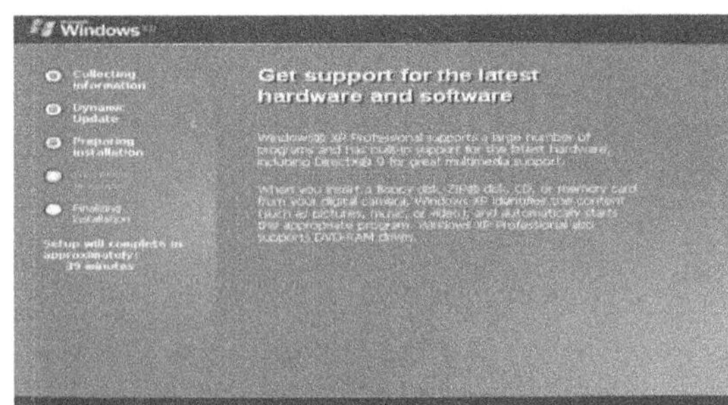

Easily move documents ….

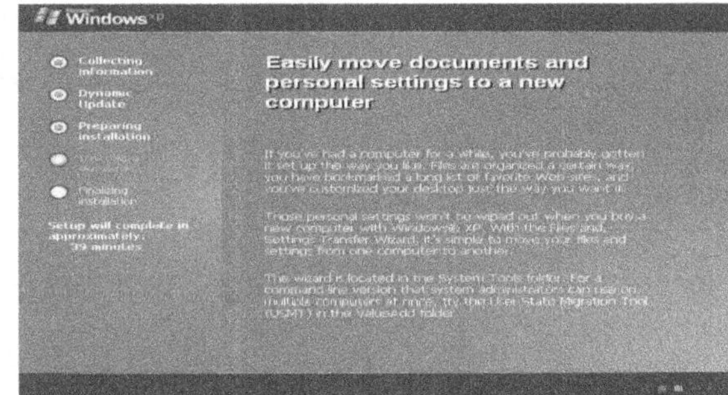

Surfing the Internet …..

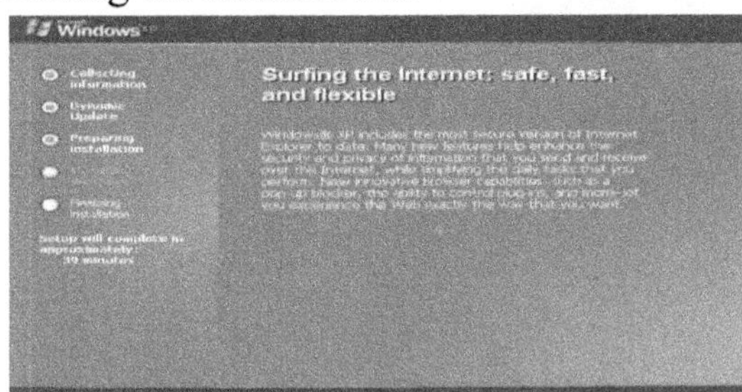

Explore your creative side with…..

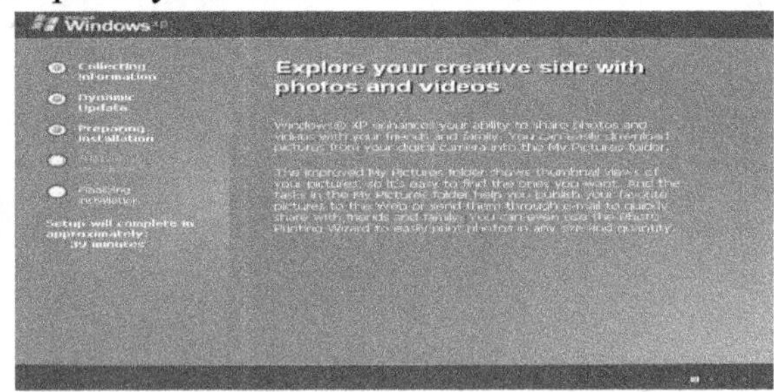

Music and entertainment…

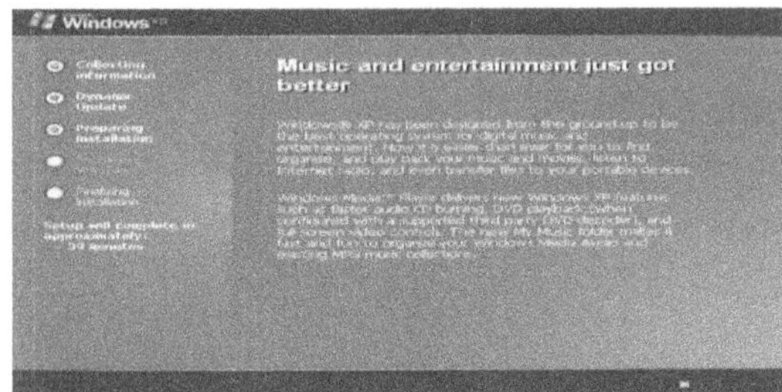

Windows Movie Maker…

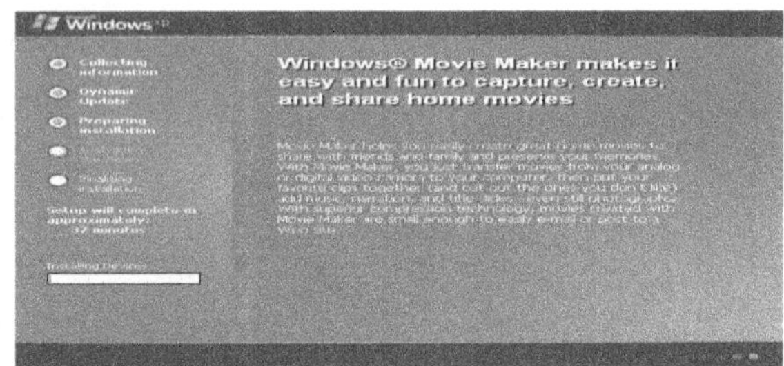

Work anytime, anywhere

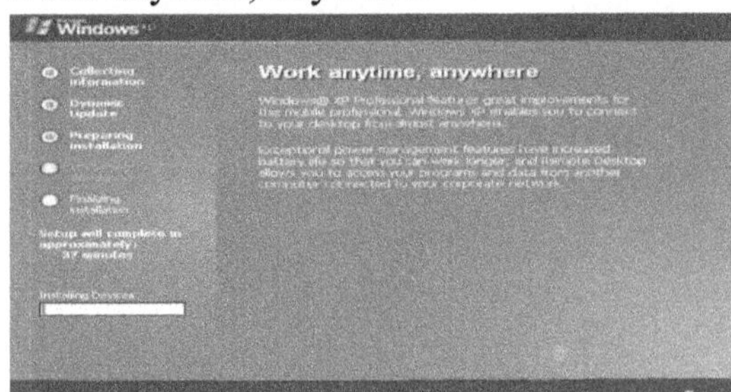

Windows XP is great….

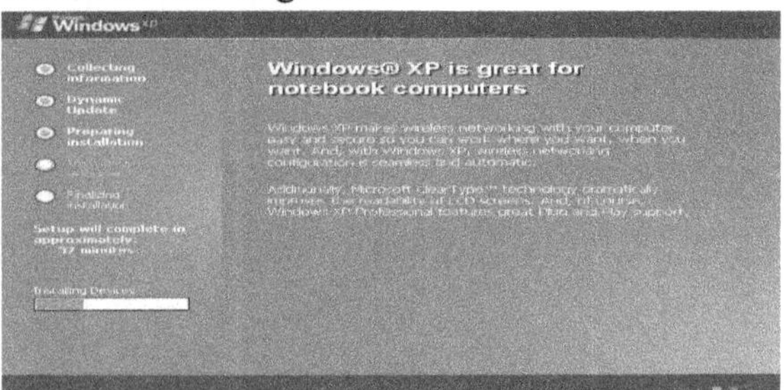

Stay connected with colleagues….

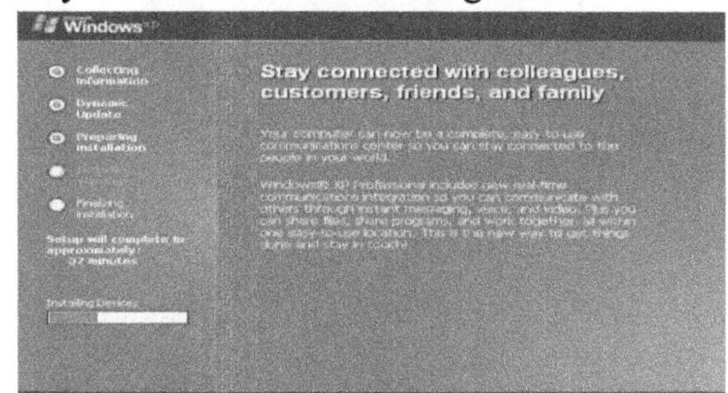

The most dependable Windows….

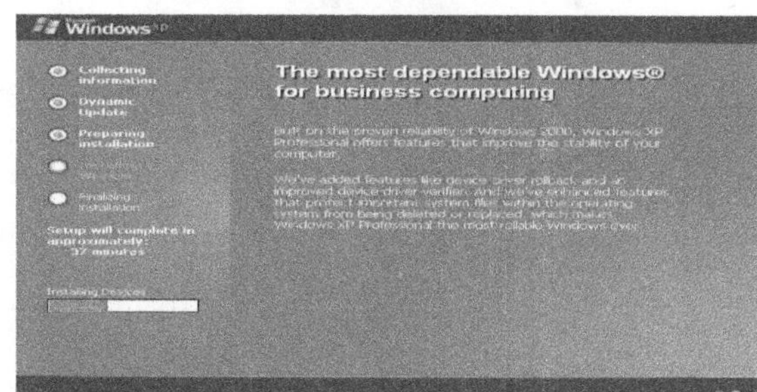

Experience the ultimate in….

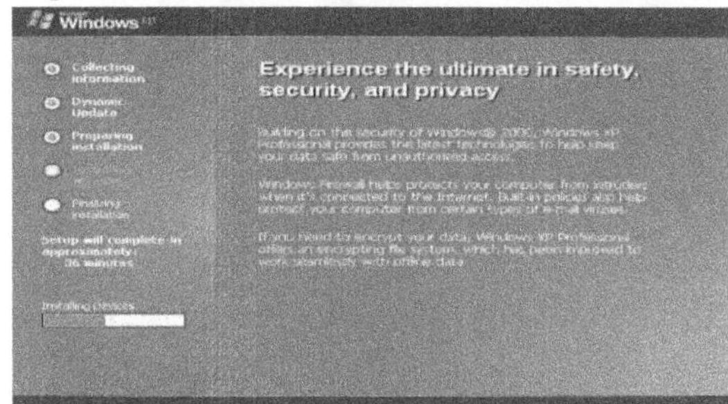

Be assured of great accessibility

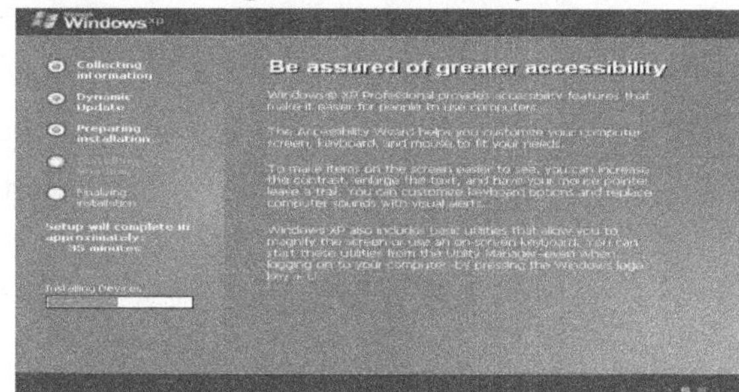

Now it's easier to get…..

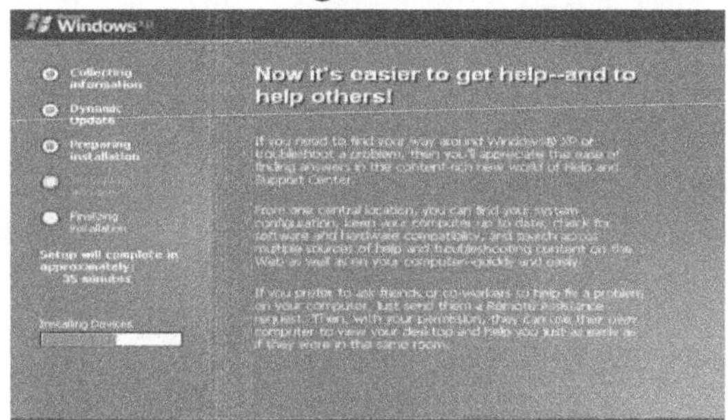

Enjoy using Windows XP

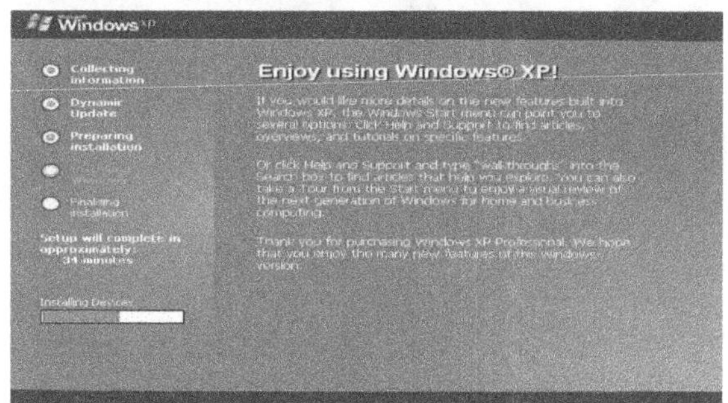

If you would like to customize Windows XP for different region and language, click on ***Customize***, otherwise click on ***Next*** to continue with default regional and language settings.

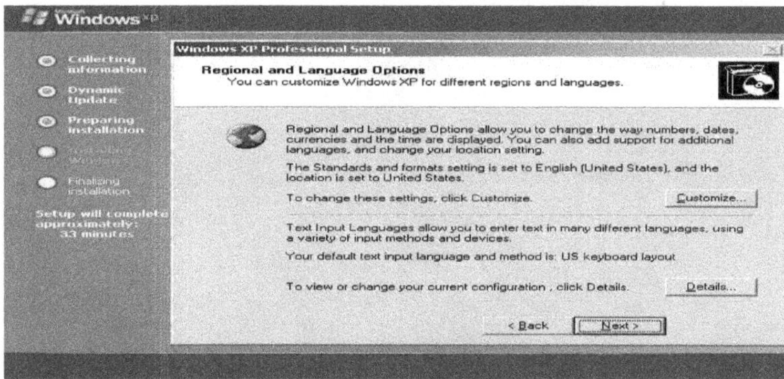

Enter your ***Name*** and ***Organization*** name to personalize Windows XP operating system, and then click on ***Next*** to continue installing Windows.

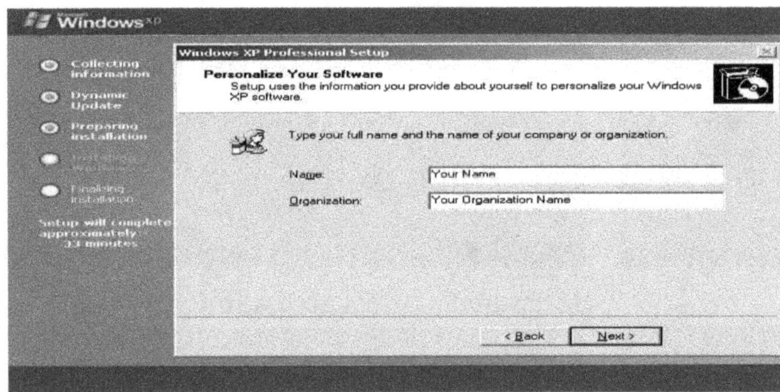

Enter the product key that came with your system and then click on ***Next***. In most cases, the product key is bundled with the software or it comes with the system. Find your 25 characters Windows product key on your computer (look at the left, right, top, and bottom of the machine to find the key sticker). A product key identifies the copy of your Windows XP and it is the unique key for every machine which needs to be entered correctly to continue further Windows installation.

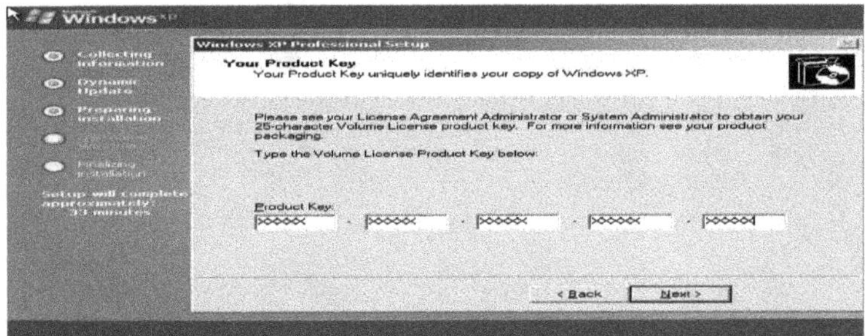

Enter computer name that should not contain spaces and periods (.) between two letters but it may contain letters (a-z), numbers (0-9) and hyphens (-). Administrator password is optional to enter but it is recommended to have a strong password to protect your system from unauthorized user access. Click on ***Next*** to continue installing the operating system.

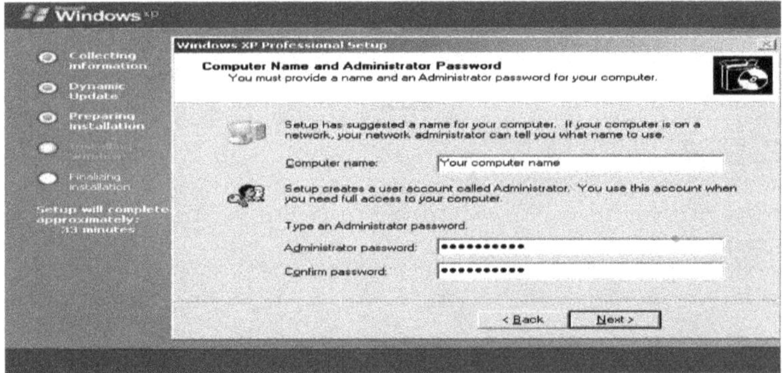

Adjust ***Date and Time*** and ***Time Zone*** settings for your system and then click on ***Next*** to continue the process.

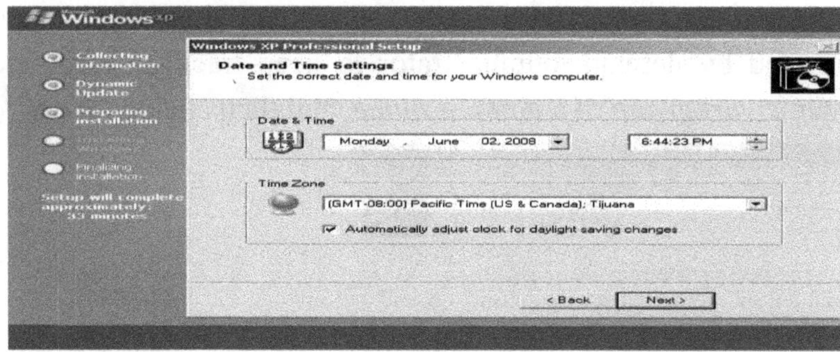

This process may take several minutes to perform necessary operations to complete Windows installation process. You may see some or all of the following screens.

Your computer will be faster….

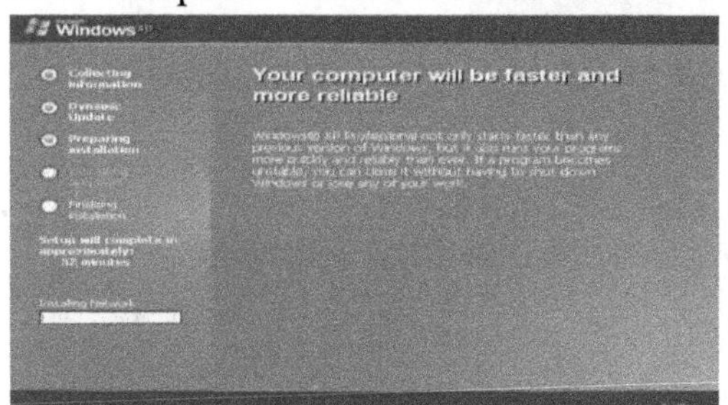

Get support for the latest….

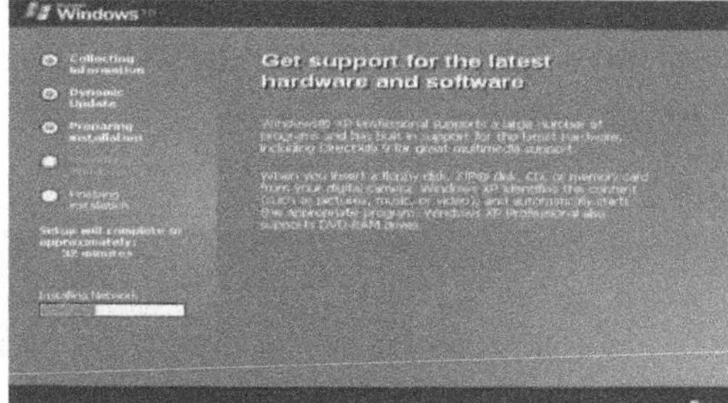

Easily move documents….

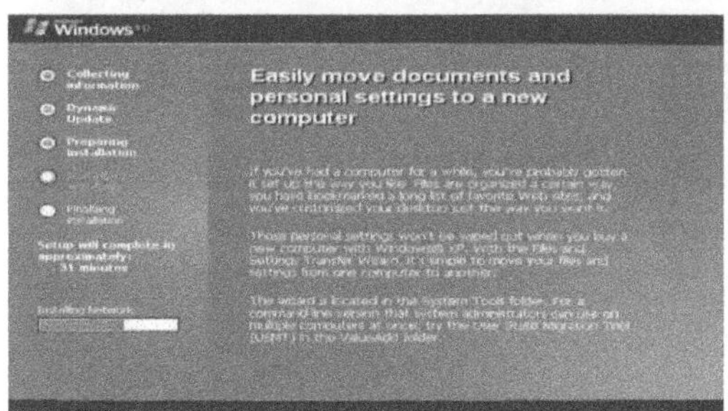

Surfing the Internet…...

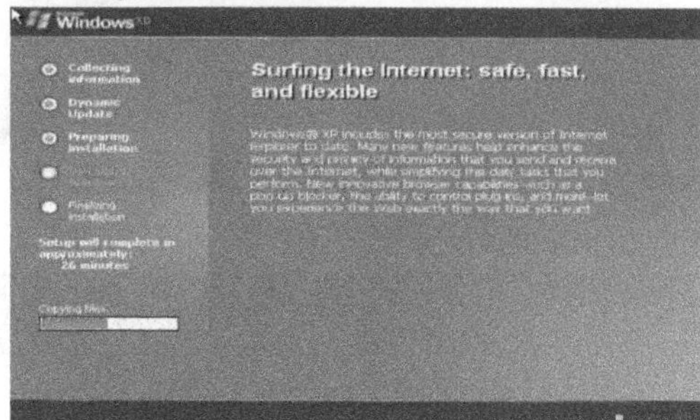

Select either ***Typical settings*** option or ***Custom settings*** option for networking. It is recommended to choose ***Typical settings*** option for your system. Click on ***Next*** to continue installing Windows. If you have specific networking needs that you know of, select ***Custom*** option and then follow on-screen instructions to configure networking components.

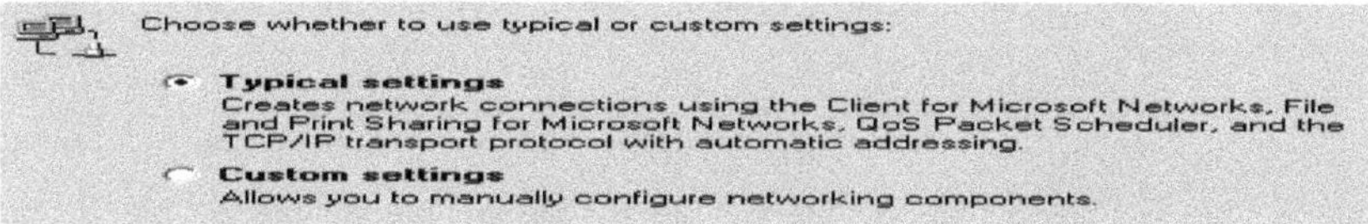

By default, every computer is a part of the ***workgroup***. A workgroup is a collection of computers which are designed to share resources with each other over the local area network. A domain is collection of computers that joined to an Active Directory domain. An Active Directory is managed by network administrator to keep track of corporate level resources for users. Enter a ***workgroup*** or a ***domain name***, and then click on ***Next***.

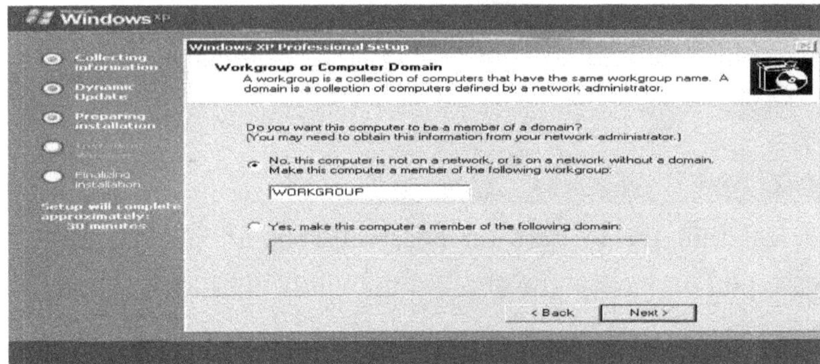

The system may take several minutes to download necessary system files. You may see some or all of the following screens.

Easily move documents ….

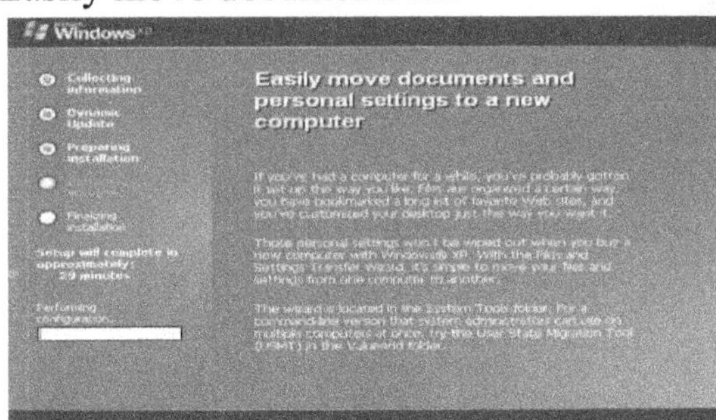

Surfing the Internet….

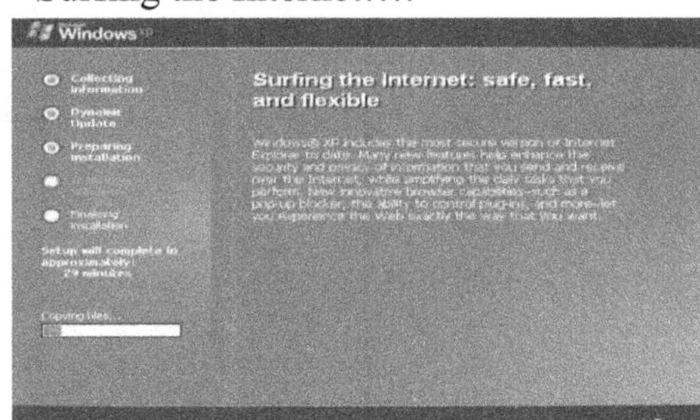

Explore your creative side….

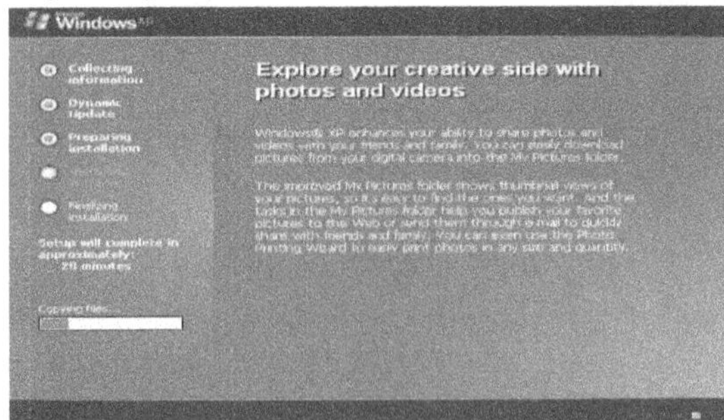

Music and entertainment….

Windows Movie Maker….

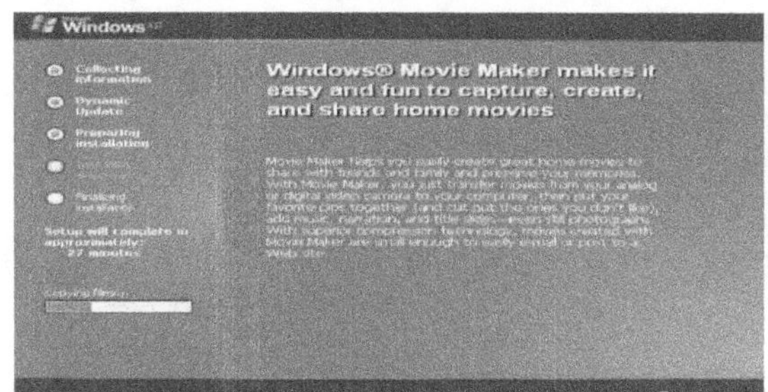

Work anytime, anywhere

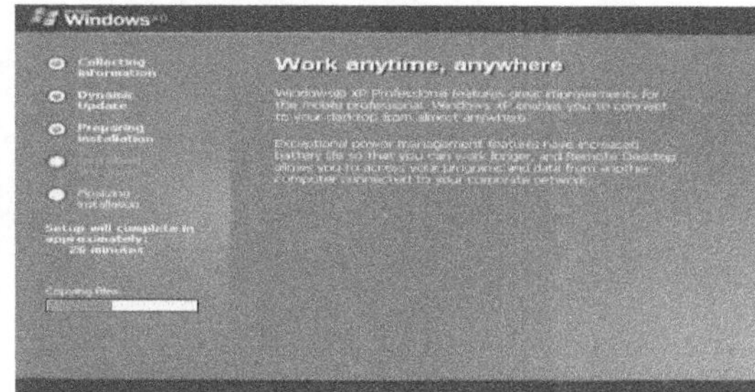

Windows XP is great….

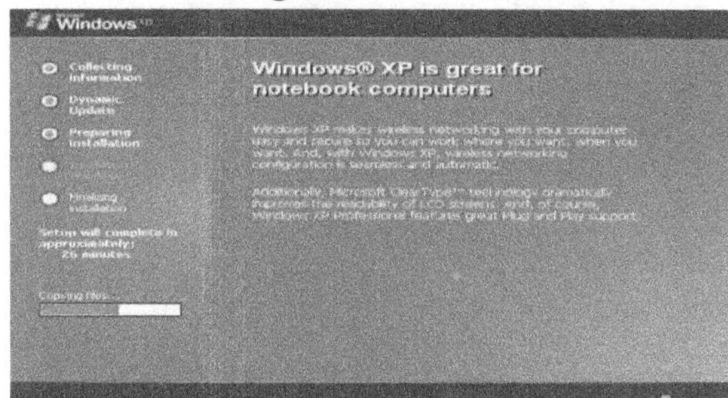

Stay connected with colleagues….

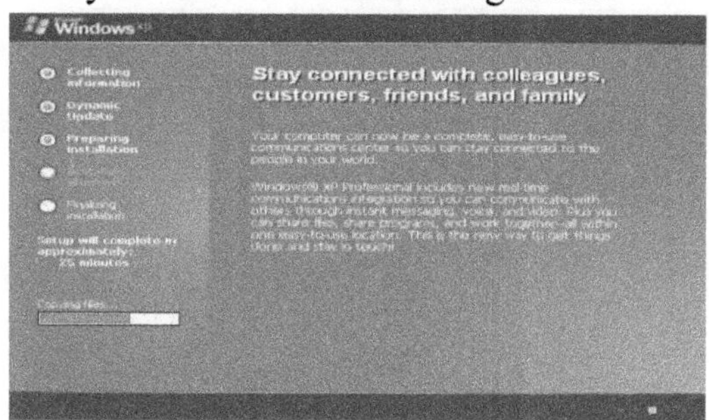

The most dependable Windows….

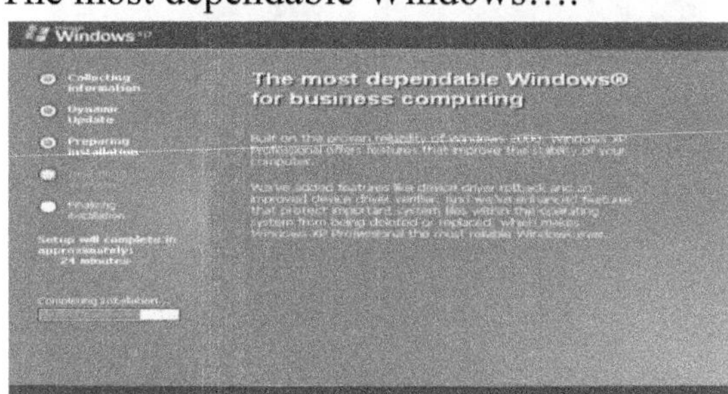

Experience the ultimate….

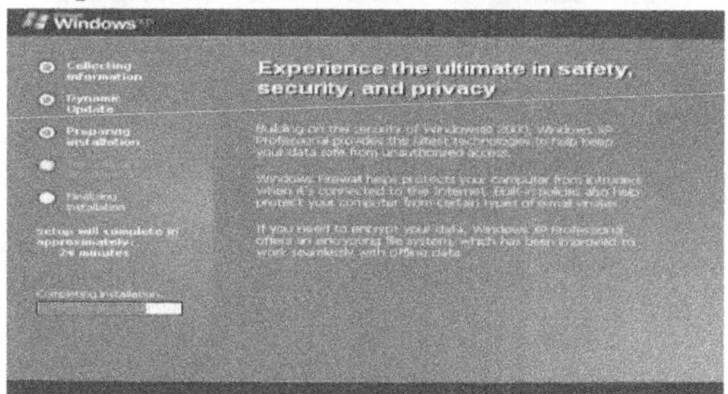

Be assured of….

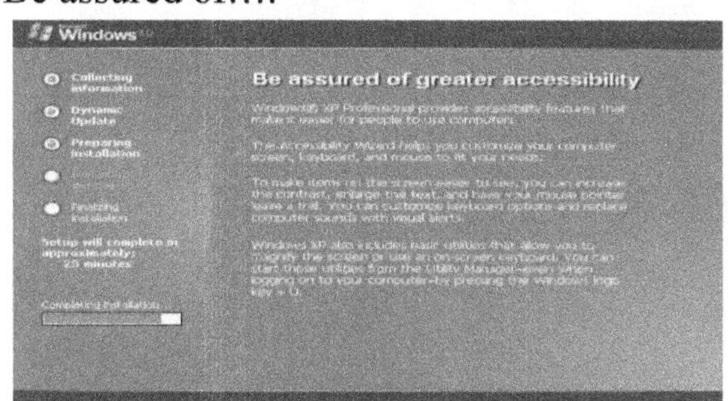

Now it's easir to get help….

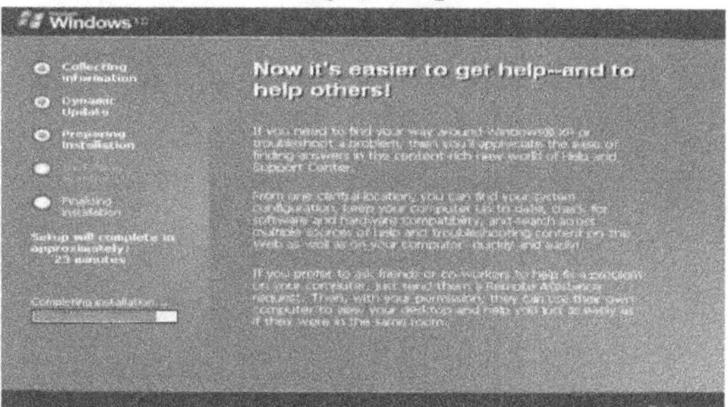

Enjoy using Windows XP

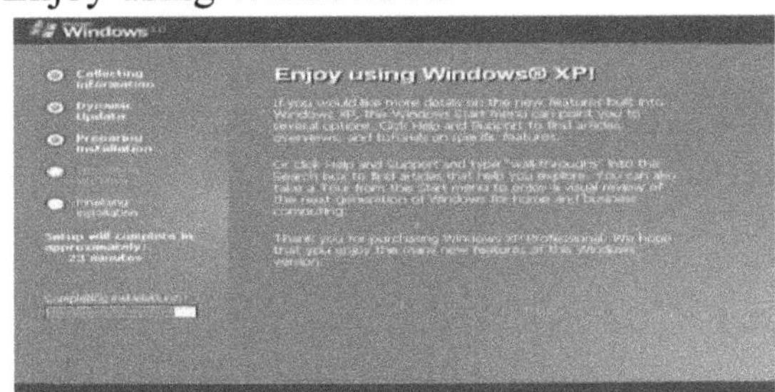

An exciting new look

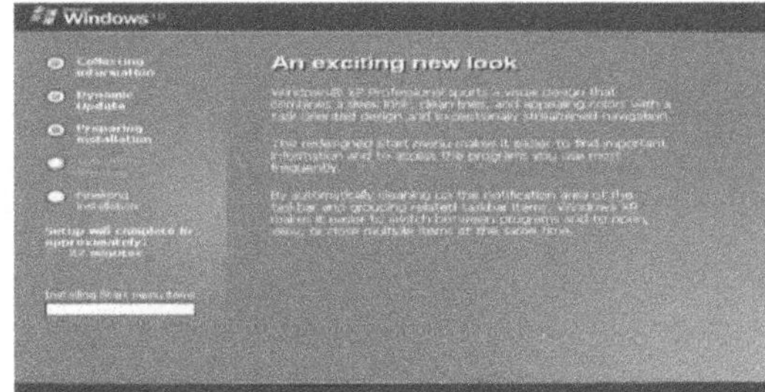

Try the easiest Windows yet

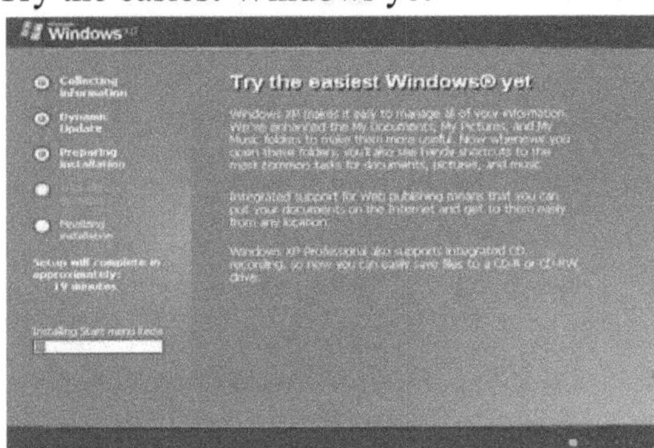

Stay up to date

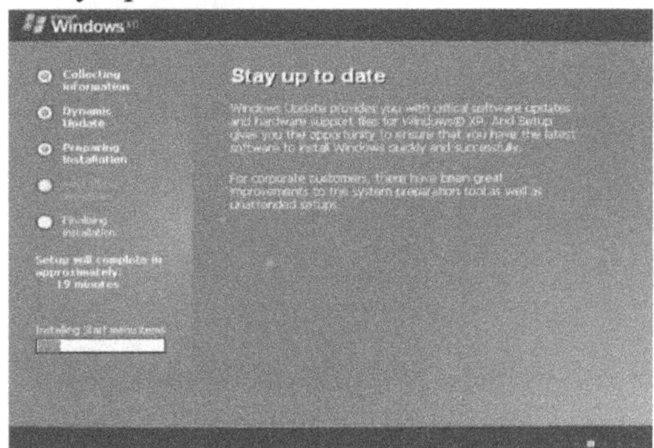

Your computer will be fastet....

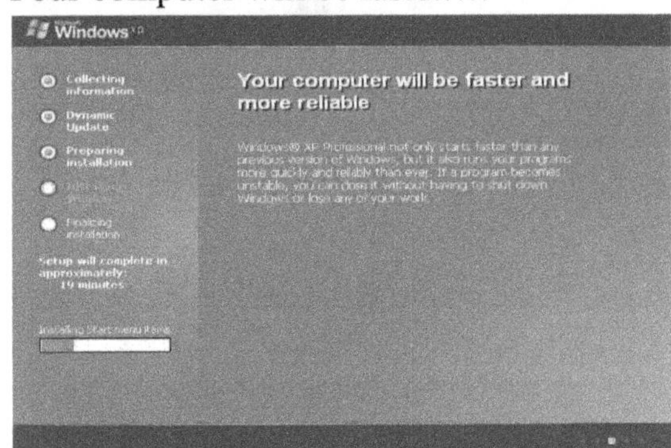

Get support for the latest....

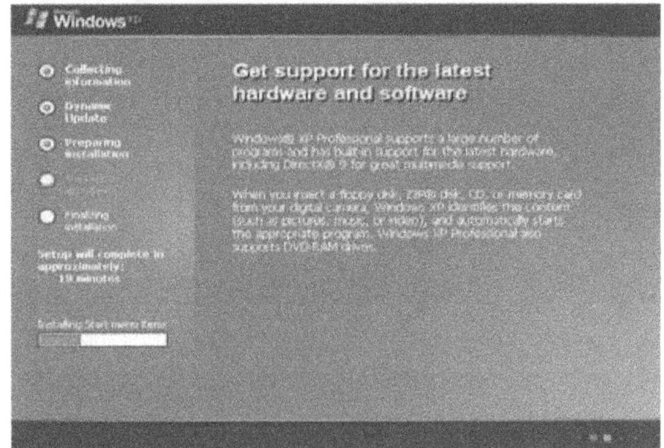

Windows XP Professional is loading…

Click ***OK*** to improve and adjust display settings.

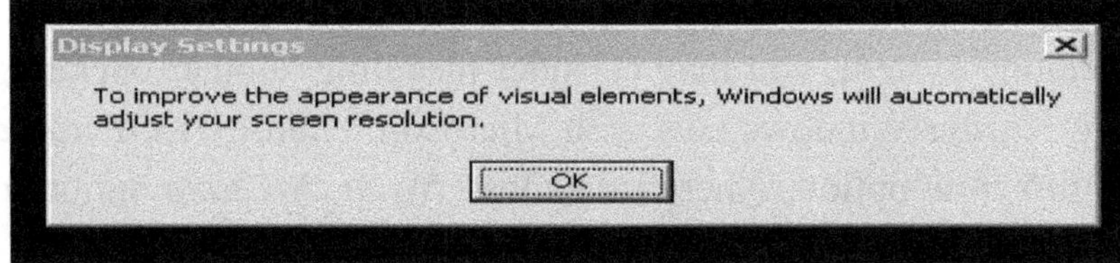

Click ***OK*** to allow system to adjust screen resolution.

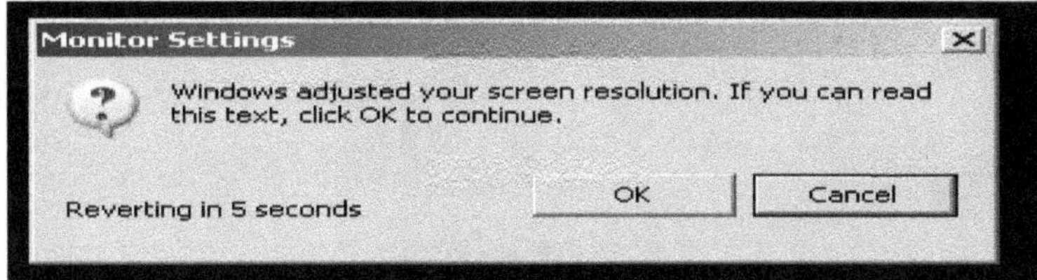

Choose ***Help protect my PC by turning on Automatic Updates now*** option and then click ***Next***.

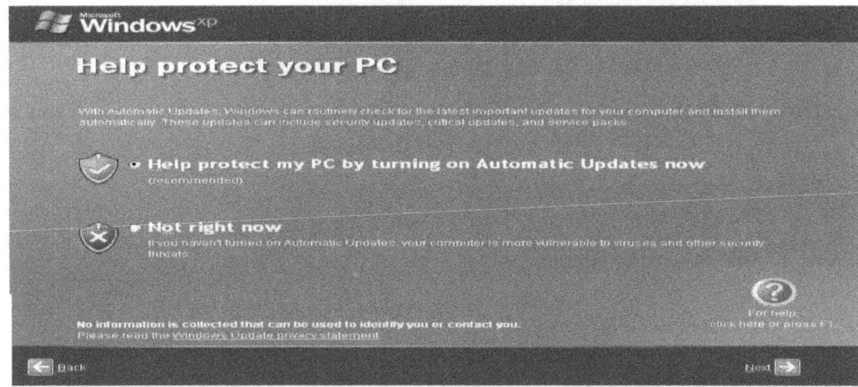

If you are asked to setup Internet conenction now, select ***Skip*** option to continue to the next step. The network and Internet connection can be configured after completing Windows installation.

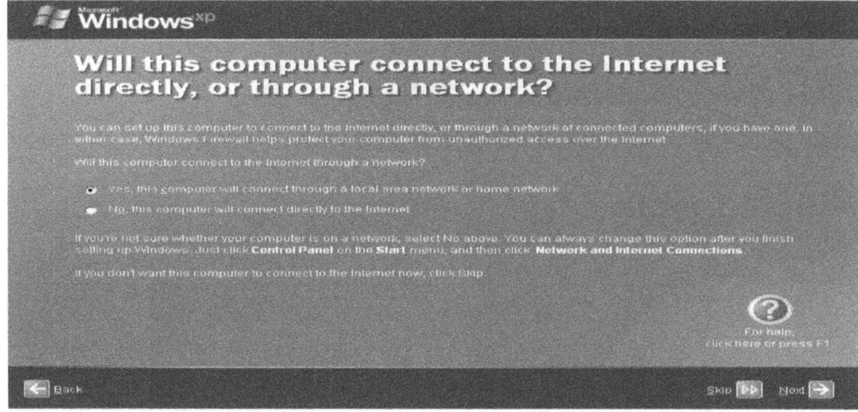

Microsoft allows you to use any Microsoft operating systems for 30 days without activating the product. If you are not completely satisfied with the performance of *Microsoft Windows XP* operating system, you may consider installing another operating system. If you would like to register Windows now with Microsoft, choose ***Yes, I would like to register with Microsoft now*** option, otherwise choose ***No at this time*** option to continue without activating the product.

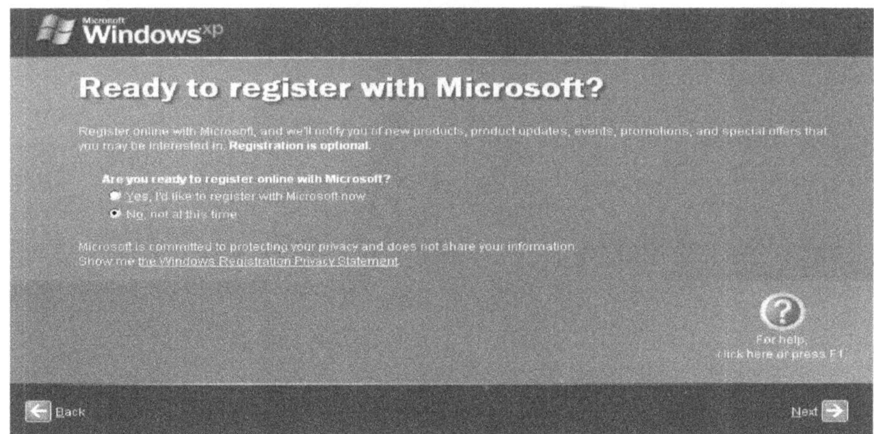

Create different account for each user who will be using this computer. Click on ***Next*** to finish setting up user's accounts.

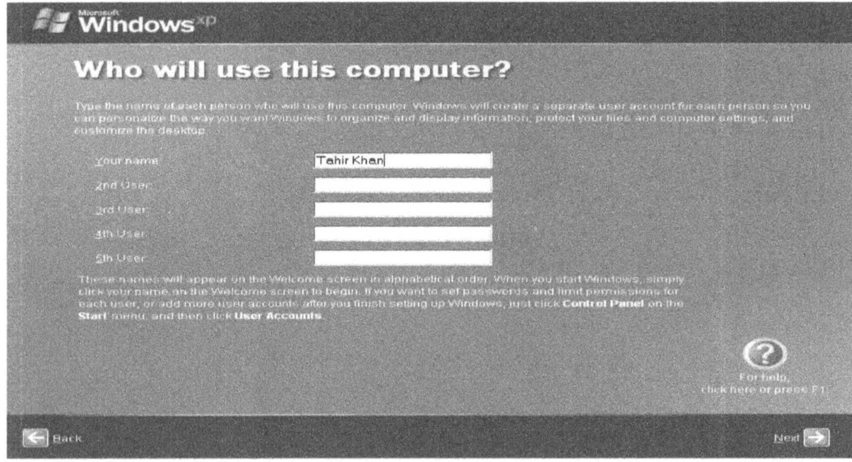

Click ***Finish*** to complete Windows XP installation and then your system will Log you in to the Windows XP.

Question: What is Windows Aero Interface?

Answer: Windows Aero is a translucent glass interface for Windows Vista users, if they meet following hardware requirements.

- Windows Display Driver Model (WDDM) for video card
- DirectX 9 capable graphics cards
- Hardware pixel shader 2.0
- 32-bit per pixel memory
- Minimum of 128 MB graphics memory

Question: Can I run Windows Vista operating system without running Vista Aero interface?

Answer: Yes, Windows Aero interface is just a computer theme which enables more visual dynamics for your system.

Question: What is Windows Vista Capable PC hardware?

Answer: A Windows Vista Capable PC is designed to meet the minimum hardware requirements to run Windows Vista features. The minimum requirements for Windows Vista capable PC are.

- A minimum of 512 MB of RAM
- At-least 800 MHz of 32-bit or 64-bit CPU
- DirectX 9 graphics processor
- Windows Display Driver Module (WDDM) with minimum of 64 MB RAM or preferable 128 MB
- 20 GB hard-disk with at-least 15 GB free space

Question: What is Windows Vista Premium Ready PC hardware?

Answer: A Windows Vista Premium Ready PC is designed to fulfill the requirement of running most of the Windows Vista built-in features. They are capable of running all built-in features of Windows Vista, such as Windows Aero interface, and ability to watch and record TV shows, etc. The minimum requirements for Windows Vista Premium Ready PC are.

- 1 GHz of 32-bit or 64-bit processor
- 1 GB of system memory

- 40 GB of hard drive with 15 GB free space
- DVD-ROM drive
- Audio output capable
- Windows Aero capable
- 128 MB of video card memory
- DirectX 9 graphics support with WDDM driver

Question: If I have an upgrade license or a full product license, would I be able to perform a custom installation?

Answer: Yes, you can perform either an upgrade installation or a custom installation by using either an upgrade license or full product license.

Question: What is Windows Flip 3D?

Answer: A Windows Flip 3D feature is designed to view open programs in 3D shape. If your system supports Windows Aero interface, you can view it by simultaneously pressing ***Windows Logo Key*** and ***Tab*** key from the keyboard.

Question: Which command to use to switch between open programs?

Answer: Press ***Alt*** key and ***Tab*** key together to switch between open programs.

Question: What are the available views to organize the contents of Windows Explorer?

Answer: The Windows Explorer views are *Tiles, Details, List, Small icons, Medium icons, Large icons, and Extra large icons*.

Question: What is Windows Easy Transfer?

Answer: Windows Easy Transfer is a data transfer utility which can be used to transfer personal data from one computer to another computer.

Question: Which programs are recommended for transferring files and settings from one computer to another computer?

Answer: Windows Easy Transfer and User State Migration Tool (USMT).

Question: What can be transferred from older computer to the new computer using Easy Transfer method?

Answer: You can transfer files, email settings, contacts, e-mail messages, program settings, and Internet Explorer favorites from older Windows XP computer to the new Windows Vista computer. In Windows 2000 system, documents, music, and pictures can only be transferred to the Windows Vista system.

Question: Does all of the Microsoft operating system support Windows Easy Transfer?

Answer: No, the Windows Easy Transfer is only supported in Windows Vista, Windows XP, and Windows 2000 operating systems.

Question: What is data transfer rate of Windows Easy Transfer cable?

Answer: The data transfer rate is 20 GB/h.

Question: What is User State Migration Tool?

Answer: It is a data migration tool that allows system administrators to move user profiles from older system to the newer system.

Question: What can be migrated from older system to the newer system using User State Migration Tool?

Answer: The USMT can migrate user's desktop shortcuts, Internet Explorer settings, outlook express settings, favorites, fonts, folder options, accessibility options, sound settings, my documents, quick launch toolbar shortcuts, regional options, mouse settings, and keyboard settings.

Question: How to access a user profile?

Answer: To access a user profile, run command prompt (*Windows Key + R*), and type *%UserProfile%* in the search bar and then click on *OK*.

Question: How to access ***C*** (*system volume drive*) using a command line?

Answer: ***C*** drive can be accessed by typing *%Systemdrive%* in search box of run command.

Question: What is BCD?

Answer: A BCD stands for boot configuration data. The boot.ini keeps track of boot configuration of the older system, e.g. Windows XP, but it is replaced by BCD in newer system, e.g. Windows Vista.

Question: What is .Net framework 3.0?

Answer: The .Net framework 3.0 defines multiple application programming interfaces.

Question: Can I upgrade my system to one of the available Vista editions from Windows XP (64-bit edition)?

Answer: No, there is no upgrade path available for Windows XP 64-bit edition.

Question: Which Windows Vista operating system supports dual-processing?

Answer: The Windows Vista Business, Windows Vista Ultimate, and Windows Vista Enterprise support dual processors.

Question: What does NTFS stand for?

Answer: The NTFS stands for New Technology File System.

Question: What does EFS stand for?

Answer: The EFS stands for Encrypting File System.

Question: Can I compress and encrypt data at the same time?

Answer: The Windows does not allow you to compress and encrypt data simultaneously. You can either compress or encrypt data but cannot use both methods at the same time.

Question: Define Standby mode?

Answer: Standby mode switches computer to the low power state. It turns off computer hard-disk and monitor to save power but provides consistent power to the memory to avoid losing your work.

Question: Define Hibernation mode?

Answer: Hibernation turns off your computer after saving all of your open applications into the non-volatile storage like hard-disk.

Question: What is sleep mode?

Answer: The sleep mode is the combination of Standby mode and Hibernation mode.

Question: What is a SRT?

Answer: The SRT stands for Startup Repair Tool. This tool is designed to fix corrupted device drivers, system files, configuration settings, registry keys, and disk boot sectors.

Question: Define standard user rights?

Answer: A standard user can perform following operations without consulting an administrator.

- Establishing a wireless or wired network connections
- Installing Wired Equivalent Privacy (WEP) for wireless connection
- Playing and burning CDs and/or DVDs
- Modifying display settings
- Configuring battery settings
- Resetting account password
- Restoring their own backups
- Synchronizing data between devices
- Establishing connection with Bluetooth devices
- Creating and configuring virtual private network (VPN)
- Viewing the system clock
- Modifying the time zone
- Adding printer and other devices

Question: What does SID stand for?

Answer: The SID stands for Security Identifier. It is a unique identity of a computer on the network.

Question: What is Windows Vista Upgrade Advisor?

Answer: Windows Vista Upgrade Advisor is designed to check your existing computer hardware and application specifications to determine whether the system can be upgraded to any of the Windows Vista editions. To run the Upgrade Advisor for you system, you must be logged-on as an administrator. The Windows Vista Upgrade Advisor hardware requirements are following.

- Must have at-least 20 MB of free hard disk
- Must have .Net 2.0 and MSXML 6.0 installed
- Need at-least 512 MB to run this utility properly

Question: Is Windows Vista Upgrade Advisor supported in all versions of Microsoft XP operating system?

Answer: No, the Windows Vista Upgrade Advisor is not supported for all earlier editions of Microsoft operating system. It does not work with Windows 98, Windows 2000, and Windows XP professional x64 edition. It is only supported for 32-bit versions of Windows XP, and Windows Vista editions.

Question: How to open Windows Anytime Upgrade files?

Answer: To open stored files of Windows Anytime Upgrade Advisor program, run command prompt (*Windows Key + R*) and type *%Systemroot%\system32* in the search bar and then click on *OK*.

Question: What is an Internet Information Server?

Answer: It is a web server. It is designed by Microsoft that hosts your websites.

Question: Does Internet Information Server (IIS) supported in all editions of Windows Vista?

Answer: No, the Internet Information Server is only supported in Windows Vista Business, Windows Vista Ultimate, and Windows Vista Enterprise editions.

Question: How many total editions of Windows Vista are available all over the world?

Answer: The eight editions of Windows Vista are available all over the world. The five editions of Windows Vista are design to sell within United States of America, and rest of them are reserved for international market, e.g. Mexico, Brazil, India, Pakistan, Thailand, China, Indonesia, Philippines and within the European Union.

Question: Name the editions of Windows Vista which Microsoft sell in United States of America?

Answer: The Windows Vista editions are, Windows Vista Home Basic, Windows Vista Home Premium, Windows Vista Business, Windows Vista Enterprise, and Windows Vista Ultimate.

Question: What is *N* version of Windows Vista?

Answer: The *N* version of the Windows Vista is designed for European Union. It is only available in Home Basic and Business versions.

Question: Define ***Starter*** edition of Windows Vista?

Answer: Windows Vista Starter edition is designed for low-end profile users. This version is not available in US market.

Question: If you decided to choose ***Custom (advanced)*** option for installing Windows Vista, what kind of an operating system are you installing?

Answer: A clean copy of Windows will be installed for your system by choosing ***Custom (advanced)*** option. This option does not keep your personal data, files, folders, and programs settings that are currently installed on your machine.

Question: If you decided to choose ***Upgrade*** option for installing Windows Vista, what kind of an operating system are you installing?

Answer: By choosing the ***Upgrade*** option performs an upgrade on your computer. An upgrade process keeps your computer files, settings, and programs but it is recommended to have a complete back up of your PC, in case your system crashes during an upgrade process.

Question: Define the difference between a Microsoft fresh installation and an upgrade?

Answer: A Microsoft fresh installation process does not keep your existing files, settings and programs that are currently installed on your computer. In simple terms, it erases data from your hard-drive and then it installs a fresh copy of a Windows for you. On the other hand, an upgrade process will keep your existing files, settings, and programs.

Question: In which order, Microsoft Windows Vista operating system copies Windows files?

Answer: It copies in the order, Windows files, expanding files, installing features, installing updates, and completing installation.

Question: Do I need to install device drivers after performing a clean Windows Vista installation on my machine?

Answer: Yes, the Windows Vista is capable of searching and downloading device drivers automatically.

Question: How to optimize Windows Vista operating system for better performance?

Answer: The following recommended settings can optimize system performance:

- Uninstall programs you never use
- Disable unnecessary startup programs
- Perform defragmentation and clean up your hard-drive on regular bases
- Turn off visual effects
- Add more memory if your system does not have sufficient memory to run all applications
- Scan your system daily for viruses and spyware or at-least once in a week
- Get Windows updates and other product updates as they release

Question: Is it recommended to have a backup of entire computer before performing a fresh Windows installation or an upgrade?

Answer: Yes, it is recommended to have a complete backup of your computer in both scenarios. If you do not have enough resources to perform a complete backup of your computer, then you must consider saving all of your personal data on an external device.

Question: What benefits would you have turning on automatic updates?

Answer: Turning on automatic updates can download latest updates as they are available for your system from Microsoft that would add improved security and reliability to your system.

Question: Does Windows Vista download automatically updates for Windows Defender spyware program?

Answer: Yes, if your system is configured properly. You must choose ***Use recommended settings*** option for Windows updates to get latest Windows Defender definitions, automatically.

Question: What are the benefits to choose ***Use recommended settings*** option for Windows updates?

Answer: The benefits are

- You join Microsoft Spynet with basic membership
- Automatically updates will be downloaded and installed for Windows Defender spyware program
- Your system will send a report to Microsoft on the detection of any potential threads for your system

Question: How to open Windows update log?

Answer: To open Windows update log, run command prompt (*Windows Key + R*) and type *%Windir%\Windowsupdate.log* in the search bar, and then click *OK*.

Question: Define the Windows Vista versions upgrade path?

Answer: The Windows Vista versions upgrade path is listed following:

- Upgrade available from Windows Vista Home Basic to Windows Vista Home Premium or Windows Vista Ultimate
- Upgrade available from Windows Vista Home Premium to Windows Vista Ultimate
- Upgrade available from Windows Vista Business to Windows Vista Ultimate or Windows Vista Enterprise
- Upgrade available from Windows Vista Enterprise to Windows Vista Ultimate

Question: Which features are not supported in Windows Vista Home edition?

Answer: The features which are not supported in Windows Vista Home edition are, aero interface, domain support, second monitor support, group policy, offline files, shadow copies, DVD maker, and has limited backup capabilities.

Question: Which features of Windows Vista are supported in Windows Vista Premium edition?

Answer: The features which are supported in Windows Vista Premium edition are, aero interface, second monitor support, group policy, offline files, shadow copies, DVD maker, media center features, and tablet PC features.

Question: Which features of Windows Vista are not supported in Windows Vista Business edition?

Answer: The features which are not supported in Windows Vista Business edition are, media center features, DVD maker, movie maker, and parental controls.

Question: Which features of Windows Vista are supported in Windows Vista Business edition?

Answer: The features which are supported in Windows Vista Business edition are, domain support, two CPU support, group policy, Internet Information Server support, offline files, shadow copies, and system recovery.

Question: What does WPA stand for?

Answer: The WPA stands for Windows Product Activation. It provides the highest level of security from Microsoft once product is activated.

Question: What is length of Windows Product Activation key?

Answer: The length of product key is 25 characters and it is always unique to each system.

Chapter 2 - Microsoft Windows Vista New Features

Topics covered in this chapter:

- Welcome Center
- Windows Experience Index (WEI) Score
- Parental Controls
- Windows Defender
- BitLocker Drive Encryption
- Windows Sidebar
- Ready Boost
- Hidden Windows Features
- Windows Meeting Space
- Memory Diagnostics Tool
- Backup Files
- Restore Files
- Complete PC Backup
- Power Management
- Windows Mail
- Windows Contacts
- Problem Reports and Solutions Tool
- Snipping Tool
- Windows Aero

Welcome Center

Welcome Center is introduced with Microsoft Windows Vista operating system that combines necessary programs such as adding new user's accounts, connecting to the Internet, transferring files and settings from the older system to the newer system, and other programs that may help Vista users to configure their computer settings. The *Welcome Center* has two sections, the ***Get started with Microsoft*** section that compiles a list of programs to view and personalize their system configurations. The ***Offers from Microsoft*** section recommends Microsoft online services to enhance the security and productivity of your system as you subscribe to their online services.

Open Welcome Center

To open ***Welcome Center*** window:

- Click ***Start*** button, and then click ***Control Panel***.
- Click ***Classis View*** from the left navigation pane.
- Double-click ***Welcome Center***.

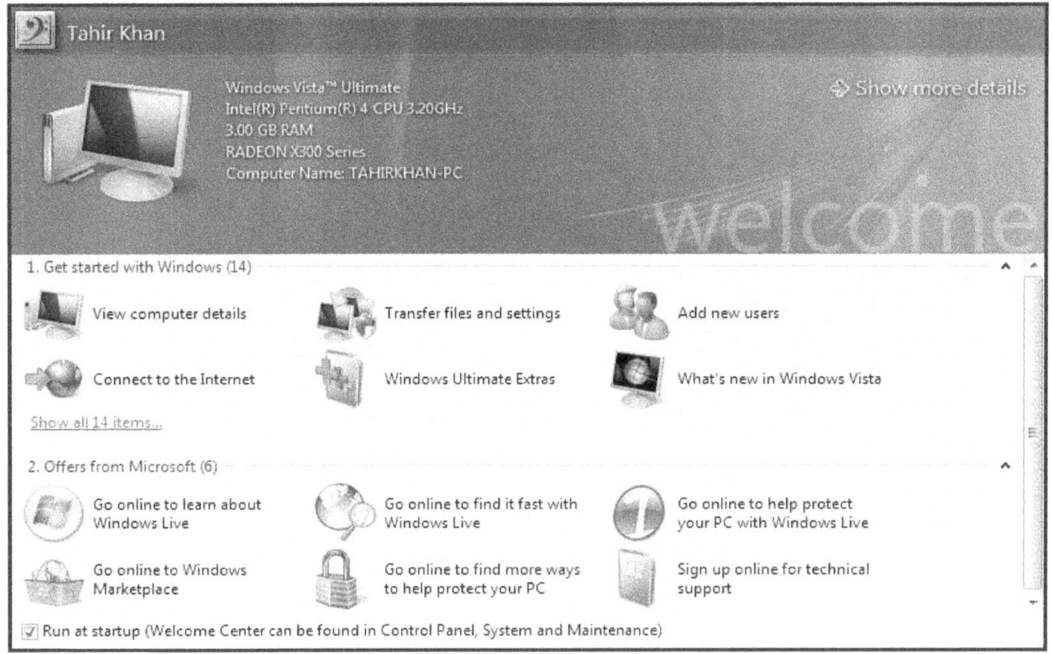

Disable Welcome Center

Welcome Center is configured to start up as soon as you log-on to your machine. The *Welcome Center* can be disabled by clearing off the ***Run at startup*** checkbox from the bottom of the *Welcome Center* panel.

☑ Run at startup (Welcome Center can be found in Control Panel, System and Maintenance)

Once the *Welcome Center* window is disabled, it will not run at the start-up of the computer

Windows Experience Index Score

The *Windows Experience Index* (WEI) score measures the performance of hardware components such as *Processor, Memory (RAM), Graphics Card, Gamming Graphics, and Primary Hard Disk.* The system performance rating falls between 1, least possible score, and 5.9, best possible base score, for your hardware system. The *base score* of the computer is determined by the lowest sub score of the weakest computer component.

Your computer has a Windows Experience Index base score of 1.0

Component	What is rated	Subscore	Base score
Processor:	Calculations per second	3.8	1.0 Determined by lowest subscore
Memory (RAM):	Memory operations per second	4.5	
Graphics:	Desktop performance for Windows Aero	1.9	
Gaming graphics:	3D business and gaming graphics performance	1.0	
Primary hard disk:	Disk data transfer rate	5.6	

Navigate Windows Experience Index (WEI) Base Score Table

To navigate the Windows Experience Index Base Score table,

- Click ***Start*** button and then click ***Control Panel***
- Click ***Classis View*** from the left navigation pane
- Double-click ***Performance Information and Tools***

The WEI base score table measures the cumulative performance of your hardware and software configurations. To improve the performance of the system, replace the computer component that has least sub score rating.

Your computer has a Windows Experience Index base score of 2.1

Component	What is rated	Subscore	Base score
Processor:	Calculations per second	4.3	2.1 Determined by lowest subscore
Memory (RAM):	Memory operations per second	4.6	
Graphics:	Desktop performance for Windows Aero	2.1	
Gaming graphics:	3D business and gaming graphics performance	3.2	
Primary hard disk:	Disk data transfer rate	5.8	

View and print details What do these numbers mean?

Parental Controls

The *Parental Controls* is designed for parents to monitor and restrict their family members from running certain programs, playing certain games, and limiting their computer usage. The *Parental Controls* is available for Microsoft Windows Vista Home, Premium, and Ultimate editions. It is only applicable to standard user accounts.

Open Parental Controls

To open *Parental Controls* program:

- Click ***Start*** button, and then click ***Control Panel***
- Click ***Classis View*** from the left navigation pane
- Double-click ***Parental Controls***

Configuring Parental Controls

From the ***Parental Controls*** window, choose ***On, enforce current settings*** option under the ***Parental Controls*** section. Once the *Parental Controls* is activated for standard users, some or all of the following policies can be enforced:

- Time limits policy
- Control games by rating and content types
- Allow and block specific programs per user need, and
- View the activity reports to monitor standard user accounts

Set up how Windows Vista will use the computer

Parental Controls:
On, enforce current settings
Off
Activity Reporting:
On, collect information about computer usage
Off
Windows Settings
Time limits
Control when Windows Vista uses the computer
Games
Control games by rating, content, or title
Allow and block specific programs
Allow and block any programs on your computer

Current Settings:
Windows Vista
Standard user
No Password
View activity reports
Web Restrictions: Windows Live OneCare Family Safety
Time Limits: Off
Game Ratings: Off
Program Limits: Off

To enforce time limits, click the ***Time limits*** link from the ***Windows Settings*** section. To activate the time restrictions policy for standard users, follow the step # 1 given below.

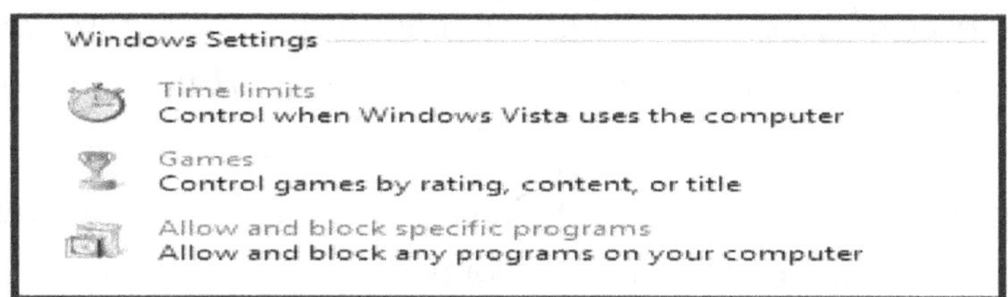

Step # 1: To apply the time restrictions for a standard user, click and drag the hours you want to block. Click ***OK*** to save preferences.

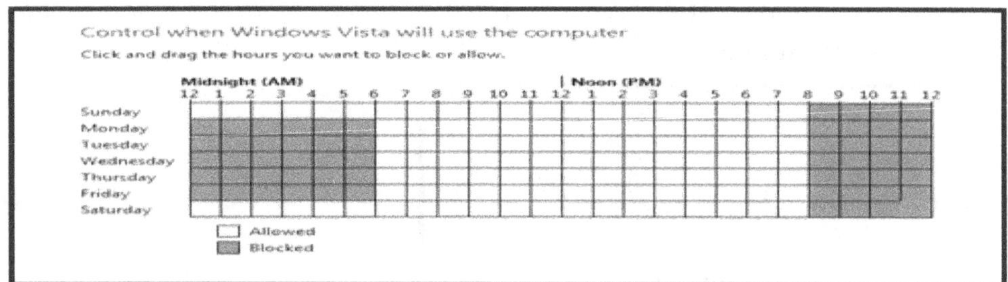

To enforce the game policy, click the ***Games*** link from the ***Windows Settings*** section, click on ***Yes*** to allow playing games, otherwise click on ***No*** to deny playing games. By default, *Windows Vista* allows a standard user to play all games. If you would like to set game ratings for a standard user, follow the step # 2 as explained below, and to block or allow specific games, follow the step # 3.

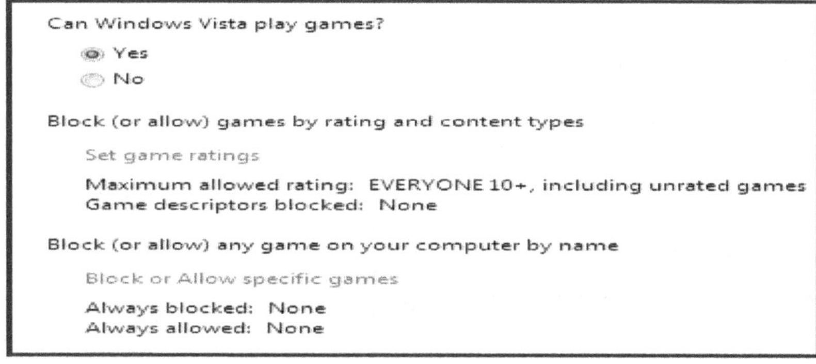

Step # 2: To set the game ratings for the standard users, click the ***Set game ratings*** link from the ***Block (or allow) games by rating and content types*** section and then choose one of the available games rating options. The available options are *Early Childhood, Everyone, Everyone 10+, Teen, Mature,and Adults Only*.

The system administrator can limit a user permission by the game's content type. The content types are: *online-experience, alcohol reference, animated blood, blood, blood and gore, cartoon violence, comic mischief, crude humor, drug reference, edutainment, fantasy violence, informational, intense violence, language, lyrics, mature humor, mild violence, nudity, partial nudity, real gambling, sexual violence, simulated gambling, some adult assistance may be needed, strong language, strong lyrics, strong sexual content, suggestive themes, tobacco reference, use of alcohol, use of drugs, use of tobacco, and violence.*

Step # 3: To block or allow a game for a user, click the ***Block or Allow specific games*** link from the ***Windows Settings*** section. You have three options (*user rating setting, always allow, and always block*) to restrict a standard user to allow or block playing games. The games you can restrict or allow for a user are: *Chess Titans, Hearts, Hold 'EM, InkBall, Mahjong Titans, Minesweeper, Purble Place, Solitaire, and Spider Solitaire*. Click **OK** to save preferences.

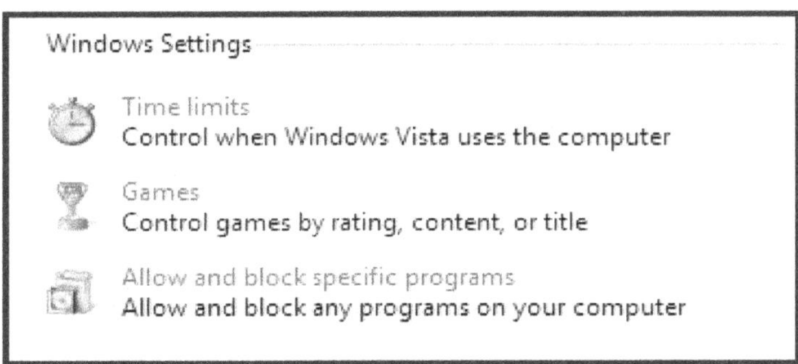

To restrict the user's permission for a program, click the **Allow and block specific programs** link under the **Windows Settings** section and then choose one of the following options:

- Windows Vista can use all programs
- Windows Vista can only use the programs I allow

Which programs can Windows Vista use?

Windows Vista can use all programs

Windows Vista can only use the programs I allow

To allow a user to use all programs, select ***Windows Vista can use all programs*** option and then click ***OK*** to save changes. Allowing a user to have access to certain programs of the machine, select ***Windows Vista can only use the programs I allow*** option and then select the programs that you wish to give access to users.

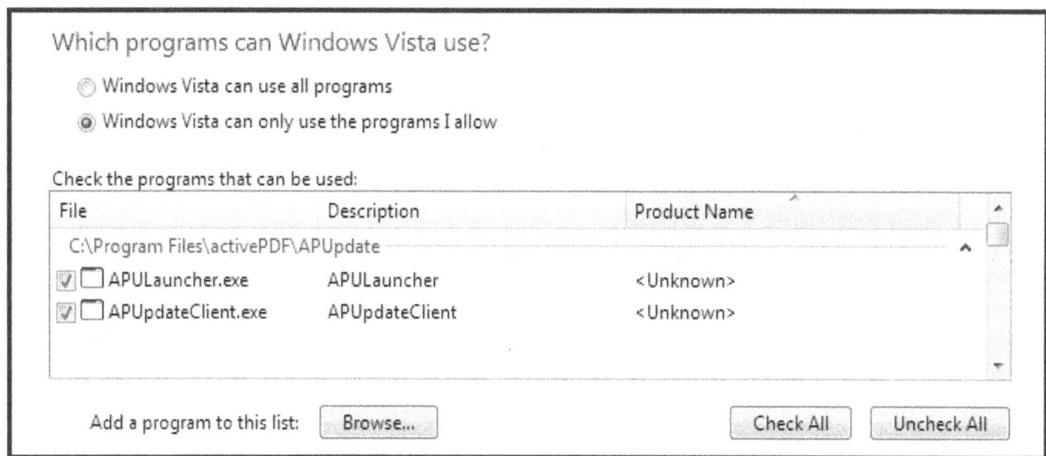

An activity report collects the information about computer usage. To activate this feature, select ***On, collect information about computer usage*** option under the ***Activity Reporting*** section. If you want to view activity reports, click the ***View activity reports*** that is located under the user account name on the right.

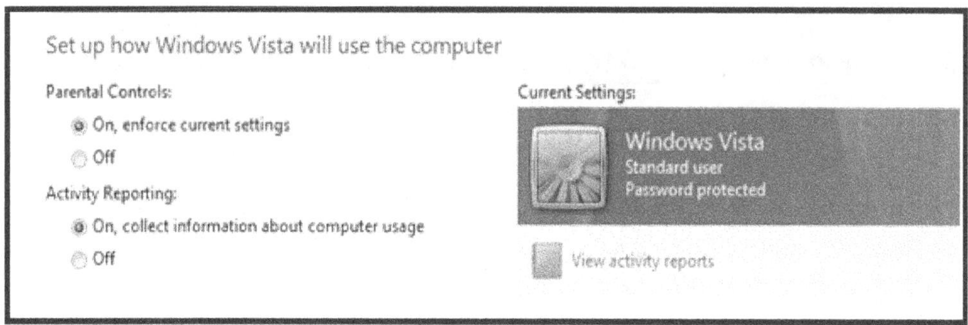

Windows Defender

A *Windows Defender* is a spyware program that helps users to protect their systems against spywares, but it does not provide any protection against viruses. It is a free program for Microsoft users. It is available to download from Microsoft website at http://www.microsoft.com/windows/products/winfamily/defender/default.mspx for earlier versions of Microsoft users. By default, this program is pre-installed for Windows Vista users.

Windows Defender Configurations

To open *Windows Defender* program, click ***Start*** button, click ***All Programs***, and then click ***Windows Defender***. From the *Windows Defender* panel, a user can perform following operations:

- Checking latest Microsoft updates for *Windows Defender* spyware program
- Quick system scan, full system scan, and customize system scan
- Joining Microsoft SpyNet community
- Automatic scanning
- Monitoring real-time for spywares
- Managing start-up programs, currently running programs, and winsock services

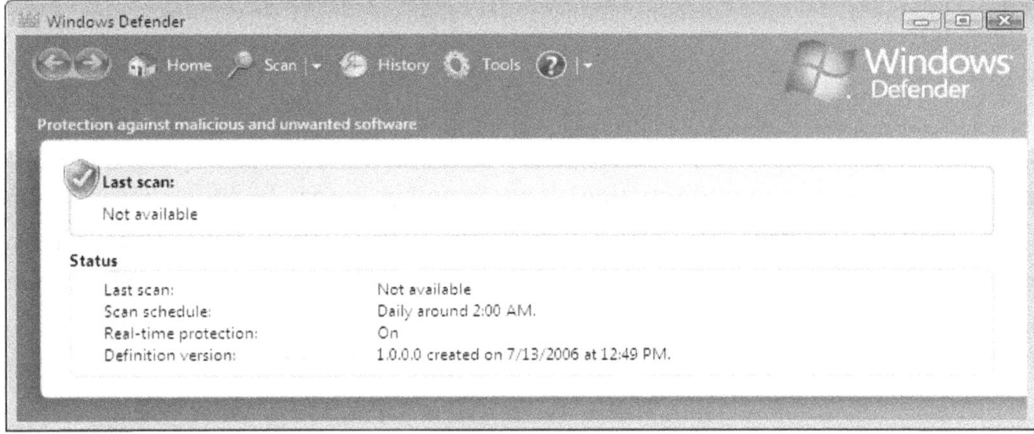

Windows Defender Updates

From the ***Windows Defender*** window, click ***Home*** tab, and then click the ***Check for Updates Now*** from the ***Check for new definitions*** section. This process may take few minutes downloading latest spyware definitions for your system. The spyware provides protection against malicious code that can be installed in your computer by a third-party.

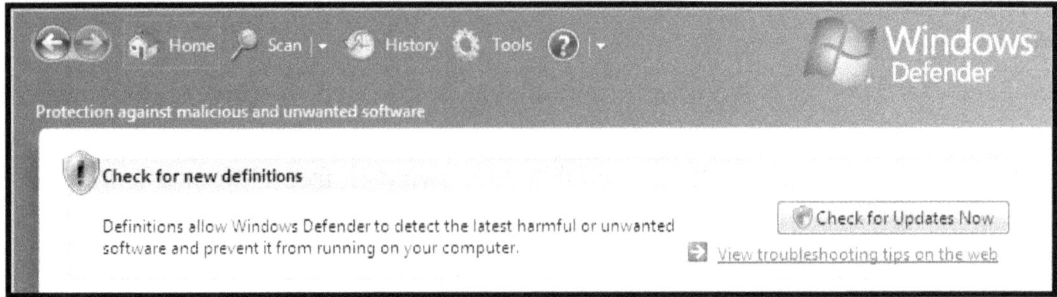

System Scanning Options

From the ***Windows Defender*** window, click the downward arrow next to the ***Scan*** tab, and then choose one of the available options (*Quick Scan*, *Full Scan* and *Custom Scan)* from drop down list. This process may take several minutes scanning your computer against malicious code, spywares, and unwanted software.

Join Microsoft SpyNet Community

From the ***Windows Defender*** window, click ***Tools*** tab, under the ***Settings*** section, click ***Microsoft SpyNet*** .

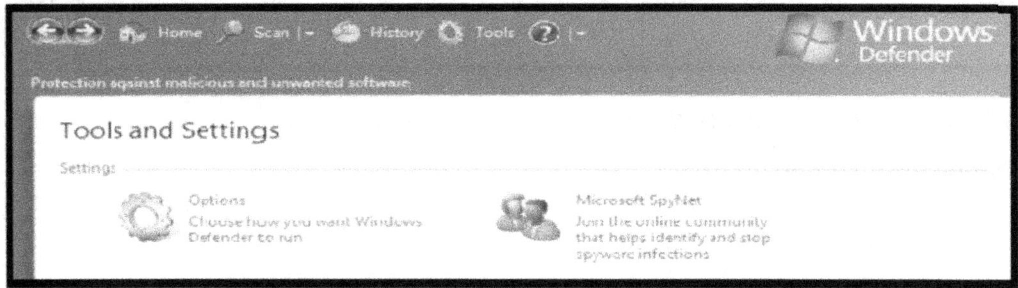

Read the benefits of having basic membership or advanced membership, and then decide which one is to join to protect your system against malicious codes, and unwanted software. You may deny joining Microsoft SpyNet community by selecting ***I don't want to join Microsoft SpyNet at this time*** option at the bottom of the window. To save preferences of the membership, click on ***Save***.

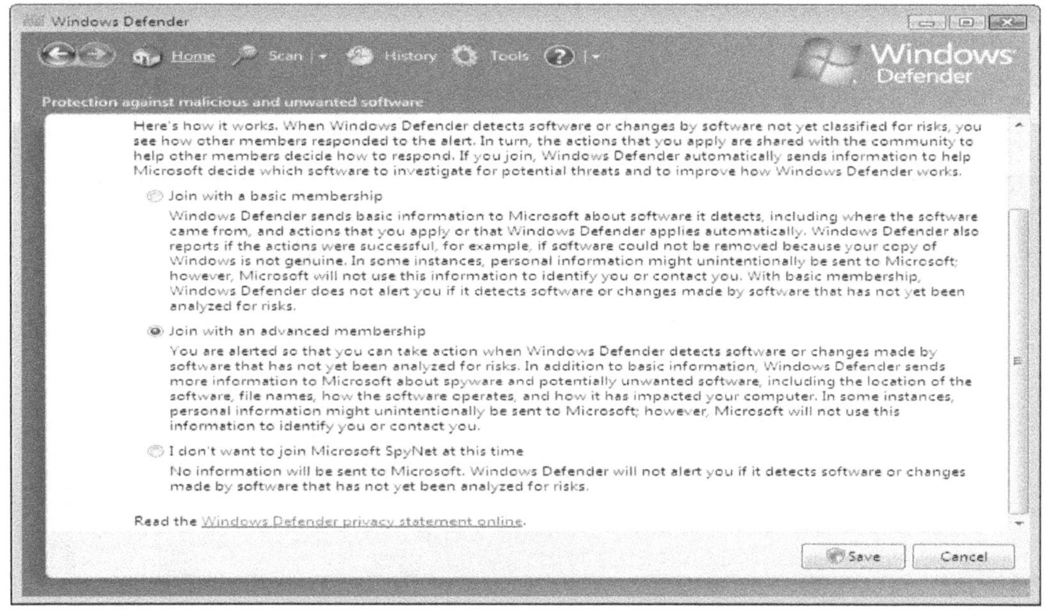

Windows Defender Options

From the ***Windows Defender*** window, click on ***Tools*** tab, under the ***Settings*** section, and click the ***Options***.

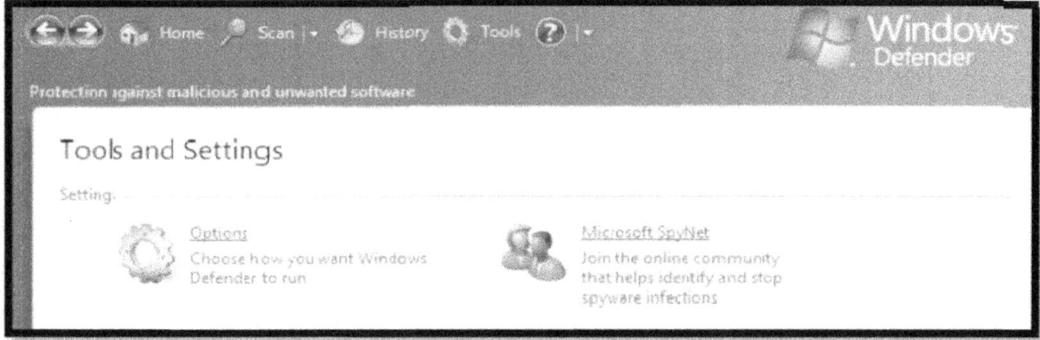

Windows Defender options are divided into following sub-sections:

- *Automatic Scanning*
- *Default Actions*
- *Real-time Protection Options*
- *Advanced Options*
- *Administrator Options*

Automatic Scanning

This section allows you to modify following preferences:

- *Automatically scan my computer (recommended)*
- *Check for updated definitions before scanning*
- *Apply default actions to items detected during a scan*

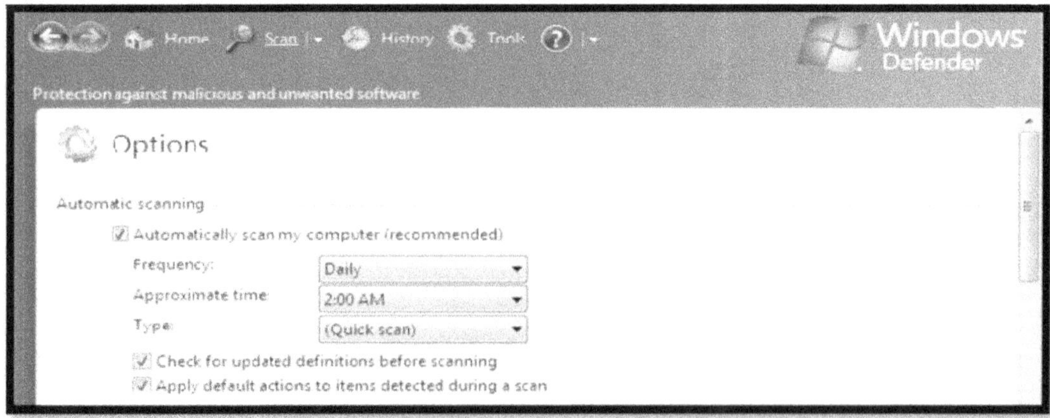

Default Actions Options

This section can adjust spyware alert level to high, medium and low.The alert items are, *high alert items, medium alert items, and low alert items.* System alerts can be removed, or ignored according to your preferences.

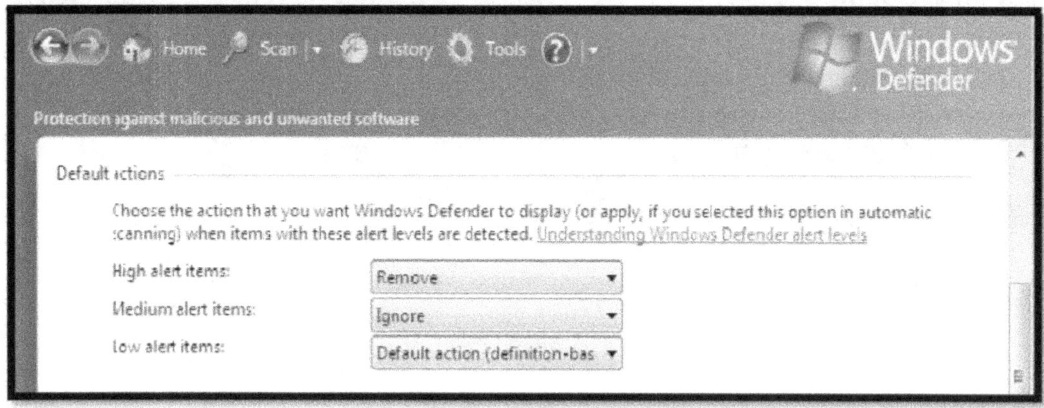

Real-time Protection Options

The real-time protection options are:

a. Use real-time protection (recommended)
   - *i.* Choose which security agent you want to run: *Auto Start, System Configuration (Settings), Internet Explorer Add-ons, Internet Explorer Configuration (Settings), Internet Explorer Downloads, Services and Drivers, Application Execution, Application Registration, and Windows Add-ons*
   - ii. Choose if *Windows Defender* should notify you about:
     1. *Software that has not yet been classified for risks*
     2. *Changes made to your computer by software that is permitted to run*
   - iii. Choose when the *Windows Defender* icon appears in the notification area:
     1. *Only if Windows Defender detects an action to take*
     2. *Always*

Administrator Options

The administrator options are:

- *Use Windows Defender:* By default, this option is set for *Windows Defender.*
- *Allow everyone to use Windows Defender:* By default, everyone has permission to review all *Windows Defender* activities to protect your computer against malicious codes and unwanted software.

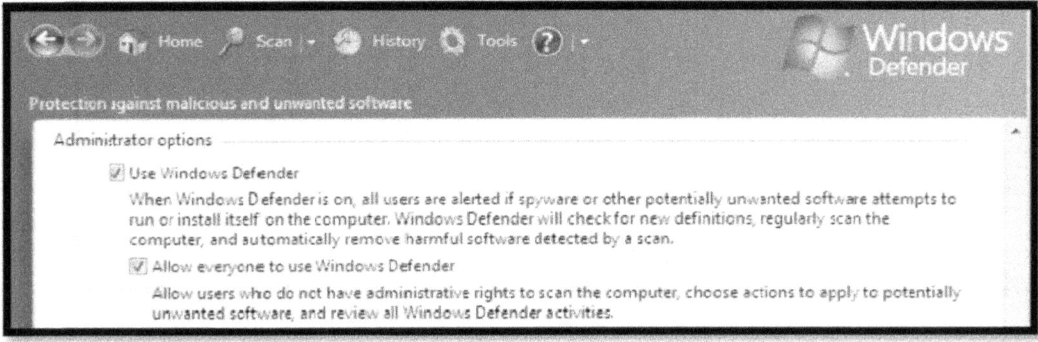

Manage Start-up Programs

To view and manage start-up programs, go to the ***Tools*** section of the *Windows Defender*, and then click the ***Software Explorer***. In the ***Software Explorer*** window, under the ***Category*** drop down menu, choose ***Startup Programs*** option. You may remove, disable or enable start-up programs. If you wish to remove, or disable a program, highlight the program from left side of the window, and then click ***Remove*** or ***Disable*** from right-bottom of the *Software Explorer* window.

Manage Currently Running Programs

To view and manage currently running programs, go to the ***Tools*** section of the *Windows Defender*, and then click the ***Software Explorer***. From the *Software Explorer* window, from the ***Category*** drop down menu, choose the ***Currently Running Programs*** option. If you wish to stop a currently running program, highlight the program from left side of the window, and then click ***End Process*** from right-bottom of the *Software Explorer* window.

Manage Network Connected Programs

To view and manage network connected programs, go to the ***Tools*** section of the *Windows Defender*, and then click the ***Software Explorer***. In the *Software Explorer* window, from the ***Category*** drop down menu, choose the ***Network Connected Programs*** option. You may stop a program or block incoming connections by clicking on ***End Process*** or ***Block Incoming Connections***, respectively . If you wish to stop a currently running program, highlight the program from left side of the window, and then click ***End Process*** from right-bottom of the *Software Explorer* window.

Manage Winsock Service Providers

A Winsock Service Provider defines how Windows network software should access network devices, e.g. TCP/IP, IPX/SPX, and DNS. To view and manage Winsock Service providers, go to the ***Tools*** section of the *Windows Defender*, and then click the ***Software Explorer***. In the *Software Explorer* window, from the ***Category*** drop down menu, choose the ***Winsock Service Providers*** option. To view the detail of the service, from the left navigation pane, click on the service to view the detail. Then the service detail will display on right section of the *Software Explorer* window.

Windows Defender Advanced Options

The advanced options for *Windows Defender* are:

- *Scan the contents of archived files and folders for potential threats*
- *Use heuristics to detect potentially harmful or unwanted behavior by software that hasn't been analyzed for risks*
- *Create a restore point before applying actions to detected items*
- *Do not scan these files or locations: Select the drive that should not be scanned against spyware threads*

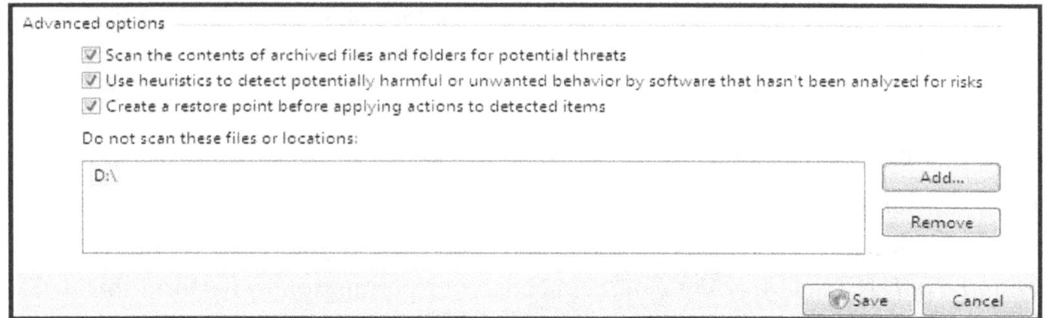

Click on **Save** after making any changes to the *Windows Defender* settings.

BitLocker Drive Encryption

BitLocker drive encryption is a new tool introduced with Windows Vista operating system that enhances the data security by encrypting entire drive of the system volume. The contents of the hard-drive get encrypted in such a way that no one will have access to it without having the proper authentication key. The key could be saved on a USB drive, in the system drive, or in BIOS (Basic Input Output System) of the computer. By default, ***C*** (system drive) drive is designated to keep Windows operating system files. BitLocker drive encryption is only available to Windows Vista Ultimate, Windows Vista Enterprise, and Windows Server 2008 operating systems.

Your system must have following configurations to use BitLocker drive encryption tool.

- At-least two hard drive partitions, one partition to start-up the system and other partition for encrypting data to protect your data privacy.
- System hard drive partitions must be formatted with ***NTFS*** (New Technology File System).
- System ***BIOS*** (Basic Input Output System) must be compatible with ***Trusted Platform Module*** (TPM) and it must support USB devices at start-up of your computer. If your computer does not support TPM and USB devices at start-up, you must upgrade ***BIOS*** of your computer.
- Requires TPM version 1.2 or higher micro chip that is designed to enhance hardware authentication to protect data privacy. BitLocker will store the cryptographic keys in the TPM, and stored keys can only be decrypted by TPM that minimizes the risk of data theft.

If your system is not TPM compatible to store cryptographic keys, then you must have a removable USB device to store keys.

BitLocker Drive Preparation Tool

To open *BitLocker Drive Preparation Tool*, click ***Start*** button, click ***All Programs***, click ***Accessories***, click ***System Tools***, click ***BitLocker***, and then double-click ***BitLocker Drive Preparation Tool***. If *User Account Control* needs your permission to perform this action, click on ***Continue***. Provide administrative credentials, if asked.

Read the BitLocker Drive preparation tool agreement, click ***I Accept***, if you accept the agreement, or otherwise click ***I Decline*** if you do not agree with terms and conditions to install BitLocker tool for your system. To continue this process, you must read and accept terms and conditions.

Read BitLocker preparing drive instructions and then click on ***Continue***.

- *Back up critical data and files before continuing.*
- *This process may require defragmentation, which may take few minutes to few hours depending on the condition of your drive.*
- *Do not store important data and files on the new active drive.*

This process may take several minutes shrinking system drive and then converting into a new active drive for BitLocker encryption process. Click on ***Finish*** and then restart the computer so changes can apply to the system.

Setup BitLocker Drive Encryption

From the ***Control Panel***, navigate to the ***BitLocker Drive Encryption*** icon, and then double-click on it. If *User Account Control* needs your permission to perform this action, click on ***Continue.*** Provide administrative credentials, if asked. The following options are available to save start-up recovery password:

- *Save the password on a USB drive:* Follow step # 1 as explained below
- *Save the password in a folder:* Follow step # 2 given below for more information
- *Print the password:* Follow step # 3 given below for more information

Step # 1: If you want to save start-up recovery password on a USB drive, connect the USB drive with your system to save recovery password on it. It is recommended to designate one USB drive to save recovery password.

You would be required connecting same USB drive with your system, every time system start-ups.

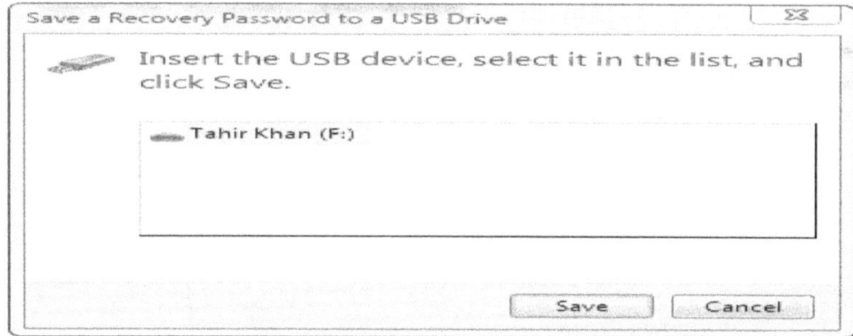

Step # 2: If you want to save recovery password in the system hard-drive, choose appropriate location for the file and then click on ***Save***.

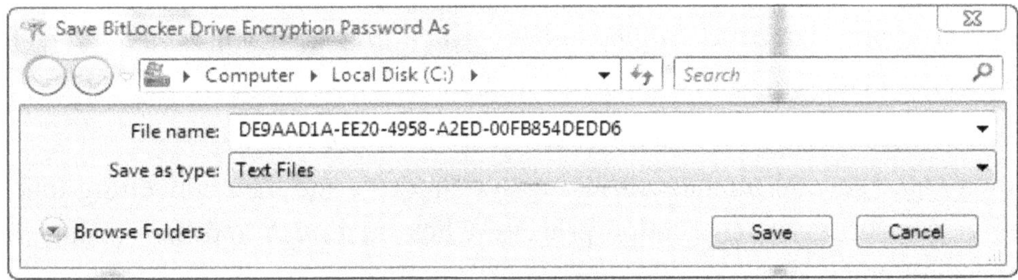

Step # 3: If you want to print the copies of the password file, select the printer you want to print, from the ***Select printer*** section, and then click on ***Print***.

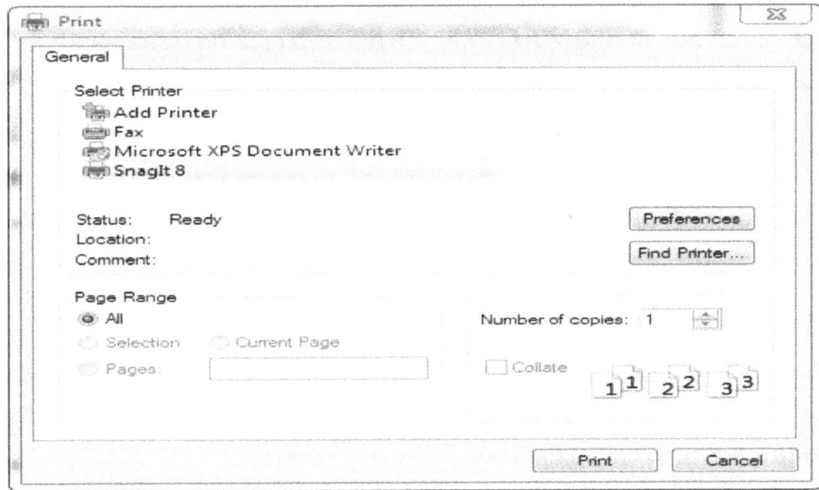

Choose one of the above methods to save the recovery password file and then click on ***Next***.

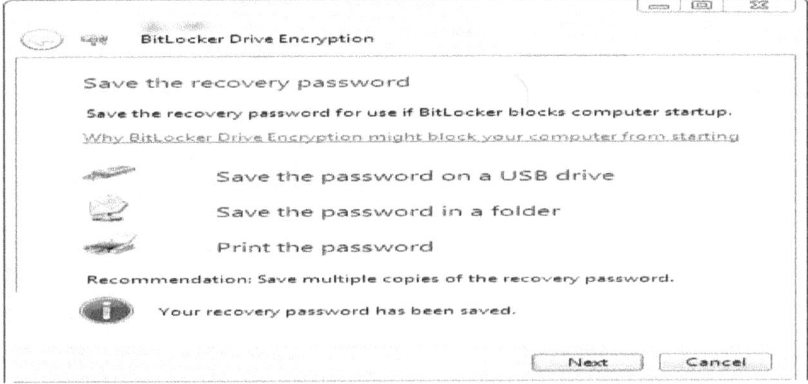

Read the instructions to encrypt system volume drive and then click on ***Continue***.

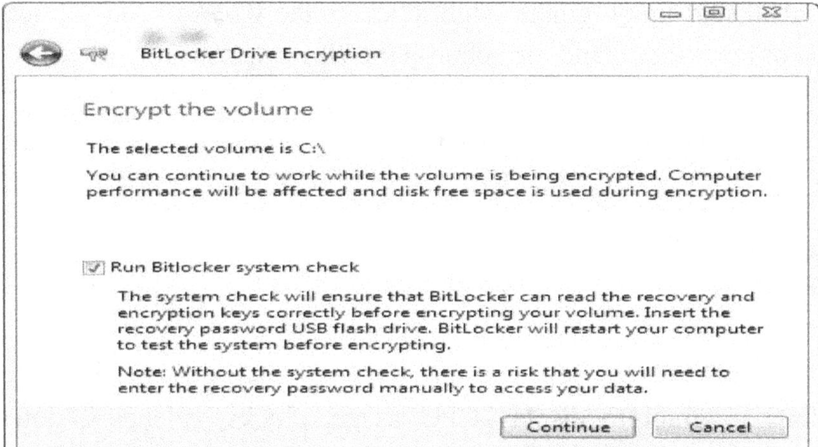

Reboot your machine so changes can apply to your system. After logging back to the machine, your system will encrypt the contents of system volume drive. It may take few hours to encrypt data depending on the size of your computer hard-drive.

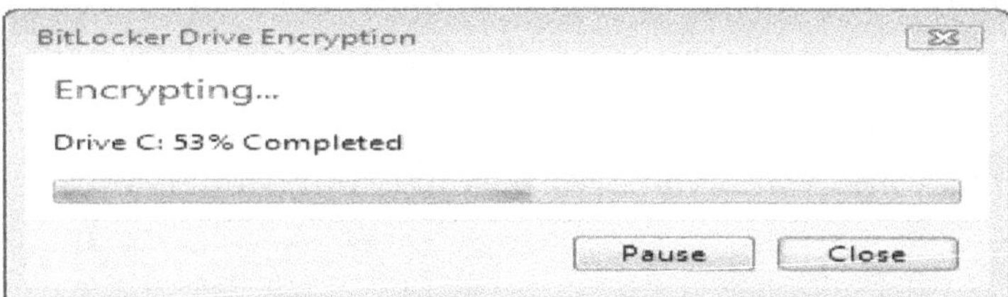

Windows Sidebar

Windows Sidebar is designed to manage and monitor computer resources by adding gadgets to the *Windows Sidebar*. By default, *Windows Sidebar* is displayed on right side of the desktop but preferred locations (the r*ight or the left*) can be adjusted to meet the user requirements. *Windows Sidebar* displays mini-programs such as weather reports, News headlines, calendar, notes, CPU and memory performance, if configured properly.

Open Windows Sidebar

Windows Sidebar icon appears in the notification area of the system by default. If you are unable to see the *Windows Sidebar* icon in the notification area of the taskbar (located at the right-bottom of the desktop), then click on arrow [<] to expand the notification area to see all start-up programs. Right-click on the *Windows Sidebar* icon from the notification area of the taskbar, and then choose the ***Open*** option from the list.

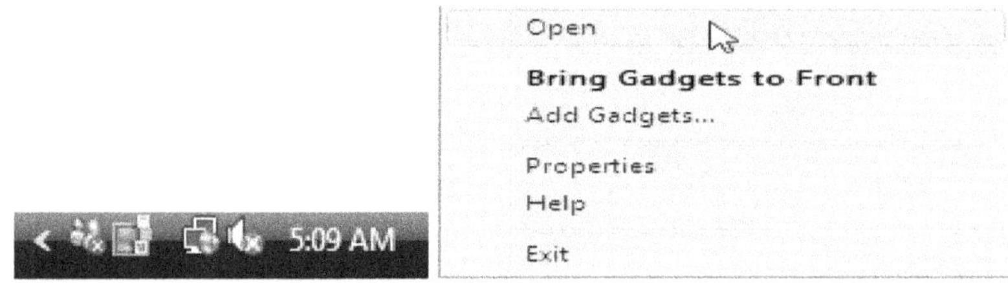

Add Gadgets on Windows Sidebar

A gadget is a stand-alone program to display CPU usage, clocks, calendars, notes, weather reports, and picture slide shows on the *Windows Sidebar*. To add a gadget, right-click on the *Windows Sidebar* icon from the system tray (right-bottom area of the desktop), and then choose the ***Add Gadgets*** option. Double-click the gadget that needs to be added to the *Windows Sidebar* from the *Sidebar Gadgets* window. If you would like to view and download available online gadgets, click the ***Get more gadgets online*** link to add more gadgets to the *Windows Sidebar*.

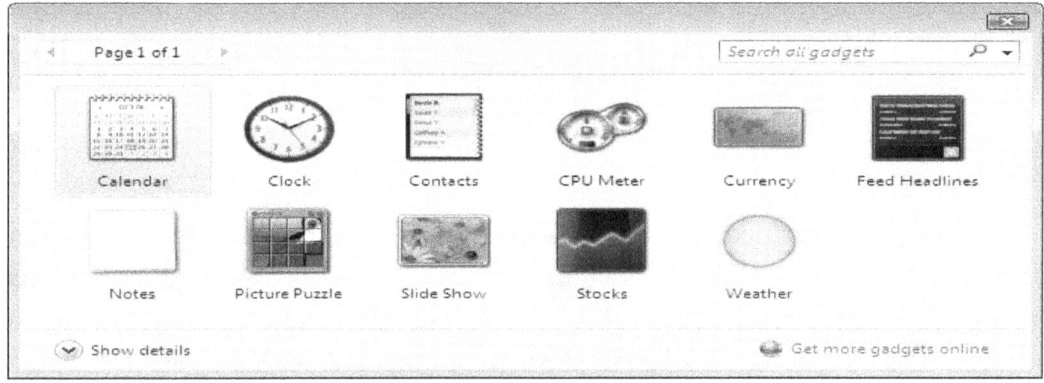

Remove Gadgets from Windows Sidebar

To open *Windows Sidebar* Properties:

- Click ***Start*** button, and then click ***Control Panel***
- Click ***Classis View*** from the left navigation pane
- Double-click ***Windows Sidebar Properties***

To remove a *Windows Sidebar* gadget, click on ***View list of running gadgets*** under the ***Maintenance*** section.

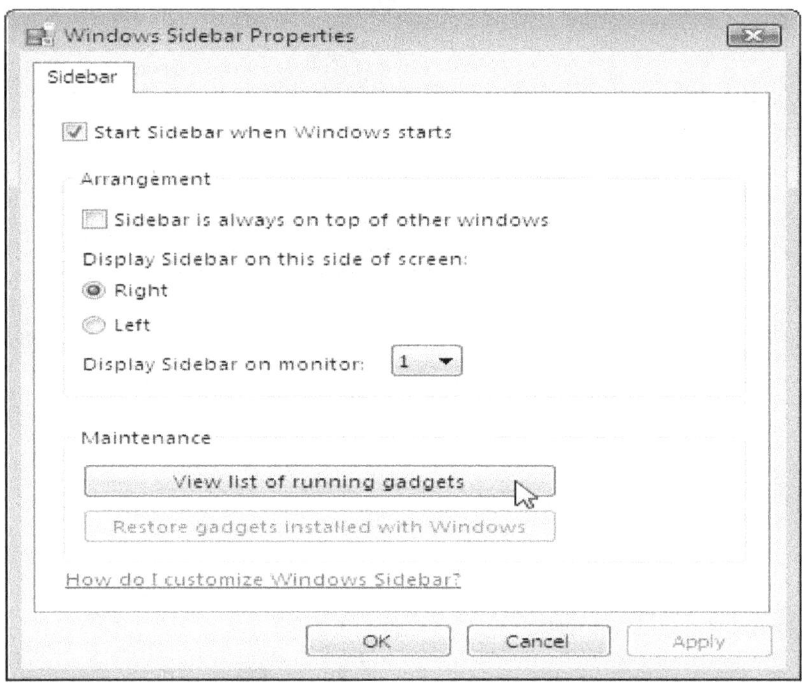

Highlight the gadget that you want to remove/uninstall and then click on ***Remove*** button. When done removing the gadgets, click on ***Close***.

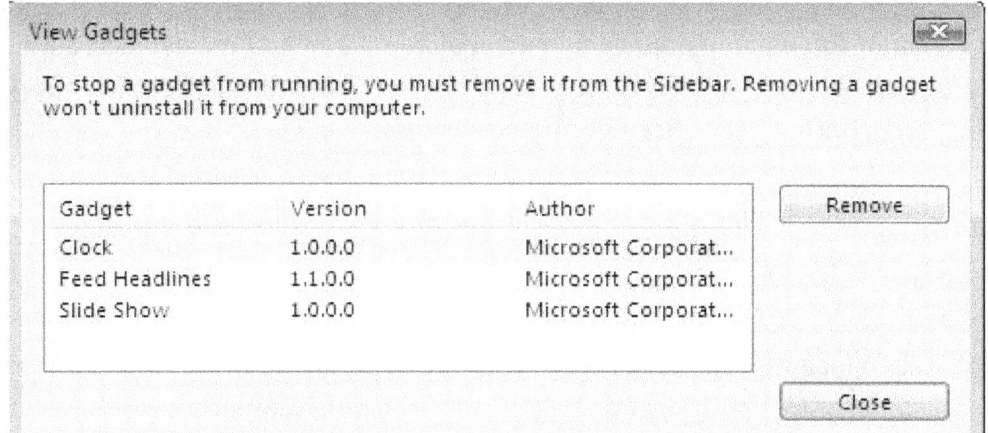

Windows Sidebar Startup Options

Open *Windows Sidebar Properties*. To enable *Windows Sidebar* start-up option, check the ***Start Sidebar when Windows starts*** box. Click on ***Apply*** and then click ***OK*** to save changes. Once the start-up option is activated for *Windows Sidebar*, it will start automatically as you log-in to the machine. To disable *Windows Sidebar* start-up feature, clear ***Start Sidebar when Windows starts*** checkbox from *Windows Sidebar Properties* window.

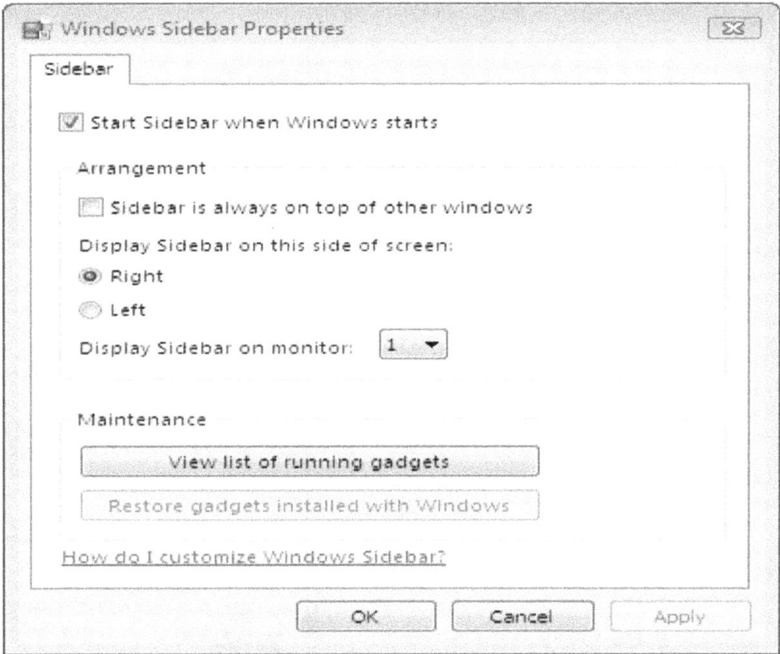

Windows Sidebar Display Settings

By default, the *Windows Sidebar* is displayed on right side of the desktop. To adjust the preferred location of the *Windows Sidebar*, open *Windows Sidebar Properties*. From the ***Display Sidebar on this side of screen*** section, choose preferred display location (***Right*** or ***Left***). Click on ***Apply*** and then click ***OK*** to save changes.

Ready Boost

Windows Vista is capable of adding non-volatile flash memory to increase the performance of your system without adding additional memory chip onto the motherboard. The Windows Vista operating system allocates the part of the USB drive's memory to speed up system performance. The Ready Boost device must meet following criteria to boost the system performance by storing file cache on the USB drive.

- Must be at-least USB 2.0 type
- Must have at-least 256 MB in size
- Should have access time of 1ms or less
- Must support NTFS, FAT16 and FAT32 formats

- Minimum of 2.5 MB/s for 4 KB random READ speed
- Minimum of 1.75 MB/s for 512 KB random WRITE speed
- Must have at-least 235 MB of free space

From the USB drive properties dialog box, click ***ReadyBoost*** tab, and then select ***Use this device*** option. Under the ***Use this device*** section, move the slider right or left to increase or decrease the space to reserve for your system speed, respectively. Click on ***Apply*** and then click ***OK*** to save Ready Boost drive preferences.

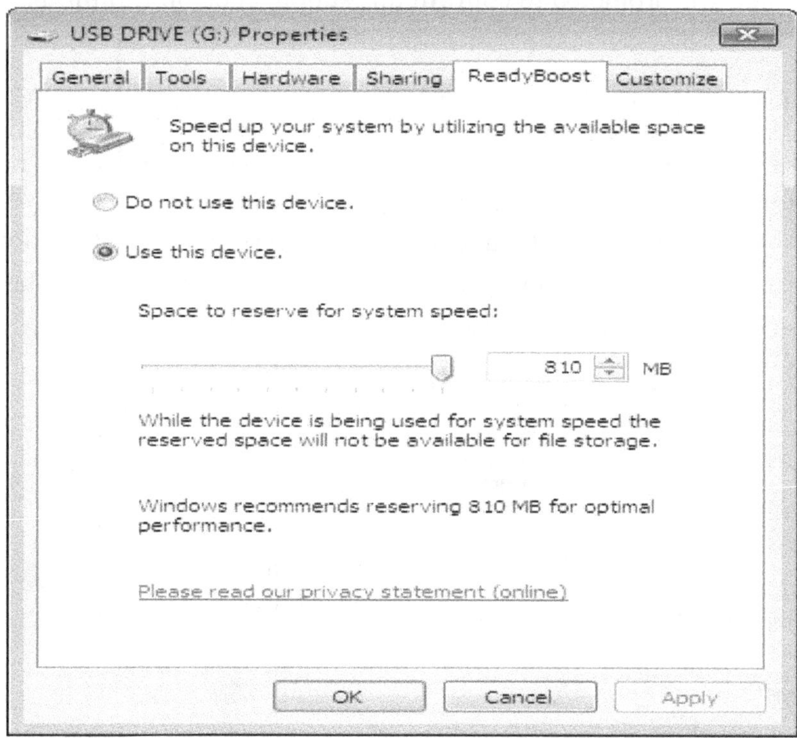

Hidden Windows Features

The *Hidden Windows Features* are pre-loaded programs that are available for your system to install as needed. The hidden Windows features are: *ActiveX Installer Service, Games, Indexing Service, Internet Information Services, Microsoft .Net Framework 3.0, Microsoft Message Queue (MSMQ) Server, Print Services, Remote Differential Compression, Removable Storage Management, RIP Listener, Services for NFS, Simple TCPIP Services (i.e. echo, daytime etc), SNMP Feature, Tablet PC Optional Components, Telnet Client, Telnet Server, TFTP Client, Windows DFS Replication Service, Windows Fax and Scan, Windows Meeting Space, and Windows Process Activation Service.*

Open Hidden Windows Features

To open *Programs and Features* template:

- Click ***Start*** button, and then click ***Control Panel***
- Click ***Classis View*** from the left navigation pane
- Double-click ***Programs***
- Click ***Turn Windows features on or off*** from ***Programs and Features*** section

If *User Account Control* window is prompted to confirm this action, click on ***Continue***.

To turn on *Hidden Windows Vista Features*, select an appropriate application that you would like to install for your system and then click ***OK*** to perform an application installation. To turn on or off a windows feature may take several minutes to complete the process. Follow the on-screen instructions to install pre-loaded hidden programs.

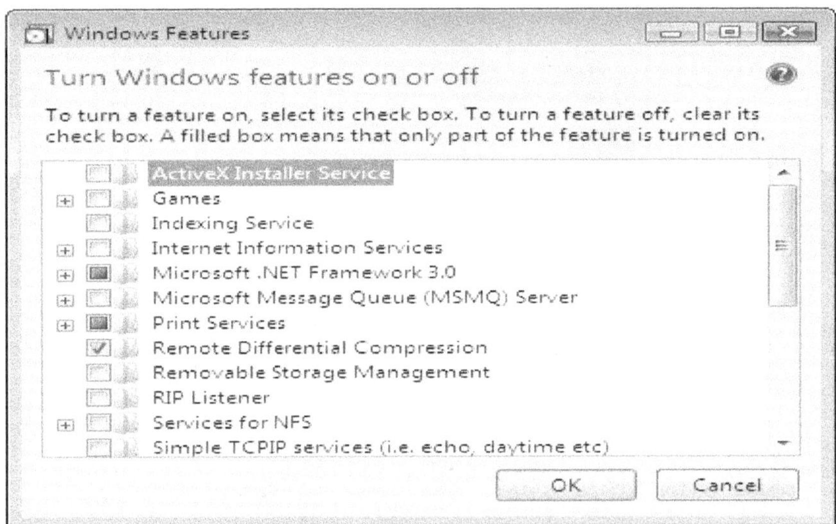

Windows Meeting Space

A *Windows Meeting Space* enables Windows Vista users to collaborate with each other by sharing handouts and the applications. The computer desktop can be shared while working on a project, if necessary. Microsoft Windows Vista Home Basic users can only view meetings but cannot create meeting sessions. Windows allows maximum of ten users to join *Windows Meeting Space* simultaneously.

Windows Meeting Space Setup

To navigate *Windows Meeting Space* path, click ***Start*** button, click ***All Programs***, and then click ***Windows Meeting Space***. From the ***Windows Meeting Space Setup*** dialog box, select ***Yes, continue setting up Windows Meeting Space*** option.

In ***People Near Me*** dialog box, type a display name so other trusted users can identify you while starting or joining a meeting. Clear the ***Sign me in automatically when Windows Starts*** checkbox, if *Windows Meeting Space* program needs to be started manually. Click ***OK*** to save preferences.

By default, your display name, computer name, and IP address are visible over the local network. If restricted security policy are enforced for your system, contact your administrator before logging-on to the *Windows Meeting Space*.

Now, you are ready to start a new meeting or join a meeting.

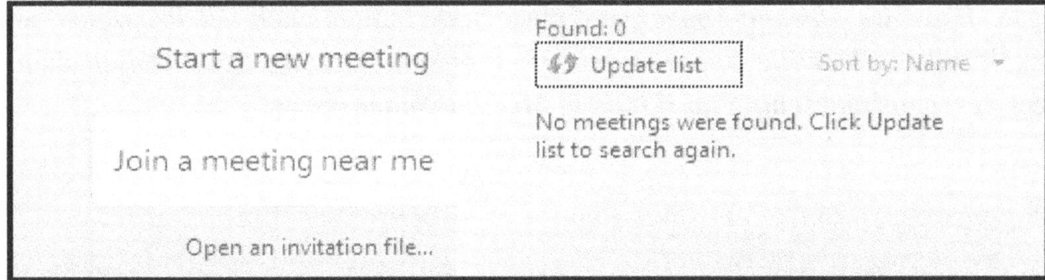

To start a new meeting, click the ***Start a new meeting*** link from left navigation pane of the *Windows Meeting Space*, and then type the new meeting name and password that must be at-least 8 characters long in length. Click on green arrow to continue creating new meeting space.

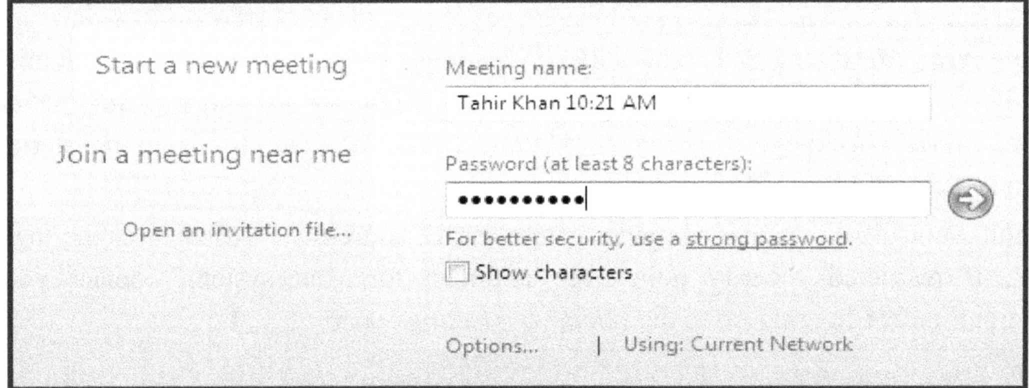

The system may take few minutes creating a new meeting space.

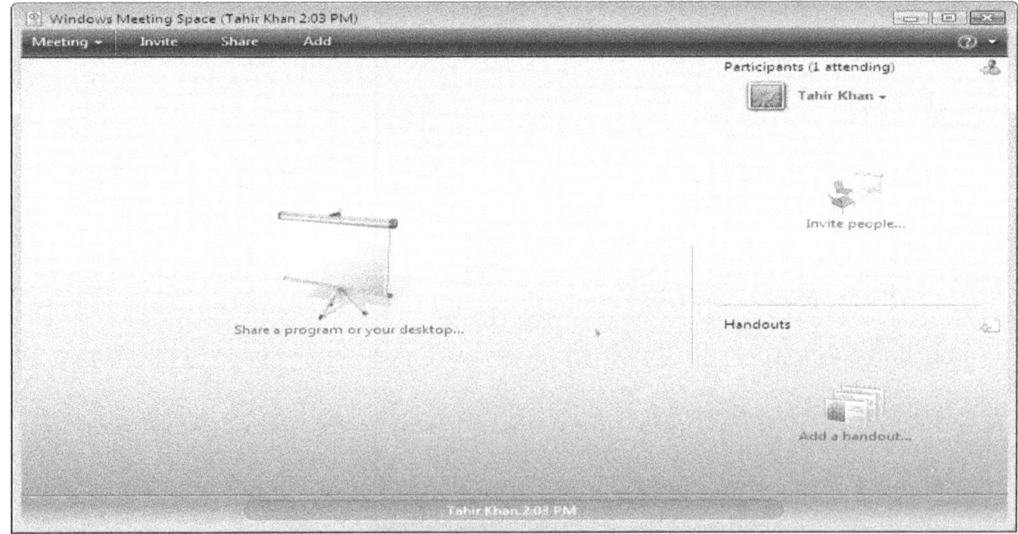

To invite trusted users to join a meeting space, choose ***Invite*** option from command bar of the *Windows Meeting Space.* From ***Invite People*** dialog box, select the ***Invite others*** option to send an invitation file to the trusted users by clicking on ***Send an invitation in e-mail*** option.

To share a program/desktop with the trusted users, click ***Share*** button from the command bar of the *Windows Meeting Space*. From ***Start a shared session*** window, click on the program that you wish to share with other users, and then click ***Share***.

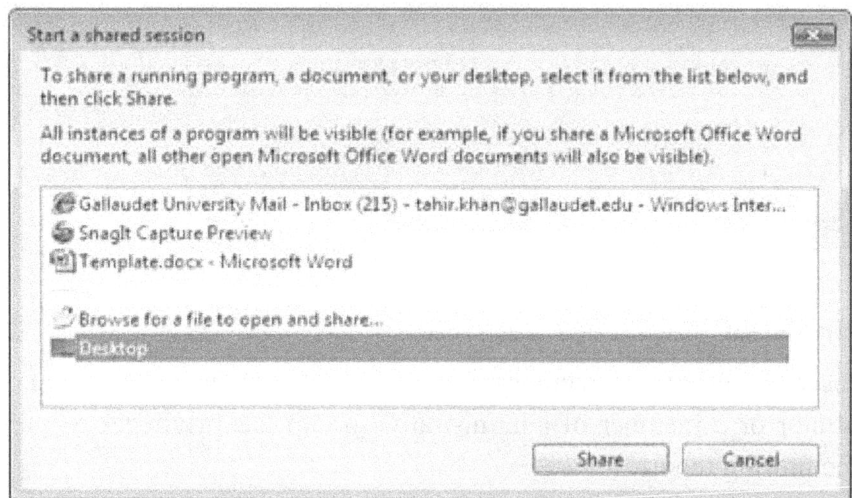

The left side of the *Windows Meeting Space* displays the status of sharing a program or desktop. If you would like to stop sharing the desktop/program, click on ***Stop sharing***.

To share a handout, click ***Add*** button from the command bar of the Windows Meeting Space. Navigate to the handout that you wish to share with trusted users and then click on ***Open*** to add handout(s) to *Windows Meeting Space*. If you are prompted to read, how the handout will be shared and how the changes made to that handout will display to the trusted users, read it carefully and then click ***OK*** to continue.

To delete a handout from *Windows Meeting Space*, click on the handout that you want to delete and then press ***Delete*** key from keyboard.

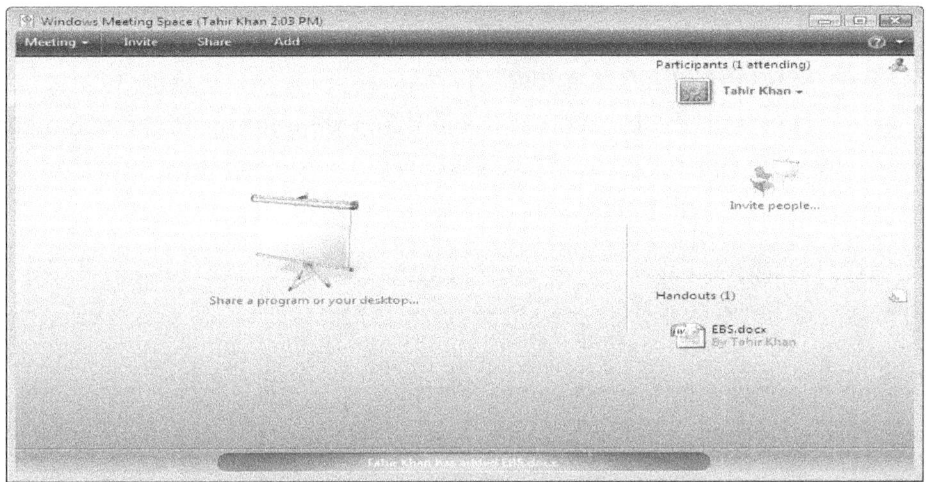

Memory Diagnostics Tool

A memory diagnostics tool checks for memory errors and then fix memory errors, if possible. An administrator or a member of administrative group has privileges to view and create real-time monitoring report.

Memory Diagnostics Scan

To open Memory Diagnostics Tool program:

- Open ***Control Panel***
- Double-click ***Administrative Tools***
- Double-click ***Memory Diagnostics Tool***

You will be asked to ***Restart now and check for problems (recommended)*** or ***Check for problems the next time I start my computer*** to perform a memory test on your system. Choose one of the above mentioned options and then click on ***Close***. It may take few minutes to few hours to perform memory test on your computer. A memory test report will be displayed at the end of the test for administrators to analyze the memory errors.

Real-time Monitoring Report

Real-time monitoring report is designed to collect important information to analyze baseline of the computer. A baseline is a snapshot of your system that determines the performance of the computer at given period of time. It helps to determine bottlenecks which is the weakest component installed in your computer that slows down your computer performance. To start system diagnostics report, click ***Start*** button and type ***perfmon /report*** [have a space between perfmon and back slash] in the search bar and then hit ***Enter*** key from keyboard to run real-time monitoring report.

Reliability and performance monitor takes about 60 seconds to collect the important information about local hardware resources, system response time, and application processes.

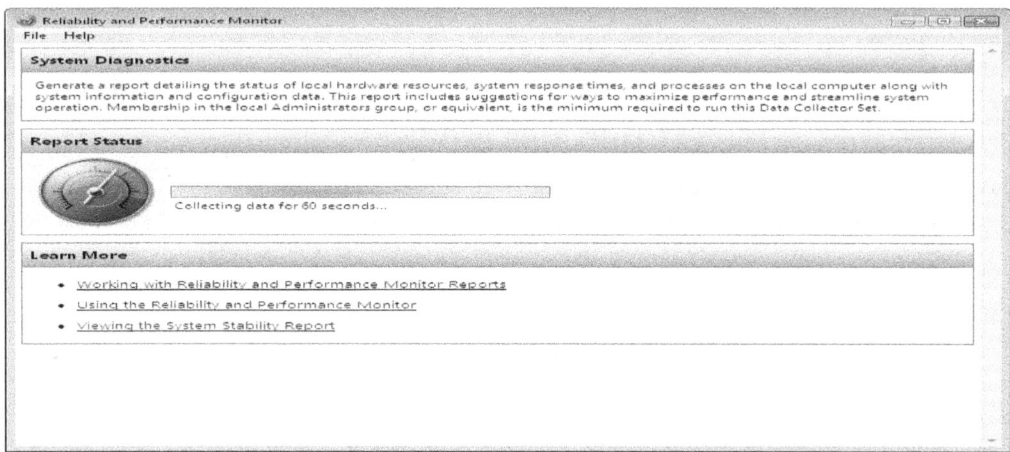

System will generate a diagnostic report with an explanation of diagnostic results. Review the results carefully and then take necessary action(s) to fix issue(s), if necessary.

Backup Files

On the corporate level, it is recommended to perform user's files and folders backup on daily basis. For home users, it is recommended to have a complete backup of their personal files and folders at-least once in a week to minimize the risk of losing personal data over a period of time. Microsoft Windows Vista Home Basic edition does not provide support for personal data backups. To backup copies of your files and folders, open the ***Control Panel Home***. In the *Control Panel* window, double-click on ***System and Maintenance***.

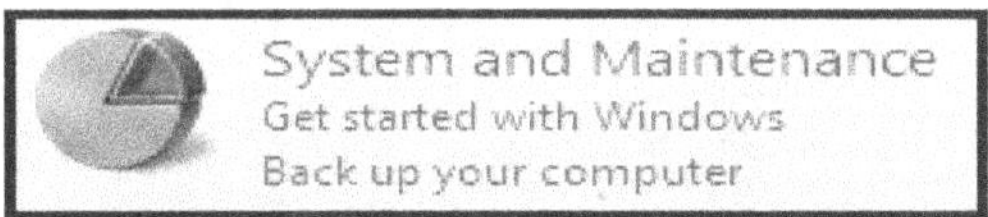

In the ***System and Maintenance*** panel, click the ***Backup and Restore Center***.

In the ***Backup and Restore Center*** panel, under the ***Backup files or your entire computer*** section, click on ***Back up files***. If *User Account Control* window is prompted to you, click on ***Continue*** to perform a backup for your system.

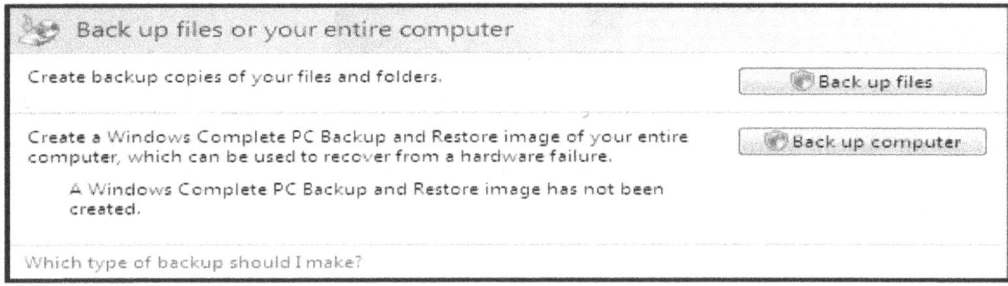

Choose a location to save the backup files and then click on ***Next***. Backup files can be saved in an external device (e.g. CD, DVD, USB drive, or any other removable device) or on a network location. To save files in an external hard-drive, connect the external hard-drive to your computer and then save backup files on it.

Choose the available file types for personal backup, and then click on ***Next*** to continue. The available backup files types are: *pictures, music files, video files, e-mail, documents, TV shows, compressed files, and any other additional files formats which have non-Microsoft extensions*. It is recommended to backup all of the file types.

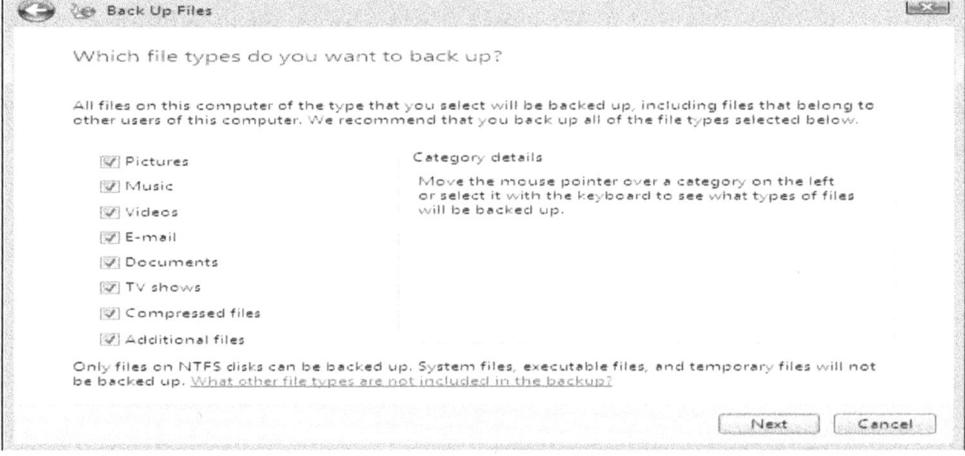

To schedule a backup, choose one of the following preferences and then click on ***Save settings and start backup***.

a. *How often:* Select Daily, Weekly, or Monthly backup option
b. *What day:* Select an appropriate day of the week
c. *What time:* Select an appropriate time

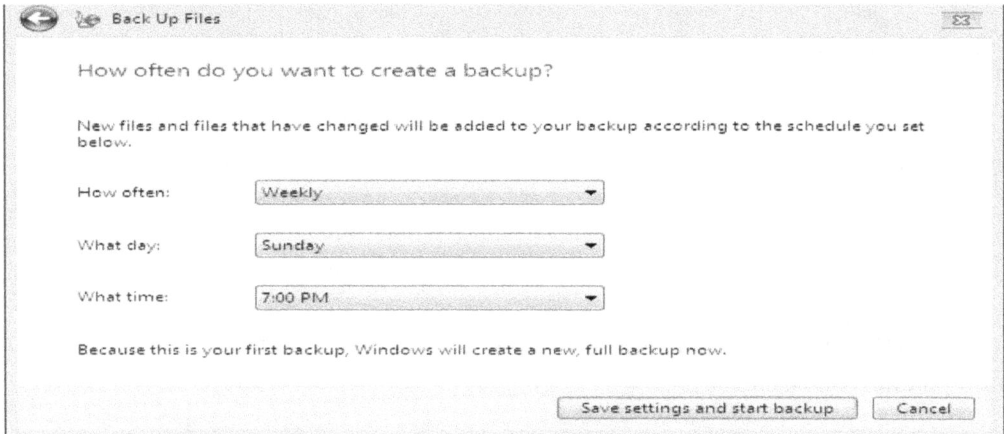

This process may take few minutes to several hours to complete the backup process depending on your computer's speed and performance. If you were successful to backup personal files and folders, you will be notified. Click on ***Close*** to complete the process.

Restore Files

Restore files are the previously backup copies of your files and folders. Microsoft Windows Vista Home Basic edition does not provide support for restoring backups. To restore user's files and folders, open *Backup and Restore Center*. In the ***Backup and Restore Center*** panel, under the ***Restore files or your entire computer*** section, click the ***Restore files***. If *User Account Control* window is prompted to you, click on ***Continue***. You may be prompted for administrative credentials, provide the administrator's username and password to restore files for your system.

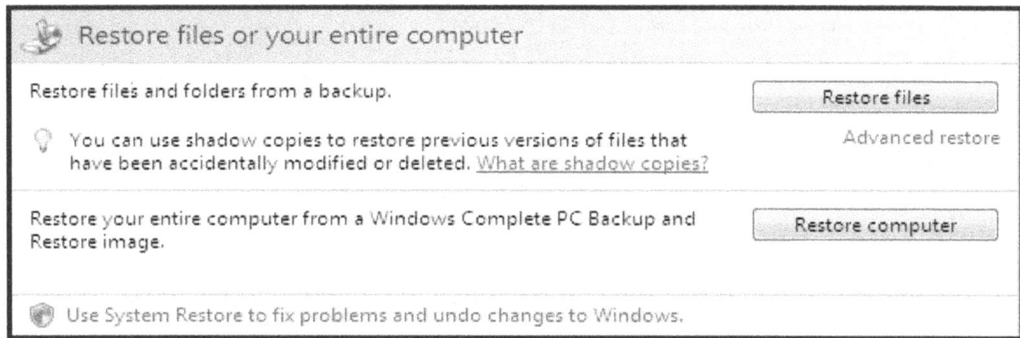

You have option to choose either ***latest backup*** option or ***older backup*** option to restore files and folders for your system and then click on ***Next*** to continue restoring files.

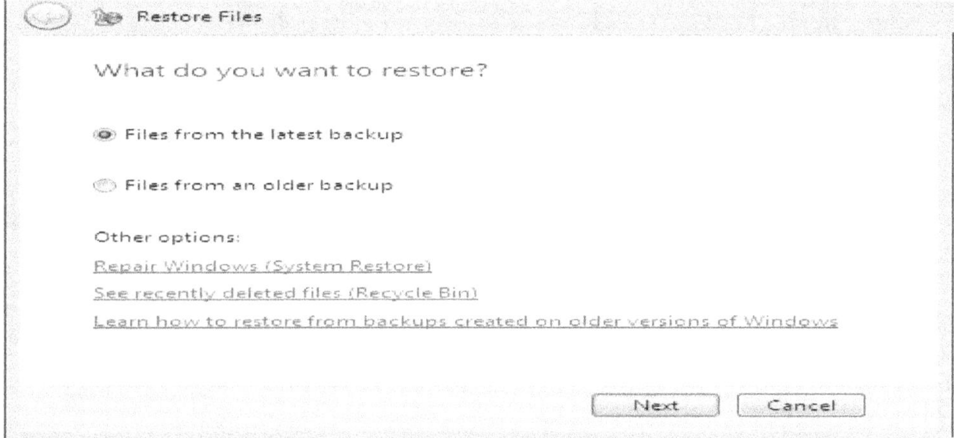

Connect the external device with your computer in which you had data backup files stored and then click on ***Next***.

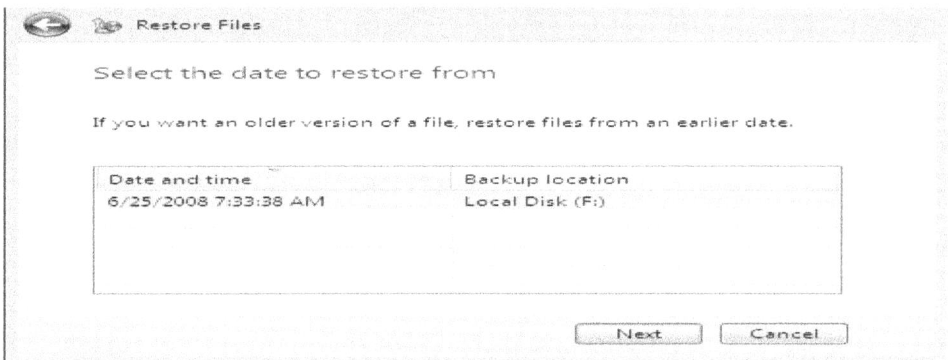

Select the files and folders that you want to restore and then click on ***Next***.

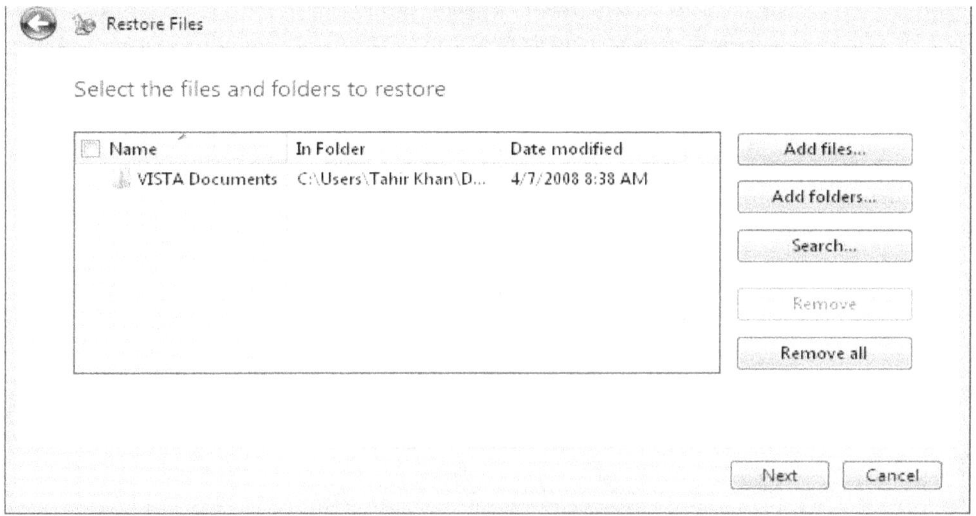

The files and folders can be restored by choosing the default option, ***In the original locations*** option in which data was previously saved or by Specifying the location of the stored files and folders. To start restoring files, click on ***Start restore***.

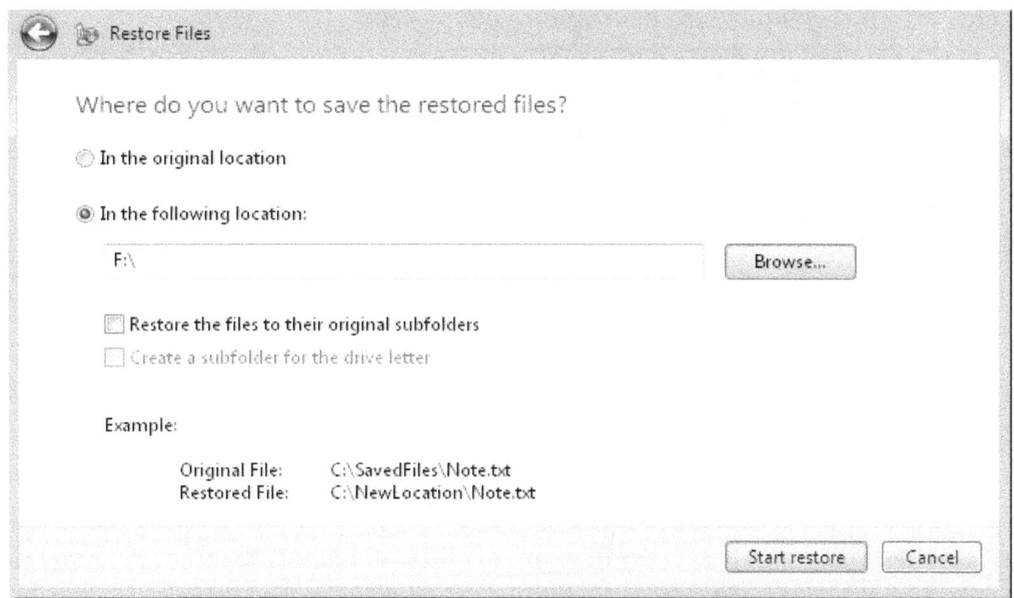

If you are prompted for NTFS file system error, you must format the external drive with NTFS file system. To format a drive with NTFS files system, right-click on the drive that you want to format with NTFS files system, and then select the ***Format*** option from the list. From drop down menu of the ***files System***, choose ***NTFS*** option and then click on ***Start*** button to format the drive. This restore process may take few minutes to several hours to complete the task depending on your computer's speed and performance. If you were successful to restore files, you will be notified. Click on ***Finish*** to complete this process.

Complete PC Backup

A *Complete PC Backup* is the backup of your personal data (documents and pictures), programs (Microsoft office), and system registry which keeps track of your hardware and software profile changes. Microsoft Windows Vista Home Basic edition does not provide support for complete PC backup. A complete PC restore is a quick way to restore all of your previously saved files, folders, programs, and hardware and software registry configurations incase of operating system failure. It is best practice to perform a complete pc backup at-least once in a week for home users to minimize the risk of losing important data if system fails.

To create a complete PC backup, open *Backup and Restore Center*. In the ***Backup and Restore Center*** panel, under the ***Backup files or your entire computer*** section, click the ***Back up computer***. If *User Account Control* window is prompted to you, click on ***Continue*** to perform a complete PC backup for your system.

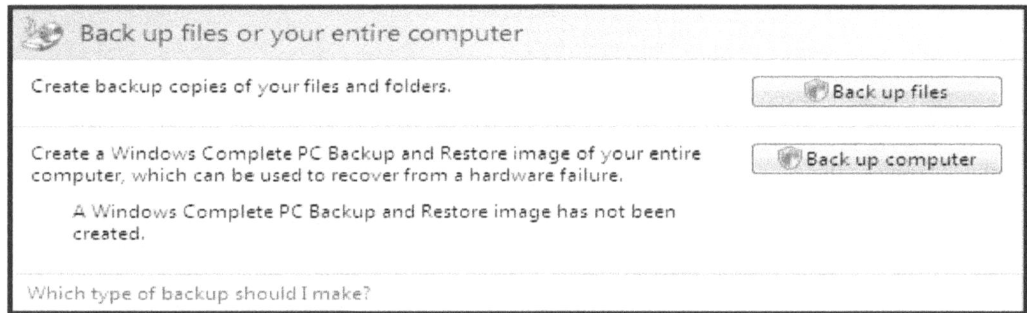

To save complete PC backup, choose a location where you want to save the backup of your computer and then click on ***Next***. Backup files can be saved in an external device (e.g. CD, DVD, USB drive, or any other removable device) or on a network location. To save files in an external hard drive, connect the external hard drive with your computer and then start saving backup files onto it. If you cannot save the PC computer backup in an external removable device, you may need to format the device with NTFS file system. If you want to save the backup files on the network, you should have access to file server to perform this action.

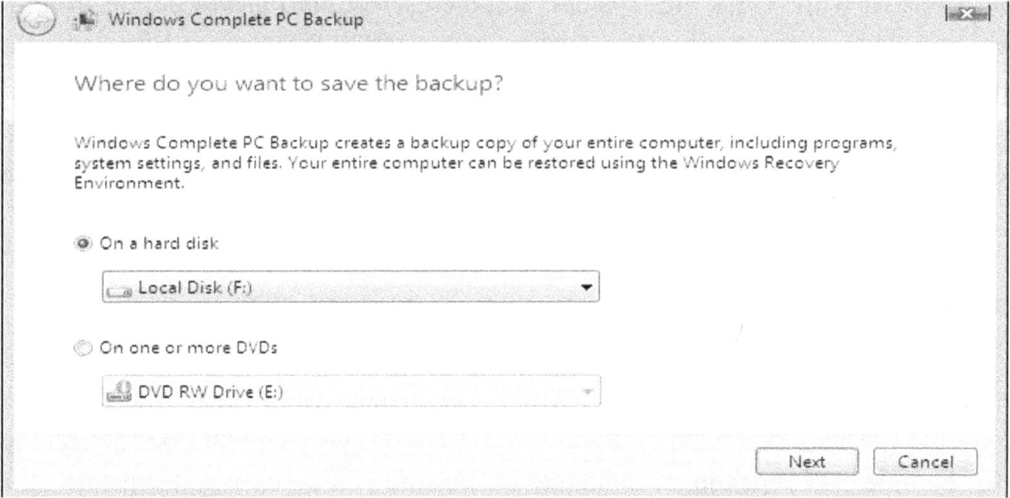

Skip this step, if you were able to save computer backup files on an external removable drive or on a network. If you cannot save the PC computer backup in an external removable device, you need to format the device with NTFS file system. To format a drive with NTFS files system, right-click on the drive that you want to format with NTFS files system, and then select the ***Format*** option from the list.

From drop down menu of the ***files System***, choose ***NTFS*** option and then click on ***Start*** to perform a format on the drive. This restore process may take few minutes to several hours to complete the task depending on your computer's speed and performance. Make sure to review the source and target disk settings before performing a complete PC backup. Click on ***Start backup*** to confirm your backup settings.

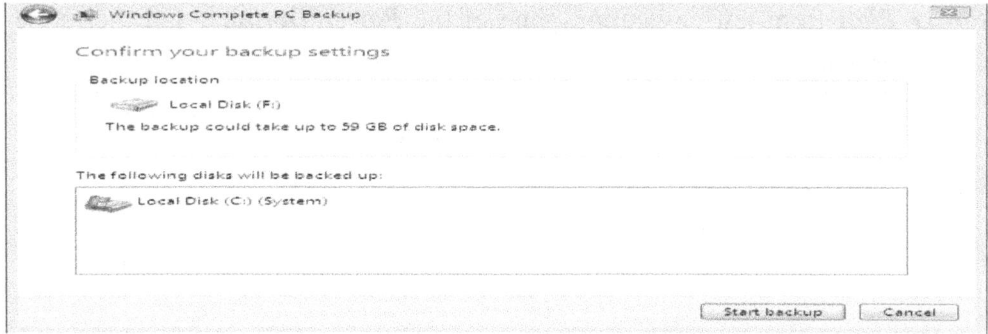

Your system may take few minutes to several hours to backup whole system. If the computer back up was successful, you will be notified. Click on ***Close*** to complete the process.

Power Management

A power management is an administrator tool to manage power plans to optimize the performance of the computer. There are three preferred power plans available for users, which are named as: ***Balanced, Power Saver***, and ***High Performance***. Your computer manufacture may have additional power management capabilities built into the system to boost the performance of your system.

Adjust Power Settings

From the ***Control Panel*** window, click ***System and Maintenance***. From the ***System and Maintenance*** window, navigate to the ***Power Options*** link and then click on it to open.

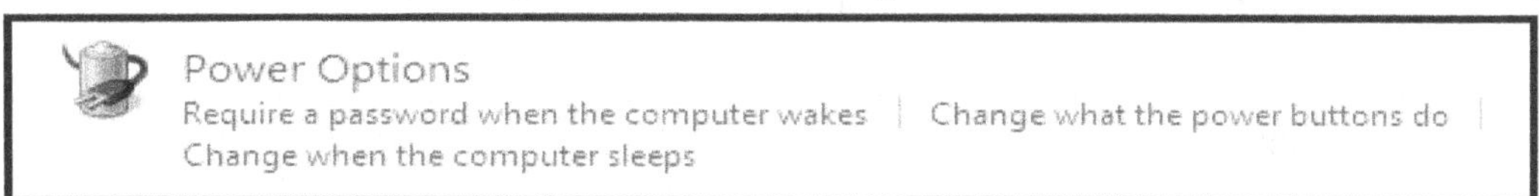

Select an available power plan for your system to optimize the performance. Windows Vista offers three power saving plans to choose from:

Balanced: Balanced energy savings and performance

Power Saver: Better energy savings over performance

High Performance: Better performance over energy savings

Power Plan Settings

Open *Power Options* from the ***Control Panel***. From the ***Power Options*** window, click on ***Change Plan Settings*** to adjust power plan settings from the ***preferred plan*** section. From the ***Edit plan setting*** window, adjust the computer display settings and computer sleep settings, and then click on ***Save Changes***. To customize a power plan, click on ***Create a Power Plan*** from left navigation pane of the ***Power Options***, and then type a name for the power plan.

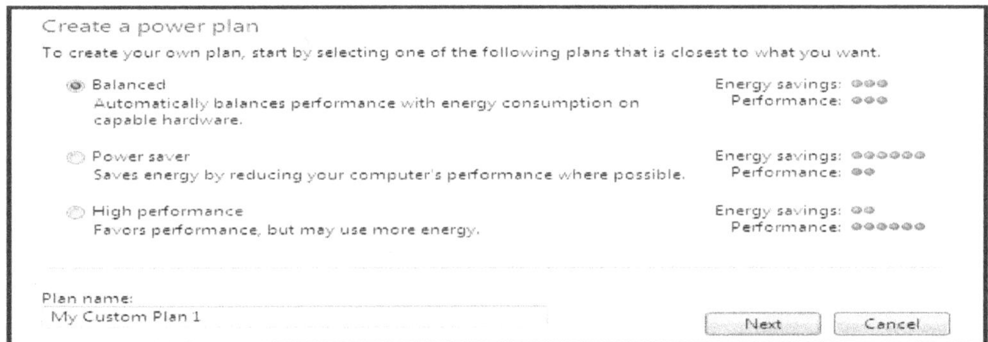

Click on ***Create*** after adjusting the sleep and display time settings. The new power plan will be your default power plan for your system, unless you change it to a different power plan.

Change settings for the plan: My Custom Plan 1
Choose the sleep and display settings that you want your computer to use.
Turn off the display: 20 minutes
Put the computer to sleep: 1 hour
Create Cancel

To remove custom power plan, click the ***Change plan settings*** under the ***My Custom Plan*** section and then click on ***Delete this plan*** to delete custom power plan. If you are prompted to delete custom power plan, click on ***OK***. The system only allows you to delete *Custom Power Plans* which are created by users. You cannot delete balanced, power saver, and high performance power plans.

Define Power Button

Power button can be defined according to the user preferences. By default, pushing the power button will result in shutting down your computer but the function of the power button can be set to hibernation mode, sleep mode, or do nothing mode. To customize power button, open the ***Control Panel*** and then navigate to the ***Power Options*** icon to open it. Click the ***Choose what the power button does*** link from left pane of the ***Power Options*** window.

You can adjust the ***Power*** button settings by selecting the options from drop down menu under the ***Power button settings*** section. It allows you to choose ***shut down***, ***sleep***, ***hibernate***, or ***do nothing mode*** options to customize the power button settings. Click on ***Save Changes*** after making any changes to the power button.

System Wakeup Password

Open the ***Control Panel*** and then navigate to the ***Power Options*** icon to open it. Click on the ***Require a password on wakeup*** link from left pane of the ***Power Options*** window.

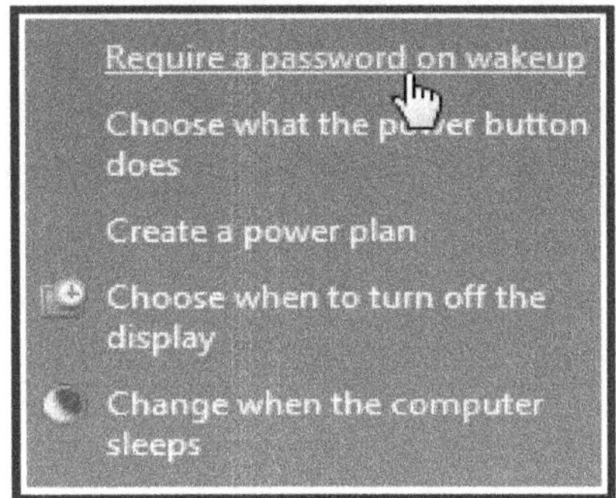

The ***required a password (recommended)*** option is grayed out (not available to choose) under ***Password protection on wakeup*** section. To change the password protection settings, click on ***Change settings that are currently unavailable***.

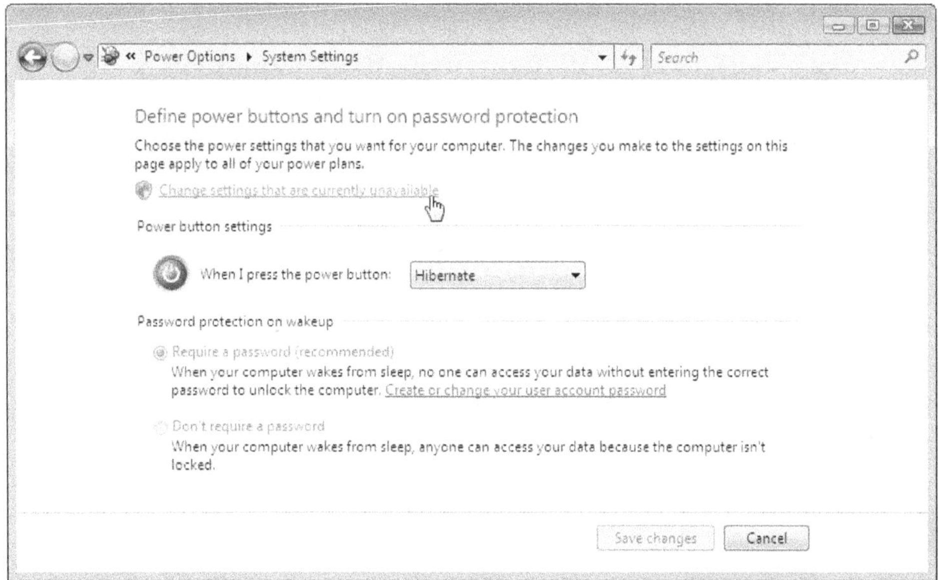

It is recommended to have a ***wakeup password*** on your system to unlock the system. Choose the password protection options for your computer and then click ***Save Changes***.

Windows Mail

Windows Mail enables users to manage, create e-mail message rules, newsgroup message rules, filter junk e-mails, and block and allow top-level domains. The POP3 and IMAP incoming mail servers are supported in *Windows Mail* but it does not provide support for HTTP e-mail accounts. In older versions of Microsoft operating system, *Outlook Express* was used to manage user's e-mail accounts but it is replaced by *Windows Mail* in new operating system of Microsoft.

Add Windows Mail Account

To navigate the *Windows Mail* path, click ***Start*** button, click ***All Programs***, and then click ***Windows Mail***. From the *Windows Mail* panel, click on ***Tools*** menu, and then choose ***Accounts*** option from the list. Click on ***Add*** to create a new e-mail account.

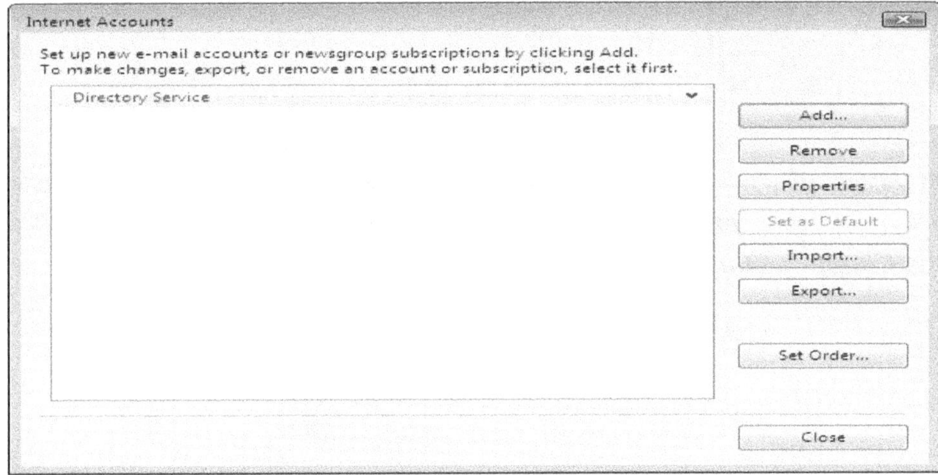

Select an account type that you wish to setup, the account types are: *e-mail accounts, newsgroup accounts, and directory services*. In this case, click on ***Email Account***. Click ***Next*** to continue.

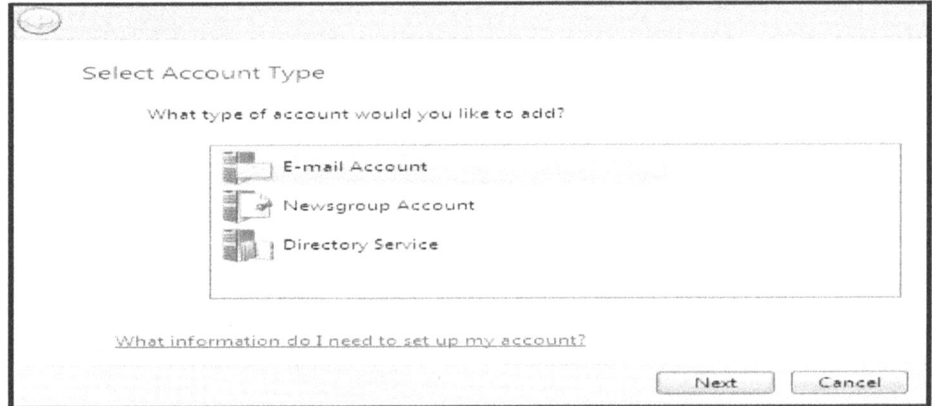

Type a display name, usually it is your name that will appear in the ***From*** field of outgoing message. To continue this process, click ***Next***.

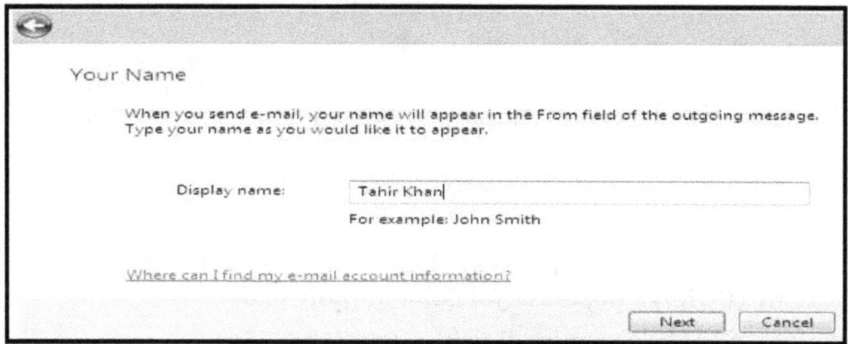

Type your personal e-mail address to setup an e-mail account. Click on ***Next*** to continue.

To setup an e-mail account, you must know the incoming e-mail server type, incoming and outgoing mail server names. If you do not have access to e-mail server information, contact your system administrator to get the necessary information to configure your e-mail accounts. To configure your *Windows Mail* account, select an incoming e-mail server, and then provide incoming and outgoing mail server names and then click on ***Next*** to continue setting up an e-mail account. If authentication needs to be activated for outgoing messages, check the ***Outgoing server requires authentication*** box.

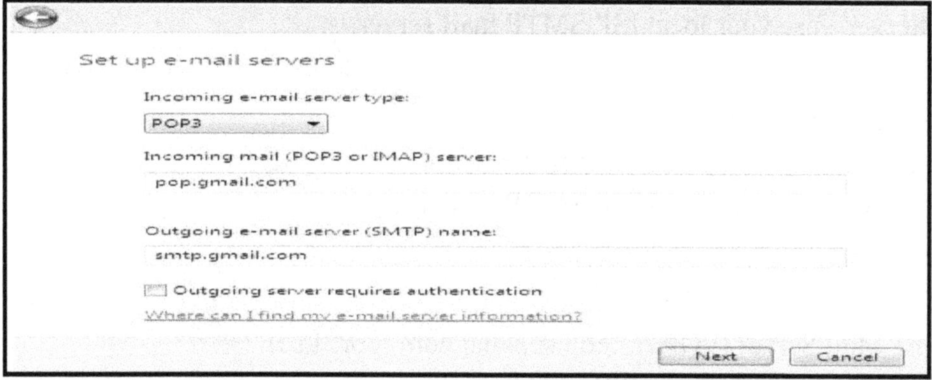

Few of the e-mail clients are mentioned following with their e-mail server types, incoming mail server names, and outgoing e-mail server names.

Hotmail Settings

Email Server Type: HTTP

Windows Mail does not support HTTP server type so you can not add a hotmail account to the *Windows Mail*.

Yahoo Mail Settings

Email Server Type: POP3

Yahoo Incoming Mail Server (POP3) - pop.mail.yahoo.com (port 110)

Yahoo Outgoing Mail Server (SMTP) - smtp.mail.yahoo.com (port 25)

Google Mail Settings

Email Server Type: POP3

Google Incoming Mail Server (POP3) - pop.gmail.com (SSL enabled, port 995)

Outgoing Mail Server - smtp.gmail.com (SSL enabled, port 465)

Lycos Mail Settings

Email Server Type: POP3 and SMTP

Lycos Incoming Mail Server (POP3) - pop.mail.lycos.com (port 110)

Outgoing Mail Server - smtp.mail.lycos.com

Mail.com Mail Settings

Email Server Type: POP3 and SMTP

Mail.com Incoming Mail Server (POP3) - pop1.mail.com (port 110)

Outgoing Mail Server - use your local ISP SMTP mail server

Tiscali Mail Settings

Email Server Type: POP3 and SMTP

Tiscali Incoming Mail Server (POP3) - pop.tiscali.com (port 110)

Outgoing Mail Server - use your local ISP SMTP mail server

Freeserve Mail Settings

Email Server Type: POP3 and SMTP

Freeserve Incoming Mail Server (POP3) - pop.freeserve.com (port 110)

Outgoing Mail Server - use your local ISP SMTP mail server

Supanet Mail Settings

Email Server Type: POP3 and SMTP

Supanet Incoming Mail Server (POP3) - pop.supanet.com (port 110)

Outgoing Mail Server - use your local ISP SMTP mail server

Create a username and a password for your e-mail account, and then click on ***Next***.

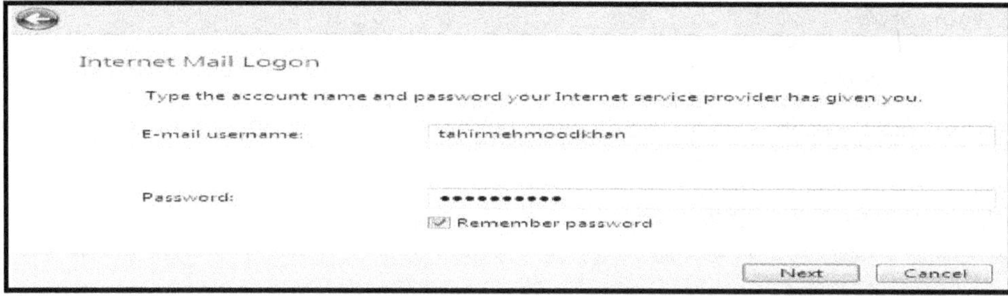

Click on ***Finish*** to start downloading e-mails form server to your computer. If you would like to download e-mails from server later, check the ***Do not download my e-mail at this time*** box.

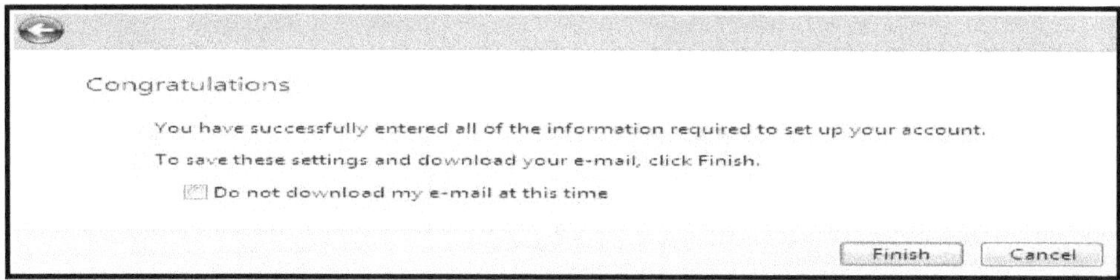

Windows Mail Options

Open *Windows Mail* to customize the ***General, Read, Receipts, Send, Compose, Spelling, Security Settings, Connection Settings, and Advanced*** preferences. From the *Windows Mail* panel, click the ***Tools*** menu and then click ***Options*** to view the *Windows Mail* options. To adjust *Windows Mail* preferences, click on each tab of the *Windows Mail* option and then select appropriate preferences. The *Windows Mail* preferences are given below.

The following sections are listed in the ***General*** tab to adjust the *Windows Mail* preferences.

In the ***General*** section, the *Windows Mail* preferences that can be selected are:

- *Notify me if there are any new newsgroups*
- *Automatically display folders with unread messages*
- *Use newsgroup message rating features*

In the ***Send/Receive Messages*** section, the *Windows Mail* preferences that can be selected are:

- *Play sound when new messages arrive*
- *Send and receive messages at start-up*

- *Check for new message every X (X represents any numeric value) minutes(s)*
- *If my computer is not connected at this time, choose one of the available options: Do not connect, Connect only when not working offline, Connect even when working offline*

In the ***Default Messaging Programs*** section, W*indows Mail* preferences that can be selected are:

- *This application is the default Mail handler*
- *This application is the default News hander*

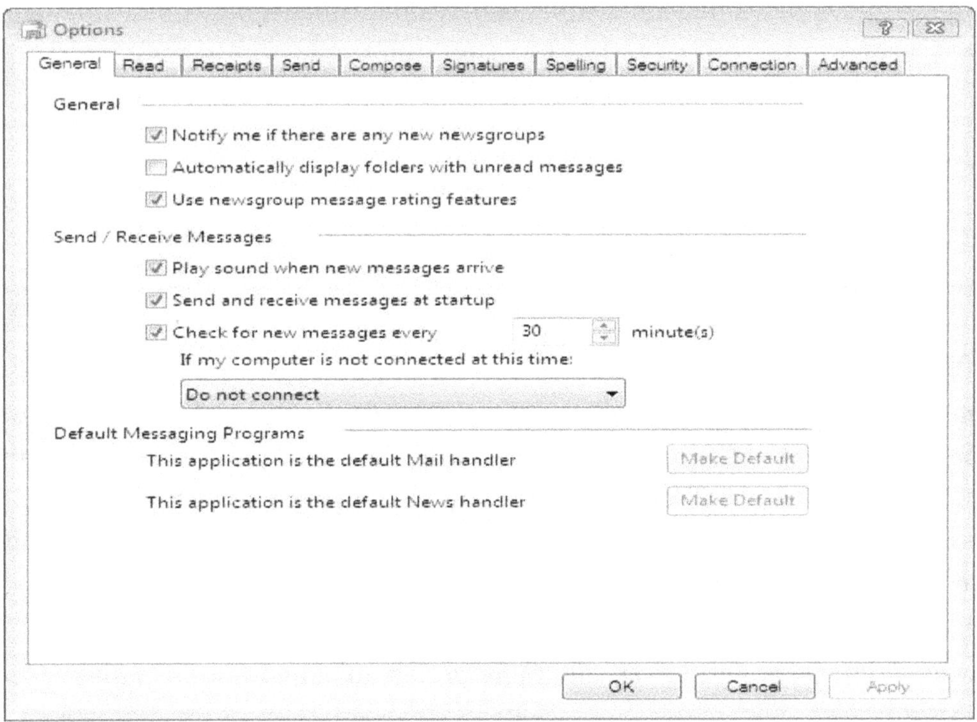

The following sections are listed in the ***Read*** tab to adjust the *Windows Mail* preferences.

In the ***Reading Messages*** section, the *Windows Mail* preferences that can be selected are:

- *Mark message read after displaying for X (X represents numeric value) second(s)*
- *Automatically expand grouped messages*
- *Automatically download message when viewing in the Preview Pane*
- *Read all messages in plain text*
- *Show ToolTips in the message list for clipped items*

- *Highlight watched messages. Choose any available color*

In the ***News*** section, the *Windows Mail* preferences that can be selected are:

- *Get X (X represents any numeric value for the header) headers at a time*
- *Mark all messages as read when exiting a newsgroup*

In the ***Fonts*** section, the *Windows Mail* preferences that can be selected are:

- *Click on **Fonts** to change fonts of a reading message*
- *Click on **International** settings to change encoding method of reading message*

The following sections are listed in the ***Receipts*** tab to adjust the *Windows Mail* preferences.

In the ***Requesting Read Receipts*** section, the *Windows Mail* preference that can be selected is:

- *Request a read receipt for all send messages*

In the ***Returning Read Receipts*** section, the *Windows Mail* preferences that can be selected are:

- *Never send a receipt*
- *Notify me for each read receipt request*
- *Always send a read receipt*

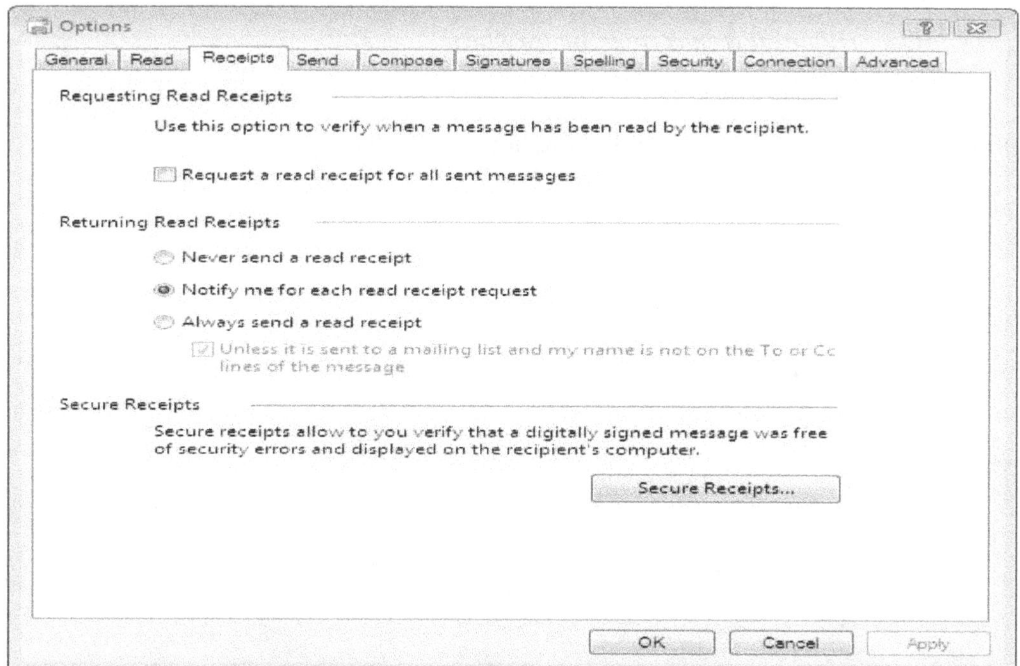

The following sections are listed in the ***Send*** tab to adjust the *Windows Mail* preferences.

In the ***Sending*** section, the *Windows Mail* preferences that can be selected are:

- *Save copy of sent messages in the Sent Items folder*
- *Send messages immediately*
- *Automatically put people I reply to in my Contacts list*
- *Automatically complete e-mail addresses when composing*
- *Include message in reply*
- *Reply to messages using the format in which they were sent*

Mail Sending Format: HTML and/or Plain Text

News Sending Format: HTML and/or Plain Text

The following sections are listed in the ***Spelling*** tab to adjust the *Windows Mail* preferences.

In the ***Settings*** section, the *Windows Mail* preference that can be selected is:

- *Always check spelling before sending*

In the ***When checking spelling, always ignore*** section, the *Windows Mail* preferences that can be selected are:

- *Words in UPPERCASE*
- *Words with numbers*
- *The original text in a reply or forward*
- *Internet Addresses*

In ***Language*** section, choose an available language for *Windows Mail.*

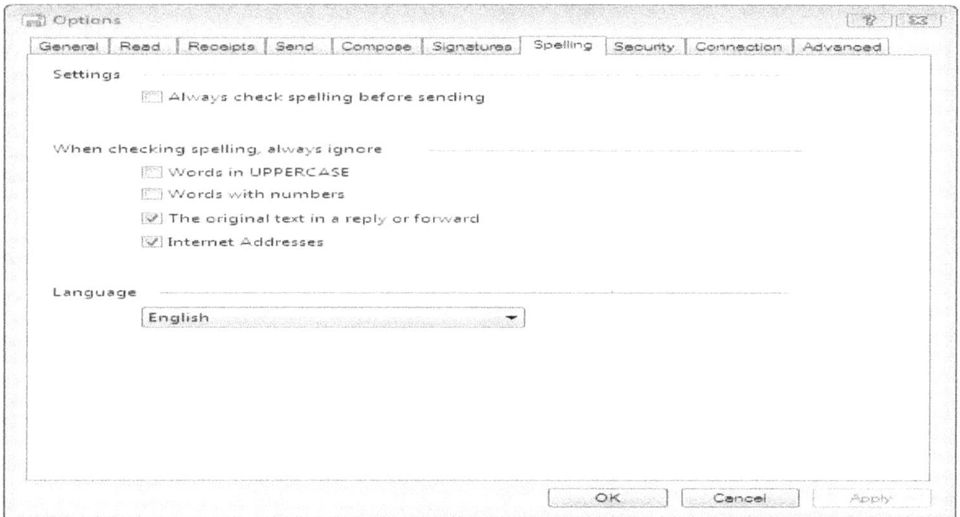

The following sections are listed in the ***Security*** tab to adjust the *Windows Mail* preferences.

In the ***Virus Protection*** section, the *Windows Mail* preferences that can be selected are:

- *Internet Explorer security zones are:*
  - ③ *Internet zone (less secure, but more functional)*
  - ③ *Restricted sites zone (more secure)*
- *Warn me when other applications try to send mail as me.*
- *Do not allow attachments to be saved or opened that could potentially be a virus*

In the ***Download Images*** section, the *Windows Mail* preference that can be selected is:

- *Block images and other external content in HTML e-mail*

In the ***Secure Mail*** section, the *Windows Mail* preferences that can be selected are:

- *Click on Digital IDs button to create or manage IDs*
- *Click on Get Digital **ID** button to read about digital ID*
- *Encrypt contents and attachments for all outgoing messages*
- *Digitally sign all outgoing messages*

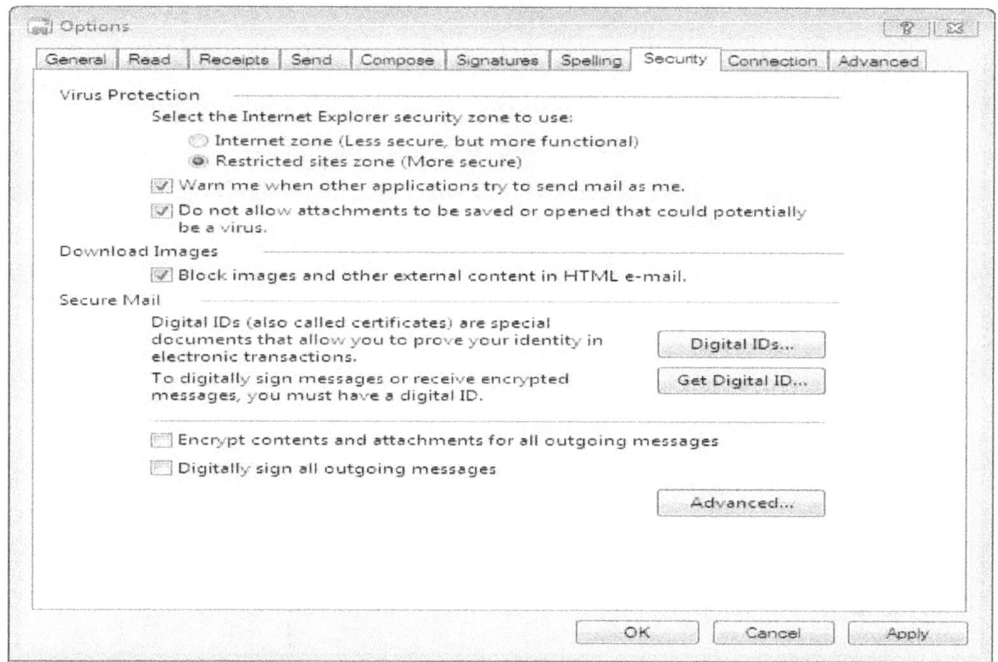

The following sections are listed in the ***Advanced*** tab to adjust the *Windows Mail* preferences.

In the ***Settings*** section, the *Windows Mail* preferences that can be selected are:

Contact Attachment Conversion: Choose one of the three available options: *Always convert Contacts attachments to vCard, ask me each time, and leave contact attachments in Contact format*

In the ***IMAP*** section, the *Windows Mail* preference that can be selected is:

- *Use the 'Deleted Items' folder with IMAP accounts*

In the ***Message Threads*** section, the *Windows Mail* preference that can be selected is:

- *Mark message threads I start as Watched*

In the ***Reply/Forward*** section, the *Windows Mail* preferences that can be selected are:

- *Compose reply at the bottom of the original message*
- *Insert signature at the bottom of a reply*

In the ***Windows Contacts*** section, the *Windows Mail* preferences that can be selected are:

- *Associate the pictures in my Windows user account and my personal contact*
- *Reduce the file size of contacts by linking to pictures on my computer*

Send/Receive Email From Server

To download e-mails from server, open *Windows Mail* program. From the *Windows Mail* panel, go to the ***Tools*** menu and then choose ***Synchronize all*** option. *Windows Mail* may take several minutes downloading messages from server to *Windows Mail* account. If *Windows Mail* did not download e-mails from server, an error message will display in ***Task*** box.

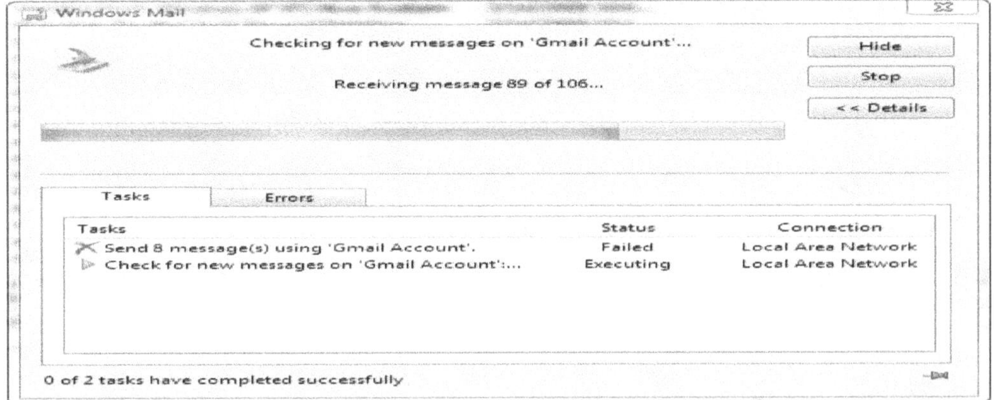

Mail Message Rules

A message rule can be defined to filter spam e-mails. Defining an e-mail message rule may reduce soliciting e-mails from unknown vendors. It is recommended to check your Junk e-mail folder for important messages which may be getting delivered to your Junk e-mail folder because of strict e-mail rules.

To create a message rule:

- Open ***Windows Mail*** program
- From the ***Tools*** menu, choose ***Message Rule*** option, and then select ***Mail***
- From the ***New Mail Rule*** dialog box, select conditions and actions rules for your e-mail account, and then type name of the rule
- Click ***OK*** to create a new message rule for your e-mail account

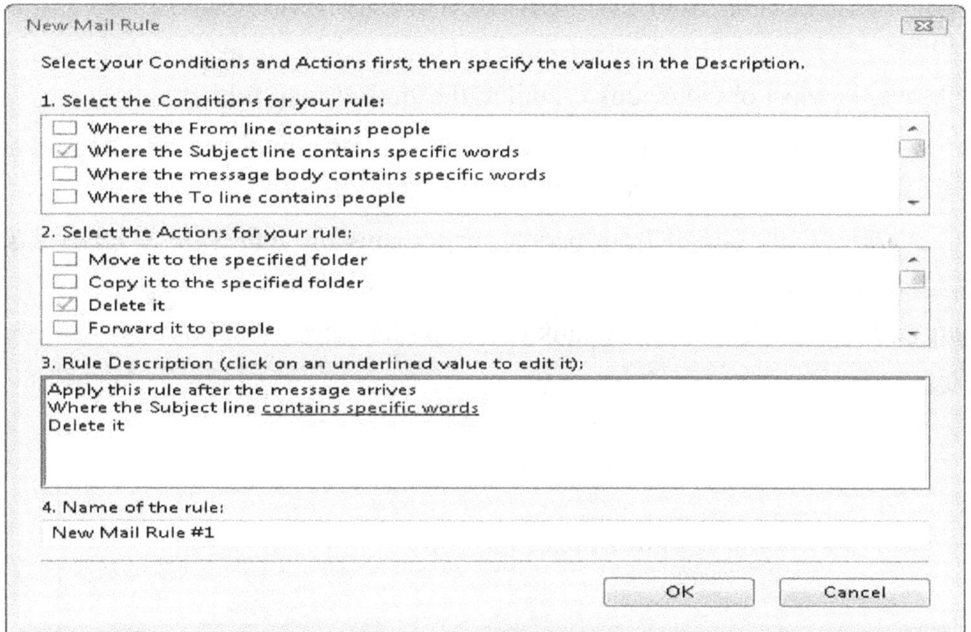

Newsgroup Message Rules

A message rule for Newsgroup is usually defined when it is necessary to move, copy, or delete the particular Newsgroup contents to a folder. To create a message rule for Newsgroup, open *Windows Mail* program. From the *Windows Mail* window, click the ***Tools*** menu, click ***Message Rule***, and then click ***News***. From the ***New Mail Rule*** dialog box, select the conditions and actions rules and then type name of the rule. Click on ***OK*** to create a new Newsgroup rule for your e-mail account.

View Windows Contact

A Windows contact card keeps track of user's e-mail ID, name, phone number, home address, etc. To view and manage Windows contacts, open *Windows Mail* program. From the *Windows Mail* window, click the ***Tools*** menu, and then click ***Windows Contacts*** to create and manage contacts.

Junk Mail Options

Junk mail can be configured to filter junk (unwanted) e-mails from your inbox. To adjust junk e-mail options, open *Windows Mail* program. From the *Windows Mail* window, click on ***Tools*** menu, and then choose ***Junk E-mail Options***.

In the ***Options*** tab, choose one of the following junk e-mail protection options.

- *No Automatic Filtering:* Mail from blocked senders is still moved to the Junk E-mail folder.
- *Low:* Move the most obvious junk e-mail to the Junk E-mail folder.
- *High:* Most junk e-mails are caught, but some regular e-mails may be caught as well. Check your Junk E-mail folder often.
- *Safe List Only:* Only e-mail from people or domains on your ***Safe Senders List*** will be delivered to your Inbox.

Click on ***Apply*** and then click ***OK*** to save junk e-mail preferences.

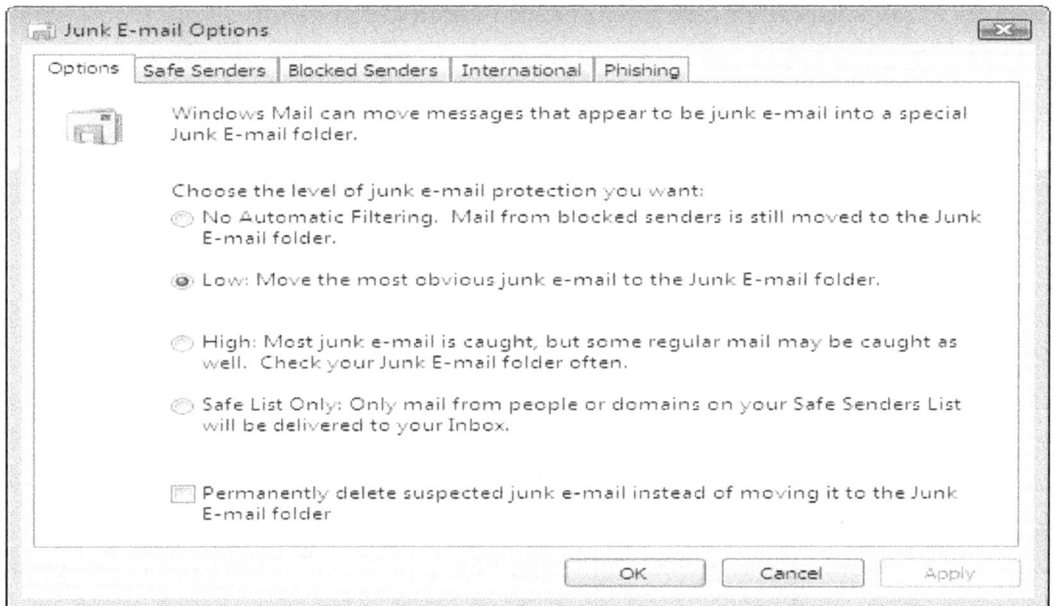

Adding User to Safe Senders List

To add a user to your safe senders list, click the ***Safe Senders*** tab from the ***Junk E-mail Options*** dialog box. In the ***Safe Senders*** tab, click the ***Add*** button to type an e-mail address that you want to add into your *Safe Senders* list. Click on ***Apply*** and then click ***OK*** to save preferences. You have option to add people automatically to the safe senders list as you e-mail them, if you would like to do so, check the ***Automatically add people I e-mail to the Safe Senders List*** box.

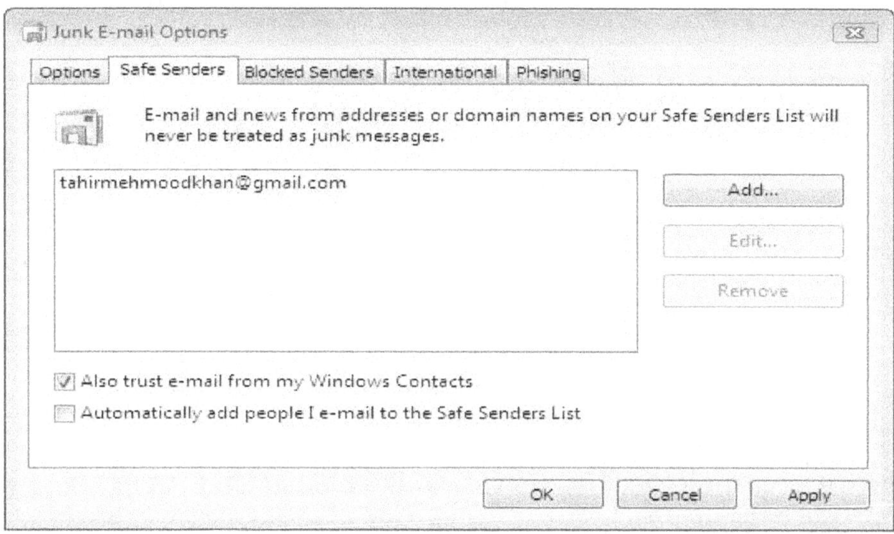

Adding User to Blocked Senders List

To add a user to your blocked senders list, click the ***Blocked Senders*** tab from the ***Junk E-mail Options*** dialog box. In the ***Blocked Senders*** tab, click the ***Add*** button and then type an e-mail address that you want to add into blocked senders list. Click on ***Apply*** and then click ***OK*** to save preferences.

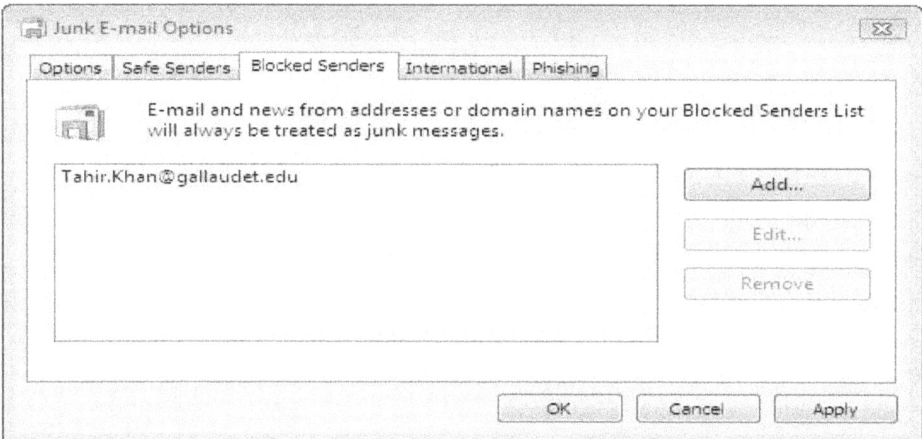

Blocking Top-level Domains

To block top-level domain, click the ***International*** tab from the ***Junk E-mail Options*** dialog box. In the ***International*** tab, click the ***Blocked Top-Level Domain List*** button and then select at-least one or more international domains that you want to block and then click ***OK***. Click on ***Apply*** and then click ***OK*** to save changes.

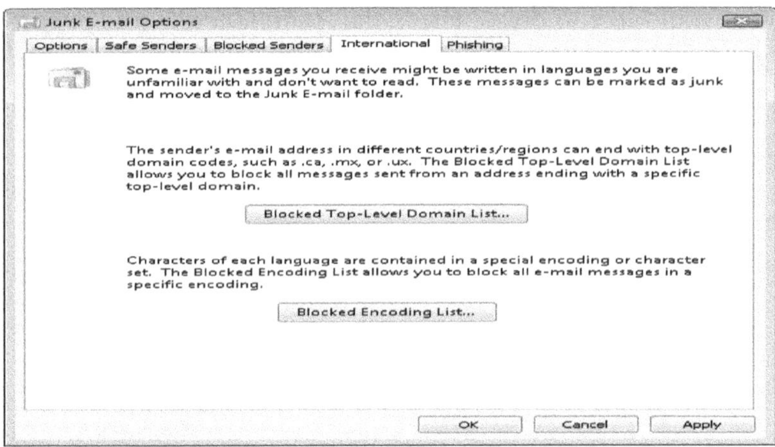

Adding Blocked Encoding List

To add an encoding list to your blocked list, click the ***International*** tab from the ***Junk E-mail Options*** dialog box. Click the ***Blocked Encoding List*** button and then select desired encoding list to add to your ***Blocked Encoding List*** and then click ***OK***. Click on ***Apply*** and then click ***OK*** to save preferences.

Customizing Phishing Filter Options

To adjust phishing options, click the ***Phishing*** tab from the ***Junk E-mail Options*** dialog box. In the ***Phishing*** tab, you can set the phishing filter to:

- *Protect my Inbox from messages with potential Phishing links*
- *Move phishing E-mail to the Junk Mail folder*

Phishing is a way to steal someone's identity and can be used for any purpose, once they have the necessary information. For example, while surfing web, an illegitimate website is asking you to provide your personal information (your name, phone number, home address, etc.) or bank information. If you have revealed personal information to illegitimate website, then they may use your personal information to hurt you financially or may sell your identify to a third party for profit.

Select one of the available *Phishing Filter* options. Click on ***Apply*** and then click ***OK*** to save changes.

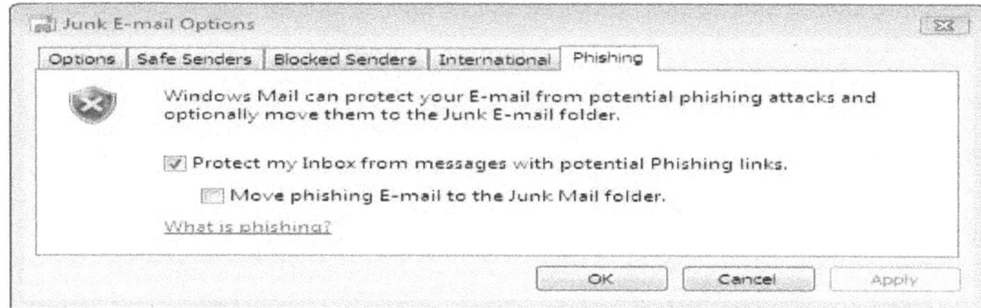

Requesting/Sending Secure Receipts

Some companies/users may request a secure digital receipt to keep track of successful delivered e-mails to your inbox. To request digital receipt, open *Windows Mail* options. From the ***Windows Mail Options*** dialog box, click ***Receipt*** tab from the ***Secure Receipts*** section and then click the ***Secure Receipts***. From the ***Secure Receipt Options*** dialog box, select the ***Request a secure receipt for all digitally signed messages*** option under the ***Requesting Secure Receipts*** section to enforce this policy to request secure receipts.

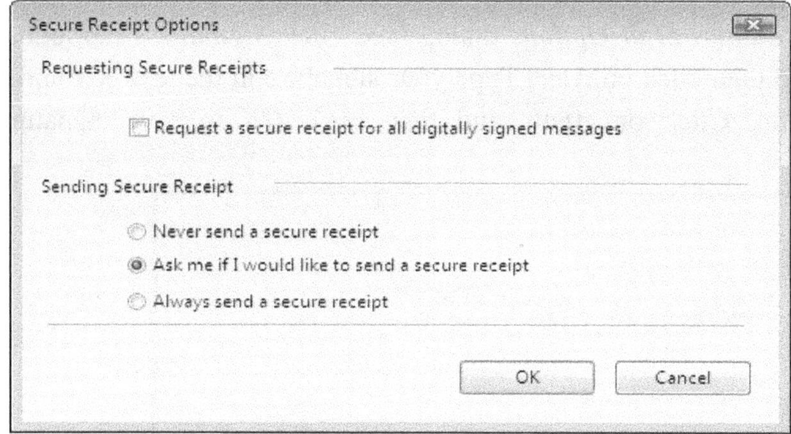

Choose one of the available sending secure receipt options (*never send a secure receipt, ask me if I would like to send a secure receipt, and always send a secure receipt*) to set sending secure receipts preferences.

Set/Change International Settings

International e-mail settings can be configured to encode outgoing messages according to the user's preferences. To adjust International encoding settings, open *Windows Mail* options. From the *Windows Mail Options* dialog box, click the ***Send*** tab under the ***Sending*** section, and then click ***International Settings***. From the *International Send*

Settings dialog box, choose an encoding setting from drop down menu of ***Default encoding*** options. Click ***OK*** to save *Windows Mail* preferences.

Add Signature

A signature sends personal information such as your job title, phone number(s), business hours, or any other information that is important for them to identify your business or job responsibilities, with all outgoing messages as an attachment or it can be viewed at bottom of the each message. To add the signature to the *Windows Mail*, open *Windows Mail* options. From the ***Windows Mail Options*** dialog box, click ***Signatures*** tab, under the ***Signatures*** section, and then click on ***New***. Type your signature in the text box under the ***Edit Signature*** section. Click on ***Apply*** and then click ***OK*** to save signature preferences.

Signatures
Signature #1 Default signature
New
Remove
Rename
Edit Signature
Text Tahir Khan
Set as Default
Advanced...
File C:\Users\Tahir Khan\Contacts\Tahir Khan.c
Browse...

Windows Contacts

The *Widnows Contacts* list is a way to manage users' information such as their names, home address, e-mail address, work information, family information, and their unique e-mail IDs.

Create Windows Contacts

To navigate the *Windows Contacts* path, click ***Start*** button, click ***All Programs***, and then click ***Windows Contacts***. From the command bar of *Windows Explorer*, choose ***New Contact*** option to create a new contact list.

From the *Windows Contacts Properties* window, click ***Name and Email*** tab, and then fill out necessary contact information. For example, contact's first, middle, last name, personal title, nickname, and e-mail address. You can customize contact preferences by clicking on ***Home***, ***Work***, ***Family***, ***Notes***, and ***IDs*** tabs. Click on each of the tabs and then fill out necessary information that would help you to organize and manage contact list. Click on ***OK*** when you are ready to apply changes to the contact list.

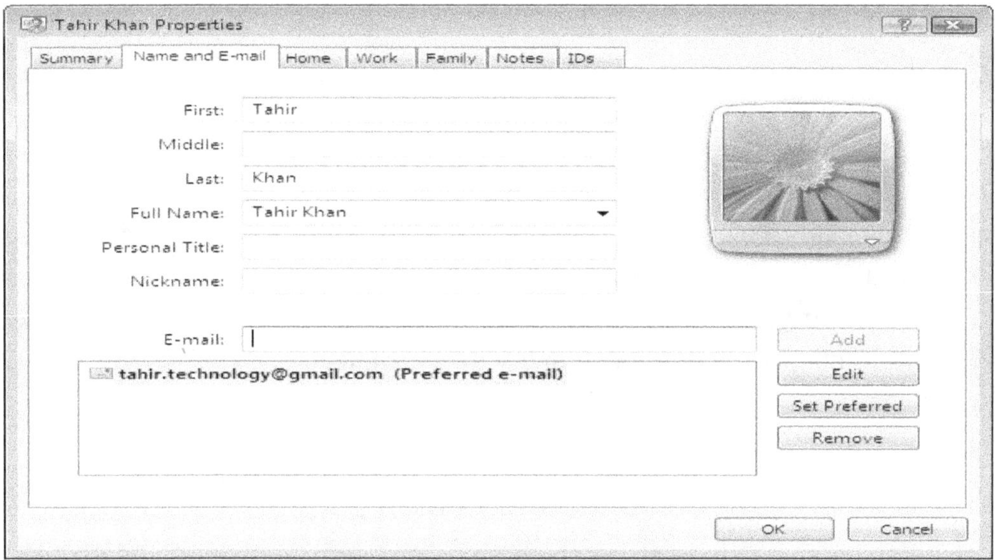

Problem Reports and Solutions Tool

Problem Reports and Solutions tool is designed to report application errors and issues to Microsoft Corporation, if your system configured properly. Microsoft consistently collects application errors to improve the performance of your operating system. Microsoft publishes solutions of the existing problems to help users to solve application issues. If Microsoft is working on a solution of the problem, the solution will be available to users as soon as Microsoft publishes it online and makes available for public.

Open Problem Reports and Solutions

Open ***Control Panel*** and navigate to the ***Problem Reports and Solutions*** icon and then double-click on it to open.

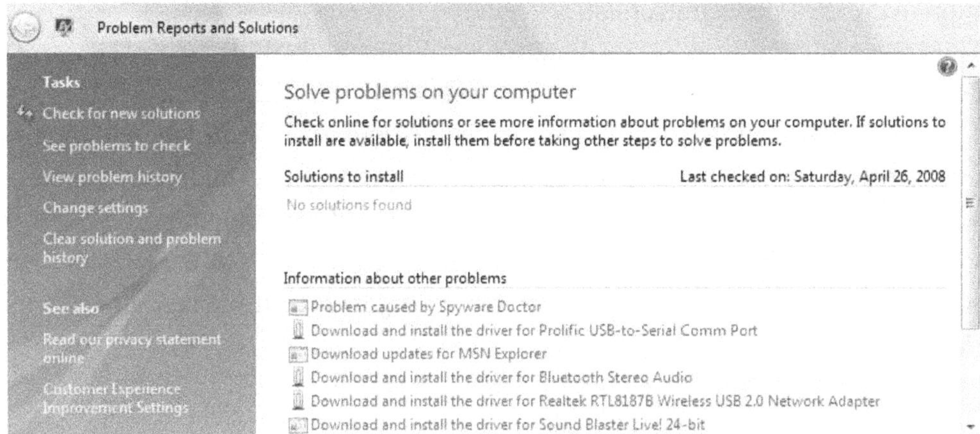

Check for New Solutions

From the *Problem Reports and Solutions* window, click the ***Check for new solutions*** link from left navigation pane. You must be connected with Internet for checking the solution of new hardware and software issues for your system. This process may take several minutes. For example, if you are unable to download updates for MSN explorer, system will check online solution of this problem and will recommend a list of solutions to fix the issue that has been tested by Microsoft.

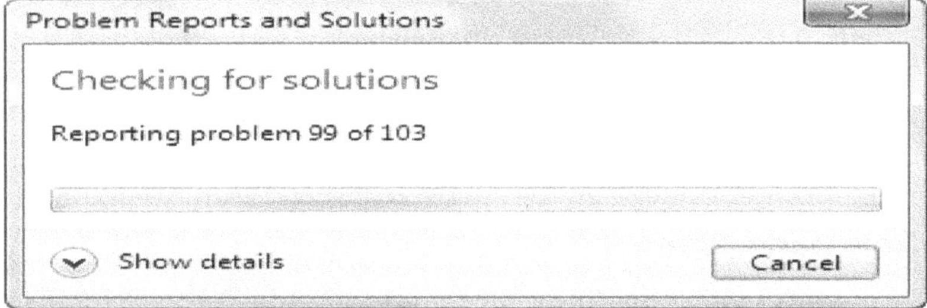

Your system lists all of the updated solutions of the issues on the right navigation pane of the ***Problem Reports and Solution*** window under the ***Information about other problems*** section. Go through the list of issues that you have had with your system and then click on solution of the problem to read about it, how to solve the issue. If Microsoft requires more information to identify the cause of the problem, you will be prompted to send a report to Microsoft.

Check Existing Solutions

From the ***Problem Reports and Solutions*** window, click the ***See problems to check*** link from left navigation pane under the ***Tasks*** section to check for solutions of the existing issues. From the dialog box, select the application that you would like to check the solution for, and then click on ***Check for solution***.

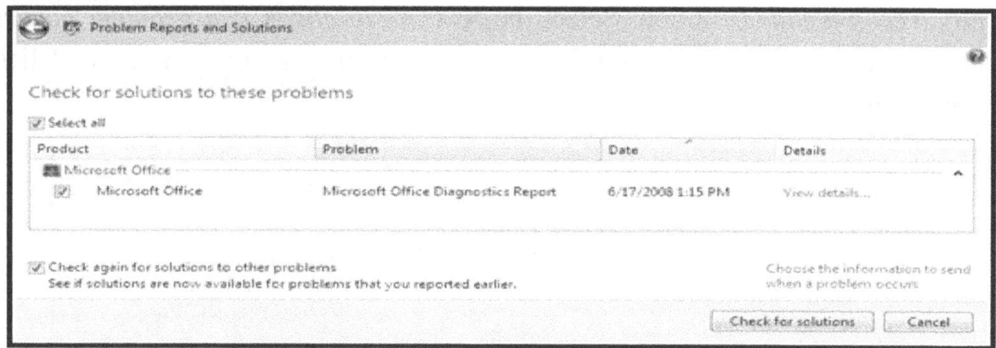

This process may take several minutes. If any new solutions of the problems are available online for your system, you will be prompted.

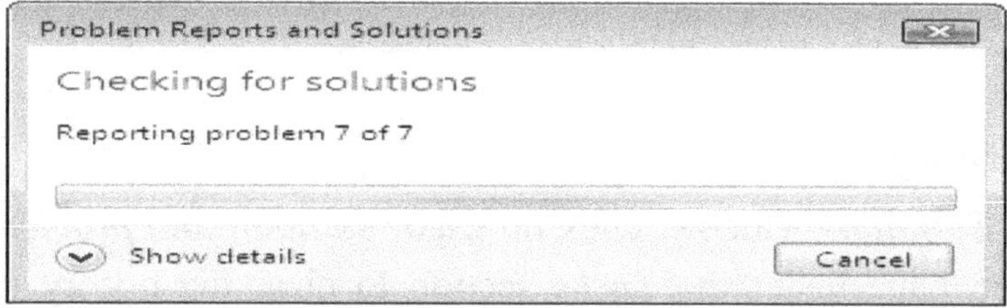

View Problem History

From the ***Problem Reports and Solutions*** window, click the ***See problems to check*** link from left navigation pane under the ***Tasks*** section to view the problems that has been identified for your system. The report shows, whether the solution is available for the problem that you are having with your system. If the solution is not available then it will show you whether it is reported to Microsoft to get any recommended solution. Click on ***OK*** to exit out of the window.

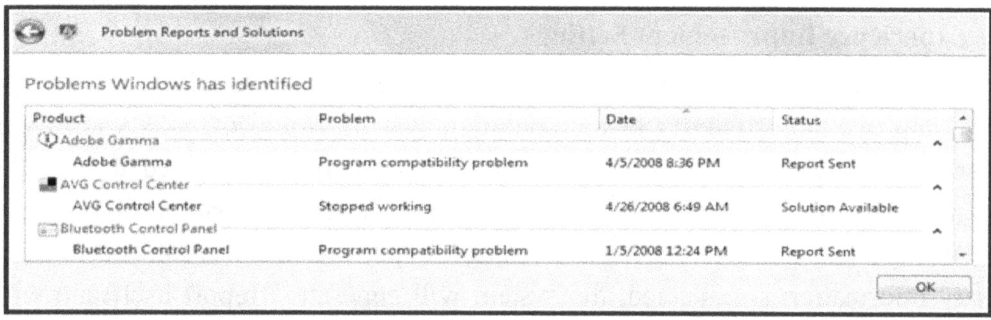

Customize Problem Reports and Solutions Settings

From the ***Problem Reports and Solutions*** window, click the ***Change Settings*** link from left navigation pane under the ***Tasks*** section. Microsoft asks you, how you would like to check the solution of the issue that you may have with your system. If you would like to check the solution of the problem automatically, select the ***Check for solutions automatically (recommended)*** option. Select the ***Ask me to check if a problem occurs*** option, if solution of the problem needs to be checked every time a problem occurs. Click ***OK*** to save preferences.

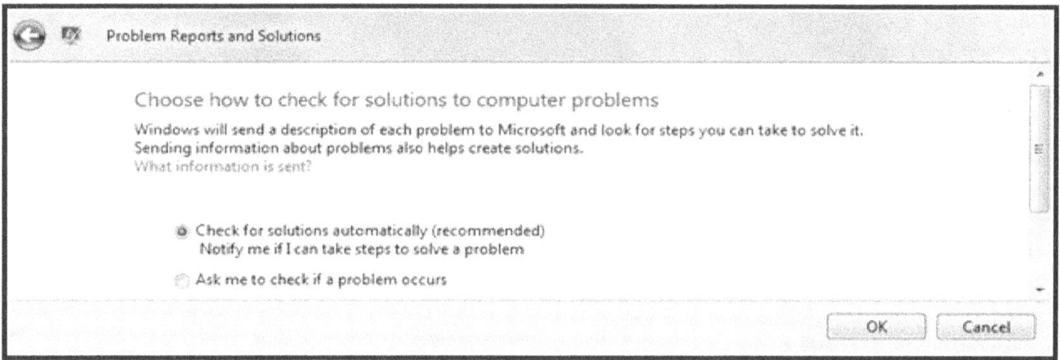

Clear Problem and Solution History

From the ***Problem Reports and Solutions*** window, click on ***Clear solution and problem history*** link from left navigation pane under the ***Tasks*** section to clear the history of solutions and the problems. Click on ***Clear all*** to delete ***Problem Reports and Solutions*** history.

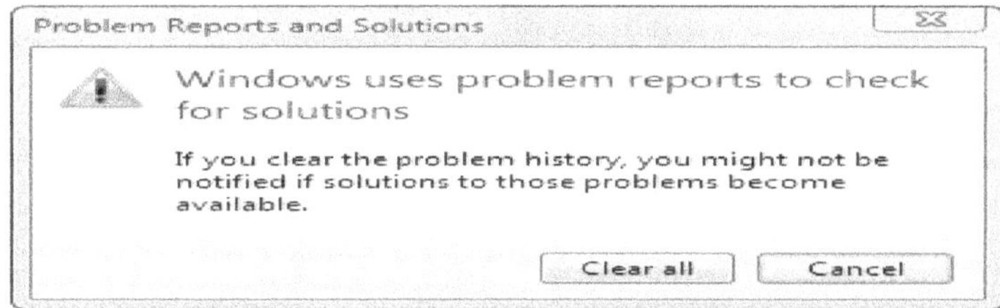

Customer Experience Improvement Settings

Customer Experience Improvement is an optional program to participate in helping Microsoft to improve the efficiency of the operating system. Microsoft asks you to join the *Windows Customer Experience Improvement* Program. If you decided to join the Microsoft improvement program, the system will collect information about your computer hardware and the behavior of the Windows application at certain times. Once the necessary information is collected, the system will generate a report itself and will send that report to Microsoft to identify the features of operating system that needs to be improved to make the Windows more reliable and efficient. Microsoft does not collect any personal information to identify you or to contact you.

To open the *Windows Experience Improvement* program, click the ***Customer Experience Improvement Settings*** link from left navigation pane of the ***Problem Reports and Solutions*** under the ***See also*** section.

To join the Microsoft improvement program, select the ***Join the Windows Customer Experience Improvement Program*** option, otherwise select ***I don't want to join the program at this time*** option to deny participation in Microsoft improvement program. Click on ***OK*** to save changes.

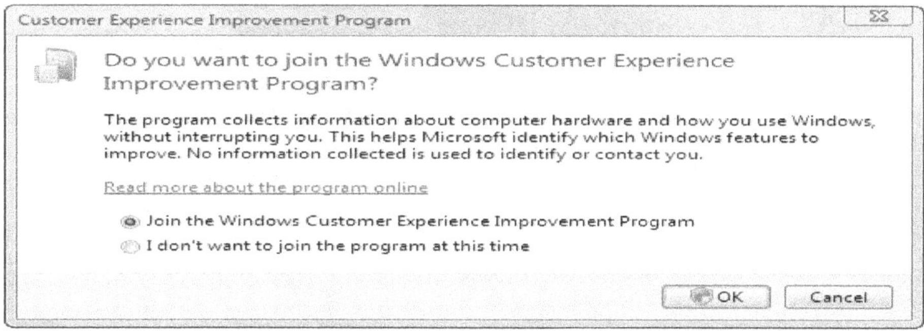

Snipping Tool

The snipping tool enables Microsoft Vista users to take snap-shots of your computer. This tool is available for all Windows Vista editions except Microsoft Windows Vista Home Basic edition. The snipping tool supports HTML, PNG, GIF, and JPEG formats.

To open snipping tool, click ***Start*** button, click ***All Programs***, click ***Accessories***, and then click **Snipping Tool**. Click on the arrow ▾ next to ***New*** tab to choose one of the following snipping options:

a. *Free-form Snip*
b. *Rectangular Snip*
c. *Window Snip*
d. *Full screen Snip*

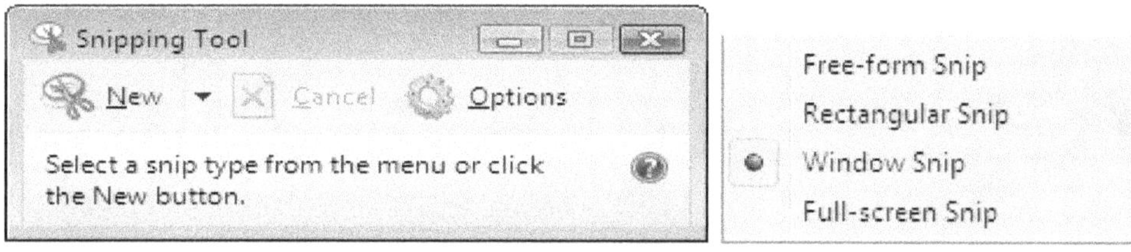

Windows Aero

Windows Aero is a translucent glass interface for Windows Vista users and it is available to users, if they meet following hardware requirements.

- Windows Display Driver Model (WDDM) driver for video card
- Directx 9 capable graphics card
- Hardware pixel shader 2.0
- 32-bit per pixel memory
- Minimum of 128 MB graphics memory

Right-click on the desktop and then select ***Properties*** option from the list to see, if your system supports *Windows Aero Interface*. If your system supports *Windows Aero Interface*, the ***Windows Color and Appearance*** window will be prompted to you and should allow you to change the color of the windows, the ***Start Menu***, and the ***Taskbar Menu***.

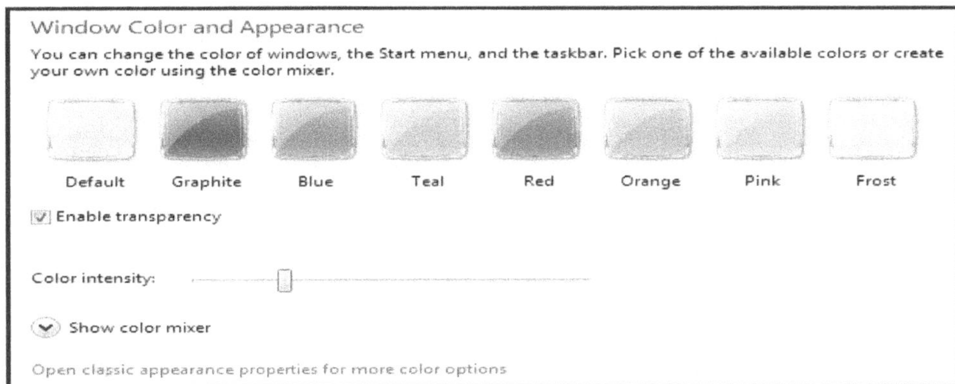

If your system does not support *Windows Aero Interface*, you would be prompted to the ***Appearance Settings*** dialog box to choose appropriate color scheme to adjust display settings.

Question: Define Windows Experience Index Base Score?

Answer: The Windows Experience Index Base Score measures the performance of your hardware and software configuration settings.

Question: Which components are based on base score?

Answer: Processor, memory (RAM), graphics, gaming graphics, and primary hard disk.

Question: How do you determine base score?

Answer: The lowest sub score of the component is the base score of your computer.

Question: Define hardware base score range?

Answer: The system performance rating falls between 1, least possible score, and 5.9 best possible base score, for your hardware system.

Question: How do I increase the base score of my hardware?

Answer: Replace the computer component that has least sub score rating.

Question: What is Parental Controls?

Answer: The Parental Controls is a new feature added to Microsoft Windows Vista operating system that allows an administrator to monitor and restrict standard users privileges. It is designed for family members who need to be restricted from running certain programs, and playing certain games. Parental Controls offers following features.

- Set time limits for computer use
- Limit Internet usage
- Restrict users from running certain programs and playing certain games
- Monitor Internet usage report

Question: Which edition of Microsoft Vista supports Parental Controls?

Answer: The Home Basic, Home Premium and Ultimate editions of Microsoft Windows Vista support Parental Controls.

Question: When a malicious program is detected by the Windows Defender, what would you do to move it to the allowed list, if it is not a malicious program?

Answer: Click the ***Add*** button under the ***Advanced*** options to add the program to the allowed list. When a program is added to the allowed list, the Windows Defender will stop scanning that program in future.

Question: Define Windows Defender allowed items list?

Answer: A allowed items displays a list of programs that should not be scanned or monitor during Windows Defender scan.

Question:What is Bitlocker Drive Encryption?

Answer: A Bitlocker drive encryption is designed to encrypt the contents of a hard-drive in such a way that no one will have access to it without proper authentication key. The key could be saved in USB drive, in the system drive, or in BIOS of the computer.

Question: Is Bitlocker Drive Encryption available in all Windows Vista editions?

Answer: No, the Bitlocker Drive Encryption is only available in Windows Vista Ultimate, and Windows Vista Enterprise editions.

Question: What is the Bitlocker encryption pin length?

Answer: The Bitlocker encryption pin length can be between 4 to 20 digits.

Question: What does TPM stand for?

Answer: A TPM stands for Trusted Platform Module. It adds extra security to your system to prevent accessing sensitive data during system startup.

Question: What is Windows Sidebar?

Answer: Windows Sidebar is an area on your desktop that displays mini-programs such as weather report, News headlines, calendar, notes, CPU and memory performance, etc.

Question: What is a gadget?

Answer: A gadget is a min-program that is designed for Windows Sidebar to display mini stand-alone programs, such as CPU usage, clock, calendar, notes, weather report, and picture slide show information, if it is configured properly.

Question: Can I add a gadget to the Windows Sidebar? **Answer**:

Yes, you can add a gadget to the Windows Sidebar. **Question**: Can

I remove a gadget from the Windows Sidebar? **Answer**: Yes, you

can remove a gadget from the Windows Sidebar.

Question: Can I view the details of a gadget before adding to the Windows Sidebar?

Answer: Yes, system lets you to view the details of a gadget before adding to the Windows Sidebar.

Question: Can I customize Sidebar?

Answer: Yes, you may download gadgets from website to customize Windows Sidebar.

Question: Can I adjust the Windows Sidebar settings so it remains on the top of other windows?

Answer: Yes, you have option to adjust the settings in such a way that it remains on the top of other Windows.

Question: Which are possible designated locations for Windows Sidebar?

Answer: The possible locations are left-hand-side and right-hand-side of the Windows desktop.

Question: Can I open Windows Sidebar from the system notification area?

Answer: Yes, right-click on the icon of Windows Sidebar and then choose the ***Open*** option from the list. You can also press (*Windows Key + G)* to bring Windows Sidebar up.

Question: What is Windows ReadyBoost?

Answer: Windows Vista system is capable of adding non-volatile flash memory for your system to increase the performance without adding additional memory chip onto the motherboard. The Windows Vista operating system allows you to allocate the part of a USB drive's memory to speed up system performance. As you connect the USB drive with your computer, Windows Vista checks to see, if attached USB drive is fast enough to work with Windows Ready Boost feature. If the USB drive is capable of Ready Boost feature, you will be asked to start the wizard to boost the performance of your system.

Question: What are the minimum requirements of the Ready Boost device?

- Must be at-least USB 2.0 type
- Must have at-least 256 MB in size
- Should have access time of 1ms or less
- Must support NTFS, FAT16 and FAT32 formats
- Minimum of 2.5 MB/s for 4 KB random READ speed
- Minimum of 1.75 MB/s for 512 KB random WRITE speed
- Must have at-least 235 MB of free space

Question: How a USB 2.0 drive improves the performance of a computer?

Answer: The Ready Boost drive only stores cache information in the USB drive which helps PC to boost the performance.

Question: If I have a removable device which has larger than 4GB storage space, would I be able to use all of the storage space for Ready Boost?

Answer: No, the device will only use 4GB of storage to improve the performance of the system.

Question: What is recommended amount of flash memory to use for Windows ReadyBoost?

Answer: The recommended amount of flash memory is one to three times of physical memory installed in your computer. You should not allocate more than 3 times the amount of RAM in the computer for Ready Boost.

Question: Define hidden Windows program?

Answer: The hidden Windows programs are pre-installed programs for your system. They can be installed as needed.

Question: Can I turn on or off hidden Windows features?

Answer: Yes, only system administrators can perform this task.

Question: What is Windows Meeting Space?

Answer: Windows Meeting Space is designed to interact with local network users effectively by sharing handouts or their computer desktops.

Question: Does all Microsoft Windows Vista operating system versions support Windows Meeting Space?

Answer: The Windows Vista Basic users can only view meetings but rest of the Windows Vista versions are capable of creating and joining meetings at any time.

Question: What is default file extension to send invitation file to join Windows Meeting Space?

Answer: The file extension is .WCINV.

Question: How many users can join one meeting session simultaneously?

Answer: Microsoft Windows Vista operating system allows maximum of 10 users to join Windows Meeting Space simultaneously.

Question: Which information you need to have before joining a meeting space?

Answer: To join a meeting space, you must have the name of the session and its password.

Question: How many users can share the document simultaneously?

Answer: Only one user can share the document simultaneously.

Question: Do I need to configure Windows Firewall for Windows Meeting Space?

Answer: No, the Windows Meeting Space configure the correct exceptions for Windows Firewall as it starts first time.

Question: When I create or join a meeting, which activities are logged by Windows Meeting Space?

Answer: The Windows Meeting Space keeps track of the following activities.

- Meeting name
- Local IP address
- Peer name

- Local user name
- Local machine name

Question: Why am I unable to start a Windows Meeting Space?

Answer: You may be using Windows Starter edition of Windows Vista that does not support this feature.

Question: Why am I unable to create a meeting session?

Answer: Check the edition of the Windows Vista you are using. If you are using Windows Vista Home Basic edition, you can not create a session because it only allows you to join a session.

Question: Why am I unable to send or receive the invitation?

Answer: The possible reasons could be one of the followings.

- You are not signed into People Near Me
- You may have limited user's rights for your account
- People Near Me is turned off for your account by an administrator
- Firewall is not configured correctly

Chapter 3 - Microsoft Internet Explorer 7.0

Topics covered in this chapter:

- Internet Explorer
- Internet Explorer General Options
- Internet Explorer Privacy Options
- Internet Explorer Security Options
- Content Advisor
- Auto Complete
- Feed Contents

Internet Explorer

Internet Explorer browser 7.0 was released by Microsoft Corporation in November 2006. It supports Microsoft Windows Vista, Microsoft Windows XP Service Pack 2, and Windows Server 2003 Service Pack 1 operating systems.

The Internet Explorer 7.0 has introduced browser tabs, safe browsing, and convenient web printing. The new browser enables users to view multiple websites in a single browser window, and provides a safe browsing Internet environment without being a victim of identity theft, if *Phishing Filter* settings are configured properly.

Internet Explorer General Options

Open Internet Explorer browser 7.0 or later, go to the ***Tools*** menu, and then choose ***Internet Options*** to open *Internet Options* window. Tools menu is located at upper-right corner of the explorer window. If tools menu is not visible on right side of the Internet Explorer window, press ***Alt*** key to display tools menu bar on top of the explorer window.

Change Internet Explorer Browser Homepage

To change Internet Explorer browser homepage, open Internet Explorer browser 7.0. From the ***Internet Options*** dialog box, click **General** tab, under the ***Home page*** section, type the URL (Uniform Resource Locator) of the website that you would like to set for Internet Explorer homepage. If multiple homepages for Internet Explorer browser needs to be added, type each website address in a new line, under the ***Home Page*** section. Each website will open its own web browser tab. Click on ***Apply*** and then click ***OK*** to save Internet Explorer settings.

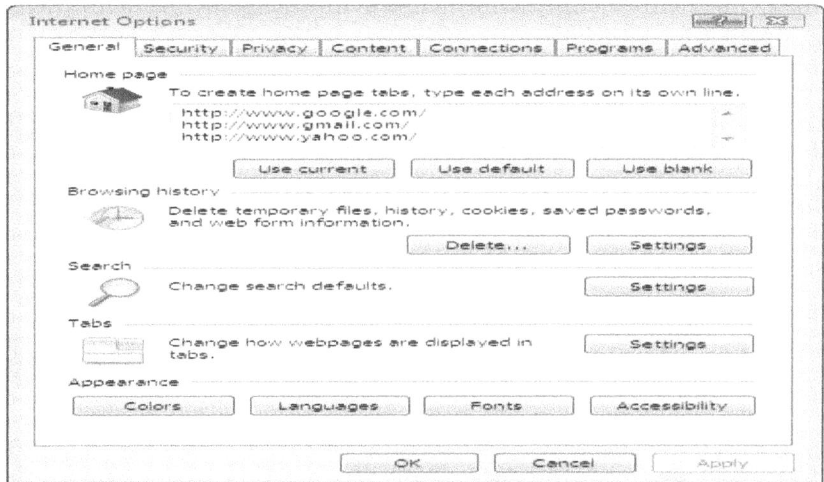

Delete Browsing History

Internet Explorer 7.0 browser keeps track of temporary Internet files, images, media files and personal information that user frequently uses online to fill out online forms. To delete Internet browsing history, open ***Internet Options*** window. From the ***Internet Options*** window, click ***General*** tab, under the ***Browsing history*** section, and then click on ***Delete*** to remove some or all of the following browsing history contents:

- ***Temporary Internet files***: Copies of saved websites, images, and media files
- ***History of saved websites***: List of previously visited websites
- ***Cookies***: Saves user's passwords, usernames, and other related information that user frequently uses online to fill out online forms

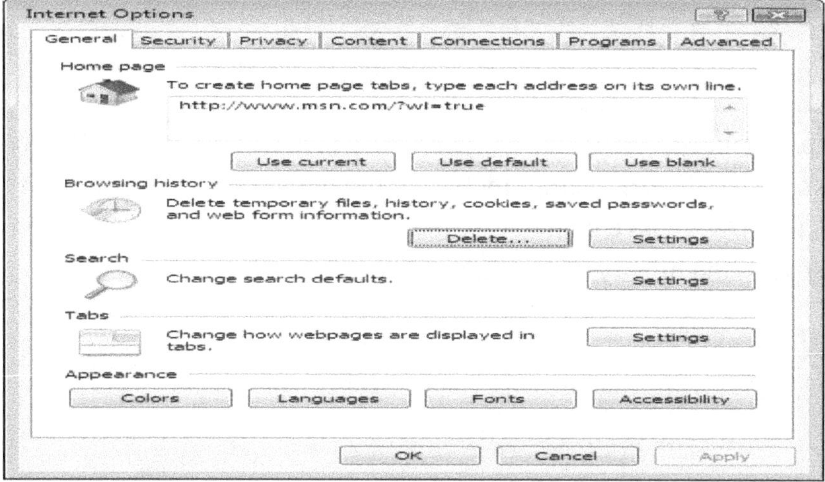

Click on ***Delete all*** from the ***Delete Browsing History*** dialog box to delete all of the temporary Internet files, cookies, and passwords that are previously saved in Internet explorer browser.

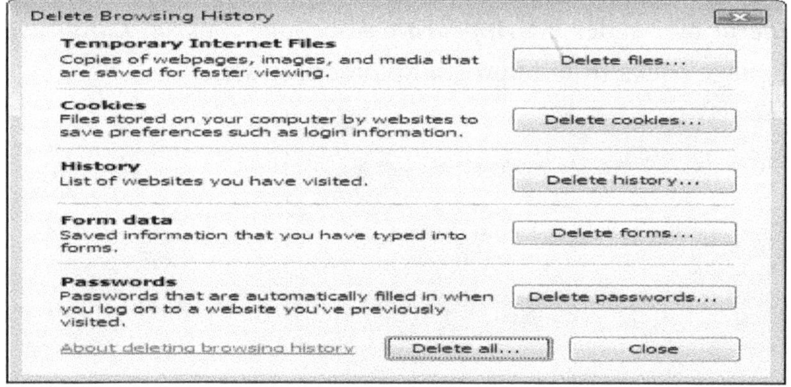

Click on ***Yes*** to confirm this action to delete all Internet Explorer browsing history. This process may take few minutes.

Customize Browsing History Settings

To adjust browsing history settings, open ***Internet Options*** window. From the ***Internet Options*** window, click ***General*** tab, under the ***Browsing history*** section, click on ***Settings*** to customize browser settings.

By default, Internet Explorer keeps record of visited web pages in history for 20 days. You can specify the days in the ***History*** section by typing the number of days you wish to keep pages in history. Click ***OK*** to save changes. If the visited web pages value is set to 0, the browser will never keep the history of websites, temporary files, and cookies.

Add/Remove Language Pack

To add or remove a language pack, open ***Internet Options*** window. From the ***Internet Options*** window, click ***General*** tab, under the ***Appearance*** section, click on ***Languages*** button to add or remove language packs from Internet Explorer browser.

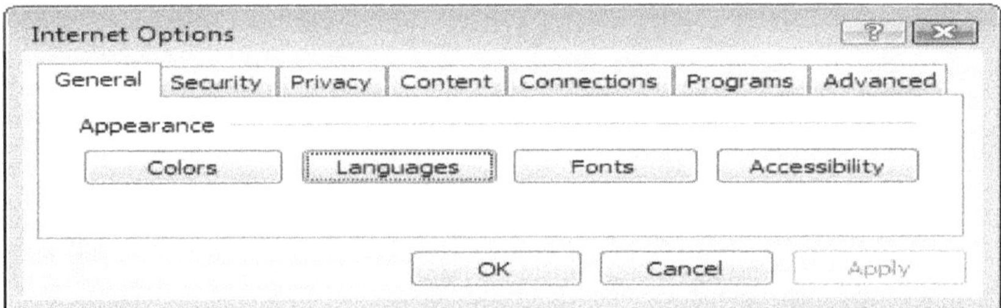

Click on ***Add*** button to continue adding another language of your choice. To remove a language, select the language that you want to remove from the ***Language Preferences*** dialog box, and then click on ***Remove***.

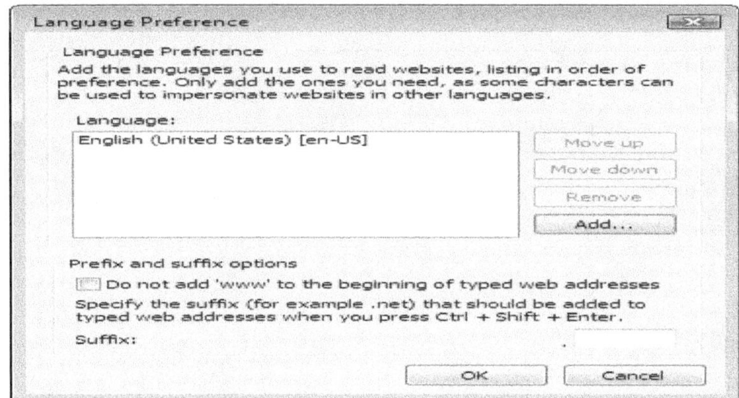

Select a language of your choice that needs to be installed and then click ***OK*** to save changes.

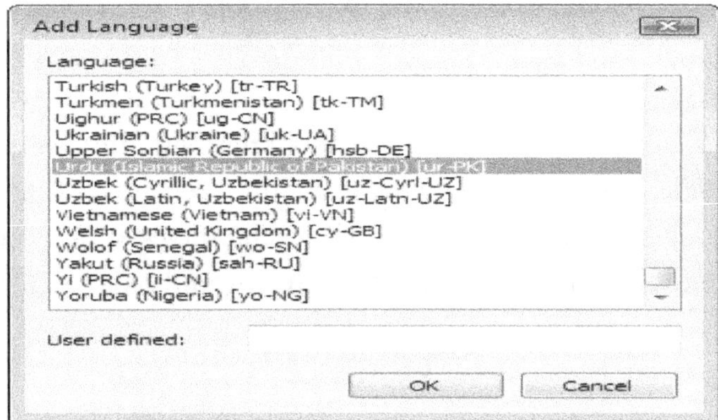

Customize Web Site Fonts

To customize web pages fonts, open ***Internet Options*** window. From the ***Internet Options*** window, click ***General*** tab. Click on ***Fonts*** under the ***Appearance*** section.

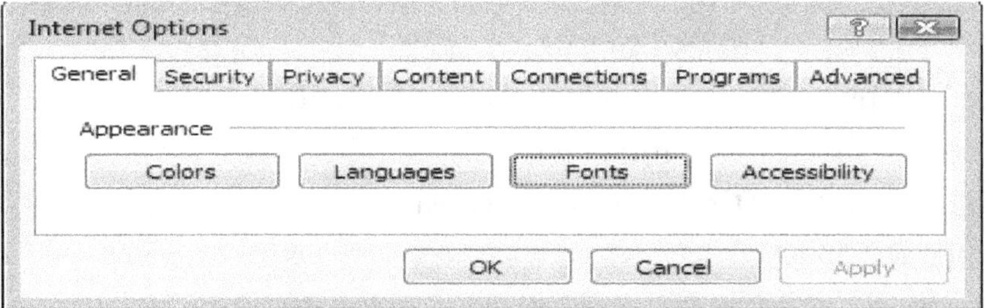

Select the webpage font, and plain text font of your choice from the ***Fonts*** dialog box. Click ***OK*** to save preferences. The ***Times New Roman*** and the ***Courier New*** are default fonts for webpage font, and plain text font, respectively for your system.

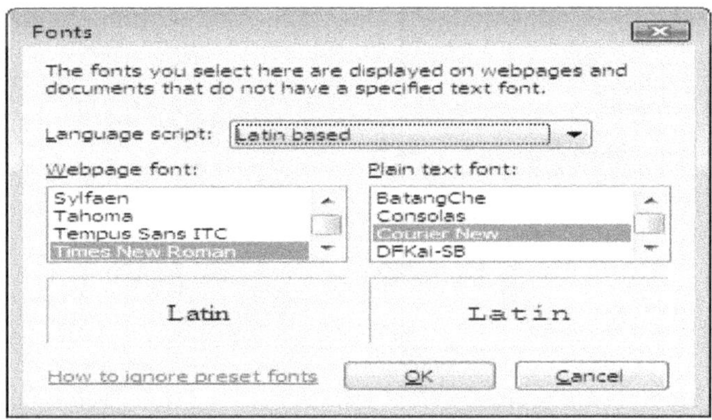

Internet Explorer Privacy Options

Internet Explorer Privacy options help users to configure pop-up blocker, and web browser cookies settings. Generally, a cookie saves usernames, passwords, e-mail addresses, and other related information that user frequently uses online. Generally, two kinds of cookies are associated with a web page, first-party cookies and third-party cookies. The first-party cookies are the cookies that come from the website you are currently visiting and third-party cookies come from websites other than the ones you are currently surfing but they are associated with the website that you are currently surfing.

Internet Privacy Settings

To adjust *Internet Privacy* settings, open ***Internet Options*** window. From the ***Internet Options*** window, click ***Privacy*** tab, under the ***Settings*** section, move the slider up and down to change settings for Internet Zones (*Internet, local intranet, trusted sites, and restricted sites*). Choose one of the following options to adjust Internet privacy settings. Click on ***Apply*** and click ***OK*** to save Internet Explorer privacy preferences.

- ***Block all cookies:*** Block all cookies from all websites. This is not a recommended setting due to the high privacy of blocking all cookies from all websites.
- ***High:*** Block cookies that save information that can be used to contact you without your explicit consent. It also blocks all cookies from websites that do not have a compact privacy policy.
- ***Medium High:*** Block third-party cookies and first-party cookies to save information that can be used to contact you without your explicit/implicit consent,

respectively. It also blocks third-party cookies that do not have a compact privacy policy.

- ***Medium:*** This option blocks third-party cookies that do not have compact privacy policy. It only restricts first-party cookies to save information that can be used to contact you without your implicit knowledge. It also blocks third-party cookies to save information that can be used to contact you without your explicit consent. This is a recommended setting for Internet Explorer browser.
- ***Low:*** This option restricts third-party cookies to save information that can be used in future to contact you without your implicit consent. It also blocks third-party cookies that do not have compact privacy policy.
- ***Accept all cookies:*** This option allows accepting all cookies from all websites. All cookies can be read by websites that are already being saved in your system. This is not a recommended setting for Internet Explorer browser due to low privacy of accepting all cookies from all websites.

Per Site Privacy

To adjust *Per Site Privacy* settings, open ***Internet Options*** window. From the ***Internet Options*** window, click ***Privacy*** tab, under the ***Settings*** section, click on ***Sites*** to set privacy settings for certain websites that are supposed to be always accepting or blocking cookies, regardless of their privacy policy.

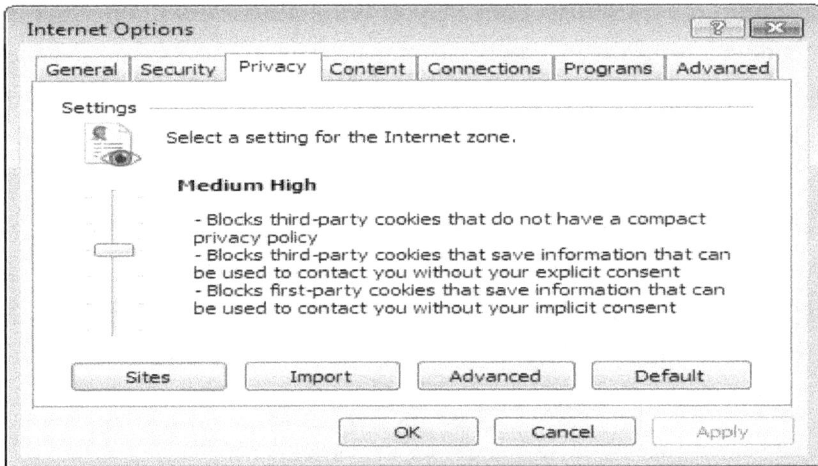

To manage a website address, type the address of that website to manage, and then click on ***Block*** or ***Allow*** button to add that website to the ***Managed websites*** category. A blocked website would never get any cookies; on the other hand the allowed websites will always get cookies regardless of their privacy policy settings. Click ***OK*** to save *Per Site Privacy* settings.

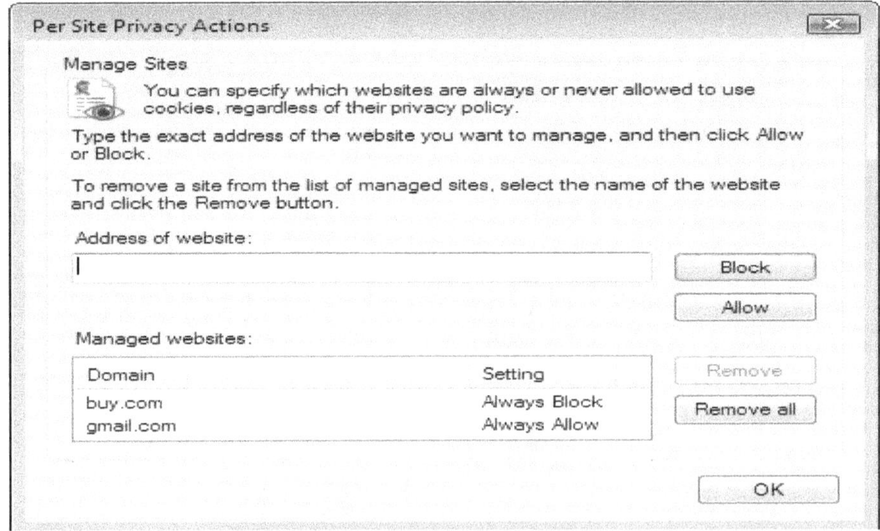

Remove Managed Websites

To remove a site from a list of the managed websites, click ***Privacy*** tab from the ***Internet Options*** dialog box, and then click on ***Sites*** from the ***Settings*** section. Select the desired website which you want to remove from the list of the managed websites, and then click on ***Remove***. If you would like to remove all of the managed websites, click on ***Remove All***. Click ***OK*** to exit out of the managed website window.

Internet Explorer Security Options

Internet Explorer security options adjust security level zone settings for Internet, local intranet, trusted sites, and restricted sites. The user will be restricted to download any materials form the website which is added to the restricted sites zone list.

Protected Mode

The Internet Explorer protected mode adds an extra layer of the security for Windows Vista users to protect their personal data while surfing web. This security is added to Internet Explorer browser to protect your system against installing any spywares, adware and malicious codes into your system without your consent while surfing web.

To enable protected mode, open ***Internet Options*** window. From the ***Internet Options*** window, click ***Security*** tab, under the ***Security level for this zone*** section, select the ***Enable Protected Mode (requires restarting Internet Explorer)*** option to enable Internet Explorer protected mode. Click on ***Apply*** and then click ***OK*** to save changes.

Reset Internet Explorer Settings

Internet Explorer settings keep track of temporary browser files, browser add-ons and toolbars, visited websites history, and cookies. A cookie saves user's passwords, usernames, Website URLs and other related information that a user frequently uses online.

To reset Internet Explorer settings, open ***Internet Options*** window. From the ***Internet Options*** window, click ***Advanced*** tab, and then under the ***Reset Internet Explorer settings*** section click on ***Reset*** button to reset browser default settings. Resetting Internet Explorer settings do not affect favorite's settings, feed settings, Internet connection settings, Group Policy settings, and Content Advisor settings.

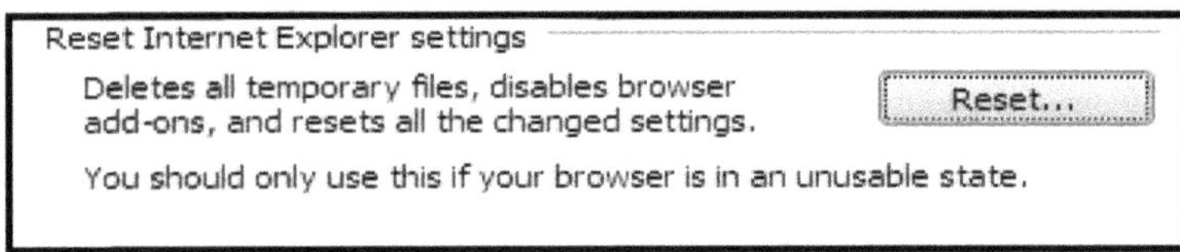

The following Internet Explorer settings can be reset by clicking on ***Reset*** button:

- *Disabling toolbars and add-ons*
- *Deleting temporary Internet files, webpage history, cookies, web form information, and passwords*
- *Resetting default web browser settings, search providers, and home pages*

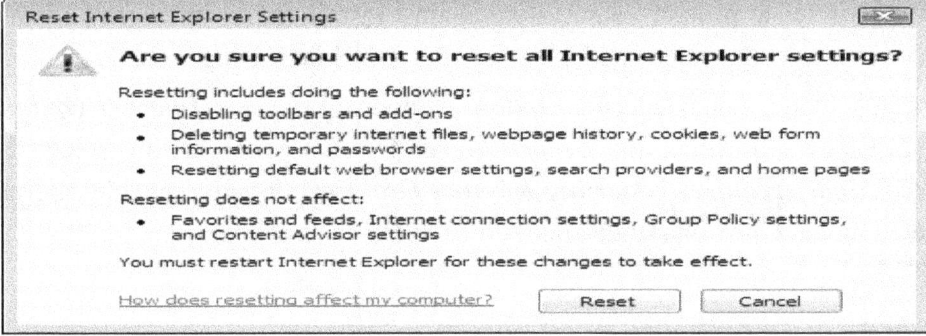

This process may take several minutes for deleting browser history, browser add-ons, and browser settings. Click on ***Close*** when it is done.

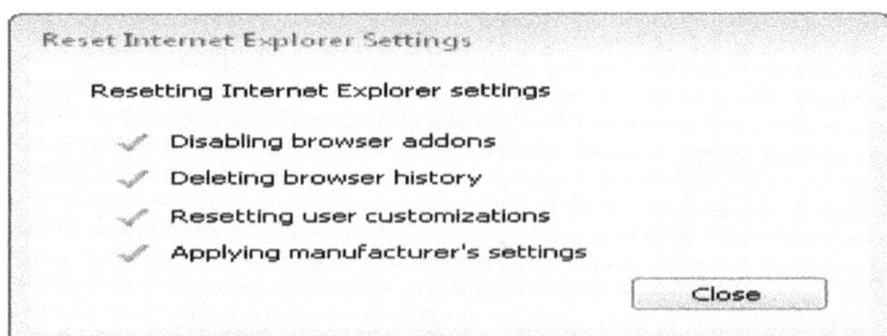

Pop-up Blocker Settings

To adjust pop-up blocker settings, open ***Internet Options*** window. From the ***Internet Options*** window, click ***Privacy*** tab, and then under the ***Pop-up blocker*** section, click on ***Settings***.

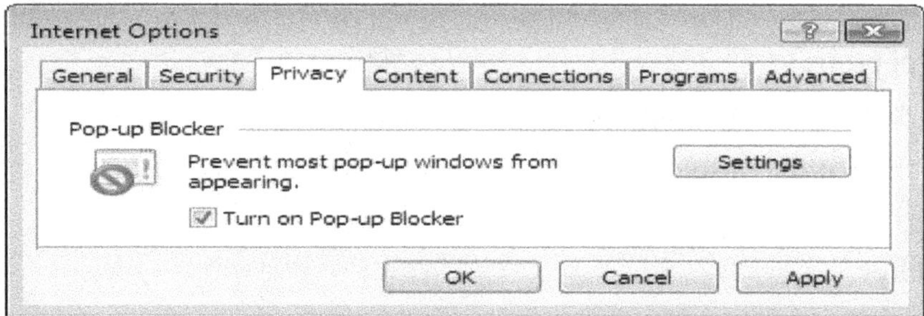

Type the address of a website that you want to allow pop-ups for, and then click on ***Add*** button to enter that website to the allowed sites list. Any website which is added to the ***Allowed sites*** will accept pop-ups. To remove a website from allowed sites list, click the website that you wish to remove, and then click on ***Remove***. If you wish to remove entire list of allowed sites, click on ***Remove all***.

If you would like to see a warning message whenever a pop-up is blocked by the browser, check the ***Show Information Bar when a pop-up is blocked*** option from the ***Notifications and filter level*** section to enable this feature. This setting will display an information bar in Internet Explorer browser to inform you about the website which is being blocked for pop-ups.

If you would like to hear a warning sound whenever a pop-up is blocked for any website, check the ***Play a sound when a pop-up is blocked*** option from the ***Notifications and filter level*** section to enable this feature. To adjust pop-up filter level setting, choose one of the following options from drop down menu of ***Filter Level*** to customize pop-up filter level settings.

- ***High***: Block all pop-ups
- ***Medium***: Block most automatic pop-ups
- ***Low***: Allow pop-ups from secure sites

Turn on Pop-up Blocker

To turn on pop-up blocker:

- Open Internet Explorer browser
- Click ***Tools*** menu
- Click ***Pop-up Blocker***
- Click ***Turn On Pop-up Blocker***
- Click on ***Yes*** to confirm this action.

It is recommended to keep the pop-up blocker turned on while surfing web.

Turn off Pop-up Blocker

To turn off pop-up blocker:

- Open Internet Explorer browser
- Click ***Tools*** menu
- Click ***Pop-up Blocker***
- Click ***Turn Off Pop-up Blocker***
- Click on ***Yes*** to confirm turning off pop-up blocker

Phishing Filter Settings

Phishing Filter settings help Internet Explorer users to protect their identity while surfing web, if *Phishing Filter* is configured properly. For example, while surfing web, an illegitimate website is asking you to provide personal information (your name, phone number, home address or bank information). If you have revealed personal information to the illegitimate website, then they may use your personal information to hurt you financially or may sell your identify to a third-party for profit.

To configure *Phishing Filter*, go to the ***Tools*** menu of the Internet Explorer browser, click ***Phishing Filter***, and click ***Turn on Automatic website checking***. From the ***Microsoft Phishing Filter*** window, select one of the following *Phishing Filter* options and then click ***OK*** to save *Phishing Filter* preferences.

- *Turn on automatic Phishing Filter (recommended)*
- *Turn off automatic Phishing Filter*

Download Internet Explorer Updates

Open Internet Explorer 7.0. Go to the ***Tools*** menu, and then choose the ***Windows update*** option from the list. From left navigation pane of the ***Windows update***, click on ***Check for updates***. Your system may take several minutes to check for new updates, and then click on ***Install Updates*** to download and install latest updates for your Internet Explorer browser. If Windows updates installation was successfully, you will be notified. Re-boot the machine so changes can apply to your system.

Manage Add-ons

Web browser add-ons add extra features to your web browser. For example, extra toolbars browser, tab effects, pop-up ad blockers, feed sidebar and so on. It is a stand-alone program that can be added to your Internet Explorer browser or any other browsers, e.g. Firefox, and Safari, to increase the interactivity between a client and a browser. It is recommended to disable or delete an add-on that is forcing Internet Explorer to shutdown unexpectedly. Deleting or disabling an add-on might prevent some sites from working properly. You must know which add-on is casing problem for your browser so you can take necessary actions to fix the problem.

To manage Internet Explorer browser add-ons, open Internet Explorer 7.0, go to the ***Tools*** menu, click ***Mange Add-ons***, and then click ***Enable or Disable Add-ons*** option. To manage add-ons, select one of the following options from drop down menu of the ***Show*** box:

- ***Add-ons that have been used by Internet Explorer***: See step # 1 below
- ***Add-ons currently loaded in Internet Explorer***: See step # 2 below
- ***Add-ons that run without requiring permission***: See step # 3 below

- ***Download ActiveX Controls (32-bit):*** See step # 4 below

Step # 1: To display a list of add-ons that have been used by Internet Explorer, select the ***Add-ons that have been used by Internet Explorer*** option from drop down menu of the ***Show*** box. If you would like to enable or disable an add-on, click the add-on that you want to enable or disable, and then click on ***Enable*** or ***Disable*** radio button. After making any changes to add-ons settings, click ***OK*** to save preferences.

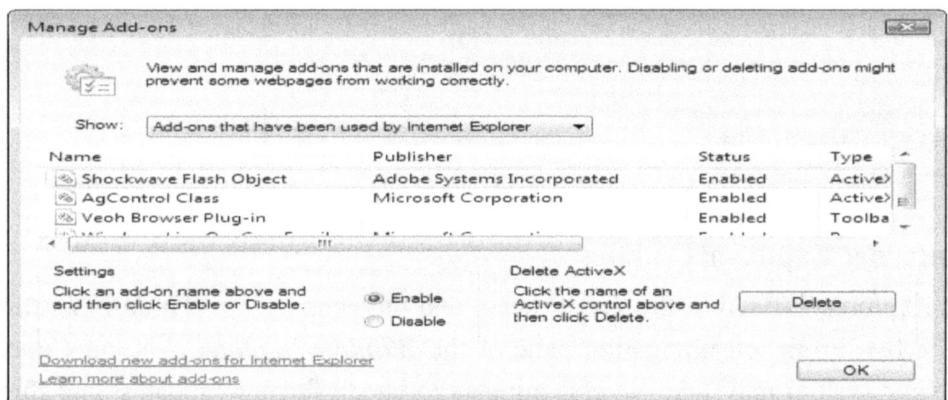

Step # 2: To display a list of currently loaded add-ons in Internet Explorer, select the ***Add-ons currently loaded in Internet Explorer*** option from drop down menu of the ***Show*** box. You can enable or disable an add-on, but it is not recommended to disable it, if it is not causing any issues to Internet Explorer browser. To disable an add-on, click the add-on that you want to disable and then click on ***Disable*** radio button under the ***Settings*** section. After making any changes to add-ons settings, click ***OK*** to save preferences.

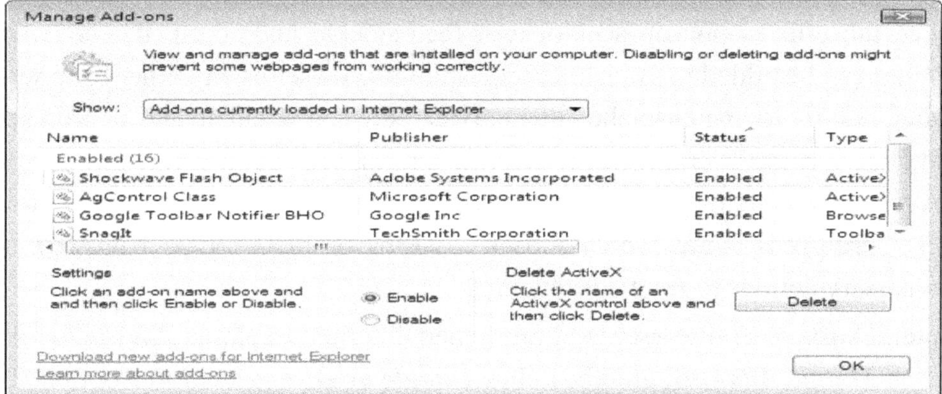

Step # 3: To display a list of Microsoft pre-approved add-ons, computer manufacture add-ons, and service provider add-ons, choose the ***Add-ons that run without requiring permission*** option from drop down menu of the ***Show*** box. It is not recommended to disable any add-ons that are pre-approved by Microsoft, unless an add-on causes unexpectedly problems for your Internet Explorer browser. If disabling an add-on solves the problem that you are having with Internet Explorer browser, it is recommended to disable that add-on temporarily. After making any changes to add-ons settings, click ***OK*** to save changes.

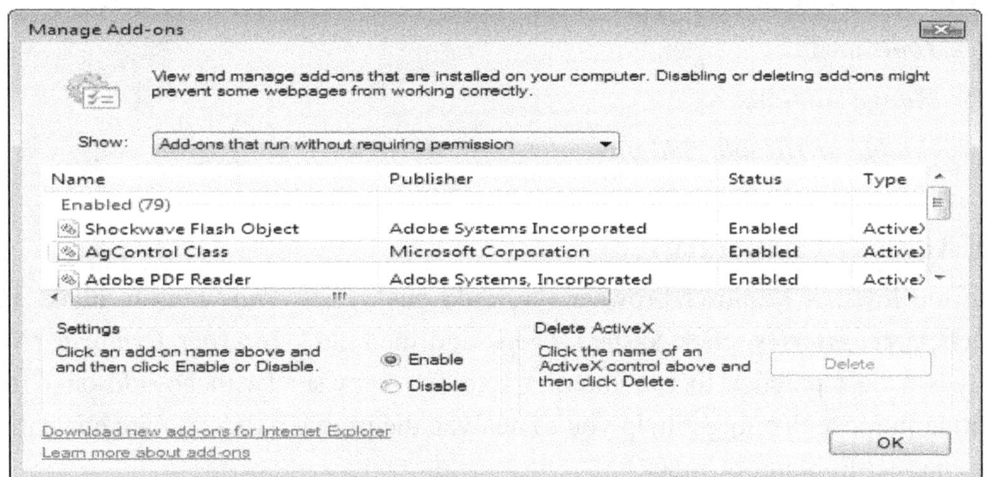

Step # 4: To display a list of ActiveX Controls that have been downloaded and installed by an administrator. Choose the ***Downloaded ActiveX Controls (32-bit)*** option from drop down menu of the ***Show*** box. The ActiveX controls can only be deleted if it is downloaded and installed with your permission. To delete an ActiveX controls add-on, click the add-on that you want to delete and then click on ***Delete*** from the ***Delete ActiveX*** section. After making any changes to add-ons settings, click ***OK*** to save changes. Internet Explorer does not add any add-ons to your system without your permissions, unless these add-ons are pre-approved by Microsoft and they are digitally signed.

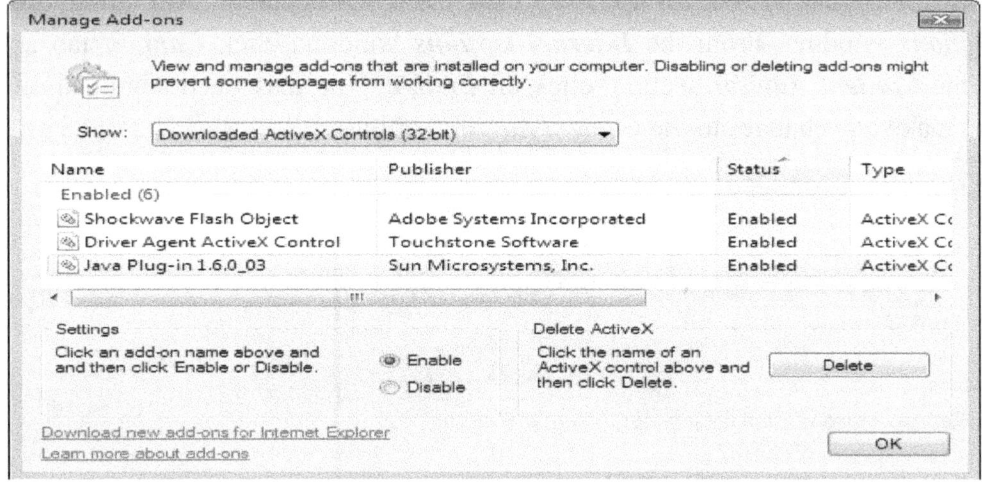

Enable/Disable Add-on Manager Window

To open add-on manager window:

- Open Internet Explorer browser
- Click ***Tools*** menu
- Click ***Mange Add-ons***
- Click ***Enable or Disable Add-ons***

Disable all Add-ons Temporarily

To navigate the Internet Explorer browser (No Add-ons), click ***Start*** button, click ***All Programs***, click ***Accessories***, click ***System Tools***, and then click ***Internet Explorer (No Add-ons)***. It is a best practice to run Internet Explorer browser (with no add-ons) for troubleshooting purpose that might help you to analyze the problem that you are currently having with Internet Explorer browser.

Content Advisor

Content Advisor blocks objectionable contents of a website. A supervisor password would require users including system administrators to view contents of a restricted website, if it is configured properly.

ICRA3 Content Level Rating

ICRA3 is an Internet Explorer browser rating system to allow or block certain pages which are not appropriate to visit for users. To view the ICRA3 content level rating, open ***Internet Options*** window. From the ***Internet Options*** window, click ***Content*** tab and then under the ***Content Advisor*** section, click on ***Enable***. You may need administrative privileges to make any changes to the *Content Advisor* settings.

In the ***Ratings*** tab, select the rating category of your choice to view the content ratings from the ***Select a category to view the rating levels*** box. To adjust content ratings, slide the slider left or right from the ***Adjust the slider to specify what users are allowed to see*** section to adjust the settings for users. It is recommended to read the rating category contents in the ***Description*** section before applying any changes to the browser. Click on ***Apply*** and then click ***OK*** to save ***Content Advisor*** preferences.

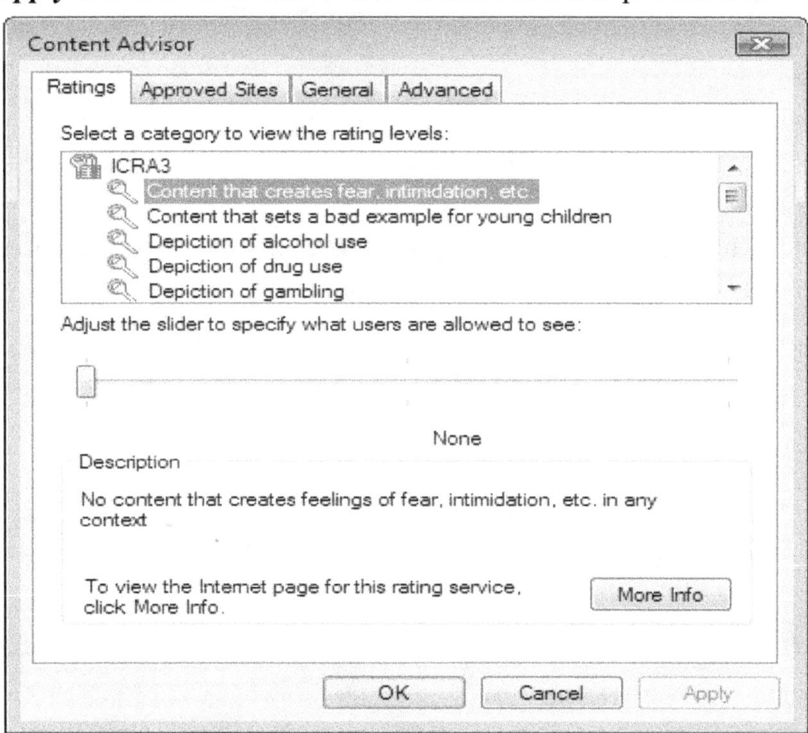

Content Advisor Approved Websites

Open ***Internet Options*** window. From the ***Internet Options*** window, click ***Content*** tab, and then under the ***Content Advisor*** section, click on ***Enable***. In the ***Approved Sites*** tab, type the address of these websites that you want for users to permit or restrict regardless of how they are rated. To allow a user to view the content of a website, type the address of that website in the search bar, and then click on ***Always*** button. On the other hand, a website which does not have appropriate contents to view can be added to the list of the disapproved sites. Type the address of that website in the search field, and then click on ***Never*** button to add that website to the disapproved list.

If a website is approved to view, a green circle with a tick mark will appear in front of it. For disapproved websites, a red circle around a white line will display in front of it. Click on ***Apply*** and then ***OK*** to save settings.

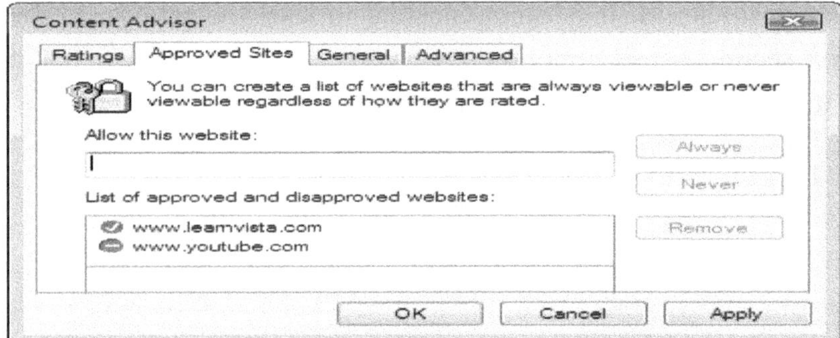

If you have not created an administrative password to manage *Content Advisor* features, you will be prompted to create a password. Type the password and then click ***OK*** to save settings.

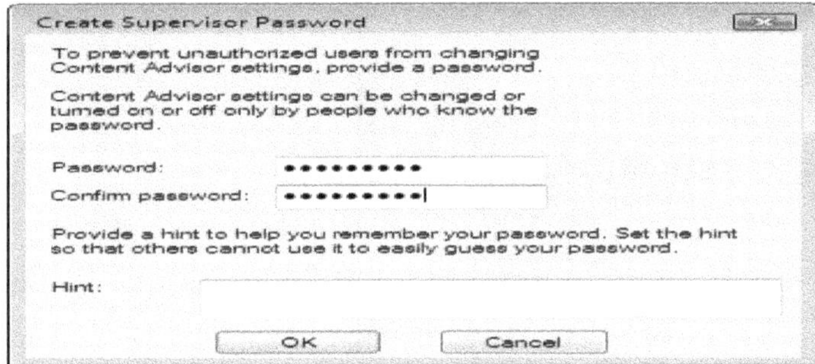

To remove approved *Content Advisor* website, select the address of that website that you wish to remove from the ***List of approved and disapproved websites*** box, and then click on ***Remove***. You can only remove one website at a time. Click on ***Apply*** and then ***OK*** to save settings.

Change Content Advisor Supervisor Password

Open ***Internet Options*** window. From the ***Internet Options*** window, click ***Content*** tab, and then under the ***Content Advisor*** section, click on ***Settings*** to change *Content Advisor* password.

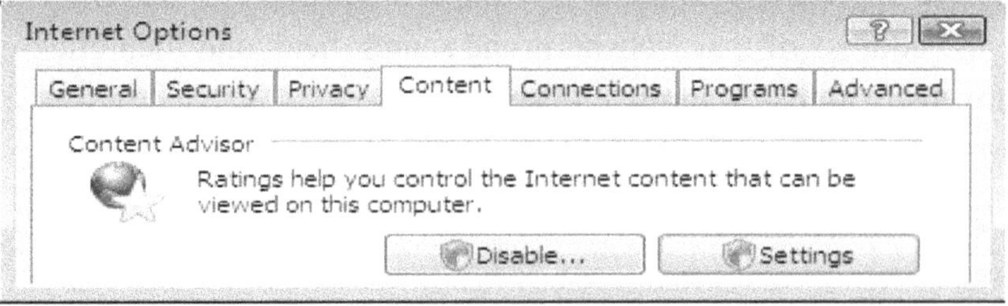

Click ***General*** tab, under the ***Supervisor password*** section, click on ***Change password***.

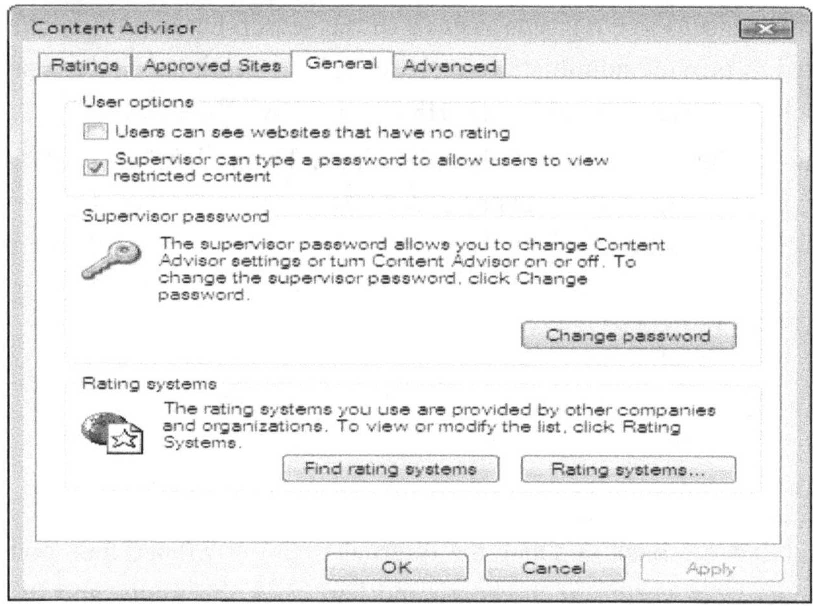

Type the old password that you had before and then type new password that you would like to set for *Content Advisor*. Type the password hint, if necessary. Click ***OK*** to save password.

Website Contents Permission

Open ***Internet Options*** window. From the ***Internet Options*** window, click ***Content*** tab, and then under the ***Content Advisor*** section, click on ***Settings***. To allow users to visit no rating website contents, check the ***Users can see websites that have no rating*** option from the ***User options*** section of the ***General*** tab. Click on ***Apply*** and then click ***OK*** to save settings.

To allow users to access restricted website contents without requiring a supervisor password. From the ***Content Advisor*** window, click ***General*** tab, and then clear the ***Supervisor can type a password to allow users to view restricted content*** checkbox, under the ***User options*** section. Supervisor password will not be asked to enter while visiting restricted contents. Click on ***Apply*** and then click ***OK*** to save *Content Advisor* preferences.

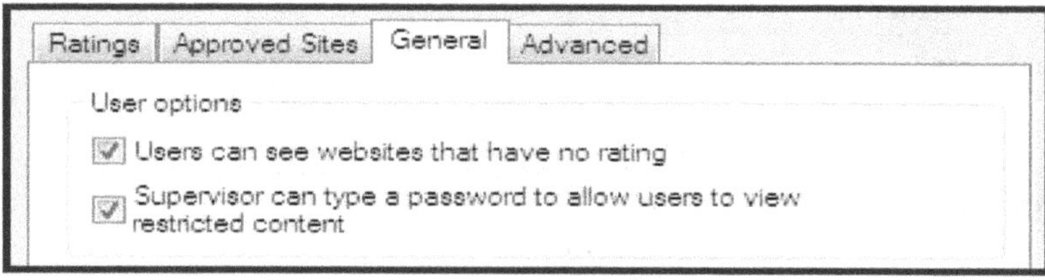

Remove Content Advisor Password

Run command prompt (*Windows Key + R*), type ***regedit*** in the search bar, and then click ***OK***. You may be prompted to provide administrative credentials to continue. To navigate the registry path, double-click on each registry folder HKEY_LOCAL_MACHINE\Software\Microsoft\Windows\Current Version\Policies\Ratings. From right pane of the ***Registry Editor*** window, right-click on the registry named ***Key***, and then choose ***Delete*** option from the list. Click on ***Yes*** to confirm delete registry value. Then exit out of *Registry Editor*.

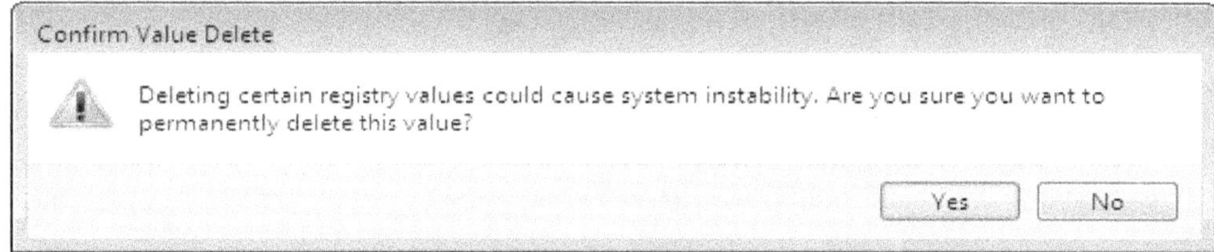

Re-boot your machine and then log back in. Open the Internet Explorer 7.0 and then go to the ***Tools*** menu in the upper right corner of the command bar, click the ***Tools***, and then click the ***Internet Option***. From the ***Internet Options*** dialog box, click ***Content*** tab, and then under the ***Content Advisor*** section, click on ***Disable***. When you are asked for a password, do not enter any password, and then click ***OK***. If above suggested solution does not work for you, you may consider downloading password remover program for removing the *Content Advisor* password.

Auto Complete

An *AutoComplete* keeps track of all previous stored entries, e.g. usernames, passwords, and URLs that you have previously used on any websites. To adjust *AutoComplete* settings, Open ***Internet Options*** window. From the ***Internet Options*** window, click ***Content*** tab, and then under the ***AutoComplete*** section, click on ***Settings***.

An *AutoComplete* options can be set for web addresses that you type into the URL of a web browser, forms that you fill out online, usernames, and passwords that you frequently use while surfing Internet. If you would like to be asked to save password every time you visit a new website, check the ***Prompt me to save passwords*** option from the ***Use AutoComplete for*** section. Check the appropriate options and then click ***OK*** to save preferences.

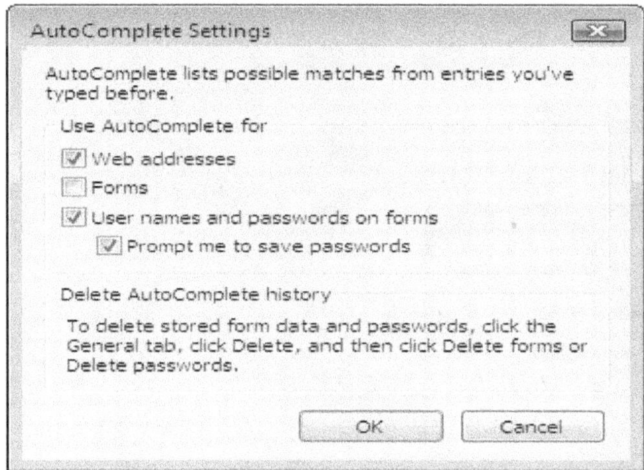

Feed Contents

Feed contents are the latest headlines that are frequently published by a website, such as blog groups, and contents of a newspaper. If you frequently visit an online newspaper to read about latest news, you can subscribe to it to only read updated contents of the website since your last visit. The feed contents are also known as Really Simple Syndication (RSS) feeds, XML feeds, syndicated content, web feeds, or channel.

Configure Feed Contents Settings

To adjust feed content settings, Open ***Internet Options*** window. From the ***Internet Options*** window, click ***Content*** tab. Click on ***Settings*** from the ***Feeds*** section.

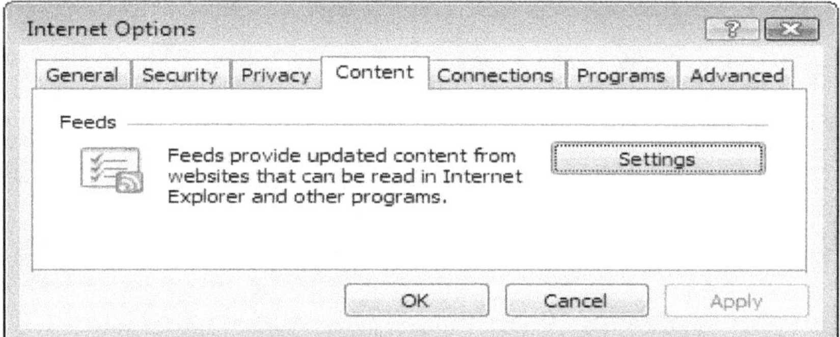

In the ***Feed Settings*** dialog box, under the ***Default schedule*** section, check the ***Automatically check feeds for updates*** option, and then select how often you want Internet Explorer to check for feed updates. You have following options to choose from: *15 minutes, 30 minutes, 1 hour, 4 hours, 1 day, and 1 week.* Choose an appropriate time frame to check for latest feed contents update.

To manage advanced feed contents, select one of the following options.

- *Automatically mark feed as read when reading a feed*
- *Turn on feed reading view*
- *Play a sound when a feed is found for a webpage*

Click ***OK*** to save feed settings for Internet Explorer browser.

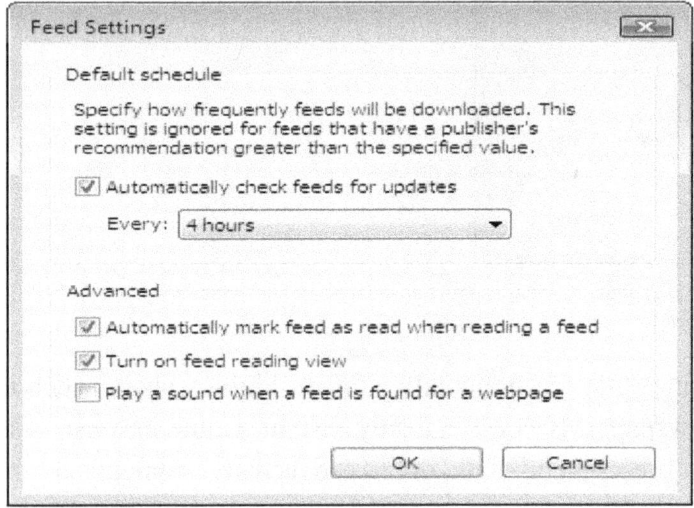

Question: What is a cookie?

Answer: A cookie is a piece of the information that your computer stores for future use. Generally, it helps a user to save its passwords, usernames, addresses, and other related information that user uses frequently online.

Question: Define cookies type?

Answer: There are two types of cookies, first-party cookies and third-party cookies. The first-party cookies are the cookies that come from the website you are currently visiting and third-party cookies come from websites other than you are currently surfing but they are associated with the website that you are currently surfing.

Question: What are the available Internet Explorer cookies settings?

Answer: The available options are:

- Block all cookies
- High
- Medium high
- Medium
- Low
- Accept all cookies

Question: What are the available filter level settings for Internet Explorer browser?

Answer: The available options are: Medium, High, and Low.

Question: What happens when a website address is added to the restricted sites zone?

Answer: The user will be restricted to download any materials form the website that is added to the restricted sites zone but website contents can be visited.

Question: What RSS stands for?

Answer: RSS stands for Really Simple Syndication.

Question: What is a feed and why is it useful to subscribe?

Answer: Feed contents are the latest headlines that are frequently published by a website, such as blog groups, and contents of a newspaper. If you frequently visit an online newspaper to read about latest news, you can subscribe to it and only updated contents of the website will display to you since your last visit.

Question: What are the other names used for feed?

Answer: It is also known as RSS feeds, XML feeds, syndicated contents, web feeds, or channel.

Question: How frequently can I download feed contents from a website?

Answer: You can configure Internet Explorer to download feed contents after 15 minutes, 30 minutes, 1 hour, 4 hours, 1 day, or 1 week.

Question: How the feed attachments normally get downloaded?

Answer: Attachments normally get downloaded when you access the feed contents.

Question: Can I configure feed settings to download the video files or attachments when downloading pointer to the feed?

Answer: Yes, from the feed properties window, check *Automatically download attached files* option.

Question: Define Content Advisor?

Answer: A Content Advisor is a way to restrict a user to only view contents of a website that are appropriate to visit.

Question: Can I enable or disable a Content Advisor?

Answer: Yes

Question: What is an AutoComplete?

Answer: An AutoComplete keeps track of all previously stored entries that you have been previously used while surfing web.

Question: What is ICRA3 content rating?

Answer: ICRA3 is the rating system that Internet Explorer uses to allow or block certain websites based on their content ratings. Internet Explorer must be configured properly to get better results.

Question: Why am I unable to access RSS feed contents while visiting certain websites?

Answer: The feed contents are not available on all websites. If a websites does not publish any feed contents, the feed icon will be inactive.

Question: What is an Internet add-on?

Answer: It is a stand-alone program that can be added to your Internet Explorer browser or any other browsers, e.g. Firefox, Safari, and Mozilla, to increase the interactivity between the user and the browser. The Internet add-ons are also known as plug-ins, extensions, and/or snap-ins.

Question: Can I manage Internet Explorer add-ons?

Answer: Yes

Question: Can I disable Internet Explorer add-on?

Answer: Yes, an add-on can be disabled if it is forcing explorer to shut down unexpectedly.

Question: If I am logged-on a machine as a standard user, and having problem with Internet Explorer add-ons, can I disable that add-on?

Answer: Yes, a standard user can disable an add-on.

Question: Can I reset Internet Explorer settings?

Answer: Yes, but it is not recommended to do so unless Internet Explorer behavior is unstable.

Question: Can I run the Internet Explorer without add-ons for troubleshooting purpose?

Answer: Yes, you can run Internet Explorer (without add-ons enabling) for troubleshooting purpose only.

Question: Can I add another language to the Internet Explorer browser?

Answer: Yes, you may install additional language pack to the Internet Explorer browser if it is necessary.

Question: Can I configure Internet Explorer page to open with multiple websites?

Answer: Yes

Question: Define Microsoft Office Document Image Write?

Answer: A Microsoft Office Document Image Write converts the documents into digital images, such as Tagged Image File Format (TIFF), or Microsoft Document Imaging Format (MDI).

Question: What is an Internet Explorer Protected Mode?

Answer: The Internet Explorer Protected Mode adds an extra layer of the security for Windows Vista users to protect their personal data while surfing Internet.

Question: Can I disable Internet Explorer Protected Mode?

Answer: Yes you can, but disabling this option is not recommended.

Question: What is Phishing?

Answer: It is a way to steal someone's identity while surfing web. For example, while surfing web, an illegitimate website is asking you to provide your personal information (your name, phone number, home address, or bank information). If you have revealed personal information to the illegitimate website, then they may sell your identify to a third-party for profit.

Question: Can I stop being a victim of Phishing sites?

Answer: Yes, make sure Phishing filter is always on.

Question: Why should I always keep Phishing filter on?

Answer: To not be a victim of Phishing websites.

Question: Internet Explorer opens briefly and then closes?

Answer: The Internet Explorer problem may go away after re-booting the machine. After re-booting the machine, if problem still exists, the problem might be related with insufficient system memory, corrupted or missing system files. If the problem is related with low system memory then you must upgrade system memory to improve the performance of your system. If your system is running in low virtual memory that can

slow down the explore performance.
If the problem is related with corrupted or missing system files, run a check disk scan to fix the problem. To perform a disk scan, run the command prompt (*Windows Key + R*) and type ***cmd*** in the search bar, and then click on ***OK***. In the DOS window, type ***chkdsk*** and then hit ***Enter*** to start the scan. This scan may take several minutes to complete, depending on the size of your hard-drive.

Question: A website is asking for a username and a password but I have never been asked for credentials before?

Answer: Clear temporary internet files, and cookies.

Chapter 4 - Microsoft Control Panel Applets

Topics covered in this chapter:

- Device Manager
- Tablet PC Input Panel
- Task Manager
- Taskbar
- Start Menu
- Classics Start Menu
- Run Command
- Windows Calendar
- Windows DVD Maker
- Hardware and Sound Control Panel Applet
- Phone and Modem Setup
- Local and Network Printers
- Appearance and Personalization Control Panel Applet
- Display Configuration
- Mouse Configuration
- Keyboard Configuration
- Scanners and Cameras Configuration
- Security Center
- Compatibility Wizard
- Clock, Language, and Region Settings
- Ease of Access Center

Device Manager

Device Manager provides an overview of installed hardware devices on your computer. It allows an administrator to change hardware configuration settings such as installing device drivers, enabling and disabling devices to troubleshoot a problem. To establish a communication between a hardware device and an application, device driver must be installed, and configured properly. Only an administrator or a member of an administrator group has privileges to make changes to the *Device Manager*.

Open Device Manager

To open *Device Manager*:

- Click ***Start*** button and then click ***Control Panel***.
- Click ***Classic View*** from the left navigation pane.
- Double-click ***Device Manager***

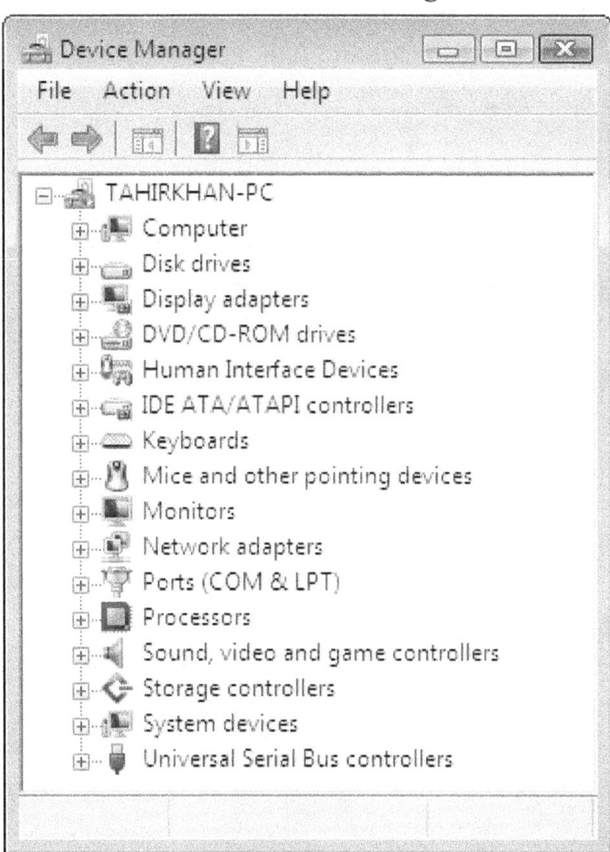

Enable Hardware Device

From the *Device Manager* window, expand the device which needs to be enabled by clicking on plus sign next to it. If a device is disabled, a downward arrow with a circle around it will appear on that device. The device can be enabled by right-clicking on it and then choosing the ***Enable*** option.

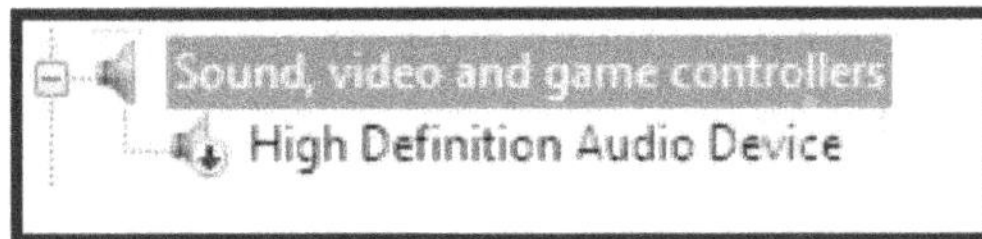

Disable Hardware Device

From the *Device Manager* window, expand the device which needs to be disabled by clicking on plus sign next to it. A hardware device can be disabled by right-clicking on the device component and choosing the ***Disable*** option from the list. If a device is disabled, the communication between a disabled device and other hardware devices will not happen until that device is enabled by an administrator. It is not recommended to disable any hardware devices unless it is required.

Wakeup Network Adaptor

To enable the wakeup option for your network adaptor, click on the plus sign next to the network adapters to expand the device components from the *Device Manager* window. Right-click on the device component listed under the ***Network adapters*** section, and then choose the ***Properties*** option from the list.

From the ***Network Adaptor Properties*** window, click ***Power Management*** tab, and then check the ***Allow this device to wake the computer*** option to allow system administrator to wake up your computer remotely to perform scheduled maintenance whenever it is necessary. Click on ***OK*** to save changes. It is not recommended to turn on this feature if it is not necessary.

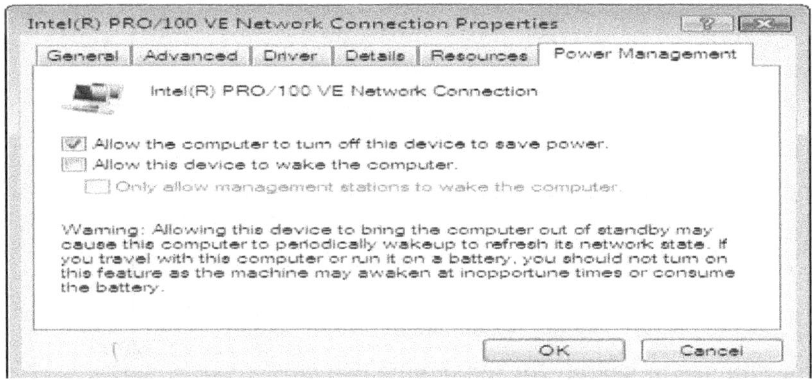

Update Device Driver

A yellow circle around the device icon means there is no communication between this device and other devices of your system. To establish a connection between this device and other devices, device driver must be installed. To update a device driver, right-click on the device you wish to update driver for, and then choose the ***Update Driver Software*** option from the list.

Windows Vista operating system is capable of searching latest driver for any device that is connected with your computer. You must be connected with the Internet to download latest device driver automatically. It also gives you an option browsing your computer to install device driver manually, if Windows Vista is unable to download latest driver automatically. Select one of the following options to download device drivers.

- To allow your system to download and install device driver automatically, choose the ***Search automatically for updated driver software*** option. - Follow the step # 1 given below for more information.
- To manually install device driver, choose the ***Browse my computer for driver software*** option. You must download device driver from the manufacture website, for example, if you have a dell computer, you must go to www.support.dell.com

to download latest device driver and save it into your local computer hard-drive. - For more explanation, follow the step # 2 as given below.

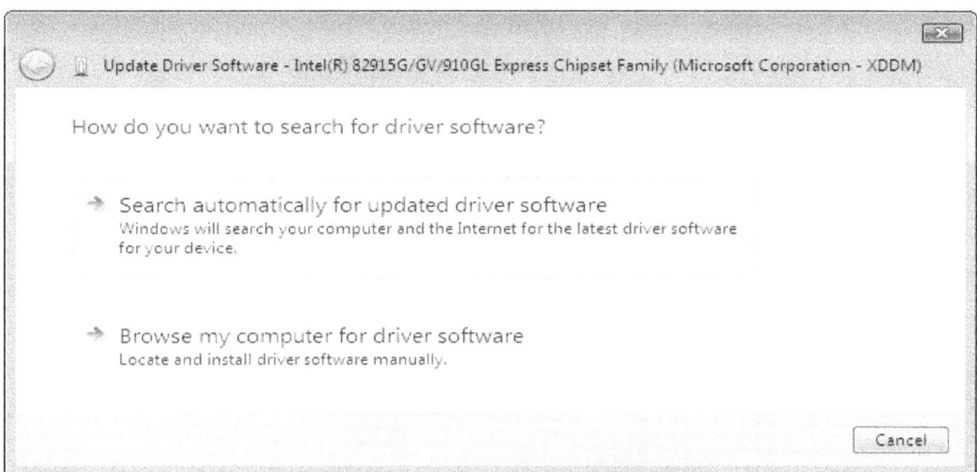

Windows may take several minutes to search for the device driver.

Step # 1: If Windows was successful to download and install the device driver, you will be notified. Re-boot the machine to apply changes to your system.

Step # 2: Navigate to the folder, in which device driver is saved, and then click on ***Next***. In earlier version of the Microsoft operating system, you were required to navigate to the subfolders of a folder in which driver were saved, but the latest Windows Vista operating system is capable of scanning subfolders itself to look for any driver that is part of the device that needs to be updated. Windows may take several minutes installing the device driver. You will be notified, if device drivers are found and installed correctly.

Rolling Back Device Driver

A device driver can be rolled back to the previously installed driver, if the device is not working properly after installing the latest driver for that device. To roll back a device driver, open the *Device Manger*. From the ***Device Manager*** window, expand the device by clicking the plus sign next to it. Right-click on that device and then choose the ***Properties*** option form the list.

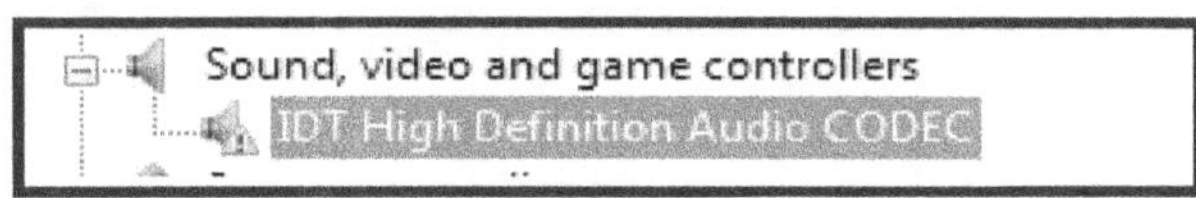

From the ***Device Properties*** window, click ***Driver*** tab, and then click on ***Roll Back Driver*** button to roll your device driver back to the previous stage. This process may ask you to re-boot your system to complete this process.

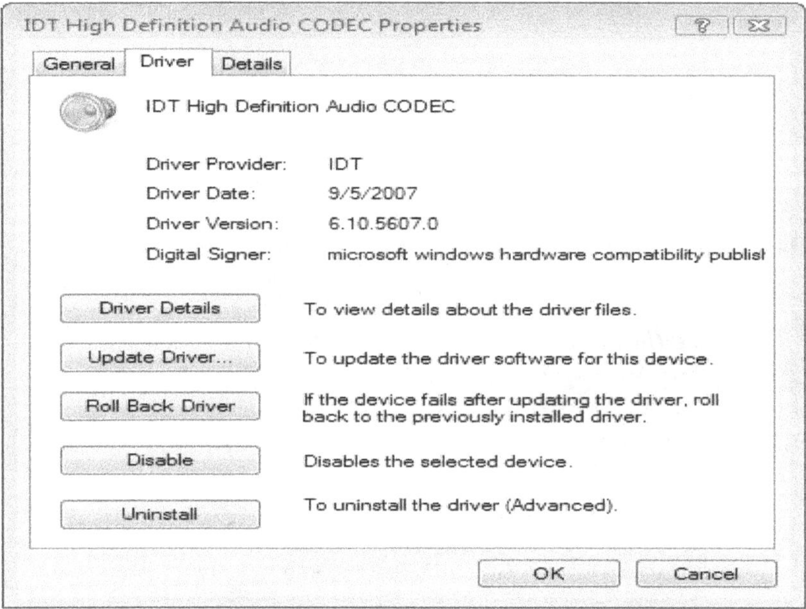

Add Legacy Hardware

Legacy hardware is compatible to work with older versions of Microsoft operating systems (Windows 95, 98, 2000, NT, and XP). Most legacy devices are not Plug-and-Play compatible. A Plug-and-Play feature automatically detects an attached device with your computer without requiring additional device drivers. To establish a communication between the legacy devices and the system active devices, the legacy hardware drivers must be installed properly. To add a legacy device, open ***Control Panel*** in classic view and then double-click ***Add Hardware***.

You may be prompted for administrative credentials to add or remove legacy device(s). To continue this process, click on ***Next***.

Choose one of the following options and then click on ***Next*** to continue this process.

a. *Search for and install the hardware automatically (Recommended).*
b. *Install the hardware that I manually select from a list (Advanced).*

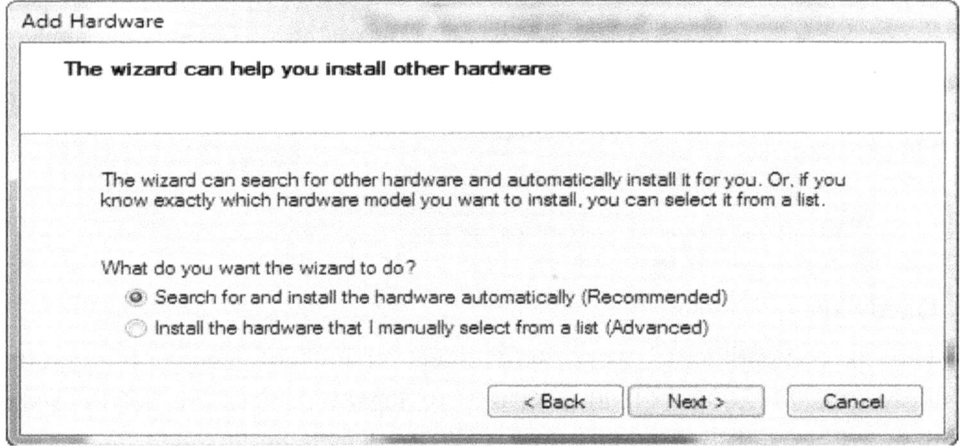

If you decided to select the option *a*, the system will search for legacy hardware and will install that device driver, automatically. This process may take few minutes searching for the legacy hardware.

If the wizard did not find any legacy hardware on your computer, click on ***Back*** button that would allow you to choose option *b* to install the device driver manually.

Choose the option *b* that would allow you to select the hardware type from the list to install the device driver manually. To continue this process, click on ***Next***.

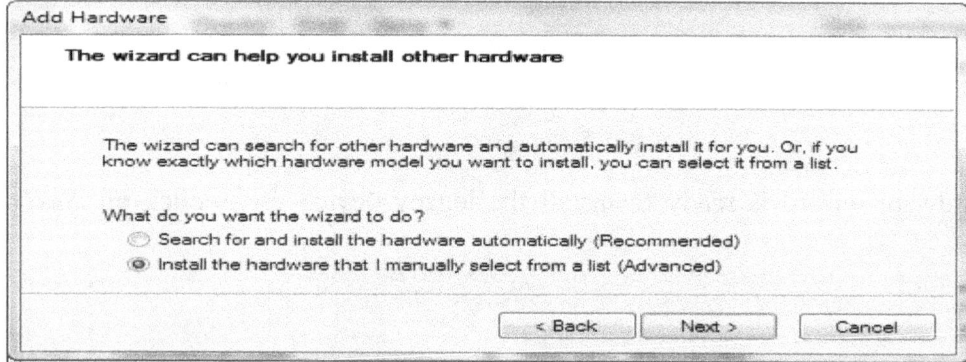

Select the legacy device that you want to install driver for, and then click on ***Next***. If legacy device is not listed, click the ***Show all devices*** under the ***Common hardware types*** box, to see all available devices for your system.

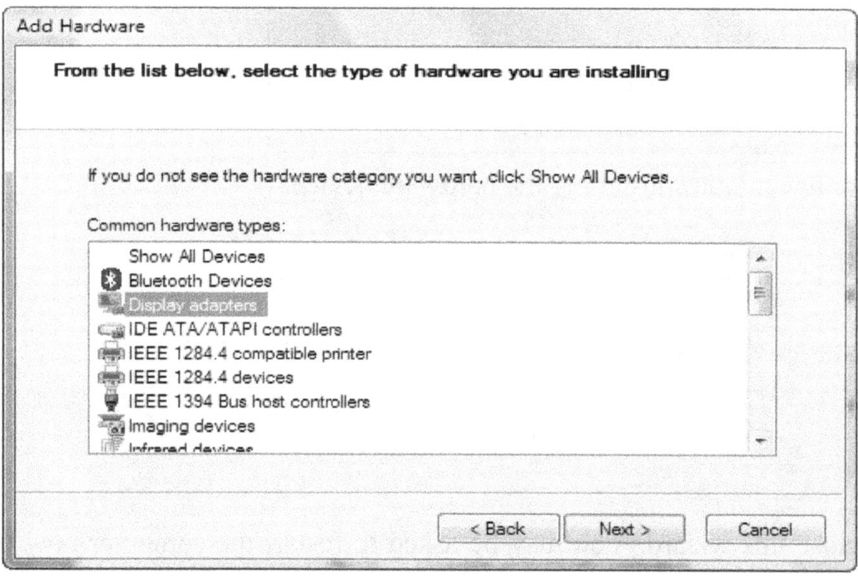

Select the manufacturer and model of the legacy hardware and then click on ***Next***. If your system did not find any device driver, click on ***Have Disk*** button to download device drivers from the disk that came with your legacy hardware system.

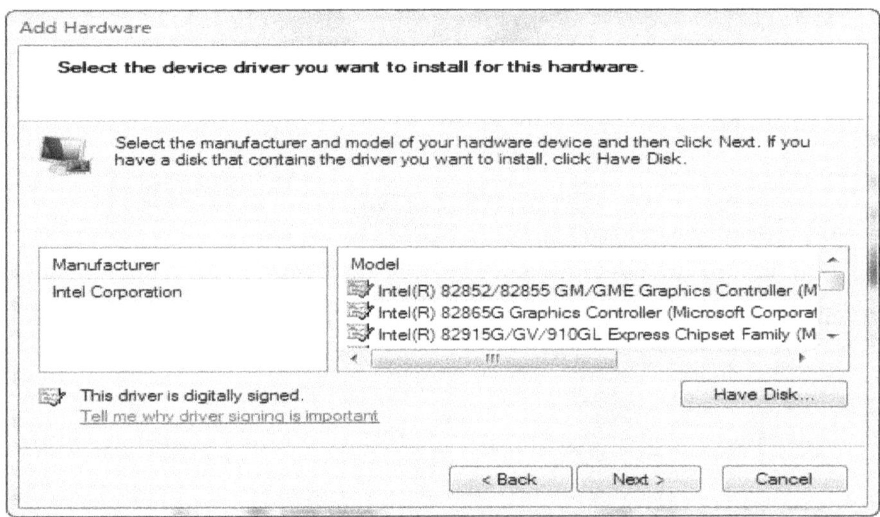

The add hardware wizard is ready to install the legacy device drive, click on ***Next*** to continue.

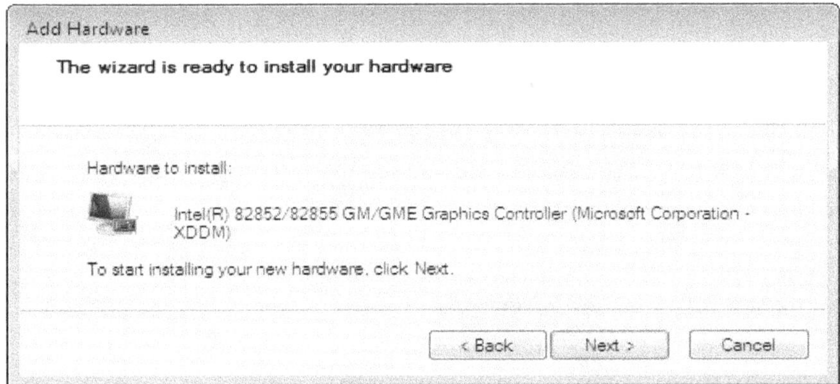

Your system may take few minutes installing the hardware device.

Click on ***Finish*** to close this wizard. You may be asked to restart the computer now or later, so hardware changes can apply to your system.

Tablet PC Input Panel

Tablet PC Input Panel is an alternative way to input the text for your system by using mouse or with stylus (Touch screen pen), or any other pointing device. This feature is available to all Windows Vista versions except Windows Home Basic edition.

Open Tablet PC Input Panel

To open *Tablet PC Input Panel*, click ***Start*** button, click ***All Programs***, click ***Accessories***, click ***Tablet PC***, and then click ***Tablet PC Input Panel***.

Tablet PC Input Panel on the Taskbar

Right-click on the taskbar (by default, located at the bottom of the desktop) and then choose the ***Properties*** option from the list. From the ***Taskbar and Start Menu Properties*** window, click on ***Toolbars*** tab, and then check the ***Tablet PC Input Panel*** option to add *Tablet PC Input Panel* to the taskbar. Click on ***Apply*** and then click ***OK*** to save settings.

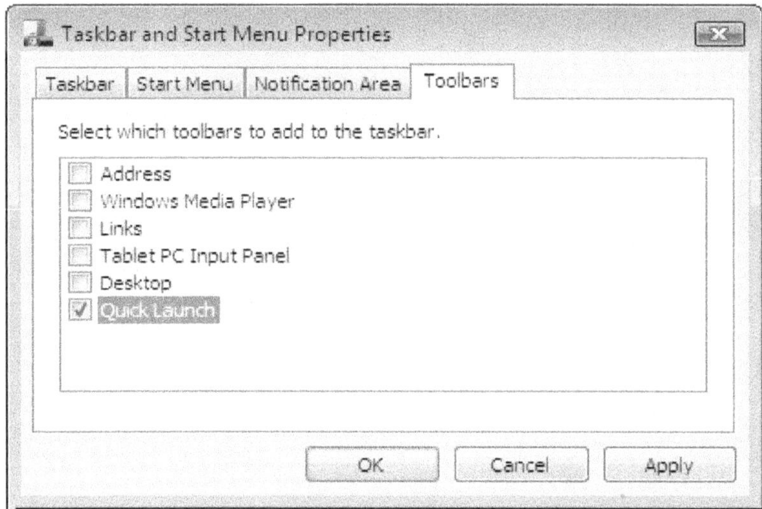

Tablet PC Input Panel icon will appear on the taskbar. Click on *Tablet PC Input Panel* icon to open the program.

Use mouse or any other pointing devices connected with your PC to write with on the writing pad. As you start writing on it, an insertion option will appear on right bottom of the pad to insert the text into another document.

To switch from *Writing Pad Mode* to *Keyboard Mode*, click the ***keyboard*** button that is located at upper left corner of the window. Use your mouse or any other pointing device to use the on-screen keyboard, if necessary.

Tablet PC Settings

To adjust *Tablet PC Input Panel* settings:

- Open ***Control Panel***
- Click ***Classic View*** from the left navigation pane
- Double-click **Tablet PC Settings**

Tablet PC Input Panel enables a user to adjust writing preferences. Select the ***Right-handed*** or the ***Left-handed*** preference under the ***General*** tab from the ***Handedness*** section. Click on ***Apply*** and then click ***OK*** to save user preferences.

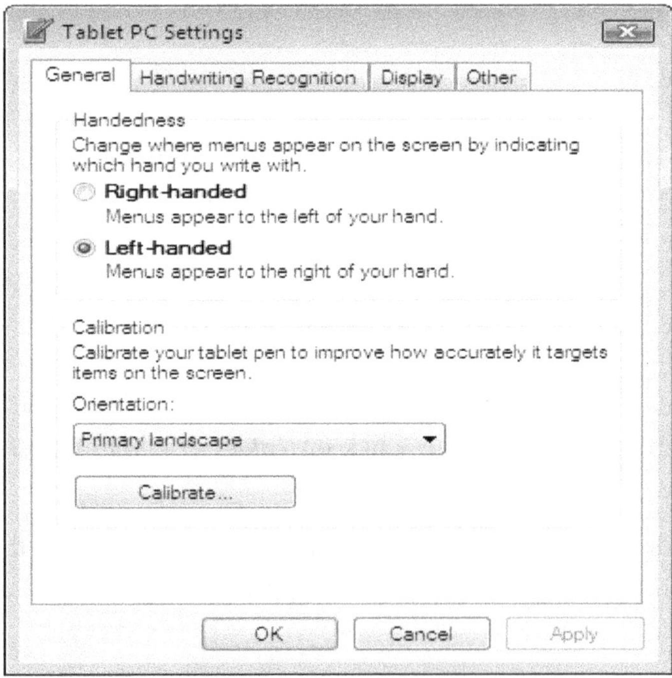

By default, handwriting recognition is enabled for users but it can be disabled by clearing off the ***Use the personalized recognizer (recommended)*** checked box in the ***Handwriting Recognition*** tab.

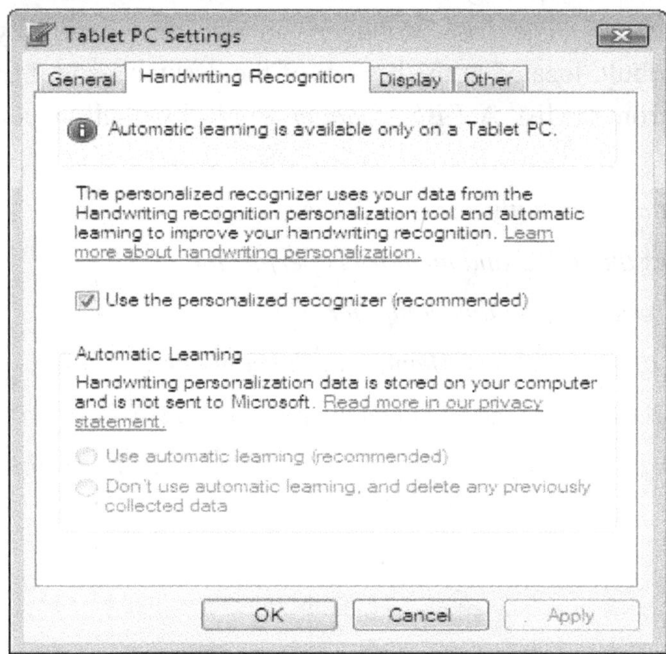

To adjust Tablet PC display settings, click ***Display*** tab from ***Tablet PC Settings*** dialog box, and then choose one of the following screen orientation options:

a. *Primary landscape*
b. *Secondary portrait*
c. *Secondary landscape*
d. *Primary portrait*

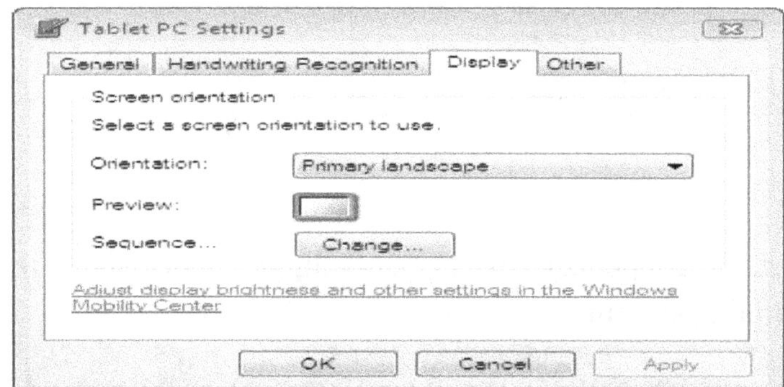

Click on ***Apply*** and then click ***OK*** to save changes.

Task Manager

Windows Task Manager allows administrators to manage currently running applications and their processes, and system services. To quickly access *Task Manager* window, press ***Ctrl, Shift, and Esc***, keys simultaneously. The *Task Manager* can also be accessed by right-clicking on the ***Taskbar*** (by default, located at the bottom of the desktop), and then choosing the ***Task Manager*** option from the list. A *Task Manager* window will allow you to perform the following operations:

- *Manage applications that are currently running in the system.*
- *Manage/monitor processes that CPU and memory is performing.*
- *Services that are currently running on this computer.*
- *Monitor the performance of the CPU and Memory of the computer.*
- *Networking (Wireless or Wired networking performance status).*
- *List of the users who are currently logged-on or were logged-on to this machine earlier.*

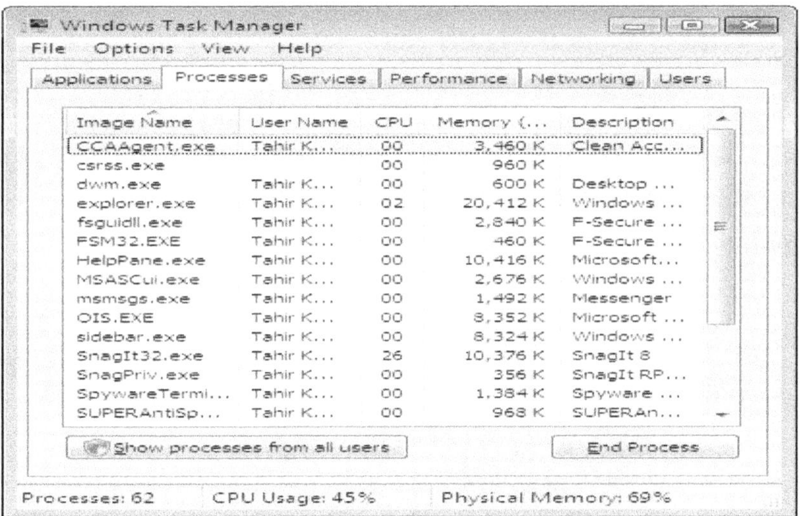

Taskbar

The Taskbar displays currently running applications. By default, it is located at the bottom of Microsoft Windows operating system.

Taskbar Properties

Right click on the taskbar and then choose the ***Properties*** option from the list. From the ***Taskbar and Start Menu Properties*** window, click the ***Taskbar*** tab, and then adjust some or all of the following available preferences:

- *Lock the taskbar*
- *Auto-hide the taskbar*
- *Keep the taskbar on top of other windows*
- *Group similar taskbar buttons*
- *Show Quick Launch*
- *Show window previews (thumbnails)*

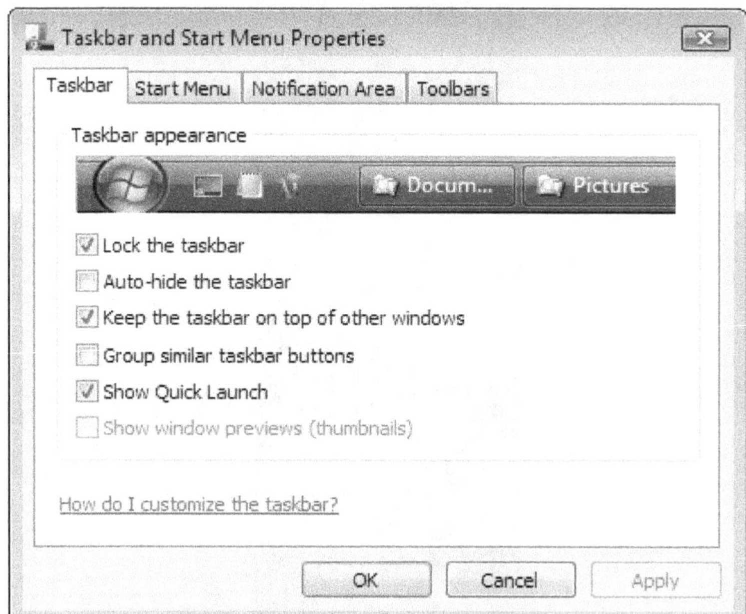

Click on ***Apply*** and then click ***OK*** after making any changes to the *Taskbar* window.

USB Drive Toolbar on Taskbar

Right click on the ***Taskbar***, point to the ***Toolbars***, and then click the ***New Toolbar***.

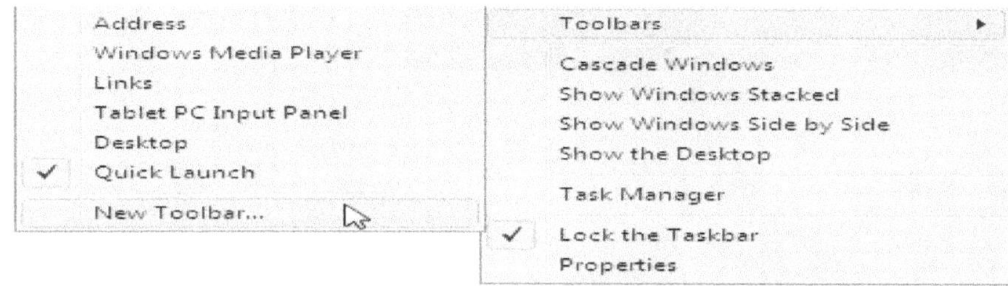

Select the USB device that you would like to add on the taskbar to access its contents. If you would like to remove the USB drive from the *Taskbar*, right-click on the *Taskbar* and point to the ***Toolbars*** and then click the ***USB Drive*** (USB drive will be removed from the *Taskbar*).

Start Menu

Windows Start Menu is a user interface for Microsoft operating systems that allows you to launch programs that are currently installed on your computer.

Start Menu Customization

Right-click on the ***Start*** button and then choose the ***Properties*** option from the list. The ***Start Menu*** folders, favorites, programs and search styles can be customized by clicking on ***Customize*** button from the ***Taskbar and Start Menu Properties*** window.

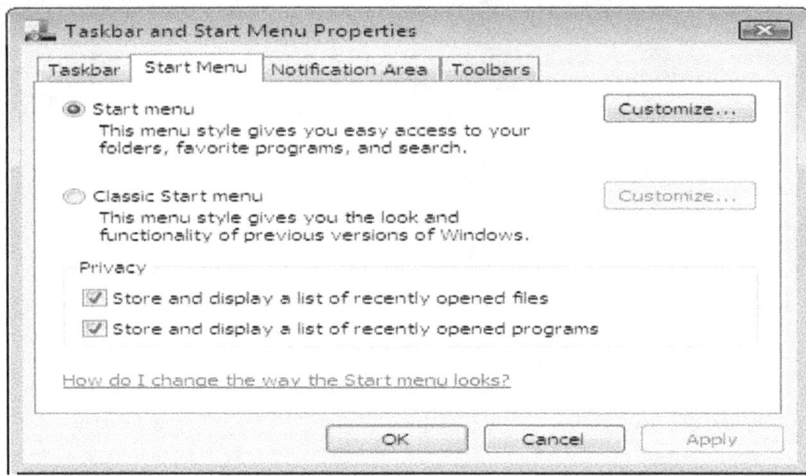

To customize Start Menu links, icons, and menus look, select some or all of the listed options from the ***Customize Start Menu*** dialog box. Click ***OK*** after making any changes.

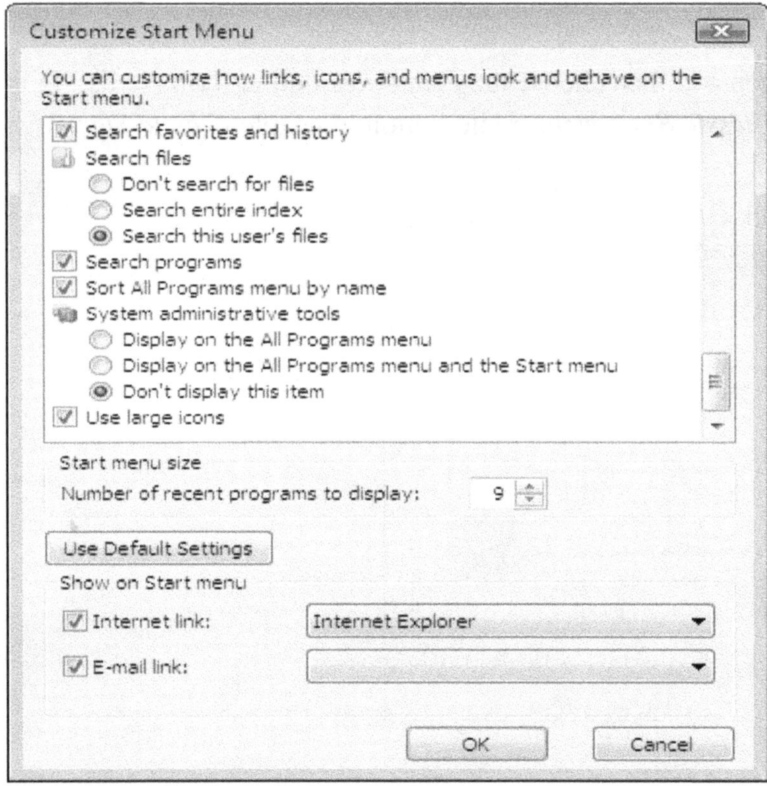

Classics Start Menu

Windows Classics Start Menu is a user graphics interface that was designed for older versions of Microsoft operating systems, such as Windows 2000, NT, and XP, to view and launch programs for your system.

Enable Classic Start Menu

Right-click on the ***Start*** button and then choose the ***Properties*** option from the list. In the ***Start Menu*** tab, select the ***Classic Start menu*** radio button to enable *Classic Start Menu* for your system.

Click on ***Apply*** and then click ***OK*** to save system preferences.

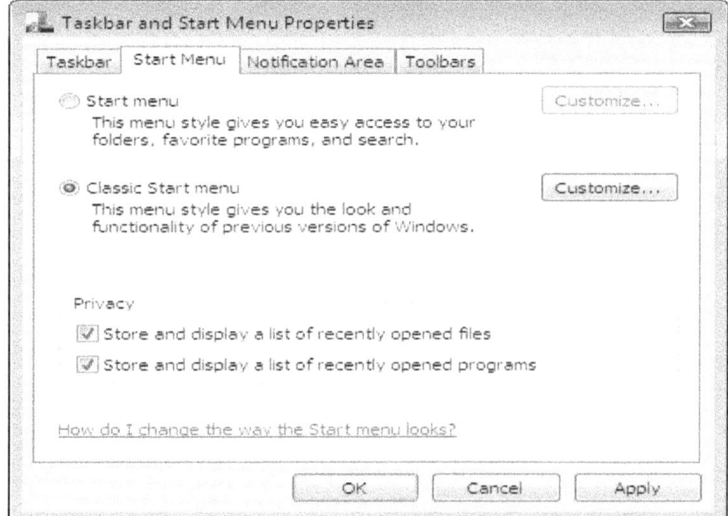

Run Command

A run command is a dialog box to access computer utilities such as DOS window, task manager, control panel, network and sharing center, device manager, etc. by typing a command line.

Open Run Command

To open *Run Command*, click on ***Start*** button and type ***Run*** in the search bar and then press ***Enter*** from the keyboard.

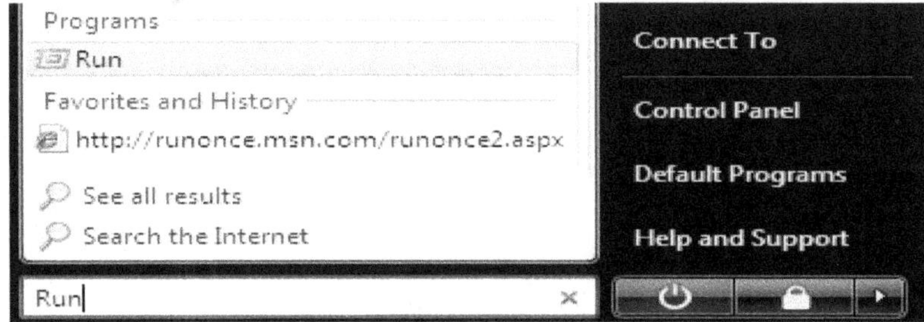

A *Run* dialog box is prompted to type the name of a program, folder, document, or Internet resource that you wish to open by typing a command line in the search bar. For example, if you would like to open DOS-window, type ***cmd*** command line in the search bar and then press ***Enter*** from keyboard to open the DOS-window.

Add Run Command in Start Menu

Right-click on the ***Start*** button and then choose the ***Properties*** option from the list. From the ***Taskbar and Start Menu Properties*** window, click the ***Start Menu*** tab, and then select the ***Customize*** radio button to add *Run Command* to the *Start Menu.*

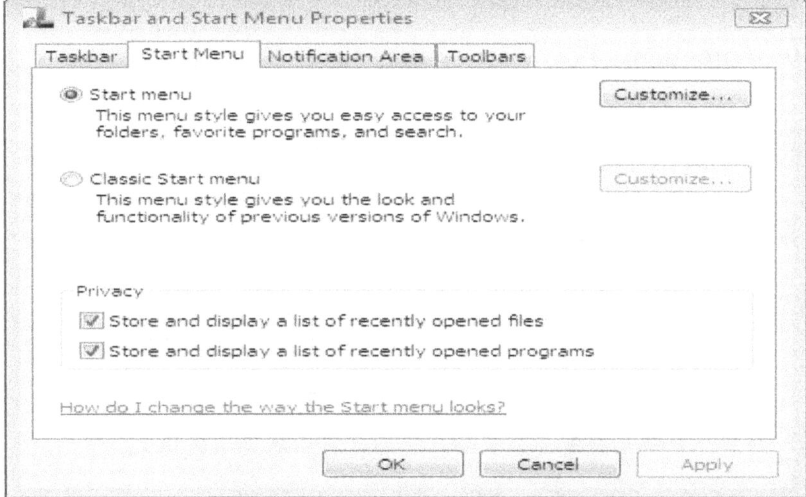

Scroll down the list to navigate the ***Run command*** option. To enable this feature, check the ***Run command*** option to activate it. *Run command* can be disabled by clearing off ***Run command*** box. Click ***OK*** to save preferences.

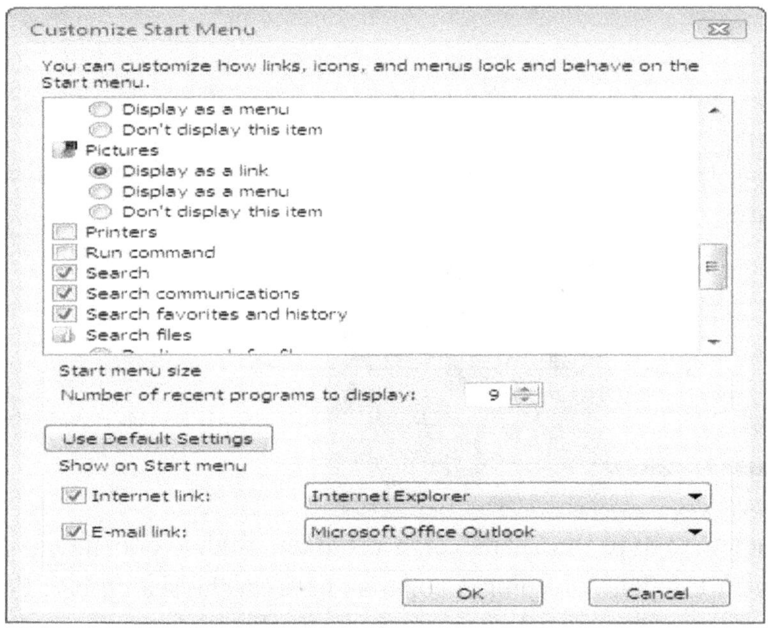

Windows Calendar

Windows Calendar is a tool that helps users to plan and manage their daily activities that includes, adding an appointment and reminder alters, adding new daily tasks, and subscribing to other's calendars to keep track of their schedule and activities.

Open Windows Calendar

To open *Windows Calendar* program, click ***Start*** button, click ***All Programs***, and then click ***Windows Calendar***.

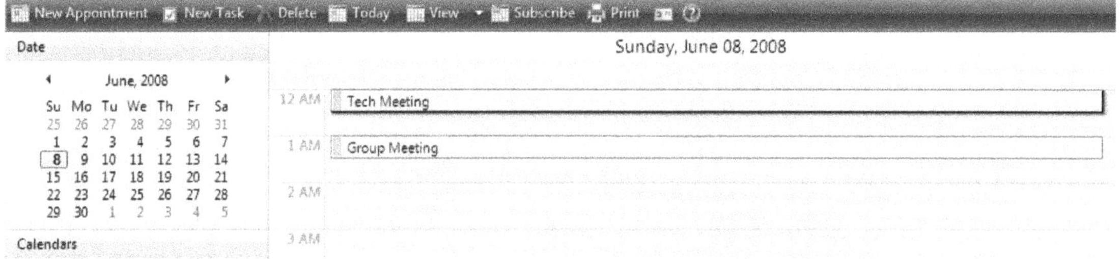

Add an Appointment

Open *Windows Calendar* program. Click the ***New Appointment*** option from the *Windows Calendar* toolbar.

Type the new name of your appointment and then adjust appointment start and end period time, from right panel of the window.

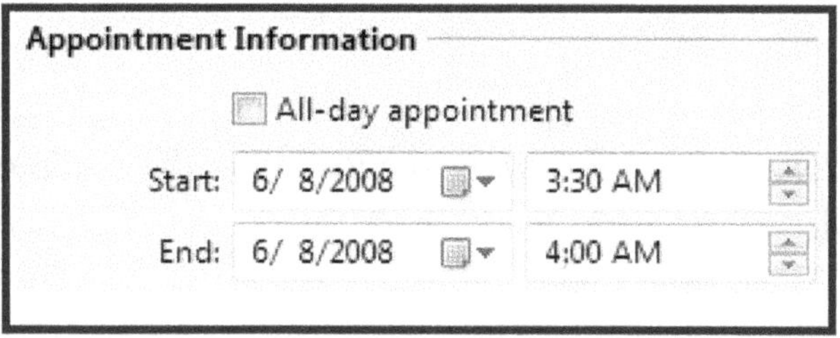

Add Recurrence to the Appointment

From the *Windows Calendar* panel, click on the existing appointment that you would like to set recurrence for, and then choose one of the available recurrence options from right navigation panel under the ***Appointment Information*** section. The available recurrence options are: *everyday, weekly, monthly, yearly, and advanced.*

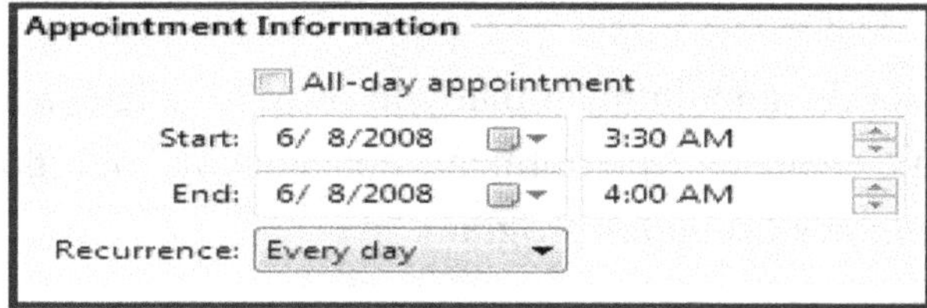

If you want to choose the advanced recurrence option for your appointment, then you must specify how many times you want the appointment to be repeated, for example, forever, or until a specific date.

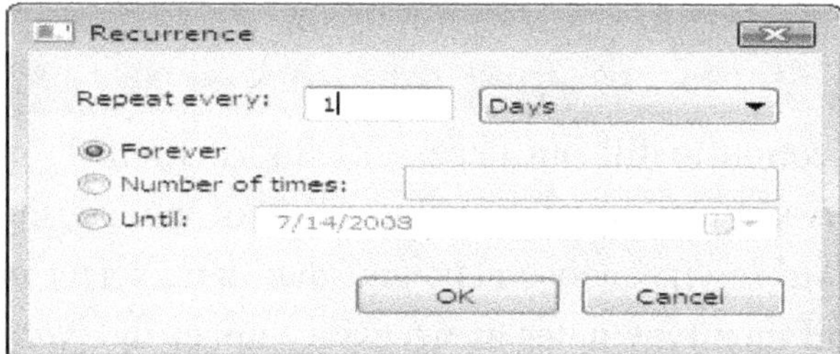

Add Reminder for an Appointment

From the *Windows Calendar* panel, click the appointment that you want to set the reminder for, and then choose the available reminder time period, from right navigation pane of the window under the ***Reminder*** section.

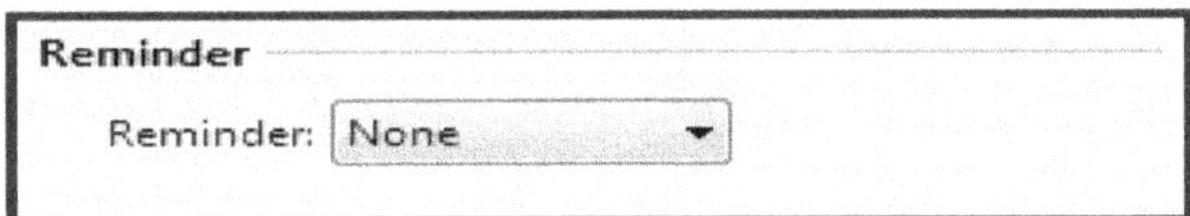

Add Location of the Meeting

From right-pane of the *Windows Calendar*, under the ***Details*** section, type the name of the meeting, location, and URL, if needed.

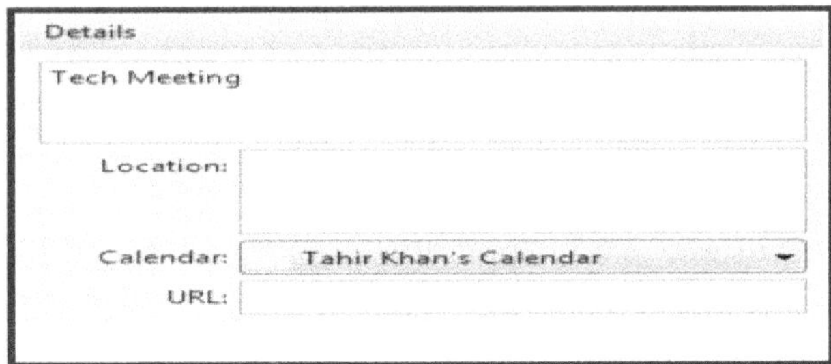

Delete an Appointment

From the *Windows Calendar* window, select the appointment that you want to delete, and then choose the ***Delete*** option from the toolbar. Appointment notes/details are not recoverable, once it is deleted from the *Windows Calendar* program.

Create New Task

From the *Windows Calendar* panel, click the ***New Task*** option from the toolbar to create a new task. New task will appear on left panel of the window under the ***Task*** section

Click on the task name under the ***Task*** section to fill out necessary information. From right-pane of the window, under the ***Details*** section, type task name, URL of the website, choose a priority option (*low, medium, and high*), choose start and due date, select ***on date*** option from the ***Reminder*** section, and then type notes as necessary under the ***Notes*** section.

Delete a Task

From the *Windows Calendar* window, select the ***Task*** from left panel of the window under the ***Task*** section that you want to delete, and then choose the ***Delete*** option from the toolbar.

Print Appointments

From the toolbar of *Windows Calendar*, click on ***Print*** option to print daily appointments and list of tasks.

From the ***Print*** dialog box, choose the name of the printer that you would like to print from under the ***Printer*** section, and then select how many copies you want to print from the ***Copies*** section. To choose printer style, choose either *day, work week, week, or month print* style from the ***Print Style*** section, and then select start and end day print ranges from the ***Print Range*** section, if necessary. Click on ***OK*** to print desired appointments.

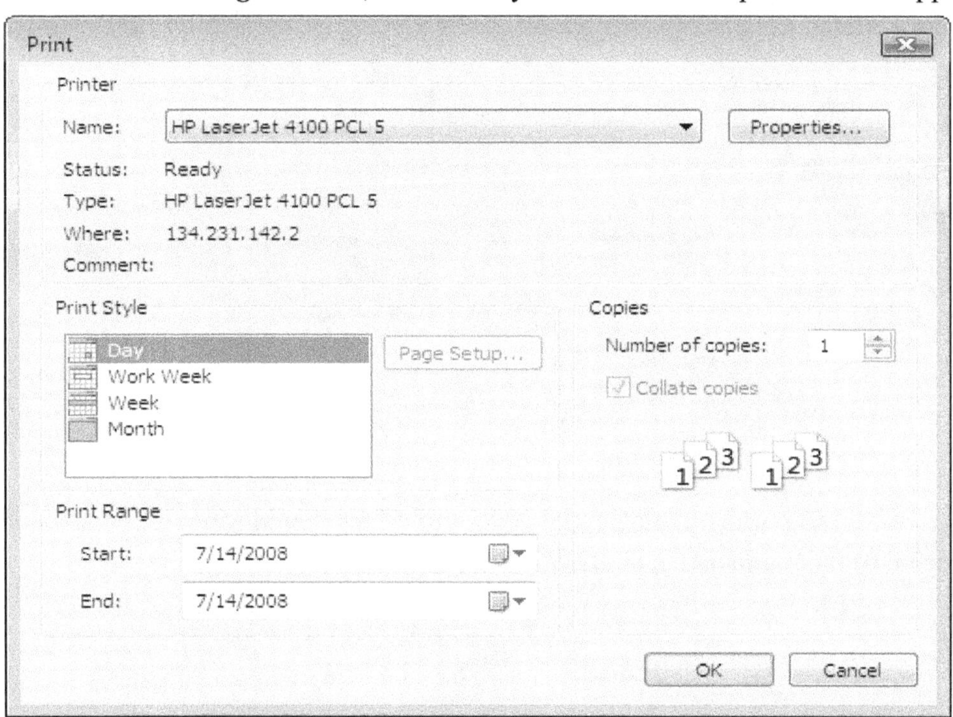

Publish Calendar

From the *Windows Calendar* window, click the ***Share*** menu, and then choose the ***Publish*** option from the drop down menu list.

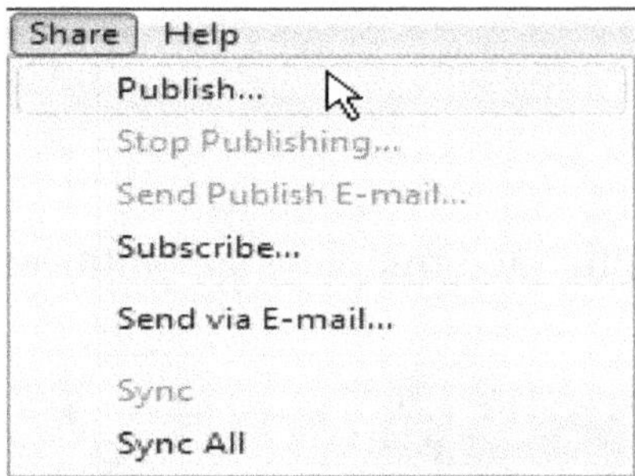

In the *Publish Calendar* window, you are required to specify the location of the publish calendar, and calendar details options that you want to share with your colleagues. For example, if you want to share the notes that are associated with a particular appointment, so your colleagues would know about the notes in advance. Click on ***Publish*** after filling out necessary information that you want to share with others.

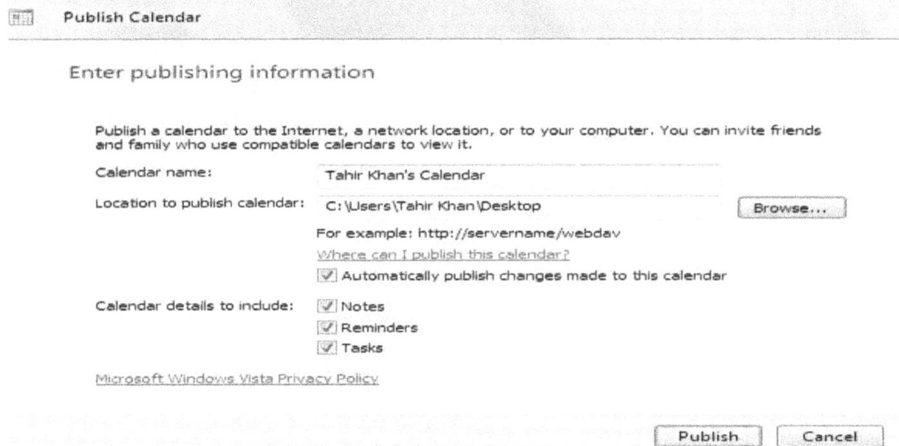

If you were successful to publish the calendar, you will be prompted to view the calendar name and location of the published calendar.

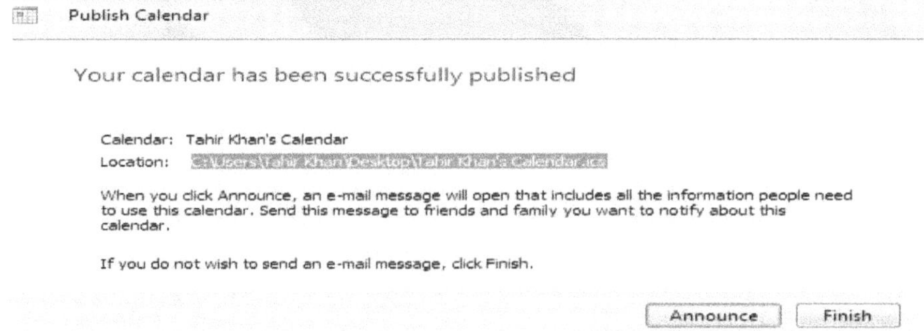

If you want to let your trusted users know about the published calendar, click on ***Announce***. *Windows Mail* will send an email to the trusted users which includes published calendar link so your colleagues can subscribe to it, if your system is configured properly for *Windows Mail.* Alternatively, you can copy the location of the published calendar, and then send them as an attachment using other email vendors e.g. Google mail, Yahoo mail, Hotmail mail, etc.

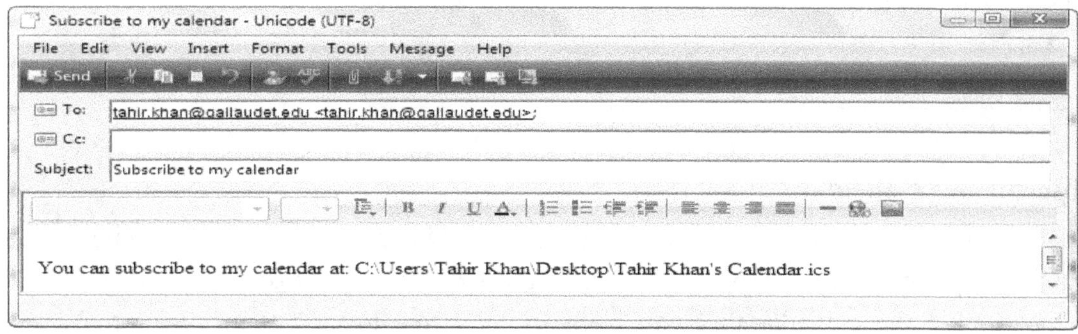

View Published Calendar Details

From left-pane of the *Windows Calendar*, select the calendar to view the published calendar details from the ***Calendar*** section. The published detail appears on the right side of the window under the ***Details*** section, you will see what is published and what features are viewable for others to view your calendar.

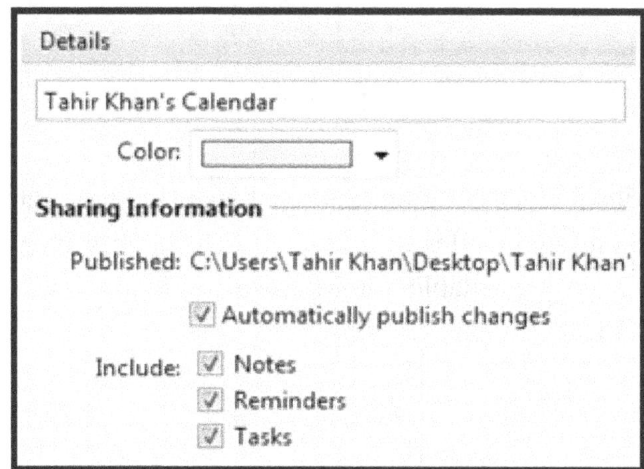

Stop Publishing Calendar

From the *Windows Calendar* window, click the ***Share*** menu, and then choose the ***Stop publishing*** option from the drop down menu list. In the ***Windows Calendar*** dialog box, click the ***Unpublish*** button to make this calendar unavailable for others. Once the calendar is unpublished, it will no longer be available to users for subscription.

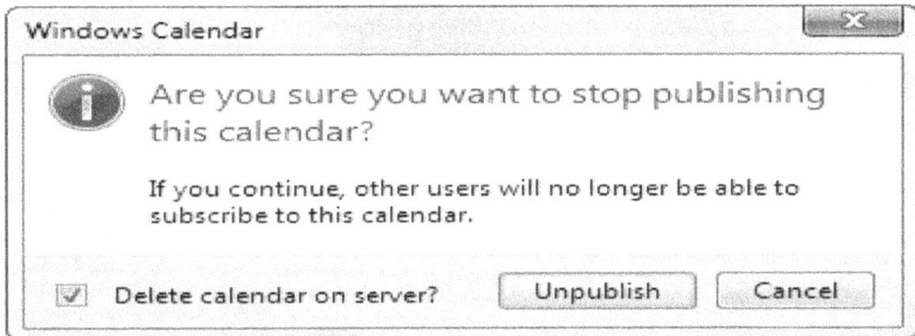

Subscribe to a Calendar

From the *Windows Calendar* window, click the ***Share*** menu, and then choose the ***Subscribe*** option from the drop down list. In the ***Calendar to subscribe to*** field, specify the location of the calendar that you want to subscribe to, and then click on ***Next*** to continue the process.

Windows DVD Maker

Windows DVD Maker is a built-in Windows Vista program that enables users to create, and customize videos files, picture files, and audio files to provide a high quality image DVD. *Windows DVD Maker* program is only available for Microsoft Windows Vista Home Premium and Microsoft Windows Vista Ultimate editions.

Open Windows DVD Maker

To open the *Windows DVD Maker* program, click ***Start*** button, click ***All Programs***, and then click ***Windows DVD Maker***.

Burn DVD

Insert the *DVD Disk* into the *DVD ROM*. Open the *Windows DVD Maker* program and then click on ***Add items*** option from the command bar of the *DVD Maker* window to add items that needs to be burned into the *DVD disk*.

Type the name of the disc title (located at the bottom of the window) and then click on ***Next***.

The *Windows DVD Maker* allows customizing the content of *DVD* by selecting available options form the *DVD Maker* command bar to adjust DVD preferences. Once the preferences are set, click on ***Burn*** button, and then follow on-screen instructions to burn the contents of the *DVD* on it. This process may take several minutes, depending on your computer performance and your DVD drive burning speed.

DVD Options

Open the *Windows DVD Maker* program. From the detailed pane of the *Windows DVD Maker*, click on ***Options***. A detailed pane is located on bottom of the *DVD Maker* window. In the DVD options window, the following preferences can be set:

- *Choose DVD playback settings. The options are: 1- Start with DVD menu, 2- Play video and end with DVD menu, 3- Play video in a continuous loop*
- *DVD aspect ratio settings. The options are: 4:3 ratio, and 16:9 ratio*
- *Video format settings. The options are: NTSC and PAL*

Click ***OK*** to save *DVD* preferences.

Hardware and Sound Control Panel Applet

Hardware and Sound panel is designed to setup and configure computer speakers, phone and modem, mouse and keyboard, power options, local and network printers, and tablet PC settings.

Open Hardware and Sound Applet

To open ***Hardware and Sound*** applet:

- Click ***Start*** button and then click ***Control Panel***
- Click ***Control Panel Home*** from the left navigation pane
- Click ***Hardware and Sound***

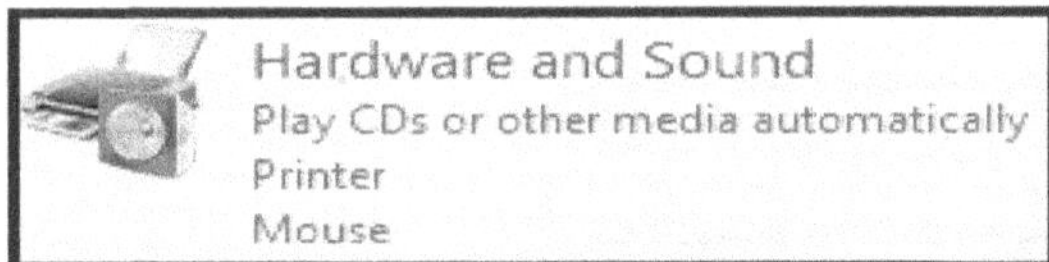

Adjust Sound Volume

Open ***Hardware and Sound*** applet, and navigate to the ***Sound*** icon, and then click the ***Adjust system volume*** link.

Click the ***Device*** menu from the ***Volume Mixer*** window, and then select one of the following audio devices.

- *Digital Audio Interface (SB Live! 24-bit)*
- *Speakers (SoundMAX Integrated Digital Audio)*
- *Speakers (SB Live! 24-bit)*

Select the device or an application to adjust the volume of, and then move the slider up or down to increase or decrease the volume, respectively. The volume of each device can be muted by clicking on speaker icon (located at the bottom of each device).

Setup Sound System

Open ***Hardware and Sound*** applet, and navigate to the ***Sound*** icon, and then click the ***Manage audio devices*** link. From the ***Sound*** window, select a speaker type that you have for your system and then click on ***Configure*** button to start configuring sound system settings.

From the ***Speaker Setup*** window, select the audio channels for your speakers, and then click on ***Next***. To test your speakers, click on ***Test*** to see if the speakers are connected to your computer properly. If the speakers are connected properly, you must hear a sound from your system speakers.

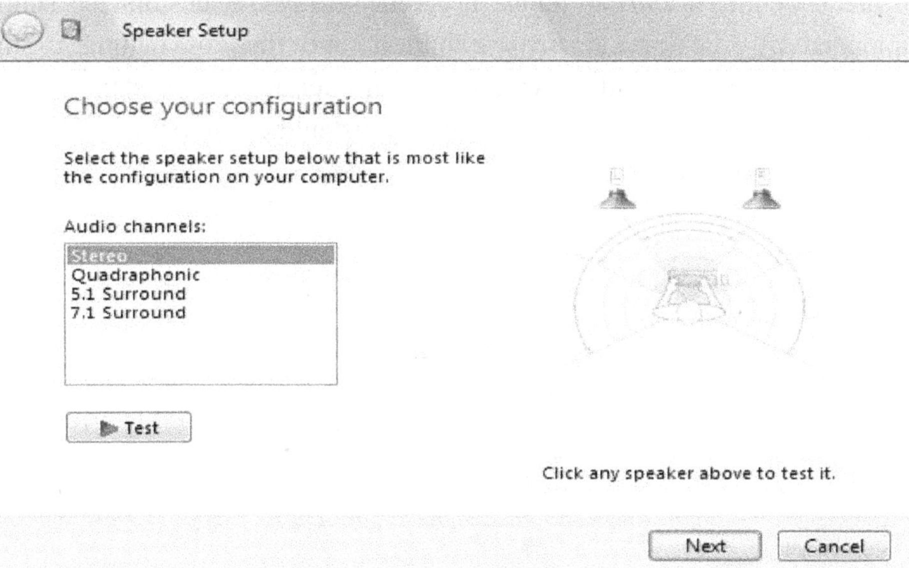

Click on ***Next*** to continue.

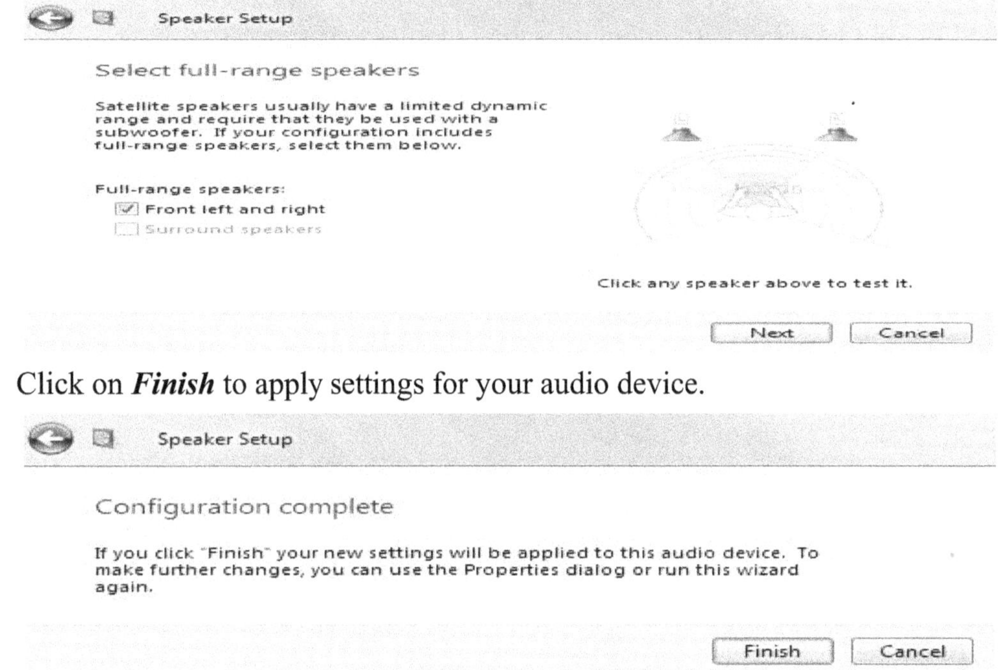

Click on ***Finish*** to apply settings for your audio device.

To adjust sound theme, click ***Sounds*** tab from the ***Sound*** window to select a sound scheme from drop down menu of the ***Sound Scheme*** and then choose a program event from the list of available programs to apply sound effects. Then select the sound track from drop down menu of the ***Sounds*** to adjust program settings. A customized sound track can be uploaded by clicking on ***Browse*** button, and then navigating to the customized sound track folder to upload customized sound track for your system. To test a sound effect for a program event, click on ***Test*** button to listen the sound track. Click on ***Apply*** and then click ***OK*** to save sound theme preferences.

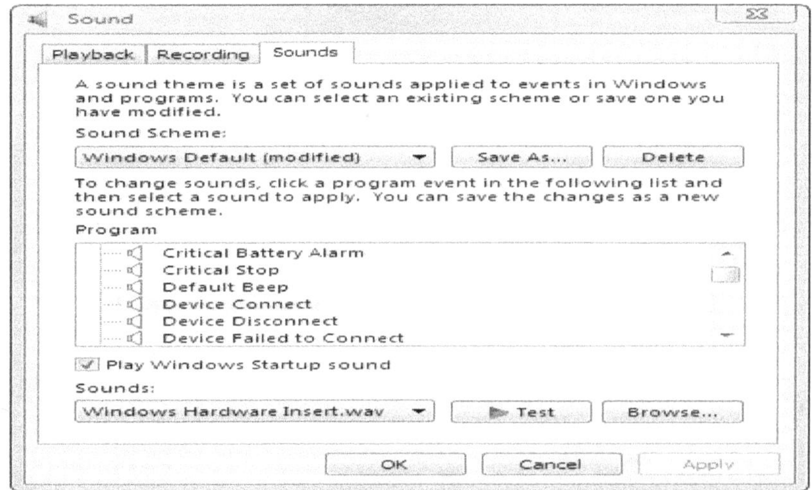

Phone and Modem Setup

To setup a phone and modem for your system, open the ***Hardware and Sound*** applet, and navigate to the ***Phone and Modem Options*** icon, and then click on it to open.

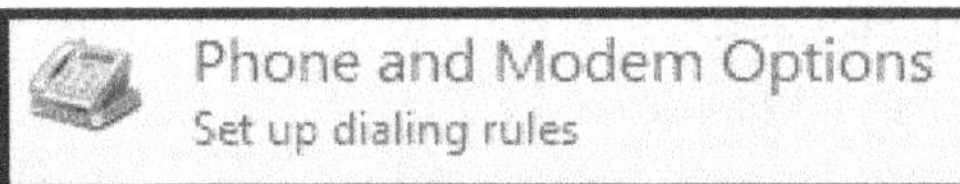

From the ***Location Information*** window, select the country/region in which you are in now, type city code in which you live in, specify a carrier code for outside dialing if provided by your carrier, and then click ***OK*** to save preferences. Now the phone modem is ready to be dialed.

Install Local and Network Printers

Open ***Hardware and Sound*** applet, and navigate to the ***Printers*** icon, and then click on ***Add a printer*** link.

If a printer is directly connected with your computer, install a local printer without creating an IP address port. A local printer can be configured with IP address, subnet mask, and default gateway using the ***Add a local printer*** option to create a new port for your printer. If a wireless or Bluetooth printer is available for your system, select ***add a network, wireless or Bluetooth printer*** option to install a network printer.

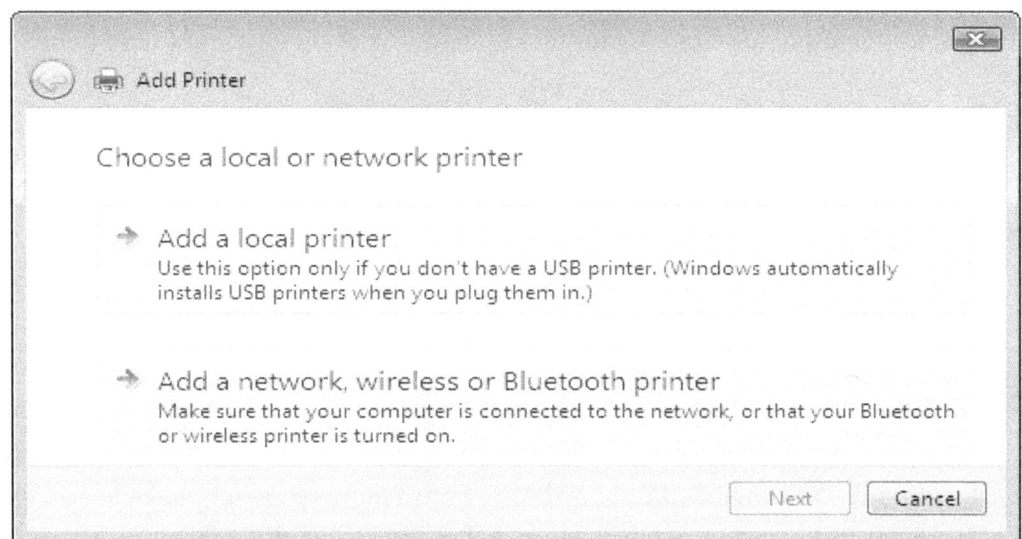

An existing port can be used to install local or network printer. Most common existing ports are LPT (*Line Print Terminal*) and COM (*Serial Port*). The designated printer's ports, such as LPT, COM, and USB (*Universal Serial Bus*) can be used to install a local printer by choosing the ***Use an existing port*** option. If a standard TCP/IP port needs to be created, click on ***Create a new port*** and then select the ***Standard TCP/IP port*** from drop down menu list. Ask the network administrator for IP address of printer that you want to connect to, if needed.

Click on ***Next*** to continue this process.

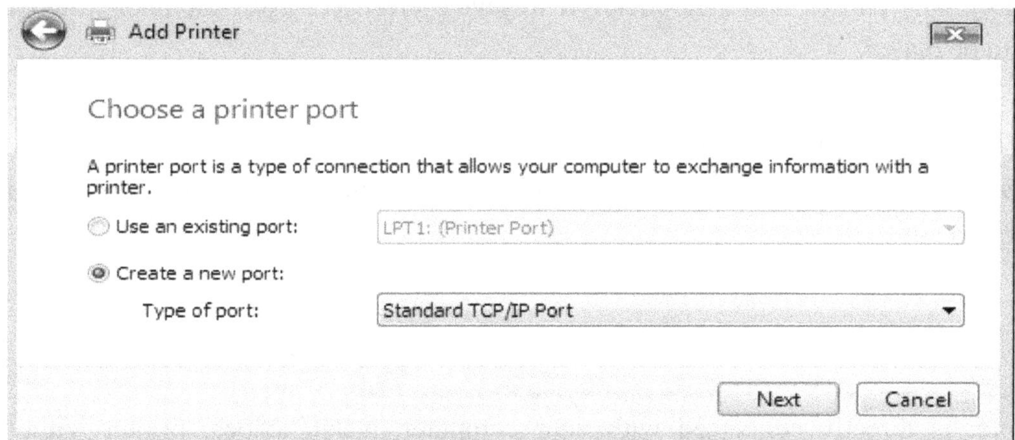

Select *the* ***TCP/IP device*** from the ***Device type*** category, and then type printer IP address. Click on ***Next*** to continue installing printer device.

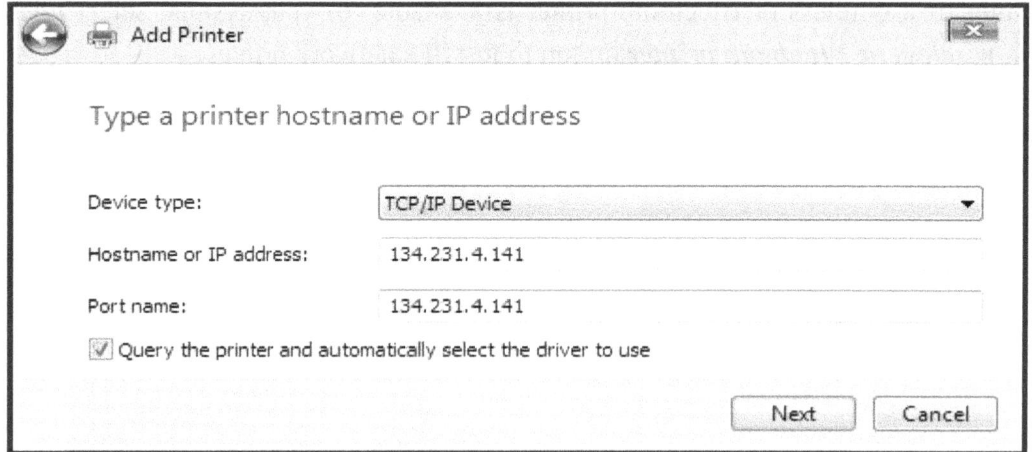

This process may take few minutes detecting your printer name and driver for your system. If your system did not detect the printer name and driver, then printer driver must be installed manually. To download printer driver from the manufacture website (get the printer name which you want to connect to, and then go to the manufacture website to download latest driver, e.g. if you have an HP printer, you would go to www.support.hp.com and click on ***Support and Driver*** link, and then type the name and model of your printer to view and download the HP printer driver) which is faster and reliable method to get the latest printer driver. If the system was successful to detect printer name and driver then click on ***Next*** to continue.

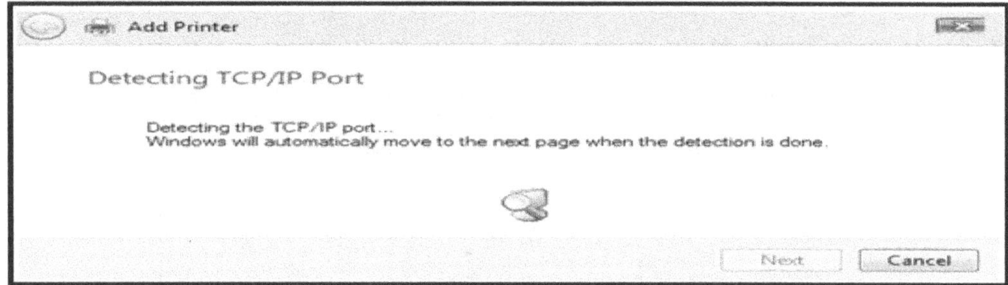

If your system did not detect printer device automatically, additional information needs to be provided to continue installing printer. Select the ***Generic Network Card*** type which is responsible to establish communication between your computer and the network. Check with network administrator to get printer configuration, if needed. Click on ***Next*** after selecting device type for your printer.

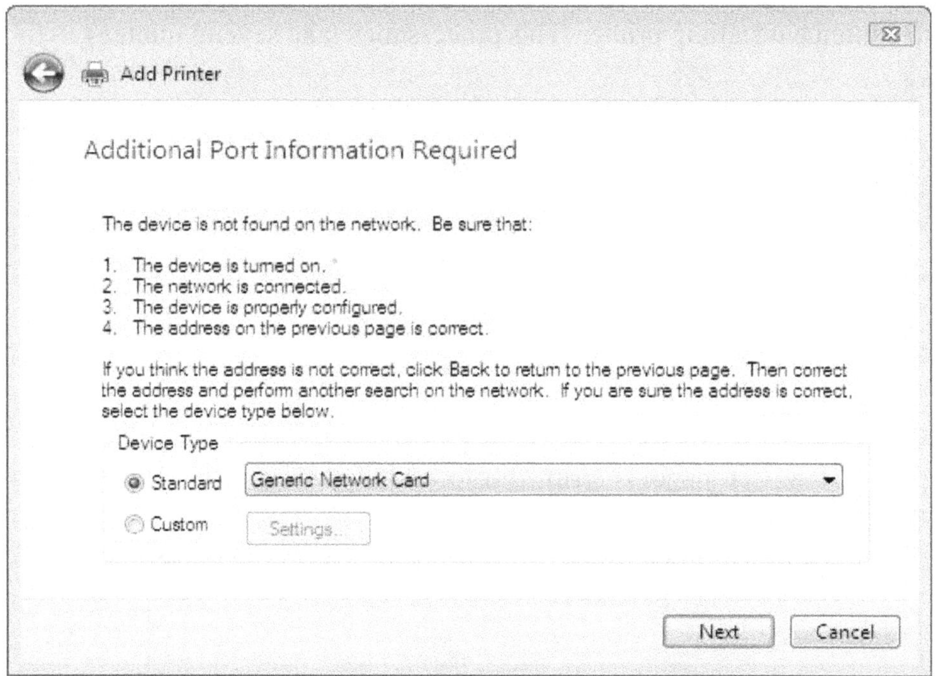

Choose the manufacture name and printer name and then click on ***Next*** to download printer device driver. If your system did not locate the manufacture name and printer name, then device driver needs to be installed manually.

To install driver manually, click on ***Have Disk***, and navigate to the driver folder in which device driver are saved, and then click on ***OK*** to start installing the device driver.

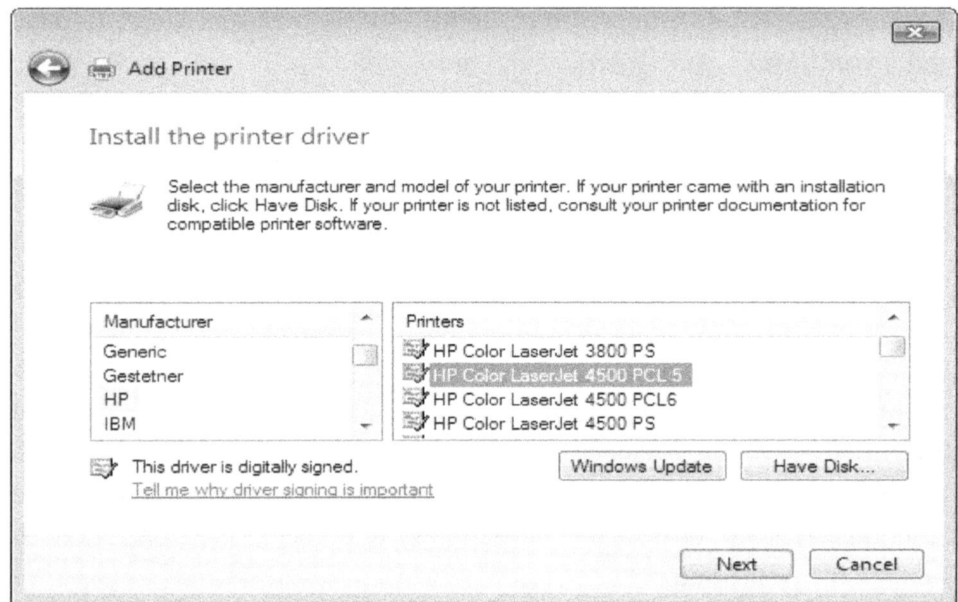

Click on ***Next*** to continue installing printer. This process may take several minutes.

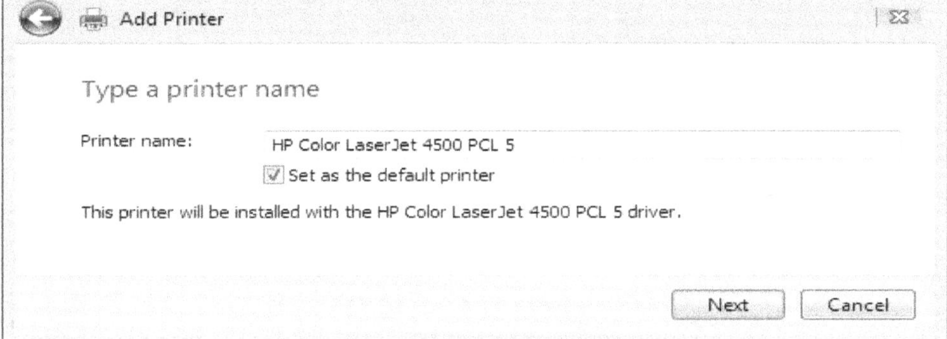

After successful installation of printer driver, click on ***Print a test page*** to see if printer is configured properly. If a test page is printed successfully, then click on ***Finish*** to complete the printer installation process.

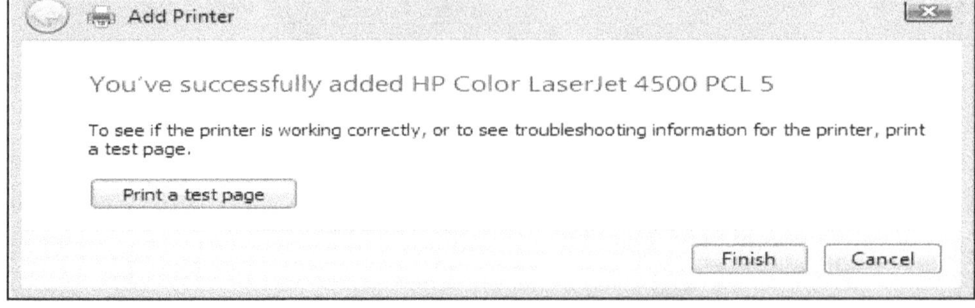

Remove a Printer

Open ***Hardware and Sound*** applet, and navigate to the ***Printers***, and then click on ***Remove a printer*** link. Select the printer that must be removed, and then click on ***Delete this printer*** option from the command bar. If you are prompted to confirm this action, click on ***Yes*** to continue. If the ***Delete this printer*** option is invisible on the command bar, click the double-arrow next to the ***Select printing preferences*** option from the command bar and then select ***Delete this printer*** option from the list.

Rename Printer

Open ***Hardware and Sound*** applet, and navigate to the ***Printers***, and then click on it to open. Select the printer that needs to be renamed, and click the double-arrow next to the ***Delete this printer*** option from the command bar to choose the ***Rename this printer*** option, and then type new name for your printer device.

Configure Printer Ports

To configure a printer port, open ***Hardware and Sound*** applet, and navigate to the ***Printers*** icon to open it. To configure a printer port, right-click on the printer icon and then select the ***Properties*** option from the list. In the ***Ports*** tab, click on ***Configure Port*** option to modify printer ports settings. Ports can be added, deleted, and configured by clicking on ***Add Port***, ***Delete Port***, and ***Configure Port***, respectively.

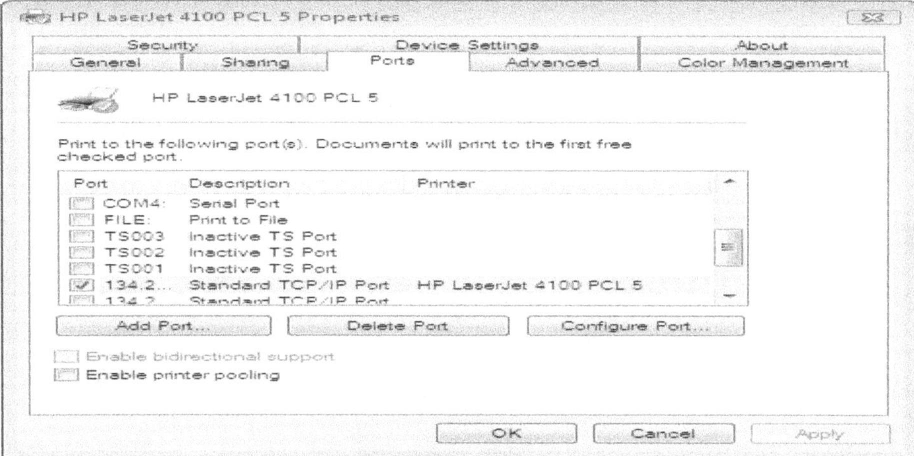

To configure port settings, type the *Port Name*, *Printer Name or IP Address*, and then adjust *Raw*, *LPR,* and *SNMP* settings. After making any changes to the printer settings, click ***OK*** to save preferences.

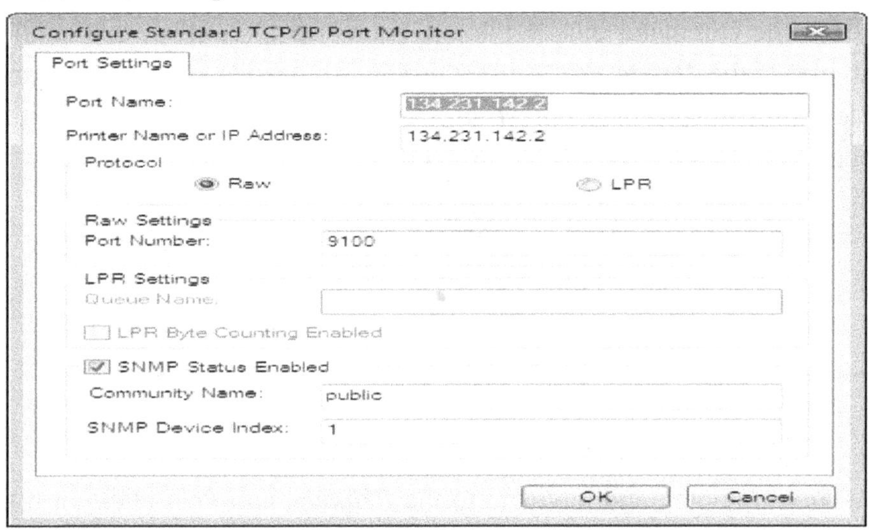

Limit Printing Time

From the ***Printer Properties*** window, click ***Advanced*** tab, and select the ***Available from*** option to adjust the printing time table. By default, printer is always available to users to print but you, as an administrator, can limit their privileges by adjusting printing hours, if necessary.

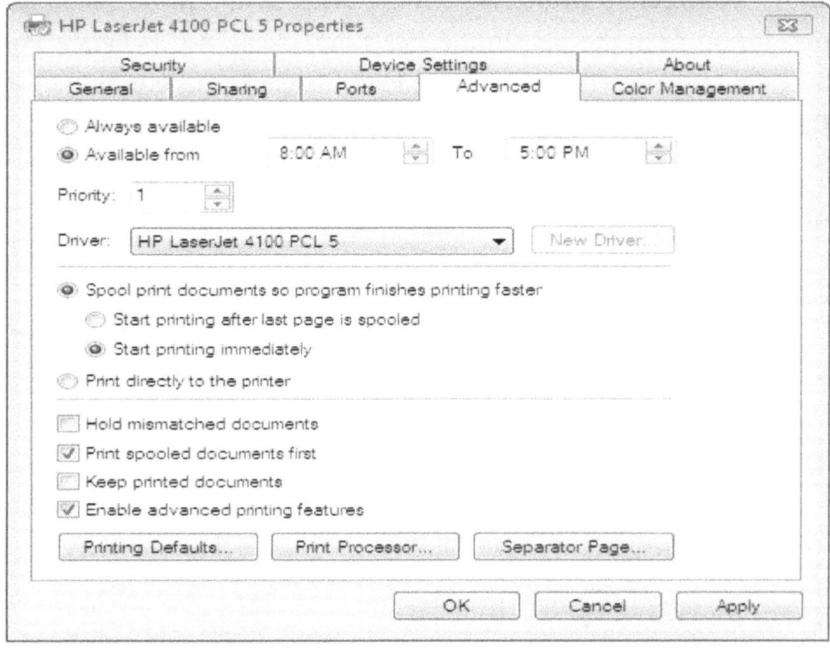

Permission to Maintain Printers

From the ***Printer Properties*** window, click the ***Security*** tab, under the ***Group or user names*** section. Select a user that needs privileges to maintain printer resources. Choose the following printer resources which can be managed by a user or a local administrator.

a. **Print**: By default, most users have permission to print.
b. **Manage printer**: Only local administrator or system administrators can manage printers.
c. **Manage documents**: By default, a system administrator has privileges to manage documents.
d. **Special permission**: If the special permissions are required to be added for a user, click on ***Advanced*** button *from* the ***Security*** tab and then make necessary changes that will affect a user but only system administrator is authorized to make such changes to a user profile.

Click on ***Apply*** to save security settings and then click on ***OK*** to close the window.

Appearance and Personalization Control Panel Applet

Appearance and Personalization applet enables administrators to change desktop background, change color scheme, and adjust screen resolution.

Change Desktop Background

To change desktop background theme, open ***Hardware and Sound*** applet, and navigate to the ***Personalization*** icon and then click on it to open. From the ***Personalization*** window, select the ***Desktop Background*** icon to adjust desktop background settings.

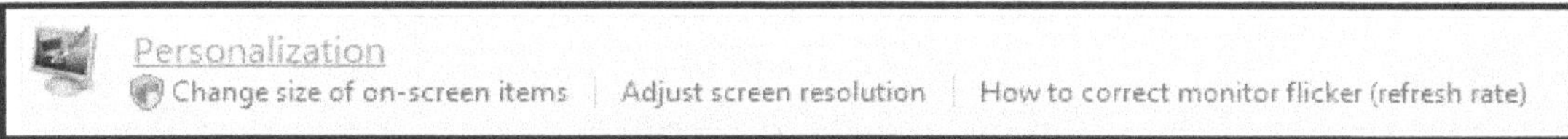

To select a desktop background theme, choose a picture file or video file that you want to set for background from the ***location*** drop down menu, and then choose position of the picture from the ***How should the picture or video be positioned*** section. Click on ***OK*** to save desktop background preferences.

Adjust Screen Resolution

Open ***Hardware and Sound*** applet from ***Control panel***. In the ***Hardware and Sound*** window, navigate to the ***Personalization***, and then click the ***Adjust screen resolution*** link.

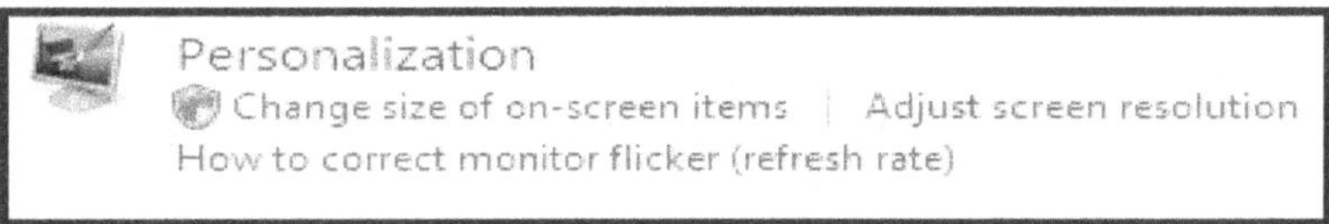

To get best color display for your monitor, select at-least 32 bit or higher color scheme from the ***Color*** section, and then adjust the resolution that meets your system requirement. Click on ***Apply*** and then click ***OK*** to save display settings.

Refresh Screen Rate

To refresh screen rate, click the ***Display Settings*** from the ***Personalization*** window. From the ***Display Settings*** dialog box, click on ***Advanced Settings*** button to adjust display settings.

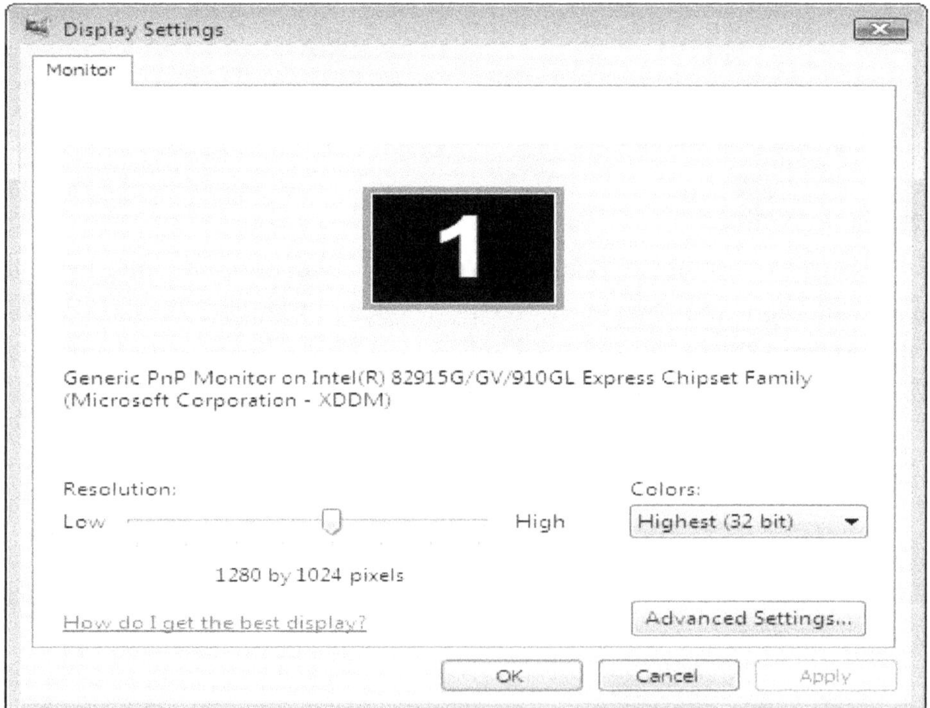

In the ***Monitor*** tab, choose the desired screen refresh rate from drop down menu of the ***Screen refresh rate*** under the ***Monitor Settings*** section. Click on ***Apply*** and then click ***OK*** to save changes.

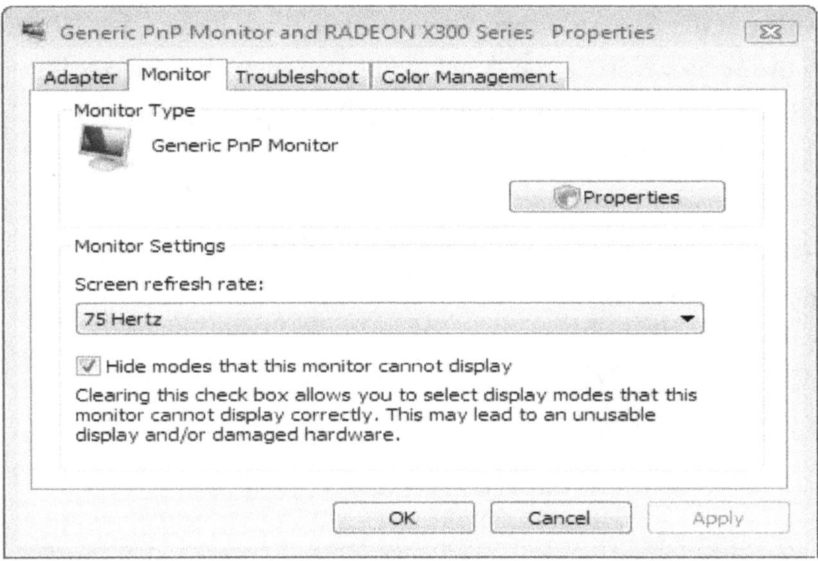

Computer Themes

A computer theme modifies the current sounds settings, icons settings, desktop screen saver settings, and other settings to change the look and feel of the computer. To change the computer theme, choose the ***Theme*** option from the ***Personalization*** window. From the ***Theme Settings*** dialog box, select a theme of your choice from the ***Theme*** drop down menu. The both *Windows Vista* and *Windows Classis* are recommended themes for your system. Click on ***Apply*** and then click ***OK*** to apply settings.

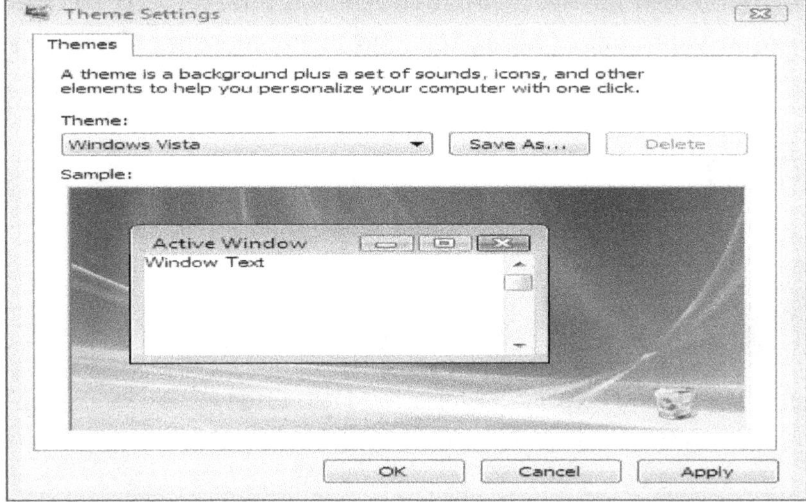

Screen Saver Customization

A screen saver is a picture or animation that covers computer screen, whenever it is in idle state. To customize screen saver, select the ***Screen Saver*** link from the ***Personalization*** window. From the ***Screen Saver Settings*** dialog box, select the ***3D Text*** screen saver option from the ***Screen Saver*** drop down menu, and then click on ***Settings*** to customize screen saver settings. To personalize your computer screen saver settings, fill out the ***text***, ***motion***, and ***surface style*** sections and then click ***OK*** to save changes.

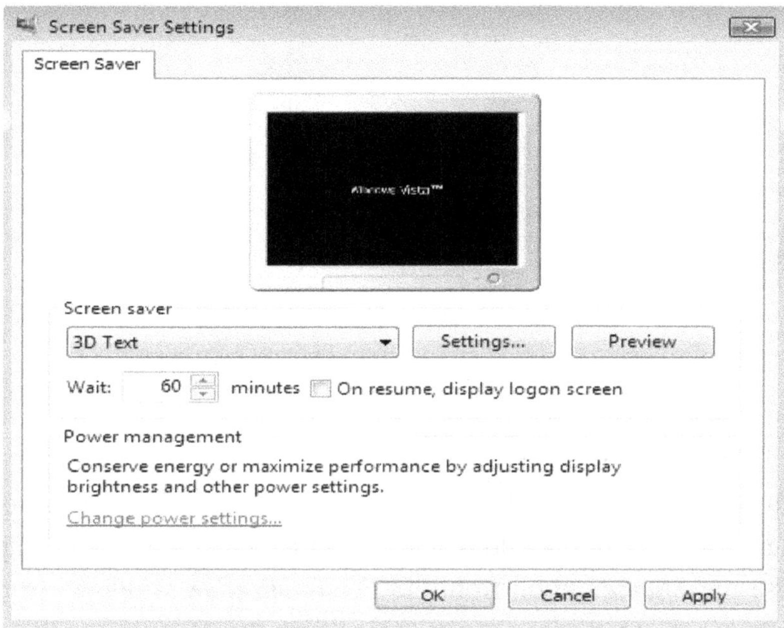

Adjust Font Size (DPI)

DPI stands for dots per inches and it measures printing or display resolution. To adjust system font size, right-click on your computer desktop, and then choose the ***Personalize*** option from the list. From the left navigation pane, click the ***adjust font size (DPI)*** link to modify DPI settings.

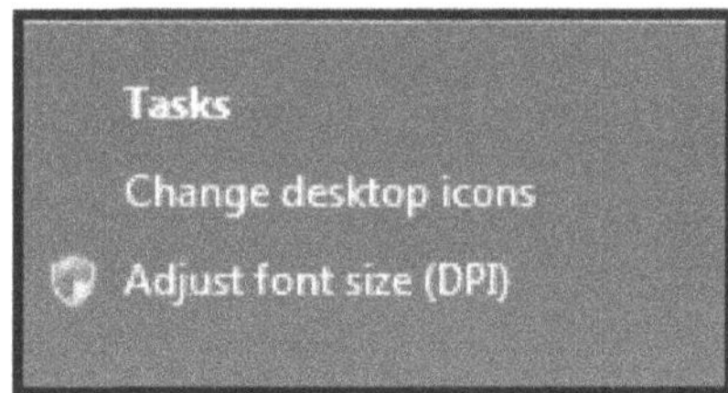

By default windows screen scale is 96 DPI, but larger scale (120 DPI) option is available to make text font appear bigger on your computer screen.

To customize DPI settings, click on ***Custom DPI*** button.

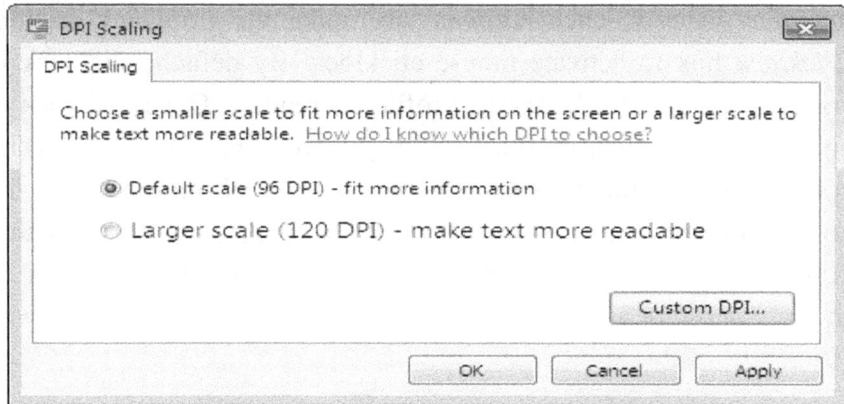

Select a percentage from drop down menu of ***Scale to this percentage of normal size***, and then click ***OK*** to save DPI settings.

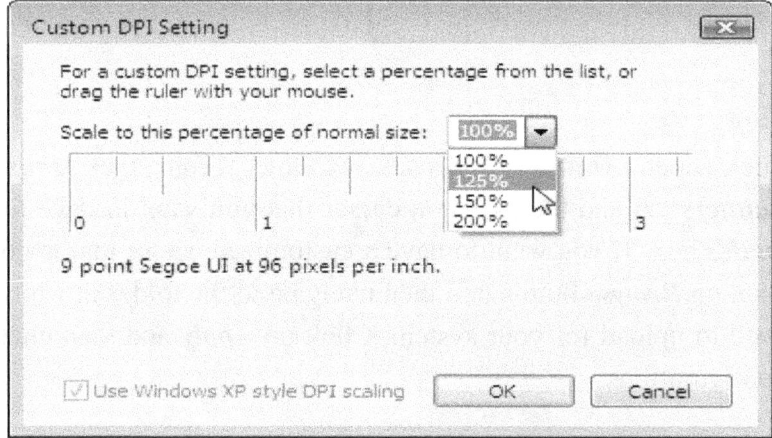

Mouse Button Configuration

To configure mouse button, open ***Hardware and Sound*** applet, and navigate to the ***Mouse*** icon and then click the ***Change button settings***.

In the ***Buttons*** tab, under the ***Button configuration*** section, check the ***Switch primary and secondary buttons*** box to change mouse button configuration. Click on ***Apply*** and then click ***OK*** to save mouse configurations.

Mouse Clicklock Configuration

From the ***Mouse Properties*** window, click ***Buttons*** tab, under the ***Clicklock*** section, check the ***Turn on Clicklock*** box to activate mouse clicklock. By default, clicklock is disabled but exceptions can be made to the user's profile on request. Once clicklock is enabled, you can drag any objects, such as files, folders, or any application shortcuts, without holding down the mouse button. You are required to press left mouse button for less than 5 seconds to activate clicklock and then it will allow you to move an object anywhere you want to, within a local user account. Click on ***Apply*** and then click ***OK*** to save changes. You can also configure advanced clicklock settings by clicking on ***Settings*** from the ***Clicklock*** section.

Mouse Pointer Configuration

To configure mouse pointer, open ***Mouse Properties*** window. From the ***Mouse Properties*** window, click ***Pointers*** tab and then select a cursor that you want to have for your system from the ***Customize*** box. If you want to have a customized cursor that is not a part of your system yet, click on ***Browse*** button and then navigate to the folder in which the customized cursor is saved to upload for your system. Click on ***Apply*** and then click ***OK*** to save mouse pointer configurations.

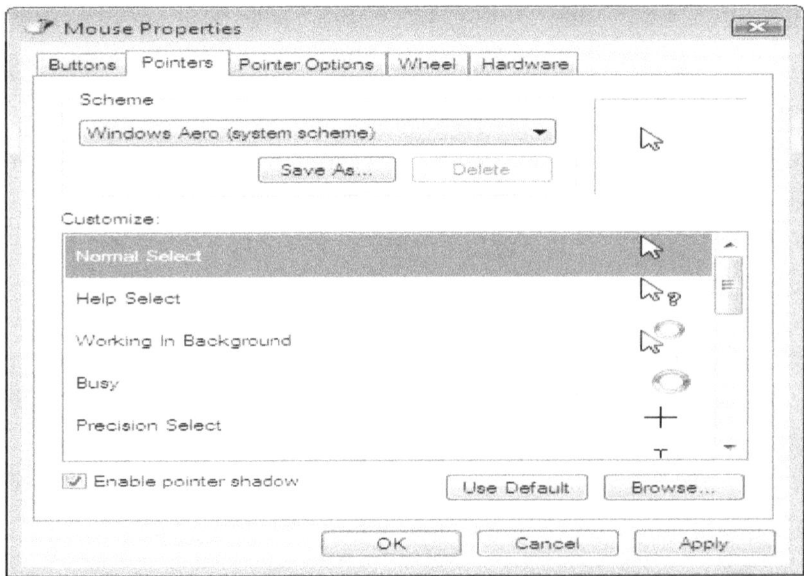

Visibility of Mouse Cursor

From the ***Mouse Properties*** window, click ***Pointer Options*** tab, under the ***Visibility*** section, check the ***Show location of the pointer when I press the CTRL key*** box to activate visibility of mouse cursor. By default, this option is disabled. It is recommended to enable this option for users who are low in vision, and are having hard time finding mouse cursor. A big round circle will appear on the location of the pointer once you press and release the ***Ctrl*** key (located at most left-bottom of a standard keyboard). Click on ***Apply*** and then click ***OK*** to save mouse cursor preferences.

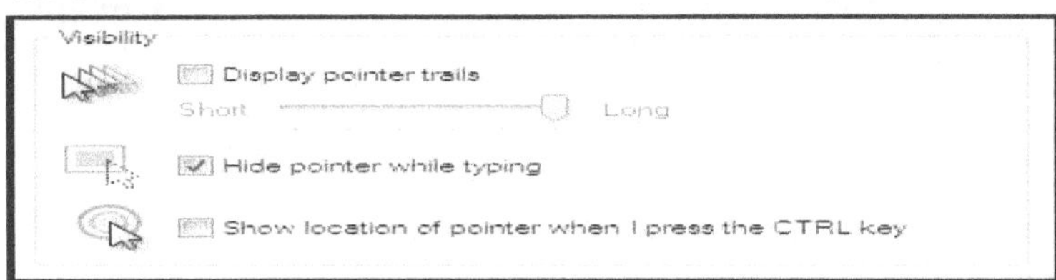

Keyboard Configuration

To configure keyboard settings, open ***Hardware and Sound*** applet, and navigate to the ***Keyboard***, and then click on it to open ***Keyboard Properties*** window.

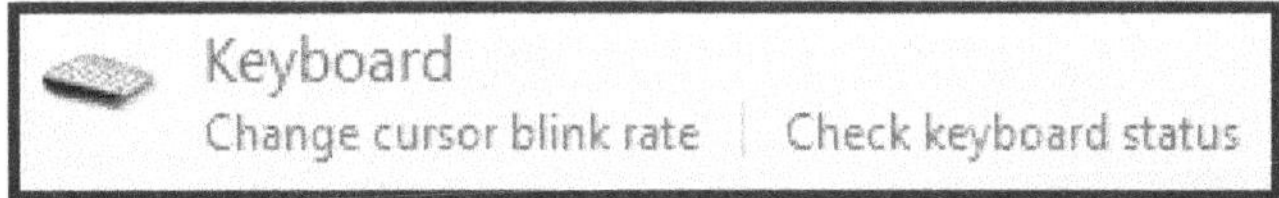

From the ***Keyboard Properties*** window, the character repeat and cursor blink rate can be adjusted by moving slider right or left to increase or decrease the speed of character repeat and cursor blinking rate, respectively. Click on ***Apply*** and then click ***OK*** to save keyboard preferences.

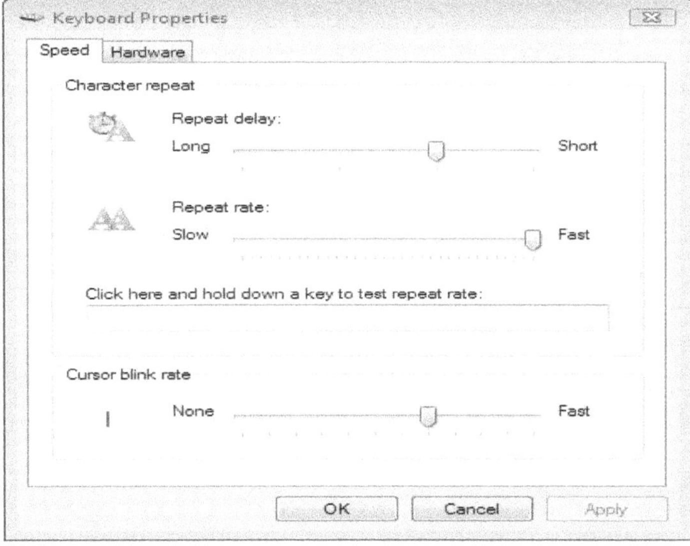

Scanners and Cameras Configuration

To run the scanner and camera setup, open the ***Hardware and Sound*** applet, and navigate to the ***Scanners and Cameras*** icon, and then click ***View scanners and cameras*** link to open ***Scanner and Camera Properties*** window.

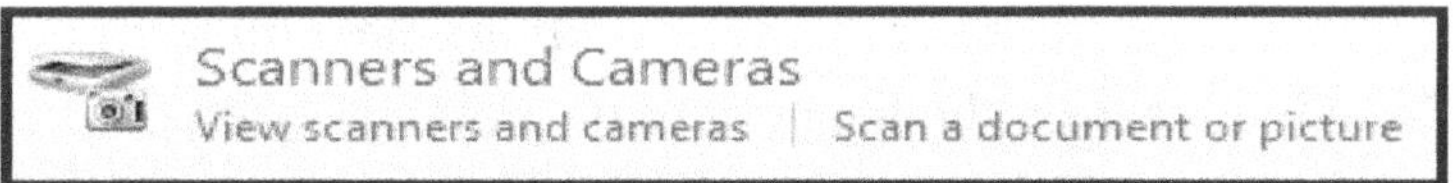

In the ***Scanners and Cameras*** window, click on ***Add Device*** button to add the device manually, if your system did not detect the attached scanner or the camera automatically.

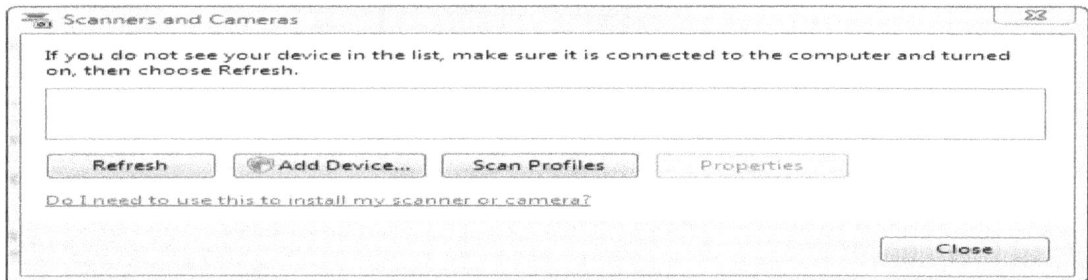

If you are prompted to confirm this action, click on ***Continue*** or provide administrative credentials to continue installing device on to your system. To start the scanner and camera installation wizard, click on ***Next*** to perform a scan to locate attached devices with your system.

Check the manufacturer and the model of the device which is connected with your system and then click on ***Next***.

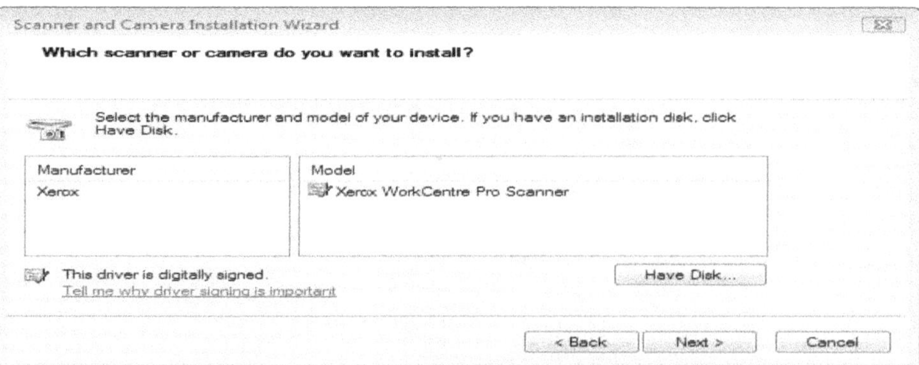

Type a name to identify the device and then click on ***Next***.

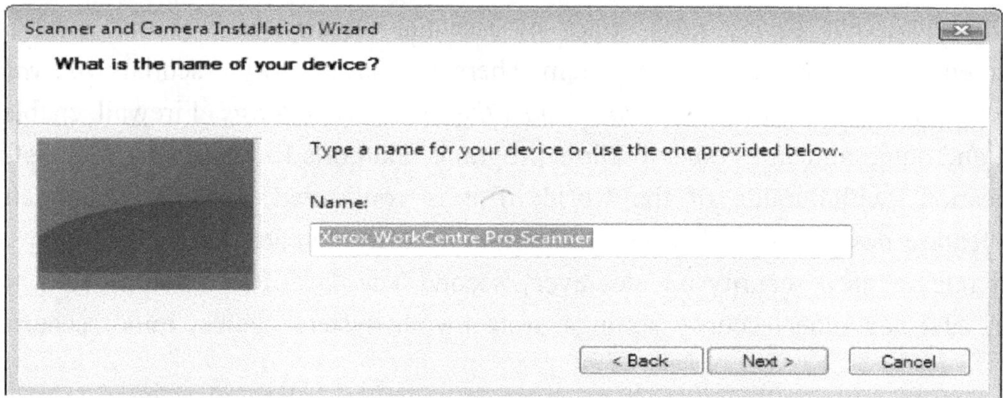

Click on ***Finish*** to complete scanner and camera installation.

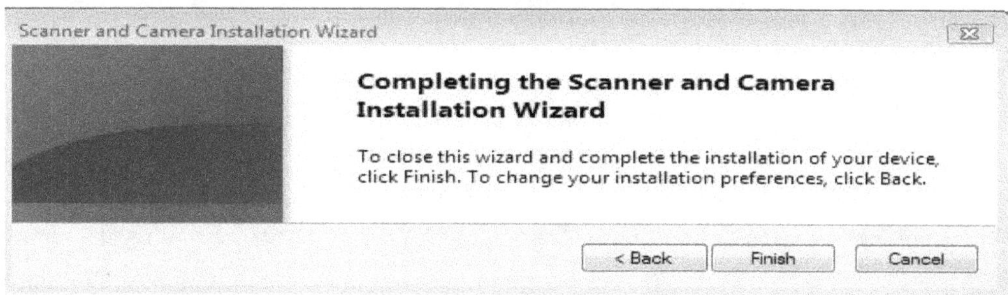

To print a test page, open the ***Scanners and Cameras*** window, and then click on ***Properties*** button.

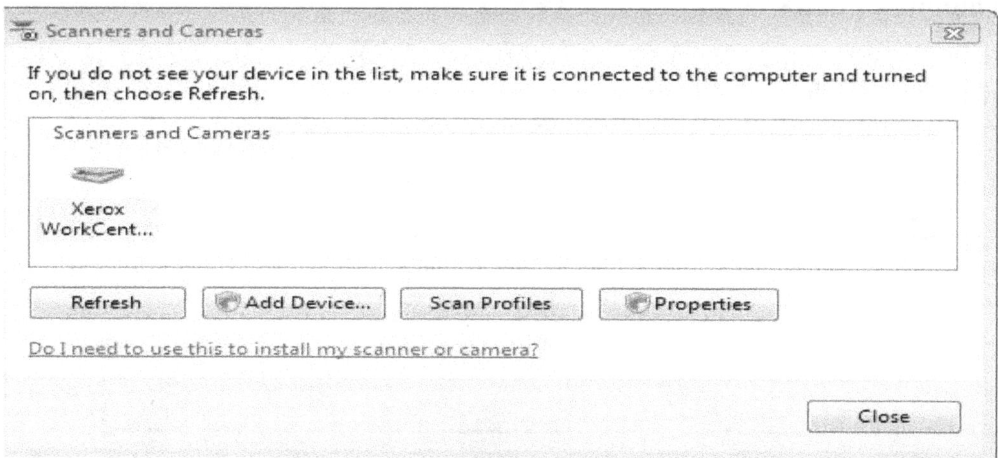

In the ***General*** tab of the ***Scanner Properties*** window, under the ***Diagnostics*** section, select the ***Test Scanner*** option to scan a test page. A test page will be scanned if the scanner is configured properly. Click on ***OK*** to close the window.

Security Center

The *Windows Security Center* keeps track of essential security settings that must be updated to enhance the security of the system. There are four security essentials, *firewall, automatic updating, malware protection, and other security settings*. Firewall enables incoming and outgoing connections to allow programs and ports to establish a successful communication with outside of the world, if it is configured correctly. Automatic updating feature downloads and installs important security patches for your system as Microsoft releases new security updates every second Tuesday of the month. Malware protection, and any other security settings protect your system against minor security threads.

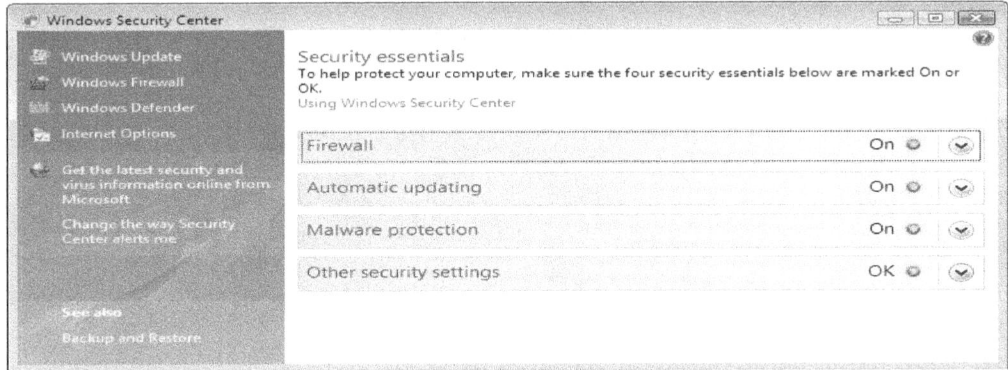

Check Windows Updates

To check for Windows updates, open the ***Hardware and Sound*** applet, and navigate to the ***Security*** icon, and then click on it to open.

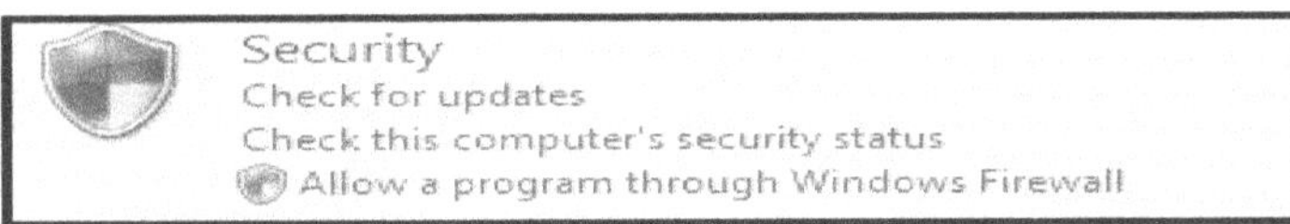

From the Security window, click the ***Check for updates*** link from the ***Security Center*** applet.

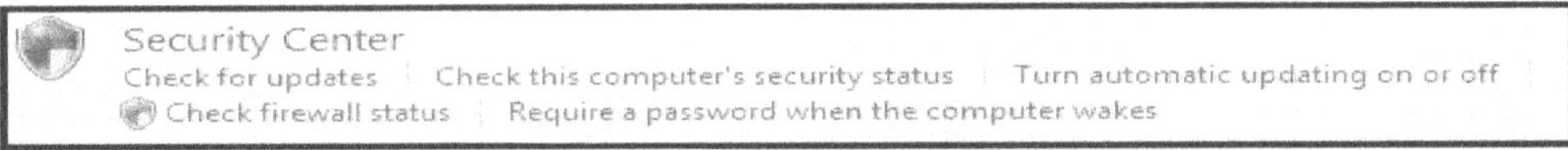

From left navigation pane of the ***Windows update***, click on ***Check for updates*** link to check for new available updates for your system, and then click on ***Install Updates*** button to download latest Windows updates. It may take several minutes downloading and installing the latest updates for your system. If Windows updates are installed successfully, you will be notified. A cold re-boot is required to apply changes to the system.

Windows Updates Configuration

To turn automatic Windows updates on or off, click the ***Turn automatic updating on or off*** link from the ***Security Center*** applet

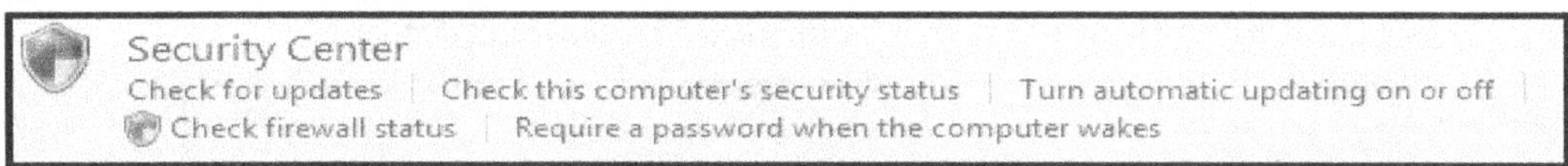

From the ***Change Settings*** window, the following options are available to choose to protect your system against any known security threads in computing industry.

- **Install updates automatically (recommended):** This is recommended setting for Microsoft users, the system will download and install updates automatically as Microsoft releases new updates.
- **Download updates but let me choose whether to install them:** The system will download the Windows updates for the system but will let you choose which updates needs to be installed for your system.
- **Check for updates but let me choose whether to download and install them:** The system will check for the updates but allow you to choose Windows updates that needs to be downloaded and install for your system.
- **Never check for updates (not recommended):** This setting is not recommended by Microsoft due to the high risk of security threads in computing industry.
- **Recommended updates:** If this option is checked, the only recommended updates from Microsoft will be downloaded and installed for your system.
- **Update service:** If this option is selected, you will be prompted to download available updates for other products of Microsoft, such as Windows Defender, a spyware program, and Windows media player, a CD/DVD movie player.

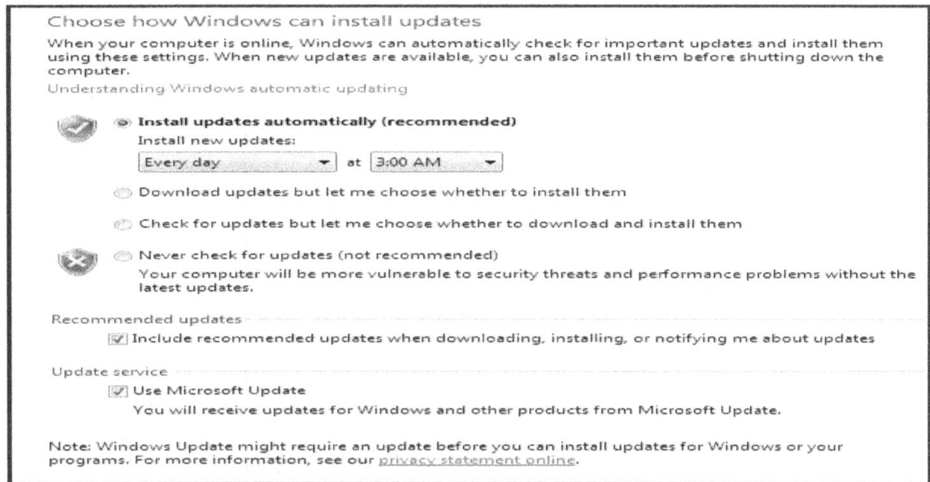

Windows Firewall Configuration

To configure *Windows Firewall*, open the ***Hardware and Sound*** applet, and navigate to the ***Security*** icon, and then click on it to open. From the ***Security*** window, click the ***Turn Windows Firewall on or off*** link from the ***Windows Firewall*** applet.

It is recommended to have *Windows Firewall* turned on to block unauthorized users connecting to your computer over the network. If someone has access to your computer, they can install malicious programs to delete, remove, and modify system registry to make your system unstable. The following *Windows Firewall* options are available to choose from.

- **On (recommended):** This is recommended option to protect your system against malicious codes that can be installed by a third-party.
- **Block all incoming connections:** This option is only recommended while connecting to the unsecured connection. A unsecured connection is available for free of charge to the public at the airport or in the coffee shop. All the incoming connections will be ignored.
- **Off (not recommended):** This is not a recommended option because it makes easier for unauthorized users to access your computer over the network.

Select one of the above options to set *Windows Firewall* settings. Click on ***Apply*** and then click ***OK*** to save preferences.

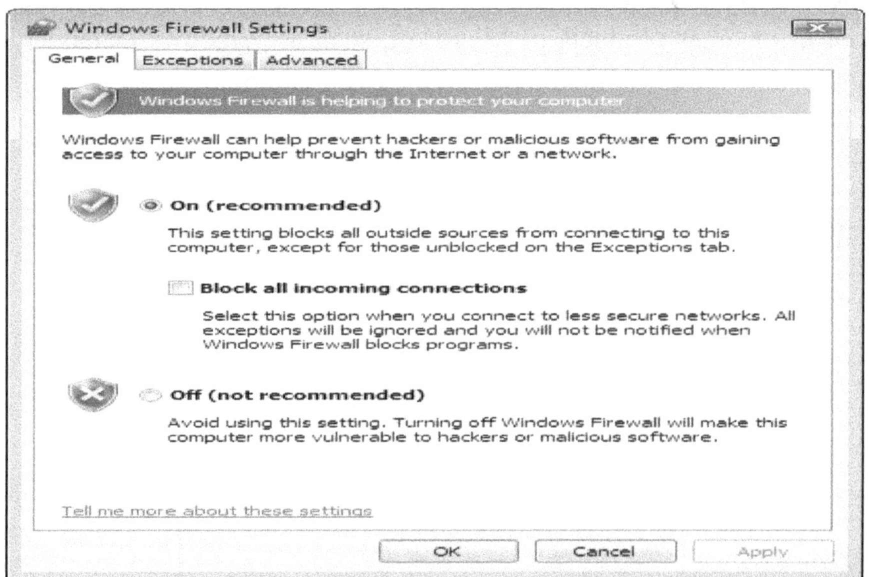

Windows has exceptions for programs and for network ports that can be blocked to restrict users to gain access to your computer or programs. To add a program to the exception list, click on ***Add program*** button and then select the program you wish to allow communication through *Windows Firewall.* To add a network port to *Windows Firewall* exception list, click on ***Add port*** button and then type name of the port, port number and then select protocol type to allow communication through the port. Click on ***Apply*** and then click ***OK*** to save changes.

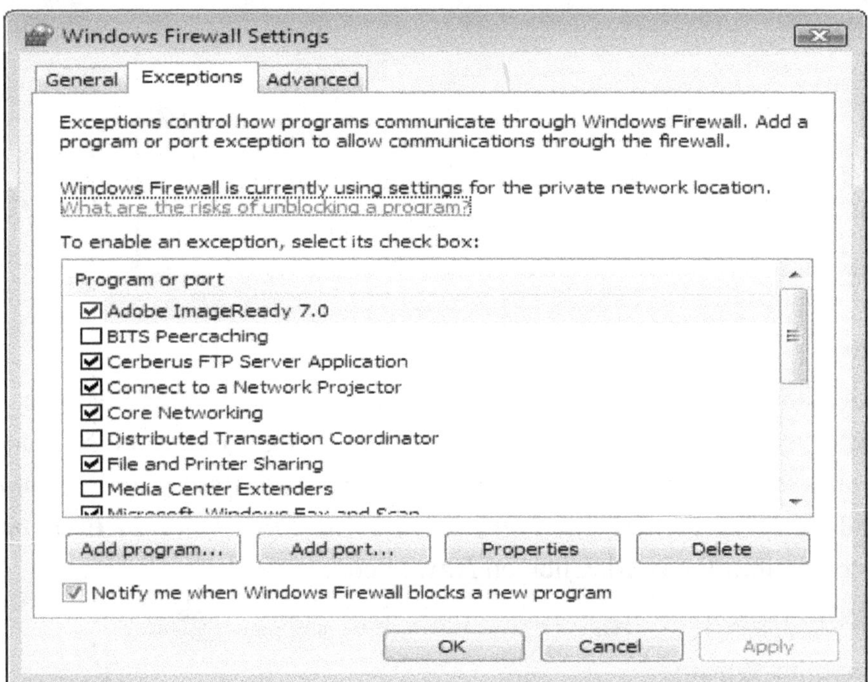

Programs and Features

Programs and Features control panel applet allows system administrators to delete, modify, install, and manage programs and Windows updates. To uninstall a program, open ***Hardware and Sound*** applet, navigate to the ***Programs*** icon, and then click on it to open. From the ***Programs*** panel, navigate to the ***Programs and Features*** icon and then click on it to open.

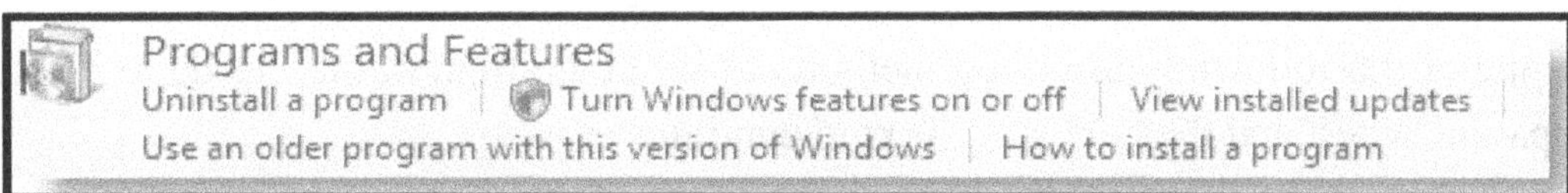

Select the application that you want to remove and then choose the ***Uninstall*** option from the command bar. You may be asked to provide administrative credentials to perform this task.

View Windows Installed Updates

To view installed Windows updates, open the ***Programs*** control panel applet, navigate to the ***Programs and Features*** and then click the ***View installed updates*** link. If any of the Windows updates are causing problems for your system. Click on the update which is causing problem and then click on ***Uninstall*** option from the command bar to remove the update to bring the system to the pervious state when it was working properly.

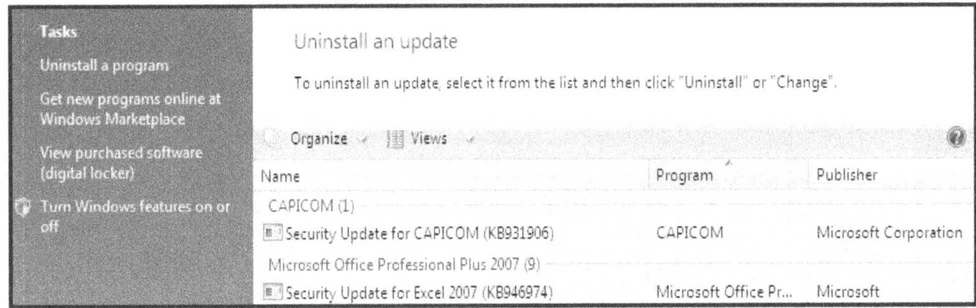

Compatibility Wizard

A compatibility mode allows an application to run with the earlier versions of Microsoft operating system such as Windows 95, 98, 2000, Windows ME, Windows NT, and Windows XP. To run a compatibility wizard for a program, open the ***Programs and Features*** window and then click the ***Use an older program with this version of Windows*** link to run program compatibility wizard. Click on ***Next*** to continue.

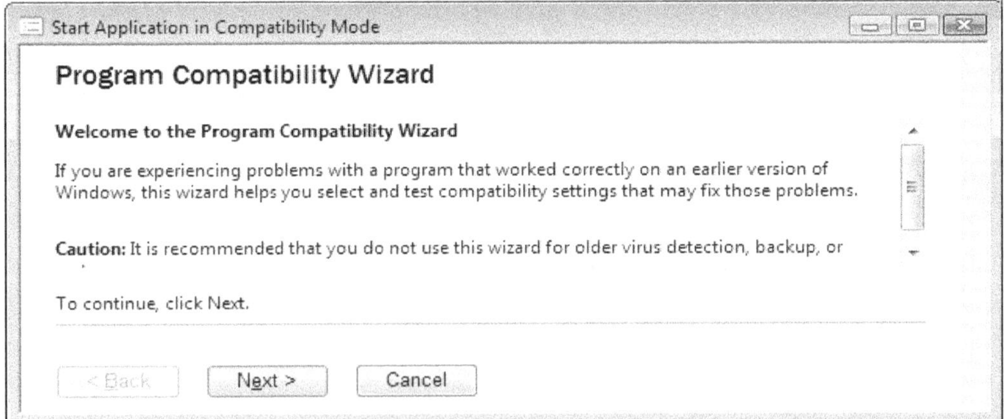

Choose one of the following described methods to locate a program that needs to be run for compatibility test and then click on ***Next*** to continue.

- *I want to choose from a list of programs*
- *I want to use the program in the CD-ROM drive*
- *I want to locate the program manually*

The compatibility wizard may take few minutes to scan your system to locate all those programs which are not compatible with the current version of Microsoft Windows Vista. Go through the list of programs to select the program that you want to run for compatibility test.

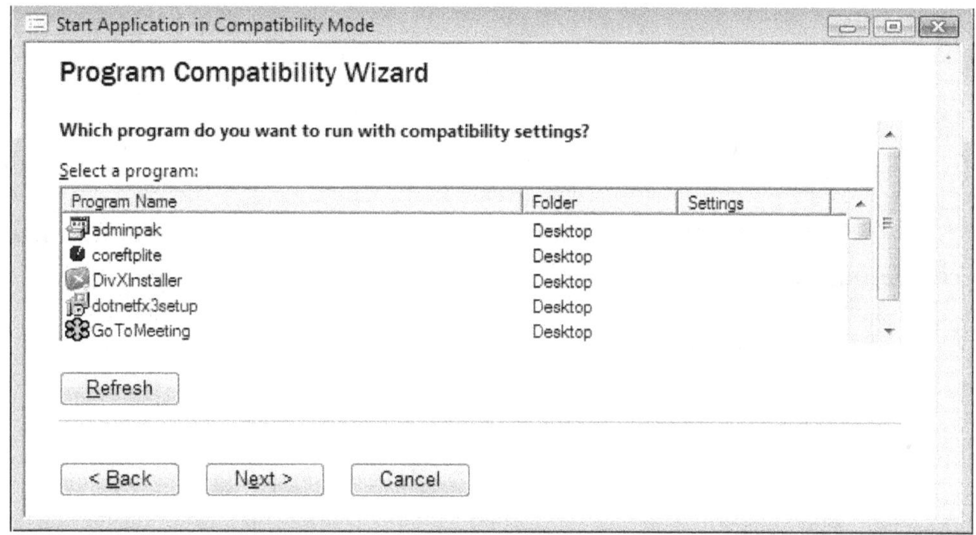

Click on ***Next*** after choosing one of the following compatibility testing modes:

a. *Windows XP (Service Pack 2)*
b. *Windows 95*
c. *Windows 98 /Windows Me*
d. *Windows 2000*

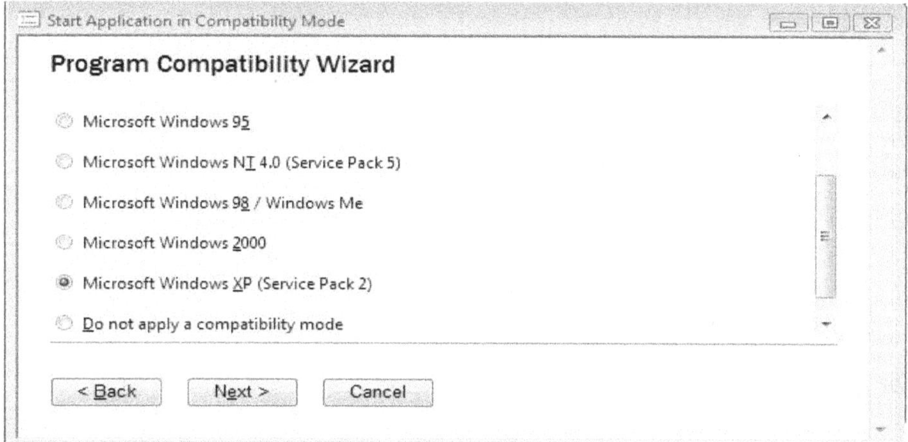

Choose an available display settings for the program and then click on ***Next***.

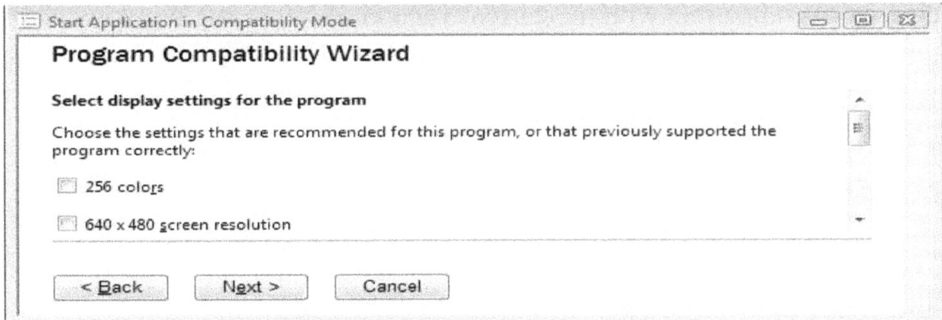

If the program needs to be run with administrator privileges in future, check the ***Run this program as an administrator*** option and then click on ***Next*** to continue.

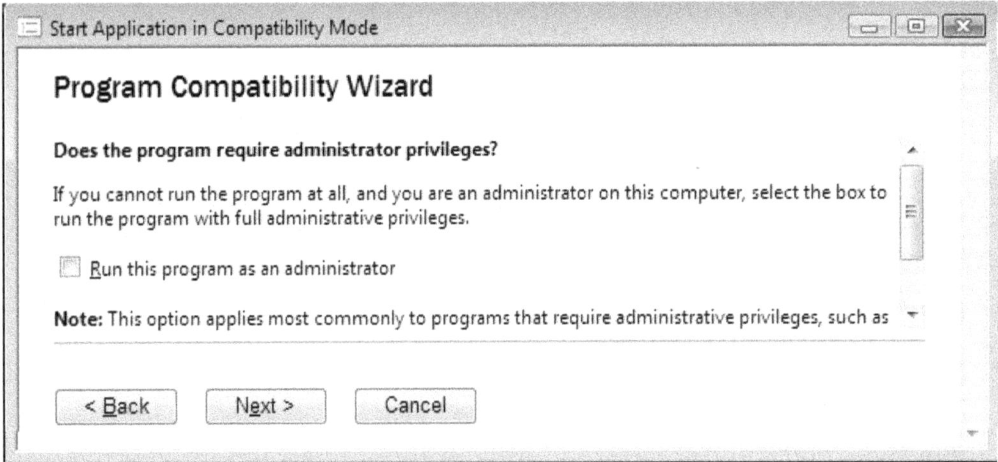

To run the compatibility test for the selected program, click on ***Next***.

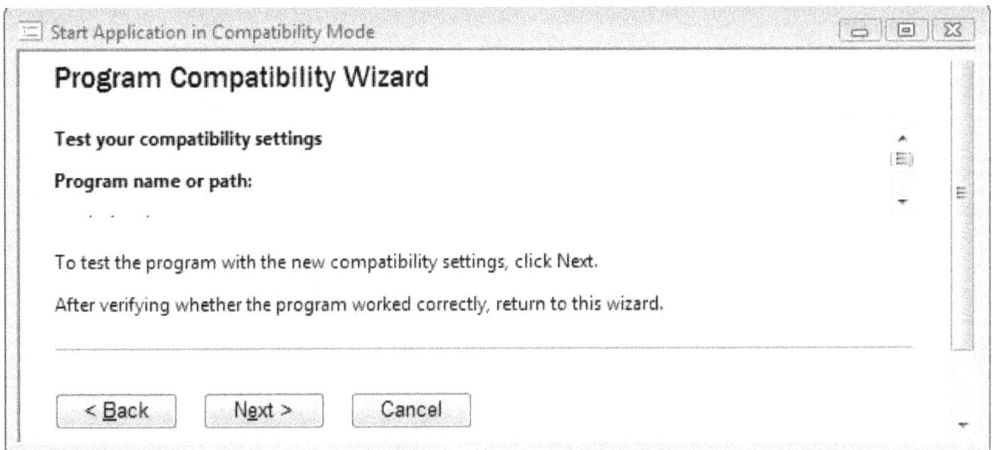

If the program works as expected, choose the ***Yes, set this program to always use these compatibility settings*** option; otherwise choose the ***No, try different compatibility***

settings option and then repeat the procedure to check for compatibility settings that might work for your system. Click on ***Next*** to apply compatibility settings.

Clock, Language, and Region Settings Configuration

Open the control panel home, and navigate to the ***Clock***, ***Language***, ***and Region*** icon, and then click on it to open to adjust clock, language, and the regional settings.

Click the ***Regional and Language Options*** applet from right-pane of the ***Clock, Language, and Region*** window.

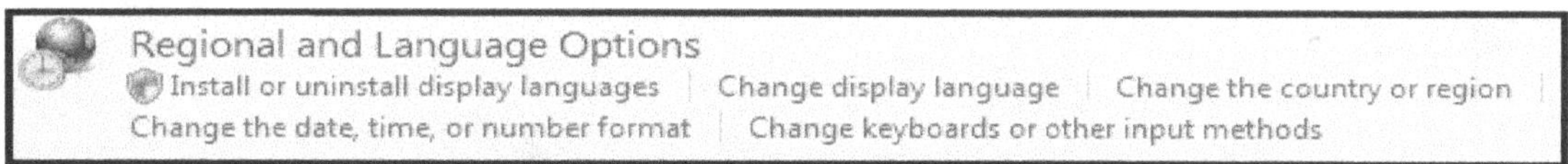

In the ***Format*** tab, choose the display format from the ***Current format*** drop down menu to adjust number, currency, and time and date formats. To customize the format settings, click on ***Customize this format*** and then set the value for each tab. Click on ***Apply*** and then click ***OK*** to save changes.

In the ***Location*** tab of the ***Regional and language*** dialog box, change the location of the current system and then click on ***Apply*** and then click on ***OK*** to save changes.

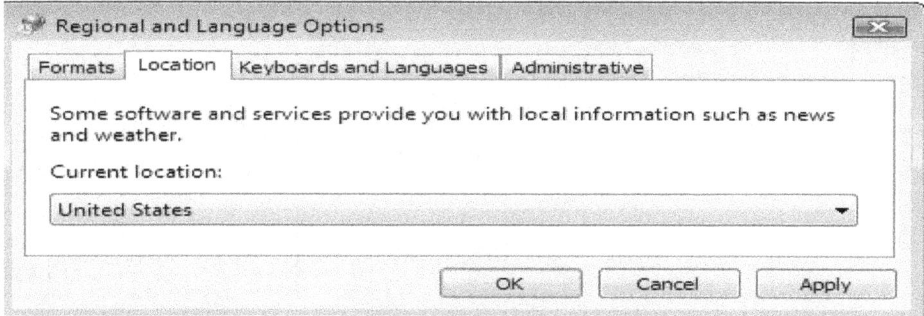

In ***Keyboard and Languages*** tab, click on ***Change keyboards*** button to change keyboard input language.

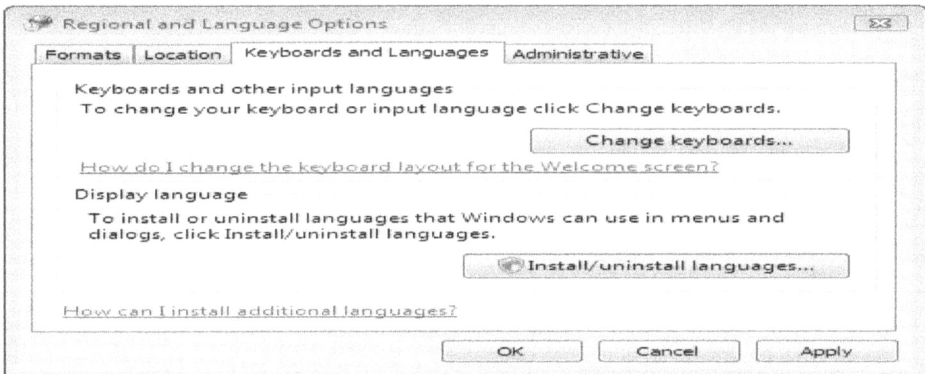

From the ***Text Services and Input Languages*** dialog box, click on ***Add*** another input keyboard language.

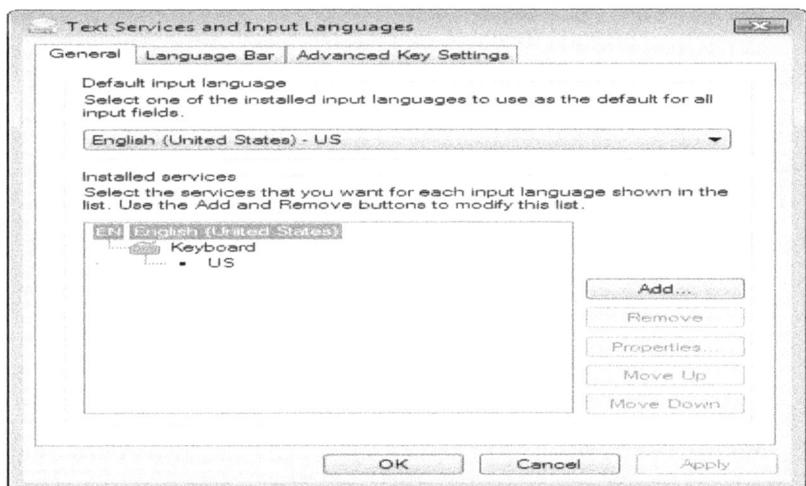

From the ***Add Input language*** dialog box, click the plus sign next to the language list to see available supported language regions. Select the language and region in which you live in, and then click on ***OK*** to add an alternative input language. To remove the language, select the input language you want to remove from the ***Text Services and Input Languages*** window, and then click on ***Remove***.

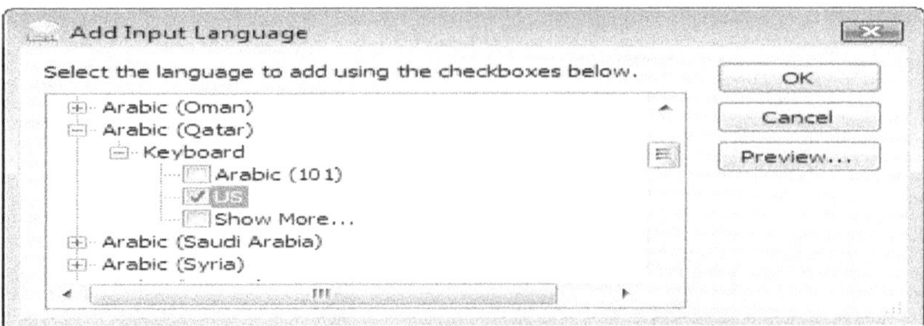

Now, a new language input pack is available for you to compose e-mails or create documents as needed. Click on ***Apply*** and then click on ***OK*** to save changes.

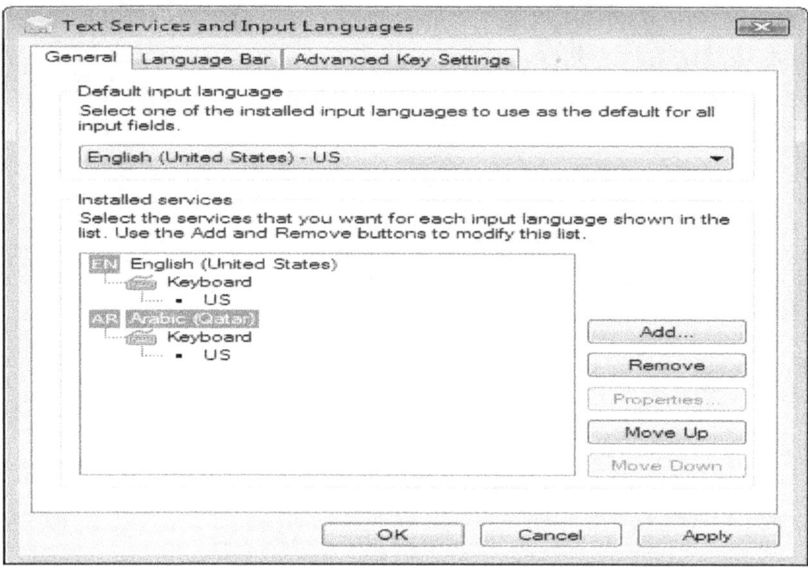

Time and Date Settings

To adjust time and date settings, open ***Control Panel Home*** and navigate to the ***Clock***, ***Language***, ***and Region*** icon, and then click on it to open the ***Date and Time*** applet.

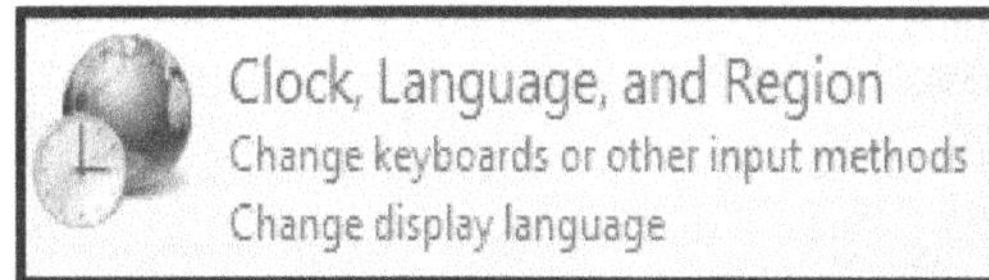

To modify date and time settings, click the ***Date and Time*** tab, and then click on ***Change date and time*** button.

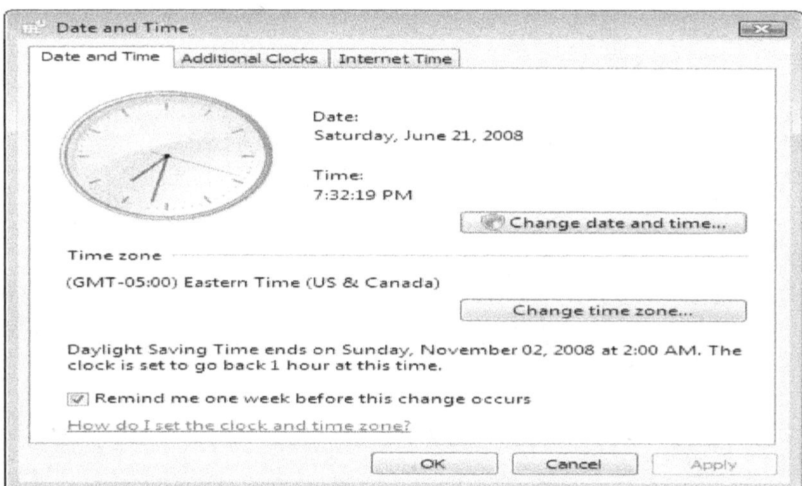

To adjust the clock time, double-click either hours or minutes or seconds, and then use up or down arrows (in front of the clock) to increase or decrease the value. To set the date, use the arrows ▸ ◂ to increase or decrease the months, and then click on today's date from the ***Date*** section. Click on ***OK*** to save date and time preferences.

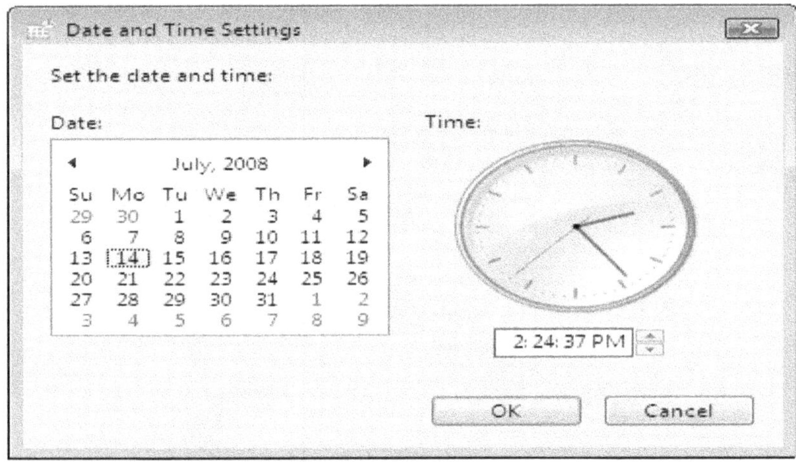

Daylight Saving Time Configuration

To change time zone and daylight savings time for the system, click the ***Date and Time*** tab, and then click on ***Change time zone*** button from the ***Time zone*** section. It is recommended to change the time zone settings when your system moves to a different location of the time zone. For example, if you moved from Minnesota (a state of United States of America) to California state (a state of United States of America), computer time zone settings must be changed. To enable daylight saving time, check the ***Automatically adjust clock for Daylight Saving Time*** option. Choose the time zone from the ***Time zone*** drop down menu, and then click on ***OK*** to save time zone preferences.

To synchronize Internet time for your system, click the ***Internet Time*** tab, and then click on ***Change settings*** button.

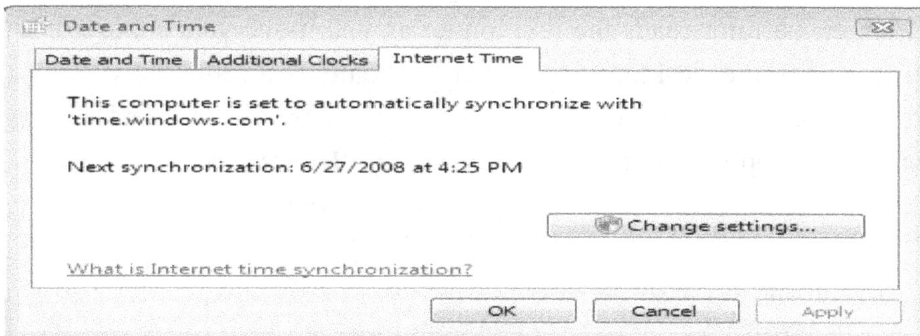

Select an Internet time server (available Internet time servers are, *time.windows.com, time.nist.gov, time-nw.nist.gov, time-a.nist.gov, and time-b.nist.gov*) from ***Server*** drop down menu and then click on ***Update now*** button to synchronize the computer clock with the server time. Click ***OK*** to save changes for the system.

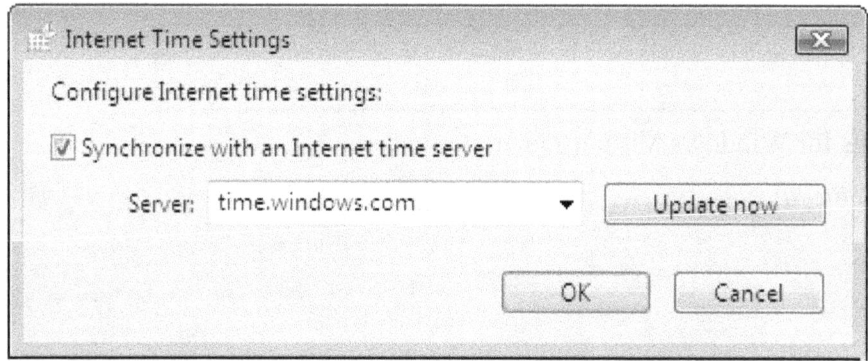

Additional Clocks Configuration

To add additional clocks for different time zones, right-click on the clock from the system tray (notification area of taskbar, located at right-bottom of the computer desktop), and then choose the ***Adjust Date/Time*** option. From the ***Date and Time*** dialog box, click the ***Additional Clocks*** tab, and check the ***Show this clock*** box. Select a time zone for your desired clock, and then enter an appropriate display name for each clock. You can add additional two clocks excluding the system clock on your system. Click on ***Apply*** and then click ***OK*** to save settings. To view additional clocks, move the mouse cursor over the system clock.

Ease of Access Center

The *Ease of Access Center* adjusts accessibility settings, such as magnifier that makes the on-screen text font larger, narrator reads the text louder as you move your mouse or any other pointing device across the desktop. On-screen keyboard is an alternative way to input text using pointing device or mouse. To open *Ease of Access Center* window, open the ***Hardware and Sound*** applet, navigate to the ***Ease of Access*** icon to open it. To quickly access *Ease of Access Center* window, press (*Windows key* + *U*) simultaneously.

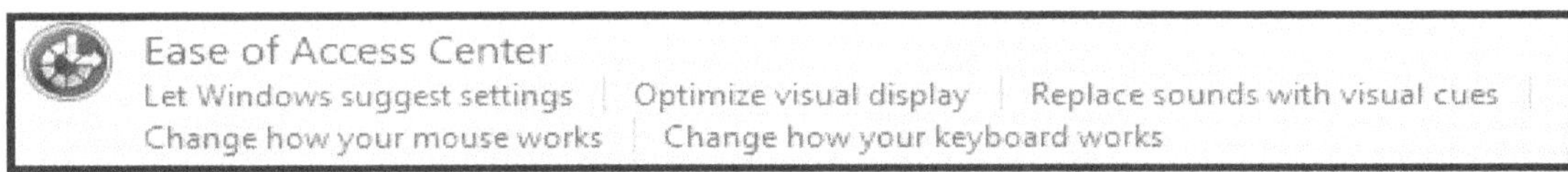

Windows Magnifier Configuration

From *Ease of Access Center* window, click on ***Start Magnifier*** to adjust the presentation, and the tracking settings.

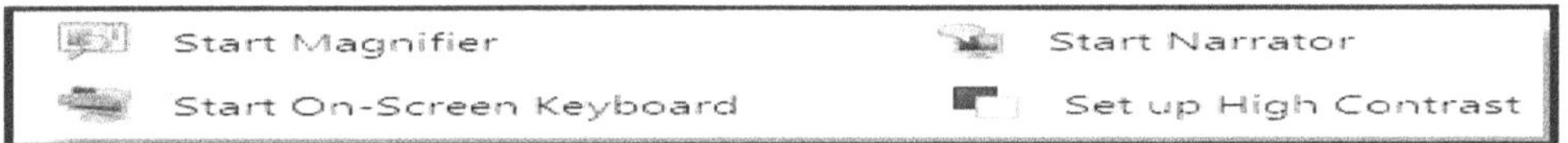

The magnifier options for Windows Vista users are:

a. *Minimize on startup*
b. *Scale factor*
c. *Invert colors*
d. *Docked*
e. *Docked position – Top, Left, Right, and Bottom*
f. *Follow mouse cursor*
g. *Follow keyboard focus*
h. *Follow text editing*

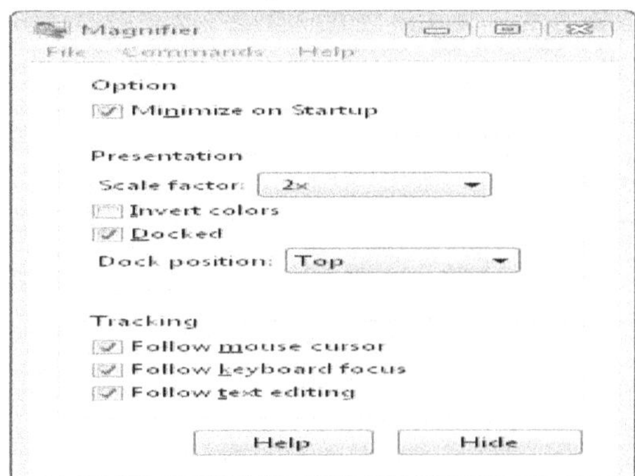

Windows Vista Narrator Configuration

From *Ease of Access Center* window, click on ***Start Narrator*** to modify narrator preferences.

Narrator starts reading the active window content as soon as it starts. It will read letter by letter as you type in the Microsoft Word document and it is useful technique for low vision users to type correctly. To stop Microsoft Narrator, click on ***Exit*** from ***Microsoft Narrator*** window.

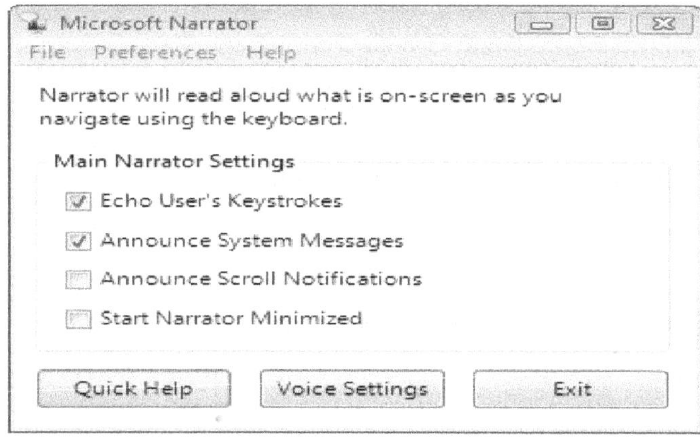

Windows Vista On-Screen Keyboard Configuration

From *Ease of Access Center* window, click on ***Start On-Screen Keyboard*** to adjust on-screen keyboard settings.

On-Screen Keyboard is designed for those users who want to input the text using the mouse or any other pointing devices.

Question: What is Windows Calendar?

Answer: Windows Calendar is a scheduling application to record appointments and tasks.

Question: What is an extension of Windows Calendar file?

Answer: The extension of the Windows Calendar file is *.ics*.

Question: Define Device Manager?

Answer: Device Manager provides an overview of hardware devices. It allows an administrator to change hardware configuration settings such as installing device drivers, enabling and disabling devices to troubleshoot a device problem.

Question: Can I enable a hardware device?

Answer: Yes you may enable a hardware device, if you have administrative privileges.

Questions: Can I disable a hardware device?

Answer: Yes, an administrator has privileges to disable a hardware device, but it is not recommended to do so unless it is necessary.

Question: Can I wake up a network adaptor?

Answer: Yes you may, if your system is configured properly.

Question: Why should I update a hardware device driver?

Answer: To establish a successful communication between two hardware devices.

Question: Does Windows Vista capable of searching hardware device driver automatically?

Answer: Yes, if your system is configured properly for Windows updates.

Question: Define code 1, 10, and 28?

Answer: The codes are explained following.

- The code 1 shows that device is not configured correctly
- The code 10 shows that device cannot start

- The code 28 shows that drivers for this device are not installed

Question: Define legacy hardware?

Answer: Legacy hardware is compatible to work with older version of Microsoft operating systems such as Windows 95, 98, 2000, NT, and XP.

Question: Define Plug-and-Play?

Answer: A Plug-and-Play feature automatically detects an attached device with your computer without requiring additional device drivers.

Question: Does legacy hardware support Plug-and-Play?

Answer: In most cases, legacy hardware does not support Plug-and-Play feature.

Question: Can I install legacy hardware on Windows Vista machine?

Answer: Yes, run the compatibility wizard to install legacy hardware.

Question: Define Tablet PC Input Panel?

Answer: Tablet PC Input Panel is an alternative way to input the text for your system by using mouse or with stylus (Touch screen pen), or using any other pointing device.

Question: Does all versions of Microsoft Vista support Tablet PC Input Panel?

Answer: Microsoft Windows Vista Home Basic does not support Tablet PC Input Panel.

Question: Can I add a Tablet PC Input Panel toolbar on taskbar on my computer?

Answer: Yes, if it is necessary.

Question: How many writing mode Table PC Input Panel support?

Answer: Two, keyboard mode and writing pad mode.

Question: Can I adjust handwriting recognition preferences?

Answer: Yes, if Tablet PC Input Panel is configured properly for handwriting recognition.

Question: Define Task Manager?

Answer: Windows Task Manager allows administrators to manage currently running applications and their processes, and system services.

Question: Define Taskbar?

Answer: Taskbar displays currently running applications. By default, it is located at the bottom of Microsoft Windows operating system.

Question: Define Start Menu?

Answer: Windows Start Menu is a user interface for Microsoft operating systems to launch programs that are currently installed on your computer.

Question: Define Classic Start Menu?

Answer: Windows Classic Start Menu is a user graphics interface that was designed for older version of the Microsoft operating systems to view and launch programs for your system.

Question: Define Run command?

Answer: A Run command is a dialog box to access computer utilities by typing a command line in the search bar.

Question: Can I publish my calendar online?

Answer: Yes, you may if you want other users to subscribe to your calendar.

Question: Define Windows DVD Maker?

Answer: Windows DVD Maker enables users to create, and customize videos files, picture files, and audio files.

Question: Does all Windows Vista editions support Windows DVD Maker?

Answer: No, it is only supported for Microsoft Windows Vista Home Premium and Microsoft Windows Vista Ultimate editions.

Question: What does LPT stand for?

Answer: LPT stands for Line Print Terminal. It is a local printer port to install printer for your computer.

Question: Define a computer theme?

Answer: A computer theme modifies the current sounds settings, icons settings, desktop screen saver settings, and other settings to change the look and feel of your computer.

Question: Define screen saver?

Answer: A screen saver is a picture or animation that covers computer screen, whenever it is in idle state.

Question: What DPI stands for?

Answer: DPI stands for dots per inches and it measures printing or display resolution.

Question: what is mouse clicklock?

Answer: A mouse clicklock is an alternative way to drag any objects, such as files, folders, or any application shortcuts, without holding down the mouse button. You are required to press left mouse button for less than 5 seconds to activate clicklock and then it will allow you to move an object anywhere you want to, within a local user account.

Question: Define Windows Firewall?

Answer: Firewall enables incoming and outgoing connections to allow programs and ports to establish a successful communication, if it is configured correctly.

Question: How would you prevent external computers from accessing your computer regardless of any Firewall rules?

Answer: Select the Block all connections option in the Inbound connection list of the Public Profile tab from Advanced Windows Firewall Security window.

Question: Define Windows Firewall exceptions?

Answer: A Windows Firewall exception controls how programs and ports communicate through Firewall.

Question: If you want to remotely manage clients by using Remote Procedure Calls (RPC), how should you configure Windows Firewall on client computer?

Answer: Enable Remote Administration exception in Windows Firewall on client computer. The Remote Administration exception allows communication through

Windows Firewall for Remote Procedure Calls (RPC), Windows Management Instrumentation (WMI), and Distributed Component Object Model (DCOM).

Question: Define Remote Assistance exceptions in Windows Firewall?

Answer: The Remote Assistance exception enables network users to send request to each other for seeking help to troubleshoot the computer issues on daily basis. The Remote Assistance exception in Windows Firewall is also design to enable Universal Plug and Play discovery protocol (UPnP), Simple Service Discovery Protocol (SSDP), and Teredo.

Question: Define Remote Desktop exceptions in Windows Firewall?

Answer: The Remote Desktop exceptions in Windows Firewall must be enabled on client computer for accessing the desktop from a remote system. If the Remote Desktop exception is enabled, the communication will pass through the Windows Firewall using RDP port 3389.

Question: Define Remote Service Management exception in Windows Firewall?

Answer: The Remote Service Management exception allows managing remote local services.

Question: Define compatibility mode of an application?

Answer: A compatibility mode allows an application to run with the earlier versions of Microsoft operating system such as Windows 95, 98, 2000, Windows ME, Windows NT, and Windows XP.

Question: Define Windows narrator?

Answer: Narrator reads the text louder as you move your mouse or any other pointing device across the desktop.

Question: Define different kinds of modems?

Answer: There are two kinds of modems, broadband modem and dial-up modem. The broadband modem provides high-speed Internet access and they use cable or DSL line to connect to the Internet. The dial-up modem connects to the Internet with much slower speeds than broadband modem and they use phone line to connect to the Internet.

Chapter 5 - Group Policy Object Editor

Topics covered in this chapter:

- User Account Control Policy
- Local Security Account Lockout Policy
- Registry Editor

User Account Control Policy

The *Group Policy Object* (GPO) allows system administrators to control hardware and software settings for user's profile to minimize the security risk for their system. A system administrator can restrict user's rights using the *Group Policy Object* (GPO) so they do not have permission to modify any hardware or software settings that can affect the security of the system. GPO can only be deployed with Windows Vista Business, Ultimate and Enterprise editions. You must be an administrator or must have administrator privileges to enforce *Local Security Policy.*

Open Local Security Setting Editor

To open *Local Security Setting Editor*, run command prompt (*Windows Key + R*), type ***secpol.msc*** in the search bar, and then click ***OK***.

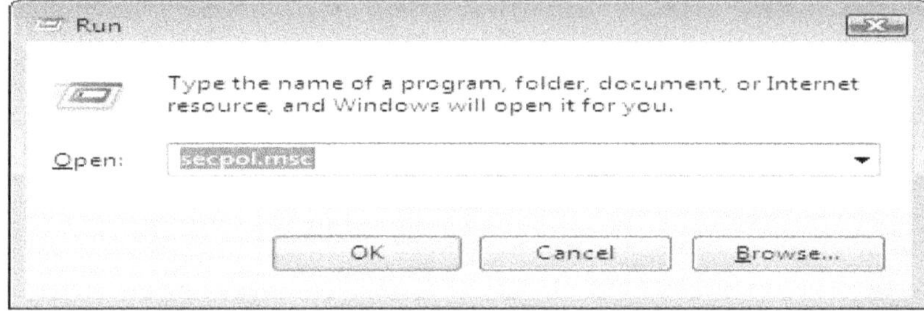

Local Security Account Policy

The local security account policy enforces the password history policy, maximum password age policy, minimum password length, password complexity requirement policy, and reversible encryption policy.

To open security account policy:

- Open *Control Panel*
- From left navigation pane, click ***Classic View***
- Double-click ***Administrative Tools***
- Double-click ***Local Security policy***
- From left navigation pane, double-click ***Account Policies*** folder
- Double-click ***Password Policy*** folder

To enforce password policy, you must be a system administrator or must have administrative privileges to make changes to the password policy. The following policies can be enforced for a local user account.

Enforce Password History - See step # 1 given below

Maximum Password Age - See step # 2 given below

Minimum Password Length - See step # 3 given below

Password Must Meet Complexity Requirements - See step # 4 given below

Store Passwords Using Reversible Encryption - See step # 5 given below

Step # 1: To enforce password history policy, double-click the ***Enforce password history*** policy and then type a numeric value between 1 and 24 in ***Keep password history for*** box. If the password history policy value is set to 0, that indicates password history is not enforced. To enforce this policy, a numeric number must be greater than 1 and less than 25. Click on ***Apply*** and then click ***OK*** to save settings.

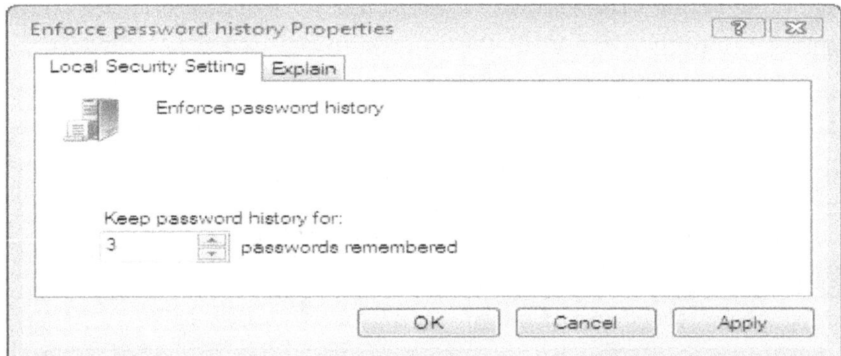

Step # 2: To enforce maximum password age policy, double-click the ***Maximum password age*** policy. Maximum password age must be between 1 and 999 days and it should not be less than minimum password age. If the maximum password age is set to 0, the password will never expire. It is recommended to set a user password policy to expire every 30 to 90 days to minimize the security risk. Click on ***Apply*** and then click ***OK*** to save settings.

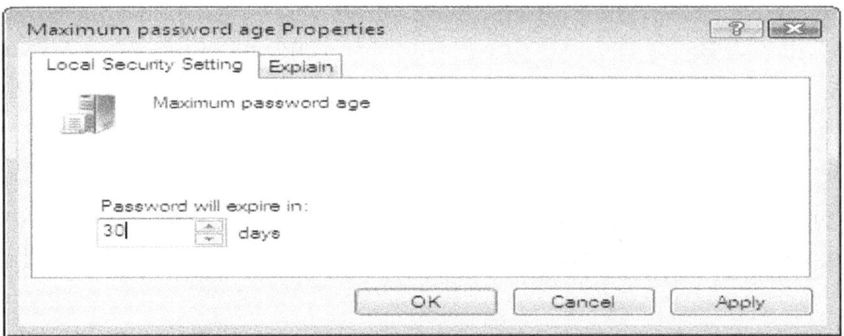

To enforce minimum password age policy, double-click the ***Minimum password age*** policy, and then type a numeric value that must be any value between 1 and 998. The minimum password age must be less than maximum password age policy. If the maximum password age is set to 0, then the minimum password can be set to any values between 0 and 998.

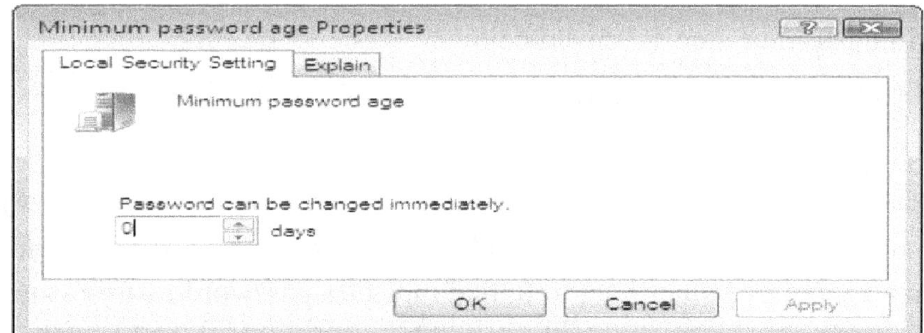

Step # 3: To enforce minimum password length, double-click the ***Minimum password length*** policy, and then type a numeric value that must be between 1 and 14. If the minimum password character length is set to 0, the minimum password length policy is not enforced. The minimum password length policy adds more security to the system which enhances overall computer security. By default, the minimum password length for the domain controller is 7 characters and 0 for the stand-alone servers.

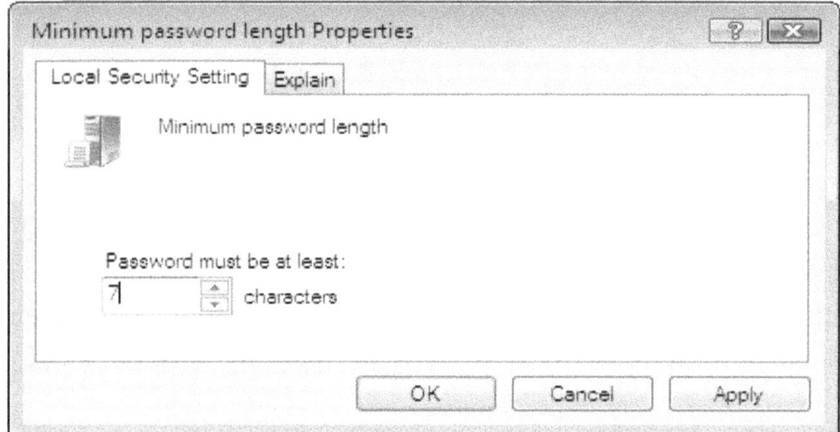

Step # 4: It is important to enforce password complexity requirements policy to add extra security to the system that helps maintaining overall network security. To activate this policy, double-click the ***Password must meet complexity requirements*** policy and then select ***Enabled*** option to enforce it. Click on ***Apply*** and then click ***OK*** to save password complexity requirement preferences. By default, this policy is enabled on the domain controllers and it is disabled on the stand-alone servers. Once you have enabled this policy to enforce it, you must explain users about the password complexity requirements. User must meet following password complexity requirements:

- User's account name should not be used as a part of the password
- User's password should not have two consecutive characters of the user's full name
- The password length must be at-least six characters long
- Should contain at-least one uppercase character (A through Z), at-least one lowercase character (a through z), at-least one digit (0 through 9) or at-least one non-alphabetic character (@, #. $, %, ^, &, *,!, etc)

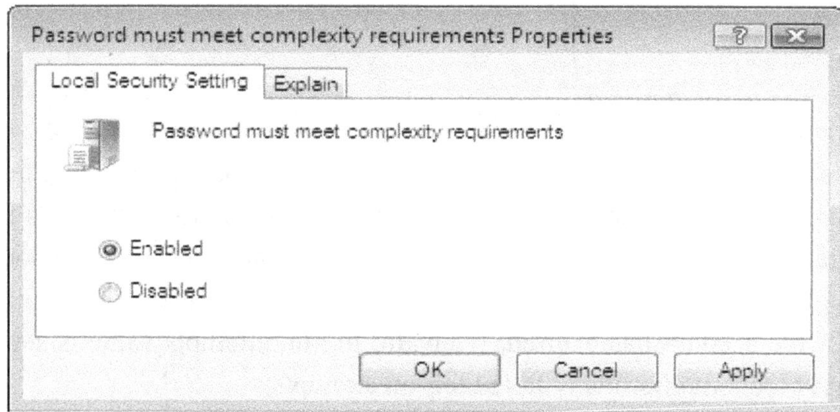

Step # 5: The ***Store passwords using reversible encryption*** policy keeps track of user's passwords for reversible encryption that provides support for applications which requires having knowledge of user's password for authentication purpose. By default, this policy is disabled and it is recommended to have this setting disabled for security reasons. To enforce this policy, double-click the ***Store passwords using reversible encryption*** policy, and then select ***Enabled*** option. Click on ***Apply*** and then click ***OK*** to save reversible encryption preferences. This policy must be enabled when it is required to perform any specific action that requires having the knowledge of stored passwords using reversible encryption.

Local Security Account Lockout Policy

The local security account policy enables system administrator to enforce account lockout duration policy, account lockout threshold policy, and reset account lockout counter after policy.

Account Lockout Threshold

Open *Local Security Settings Editor*. From the left navigation pane, under the ***Security*** settings section, click the ***Account Lockout Policy*** folder.

From the right navigation pane, double-click the ***Account Lockout Threshold*** policy, and then type any value between 0 and 999 in the ***Account will lock out after*** box. Click on ***Apply*** and then click ***OK*** to save changes. It is best security practice to limit user's logon attempts that may reduce unauthorized user access to your computer resources. A locked-out account can only be reset by a system administrator or user must wait until the lockout duration for the account has expired. If invalid log-on attempts value is set to 0, the account will never lockout after many failed log-on attempts.

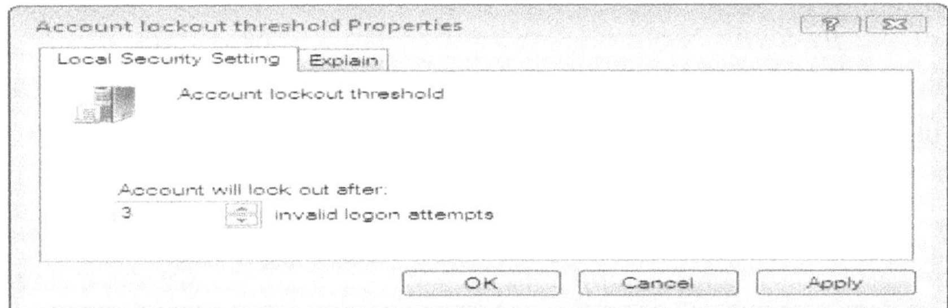

An account lockout threshold policy may affect ***Account lockout duration*** policy and ***Reset account lockout counter after*** policy, if you accept the suggested 30 minutes value for each policy. Click ***OK*** to save changes.

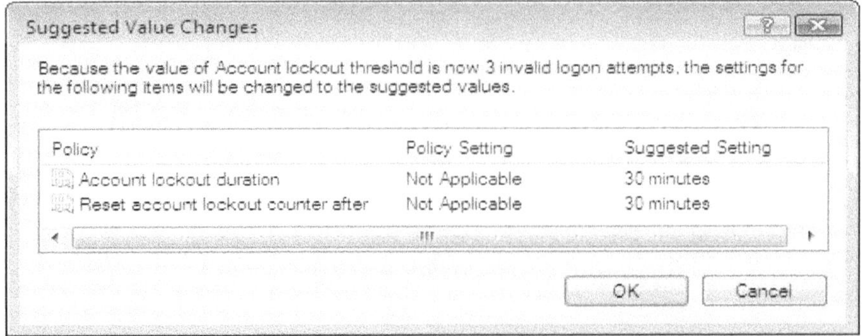

Audit a User

A system administrator can audit a user to keep track of changes that can be made to a file, document, and the system registry. Auditing a user for an item is the best way to limit user privileges to enhance the security of the system. To monitor a document changes, right-click on the document that you want a user to audit for, and then select the ***Properties*** option from the list. Click the ***Security*** tab, and then click on ***Advanced*** button to set special permission for the user.

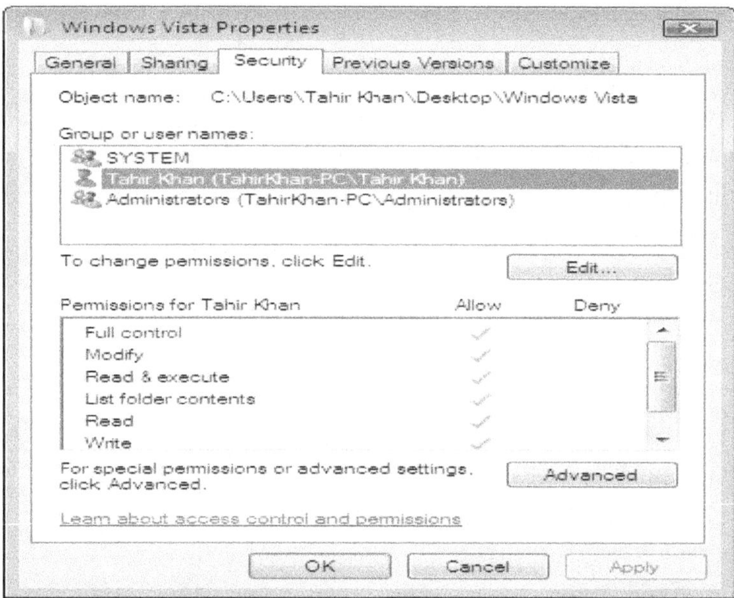

Click the ***Auditing*** tab, and then click on ***Continue*** the process. You must be an administrator or a member of an administrative group or must have administrative privileges to perform this task.

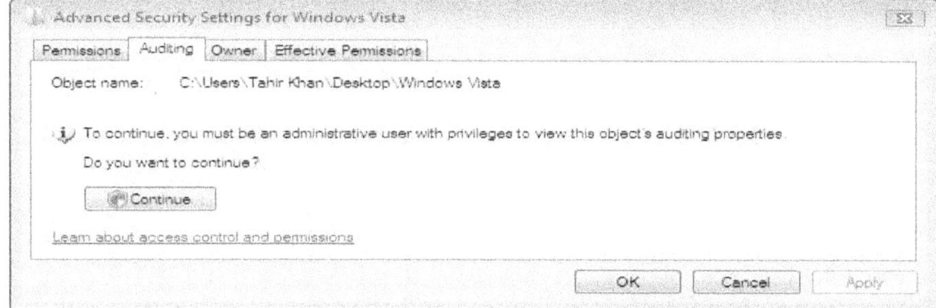

Click on ***Add*** button to add a user which needs to be audited.

Type the name of a user or a group in the ***Enter the object name to select*** box, and then click ***OK***. You can only audit an active user. If you select a user or a group who is not an active user, a warning message will be prompted.

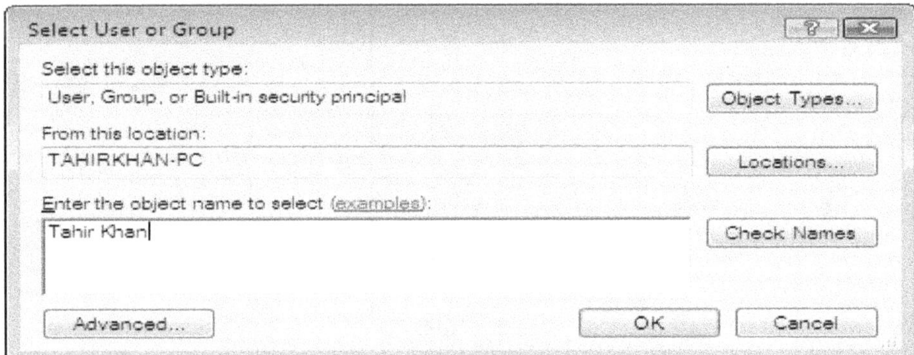

Go through the list of auditable actions from the access section to select appropriate action for a user that must be audited. Click ***OK*** to save preferences.

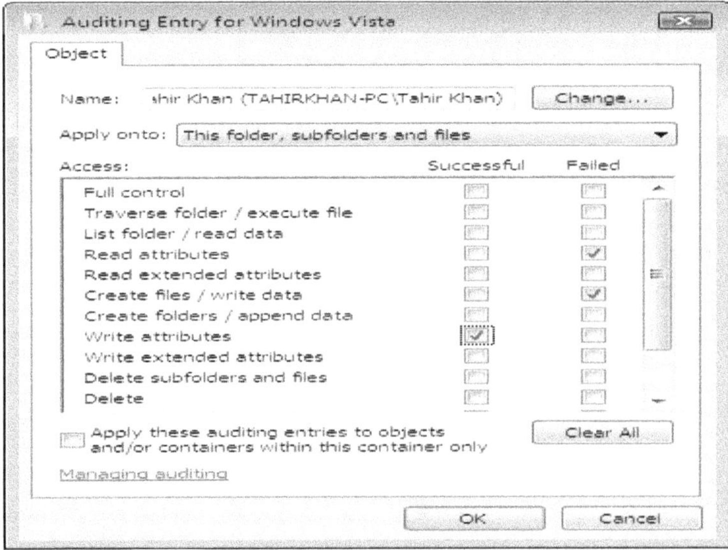

View Audit Log

Open ***Administrative Tools*** from the *Control Panel*. In the ***Administrative tools*** panel, navigate to the ***Event Viewer*** icon and then double-click on it to start the program. If you are prompted for administrative credentials, provide administrative credentials to continue this process.

In the left navigation pane, under the ***Event Viewer (Local)*** section, double-click the ***Windows Logs*** folder and then click on ***Security*** option.

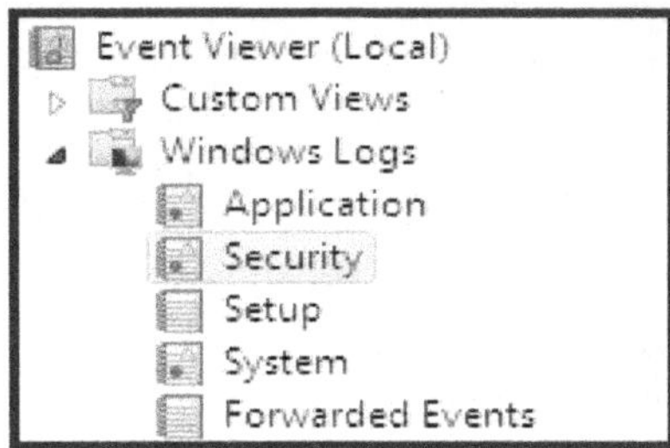

In the right navigation pane under the ***Security*** section, double-click the desired event to view the changes that were made to the document by an audited user. In addition, an audit report informs you about the log name, source, event id, level, user (if applicable), OpCode, users last logged-on date and time, task category, keywords (audit success or fail), and the computer name. The event information can be copied by clicking on ***Copy*** button (located at the left-bottom of the *Event Properties* window). The copied information can be saved into a word document file for future reference. Click on ***Close*** to exit out of the window.

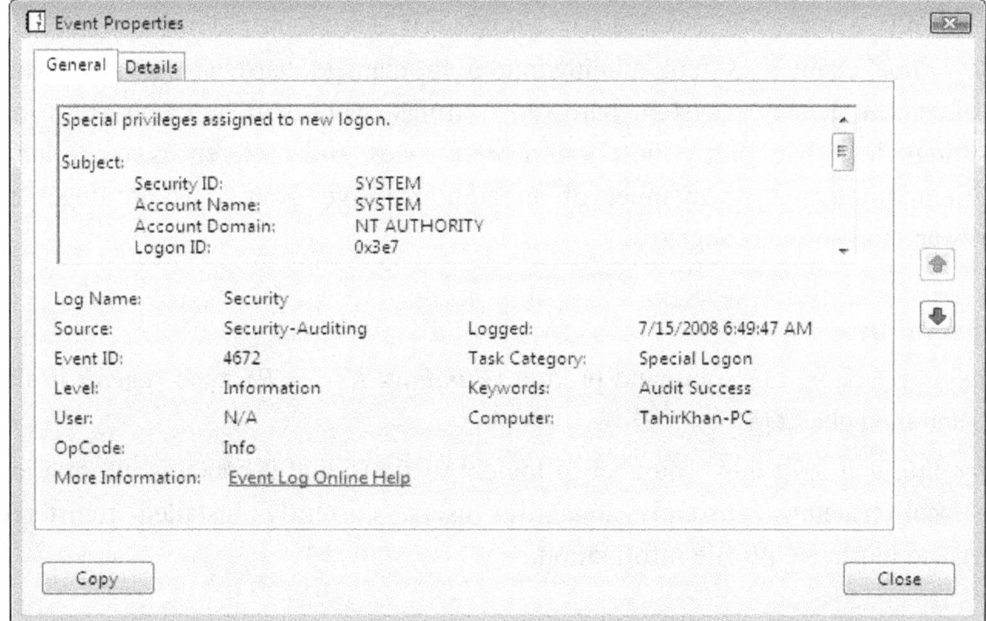

Event Viewer enables an administrator to view the audited event information in friendly view or in XML view. Click the ***Details*** tab, and select the ***Friendly View*** radio button and then click the plus sign (+) to expand the system and ***EventData*** category to view the detailed information of an event. If you would like to view the information in XML view, click on ***XML View*** radio button. To copy the event information, click on ***Copy*** button (bottom-left hand side) and paste into word document to save it for future reference.

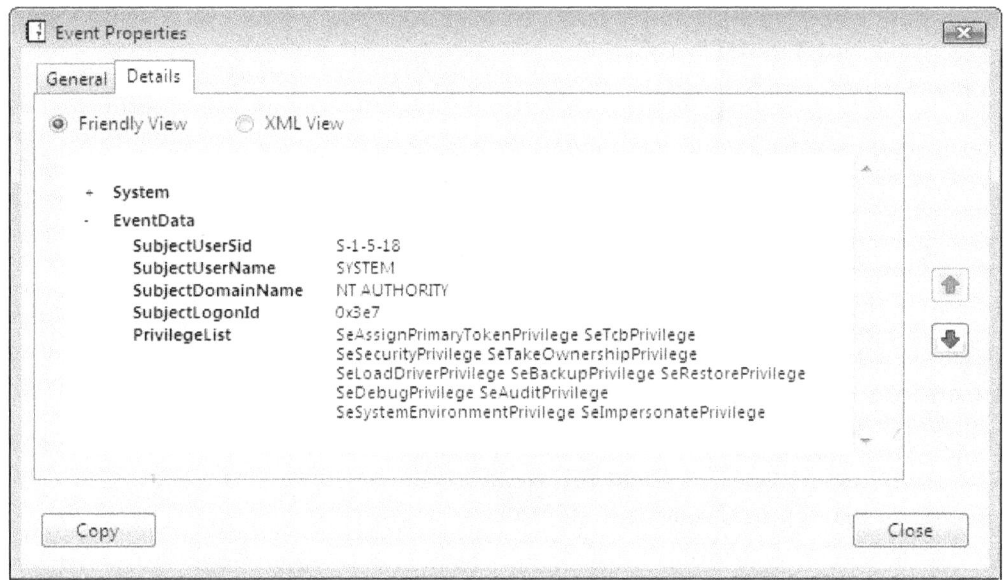

Registry Editor

A *Registry Editor* enables system administrators to manage hardware and software registry preferences. It stores system hardware settings, Microsoft and non-Microsoft software settings, local user and remote user's preferences, and preferences of the local machine. An administrator or member of an administrative group has privileges to modify hardware and software registry.

Open Registry Editor

To open *Registry Editor*, run command prompt (*Windows Key + R*), type ***regedit*** in the search box, and then click ***OK***.

The *Registry Editor* is split into a number of logical sections, and it contains information about the local machine, currently logged-in users, currently installed registered applications, and hardware profile information.

HKEY_CLASSES_ROOT

The ***HKEY_CLASSES_ROOT*** key is abbreviated as HKCR. It stores information about applications to keep information of file associations, file extensions, ActiveX and plug-ins detail.

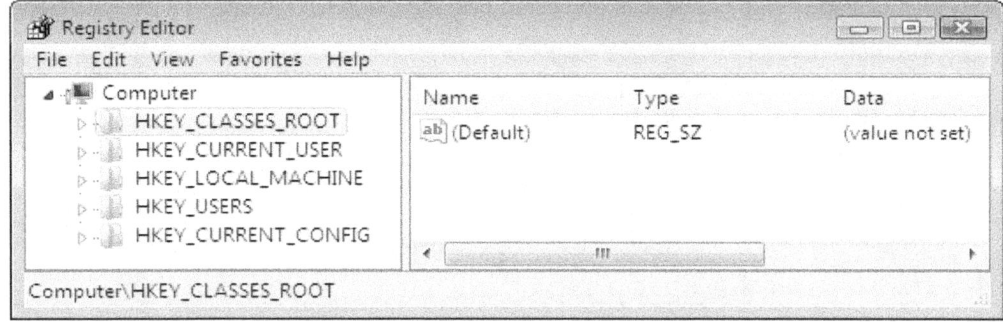

HKEY_CURRENT_USER

The ***HKEY_CURRENT_USER*** key is abbreviated as HKCU. It stores currently logged-in user profile settings. The configuration will only apply to the currently logged-in user profile. Each user will have separate configuration settings for their profiles.

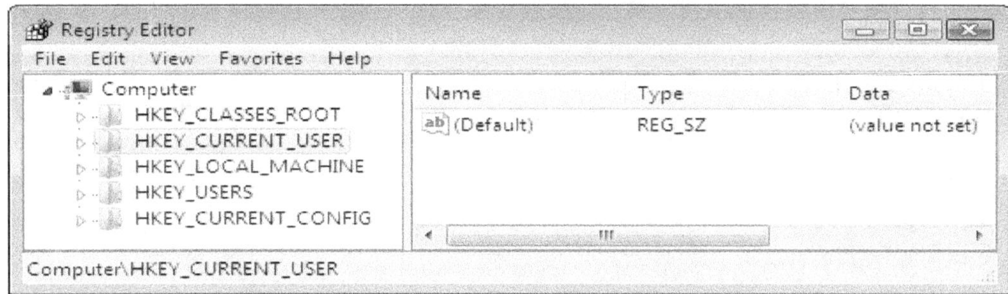

HKEY_LOCAL_MACHINE

The ***HKEY_LOCAL_MACHINE*** key is abbreviated as HKLM. It stores all hardware configuration profile settings for your local machine. The configurations will be applied to all users' profiles.

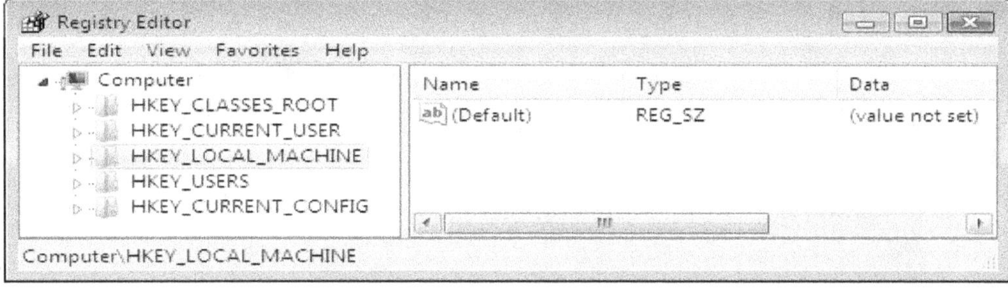

HKEY_USERS

The ***HKEY_USERS*** key is abbreviated as HKU. It stores users and programs configuration settings that include configuration setting of the screen saver, fonts, and folder view preferences.

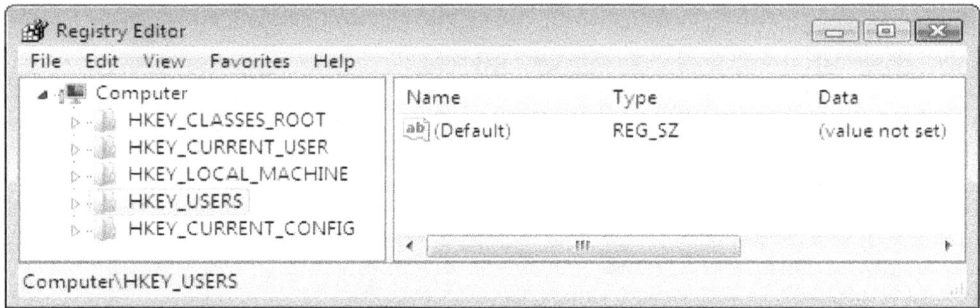

HKEY_CURRENT_CONFIG

The ***HKEY_LOCAL_MACHINE*** key is abbreviated as HKCC. It stores all current hardware profile configuration settings for your local machine.

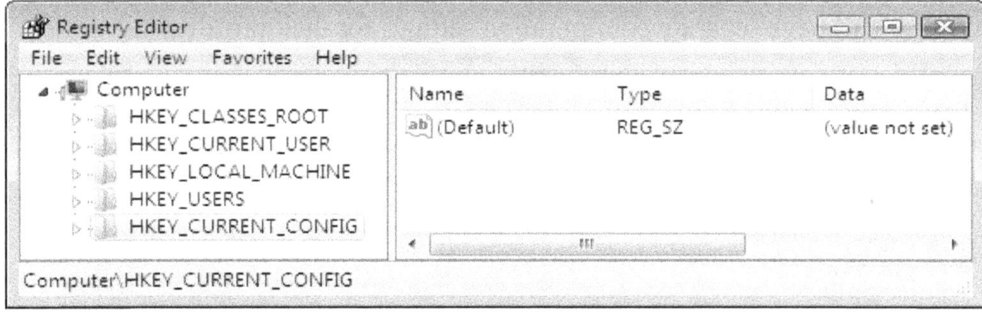

Add User Permissions

Open *Registry Editor*. From left navigation panel of the *Registry Editor*, click the registry tree folder and then navigate to the registry key file that you would like to add permission for. To add permission for a user or a group, click on ***Edit*** menu and then select the ***Permissions*** option.

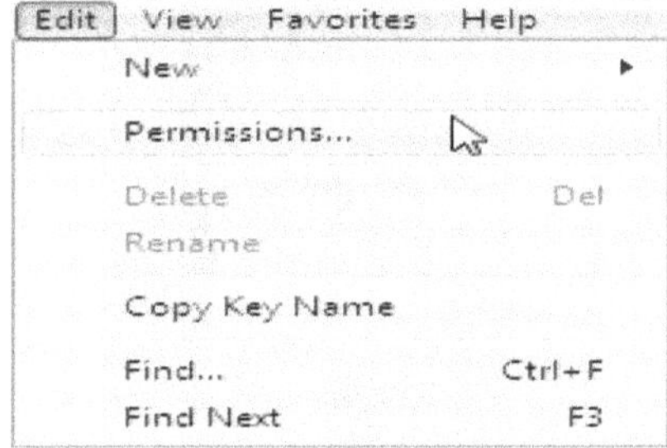

To specify the permission for everyone (for all users), click on ***Everyone*** from the **Group or user names** box and then set appropriate permission rules from the ***Permissions for Everyone*** section. To set the special permission or advanced permission for a user, click on ***Advanced***.

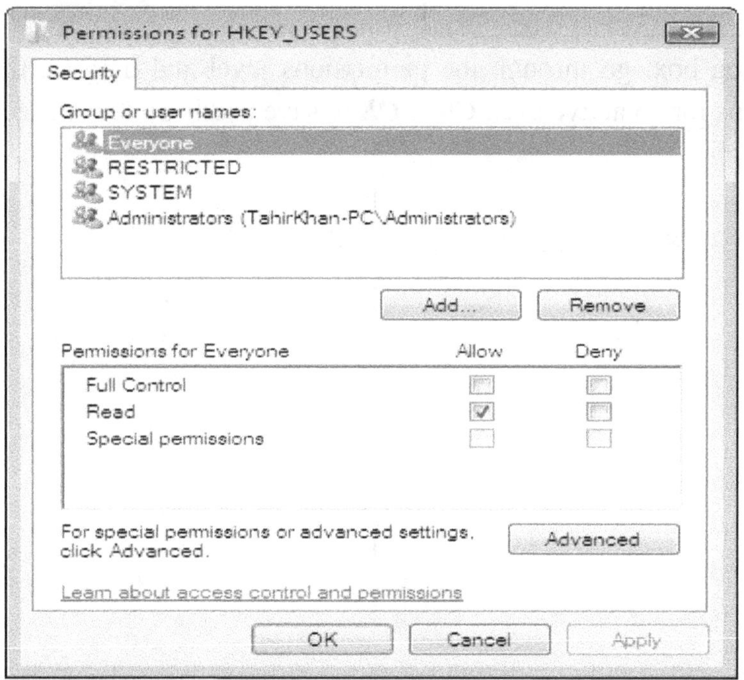

In the ***Permissions*** tab, you have option to modify, remove, and add new user permissions for a standard user. To add a new user, click on ***Add***.

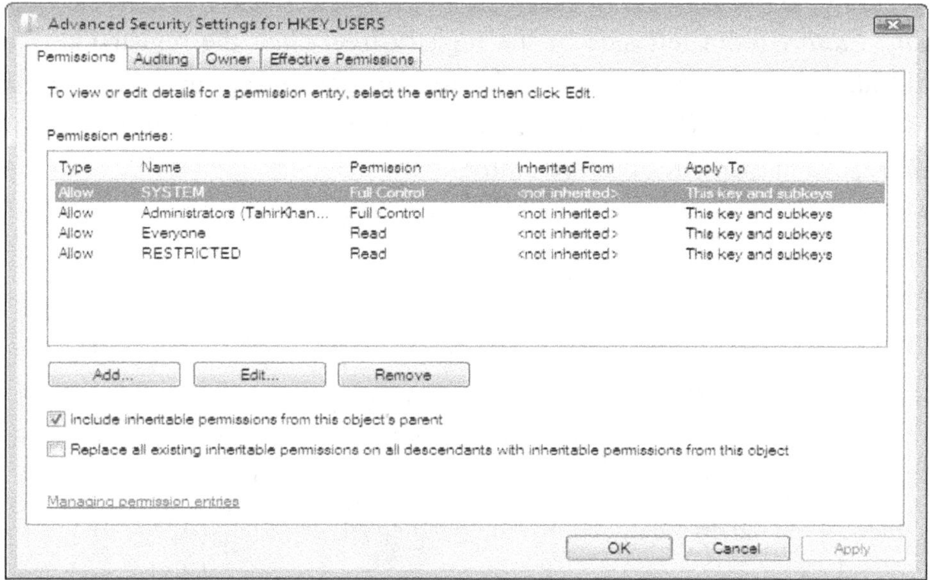

To set the permission for an active local user, type the username in the search box to check the validity of an existing active user, and then click ***OK***.

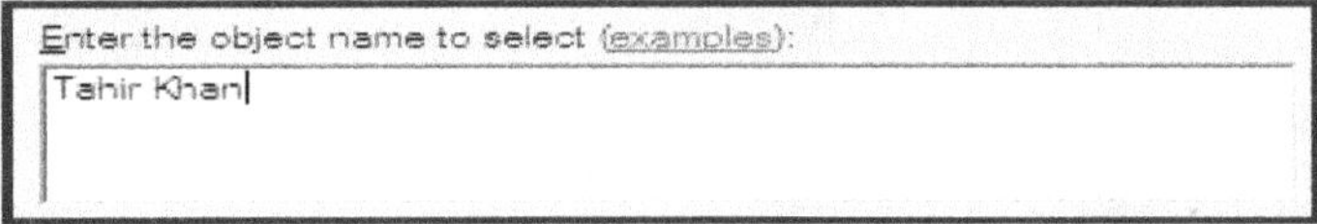

In the ***Permissions level*** dialog box, go through the permissions level and then set the appropriate level of permissions for an active user. Click ***OK*** to save user's preferences.

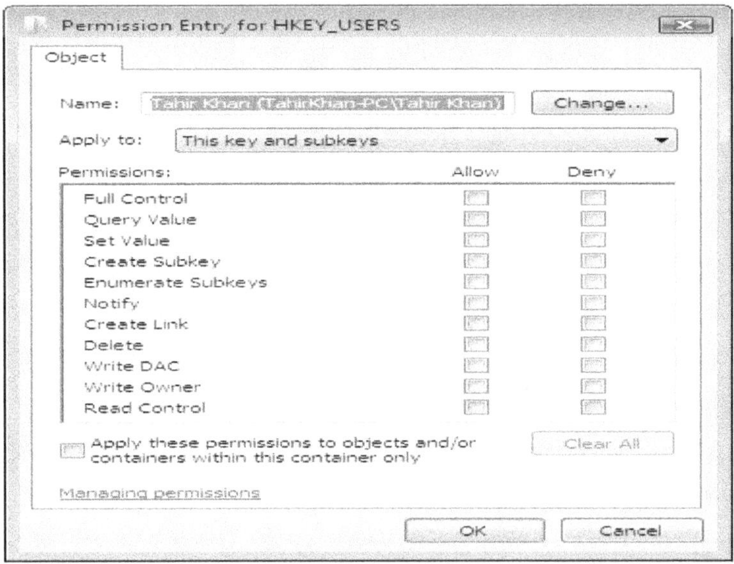

Auditing for System Registry

Open the *Registry Editor*. From left side of the registry tree, click the registry key for which you would like a user to be audited for. To audit a user or a group, click on ***Edit*** menu and then select the ***Permissions*** option. To audit a user, click on ***Advanced*** button. Click the ***Auditing*** tab, and then click on ***Add*** button.

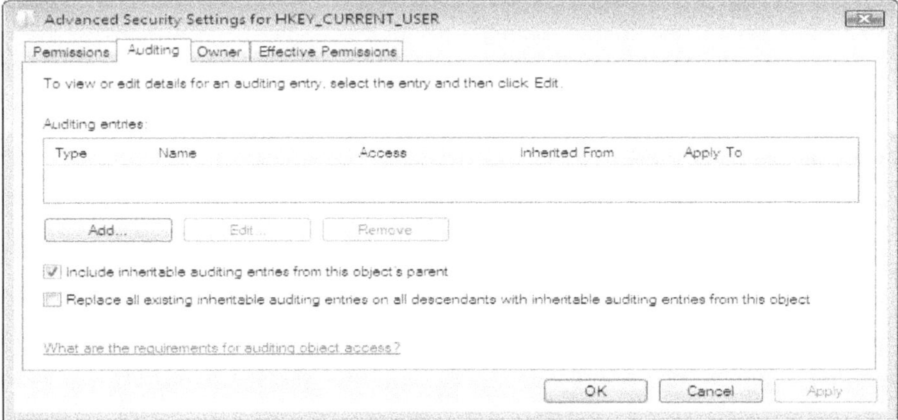

Enter the name of the user that needs to be audited in the search box and then click on ***OK***. If you have entered the correct username, you will be prompt to a permission level window that will allow you to audit successful and failed user attempts to log-on, create, delete, and modify system registry key, otherwise you will be asked to correct the username to continue the process.

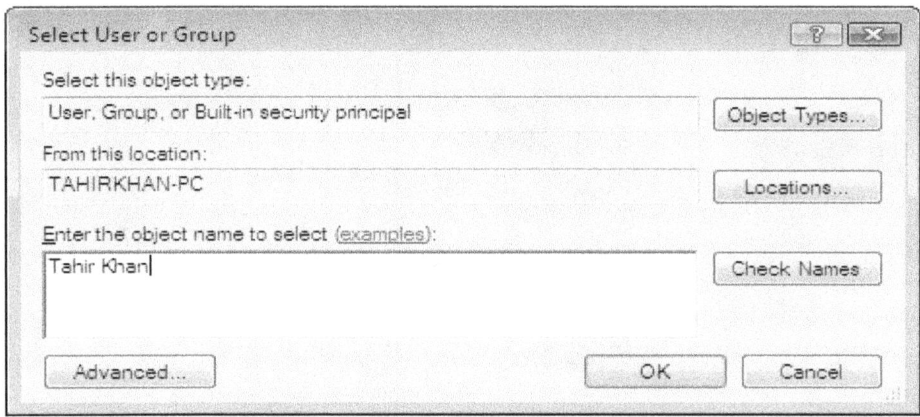

In the ***Auditing Entry*** dialog box, from the ***Access*** box, select the appropriate audit level and then click ***OK*** to save user's auditing preferences.

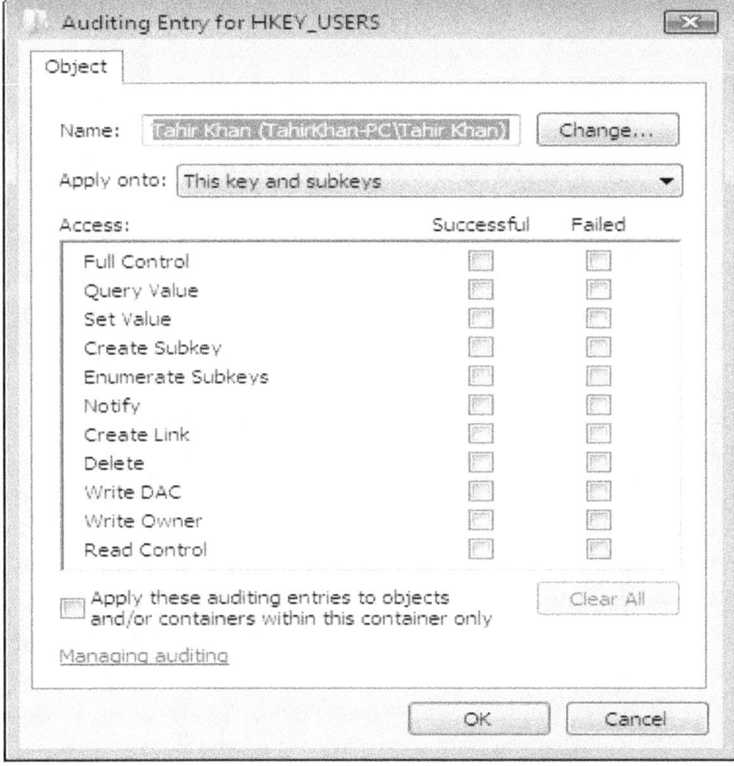

Registry Key Owner

Open the *Registry Editor.* From the left side of the registry tree, click the registry key, for which you want to take ownership of. To add a new owner for a registry key, click on ***Edit*** menu and then select the ***Permissions*** option. To add a new owner for a registry, click on ***Advanced*** button.

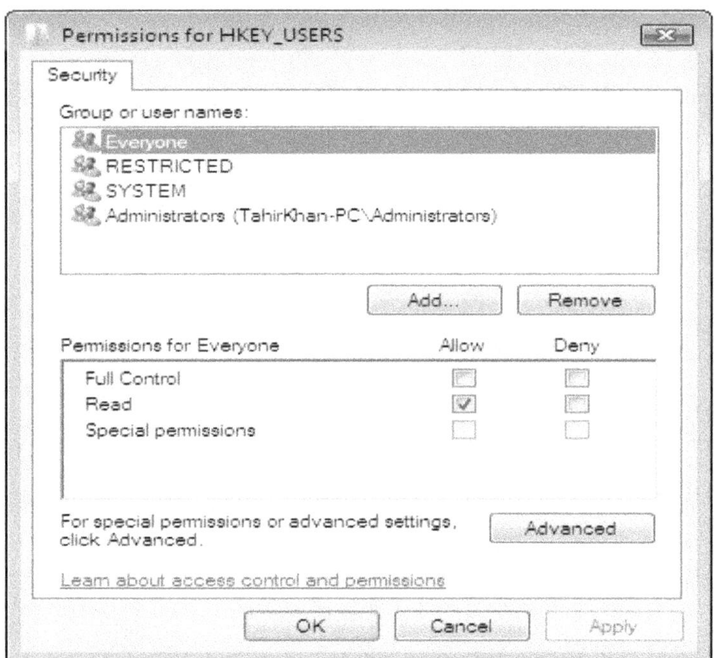

In the ***Owner*** tab, click on ***Other users or groups*** button to add another owner.

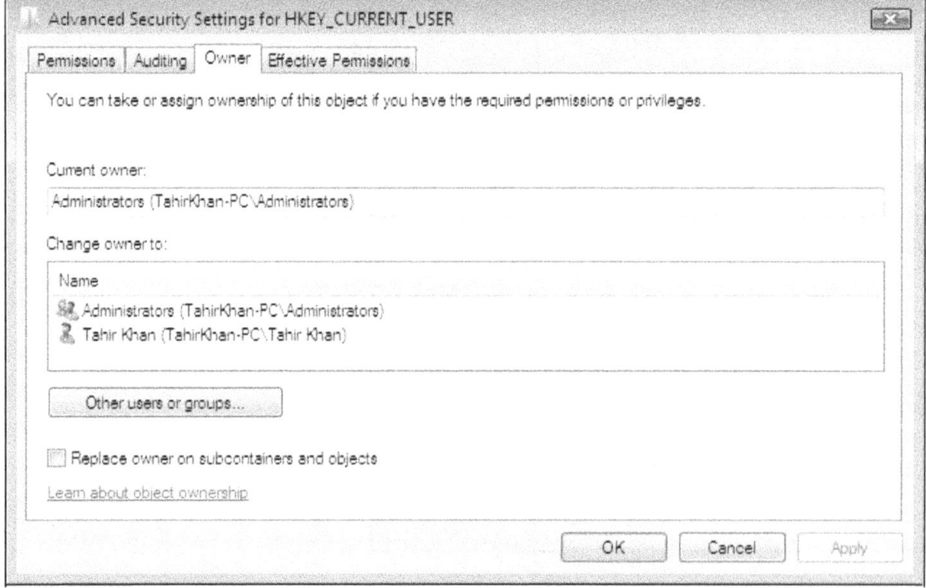

Enter the name of the new registry owner in the search box which needs permission to modify, delete, and create new system registry keys within the registry folder. Click ***OK*** to save preferences.

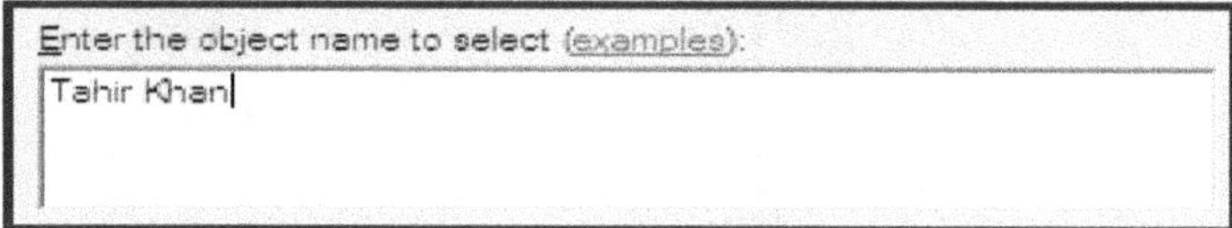

Click on ***Apply*** and then click ***OK*** to save registry settings.

Ownership Effective Permissions

Open the *Registry Editor* and from left side of the registry tree, click the registry key which you want to view and manage effective permissions. To manage and view the effective permissions, click on ***Edit*** menu and then select ***Permissions*** option. Then click on ***Advanced*** button.

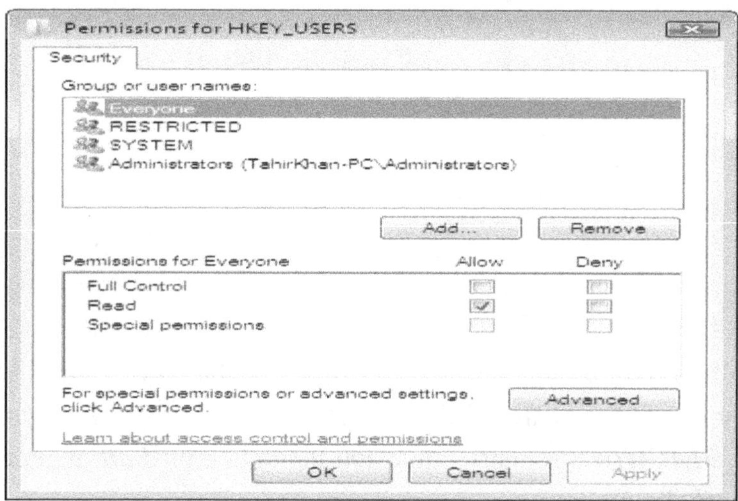

Click the ***Effective Permissions*** tab, and then click on ***Select***.

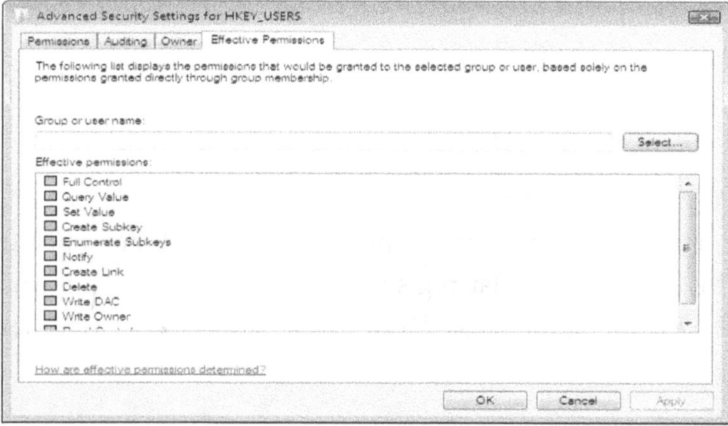

Enter the username of the owner that has been previously associated with this registry. Click ***OK*** to view the effective permissions.

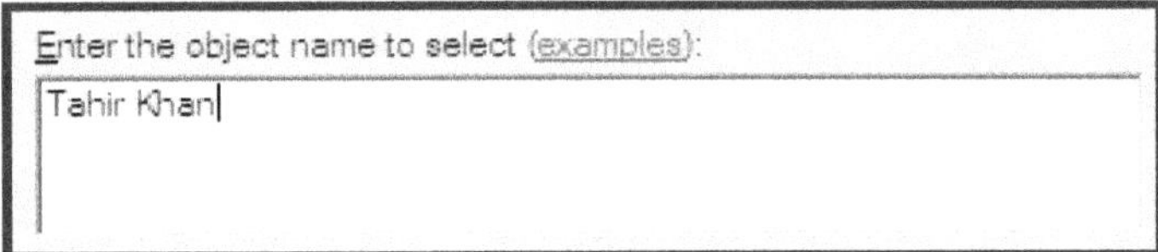

Add Registry Key

From left navigation panel of the *Registry Editor*, click the registry tree and then navigate to the registry key under which you would like to create a new key. To create a new registry key, go to ***Edit*** menu, click ***New***, and then click the ***Key*** to create a new key for your system.

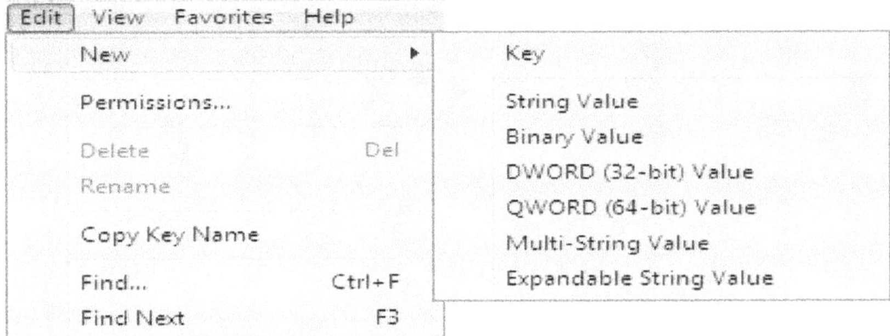

Find Registry Key

Open *Registry Editor* and then highlight the name of the registry key that you would like to search for. For example, if you want to search for the local machine registry key, you must click on ***HKEY_LOCAL_MACHINE*** registry name and then click on ***Edit*** menu to select ***Find*** option to open ***Search*** dialog box.

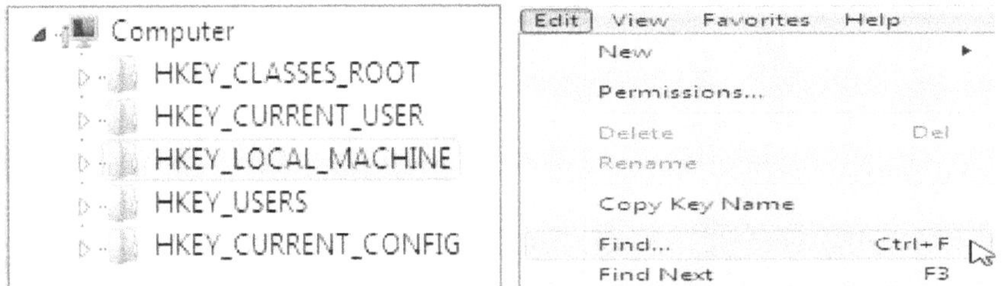

In the ***Search*** dialog box, type the name of registry key in search box, and then click on ***Find Next***. If you would like to find more similar registry key values, either go to ***Edit*** menu and then select the ***Find Next*** option or press ***F3*** key from keyboard to find next registry value.

Print Registry Key

From left navigation panel of the *Registry Editor*, click the registry tree folder and then navigate to the registry key file which you would like to print. For example, if you want to print registry key named ***HKEY_CURRENT_CONFIG***, select the registry name and then go to the ***File*** menu to choose the ***Print*** option. If you have multiple printers installed on your machine, make a choice of correct printer under the ***Select Printer*** section and then click on ***Print*** button.

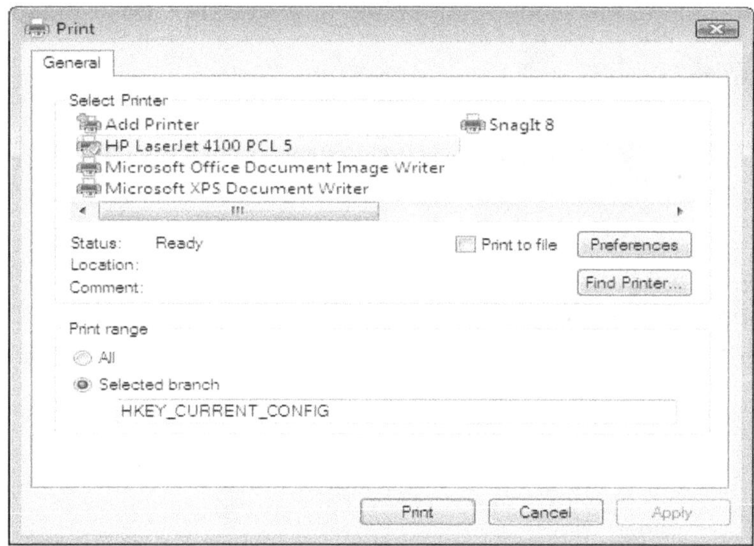

Copy key Name

From left navigation panel of the *Registry Editor*, choose the name of the registry folder that you would like to copy. For example, if you want to copy the name of ***HKEY_LOCAL_MACHINE*** registry, select the registry name and then select the ***Copy Key Name*** option from the ***Edit*** menu to copy the name of the registry. After copying the registry, you can paste it into any programs such as Microsoft Word document, notepad, etc.

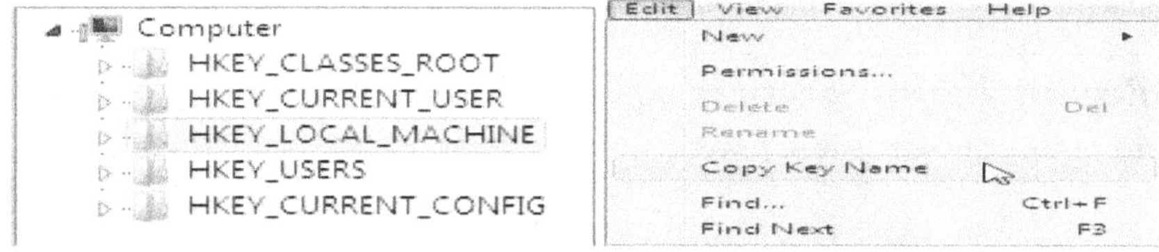

Registry Favorites

From left navigation panel of the *Registry Editor*, select the name of the registry that you would like to add to the *Registry Editor* Favorites. For example, if you want to add the

HKET_CLASSES_ROOT registry to favorites, click on it and then click on ***Favorites*** menu from registry menu bar and then select the ***Add to Favorites*** option to add it to the ***Registry Editor Favorites***.

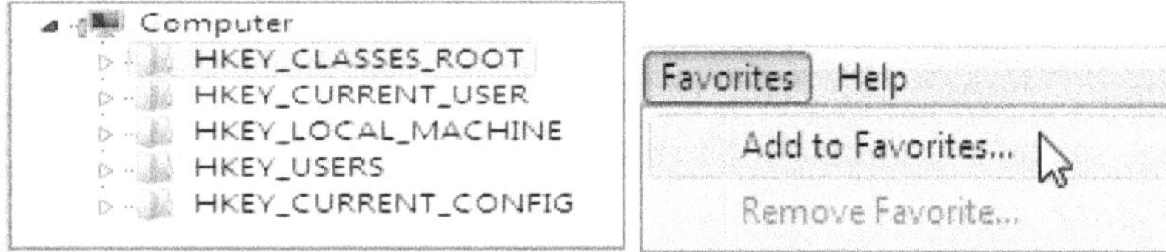

Click on ***OK*** to add registry name to the favorite's folder.

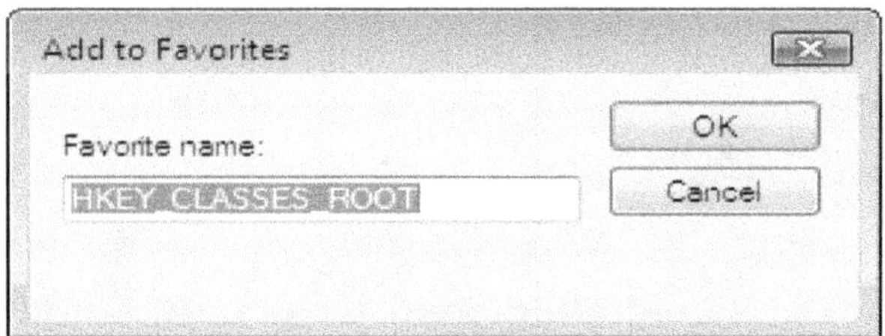

To remove a registry name from favorites, go to the ***Favorites*** menu and then choose the ***Remove Favorites*** option to remove the registry name from the ***Registry Editor Favorites***.

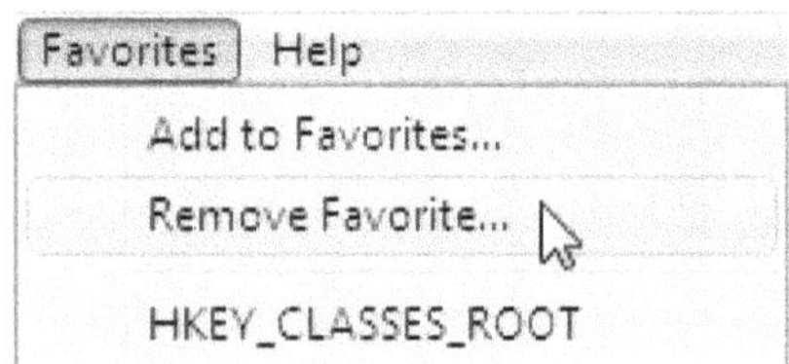

Highlight the registry name that needs to be removed from ***Select Favorite(s)*** box and then click ***OK***.

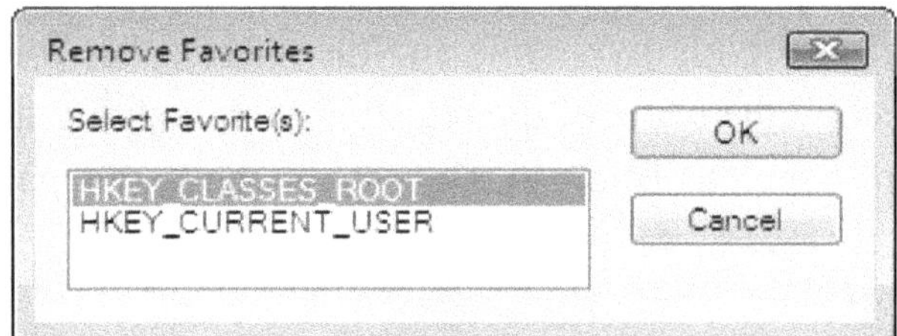

To view the list of the ***Registry Editor Favorites***, click on ***Favorites*** menu to see a list of favorites that has been added to the favorites list.

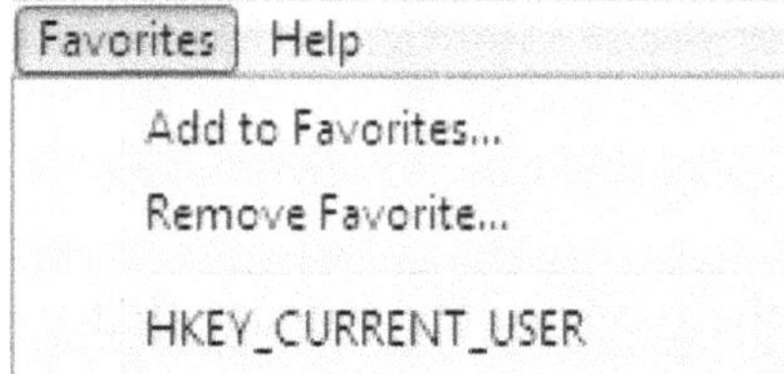

Edit Registry Key Value Data

From left navigation panel of the *Registry Editor*, click the registry tree folder and then navigate to the registry key that you would like to modify. Click the registry value from right navigation panel of Registry Editor that you want to modify and then go to the ***Edit*** menu and choose the ***Modify*** option.

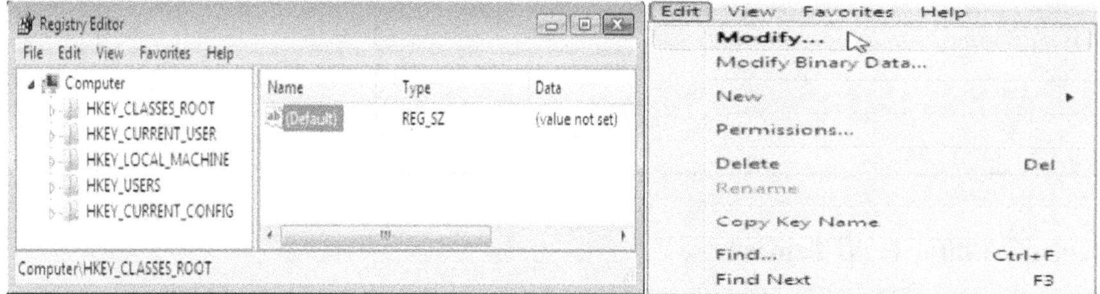

Enter the value data in the ***Value data*** field and then click on ***OK*** to save changes.

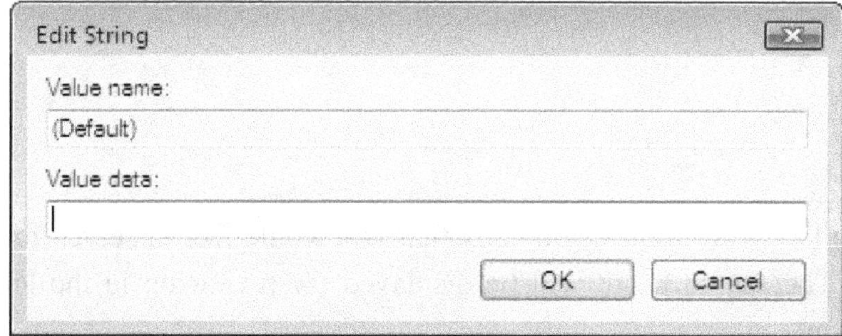

Modify Registry Key Binary Data

From left navigation panel of *Registry Editor*, click the registry tree folder and then navigate to the registry key that you would like to modify, and then go to the ***Edit*** menu and choose the ***Modify Binary Data*** option.

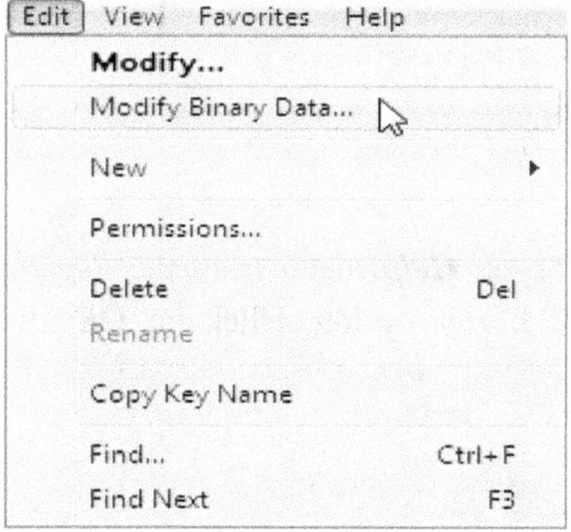

Edit the binary value and then click on ***OK*** to save changes.

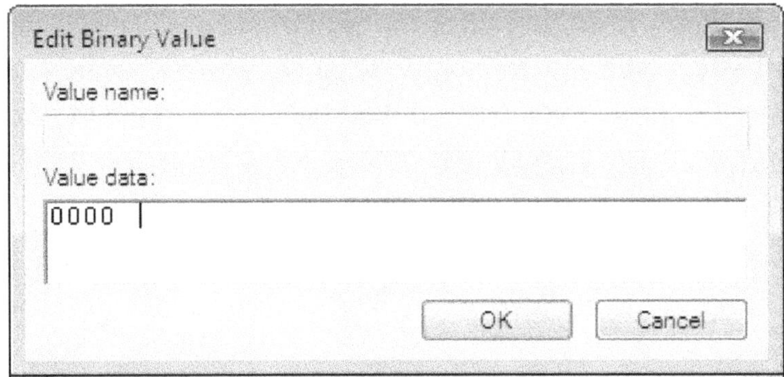

Registry Editor Help Topics

Open *Registry Editor*. To get help using *Registry Editor*, click on ***Help*** menu from *Registry Editor* menu bar, and then choose the ***Help Topics*** option.

Click on ***Index*** tab to type a keyword in the search box that you would like to search for, and then click on ***Display***. The search result will be displayed for reviewing in the left navigation pane of the window.

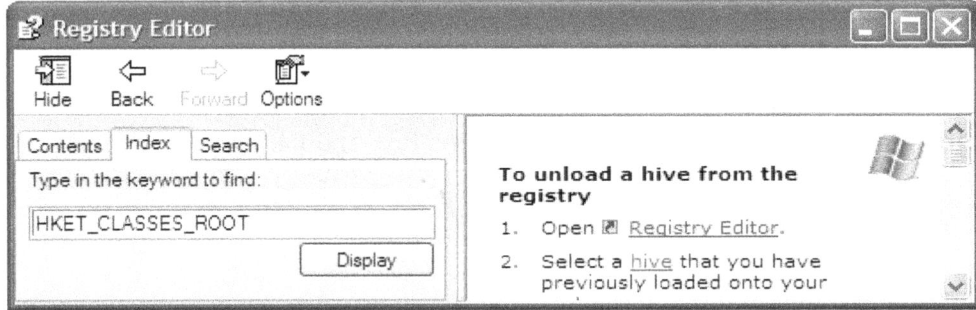

About Registry Editor

If you want to know about the *Registry Editor*, click on ***Help*** menu from the *Registry Editor* menu bar, and then choose ***About Registry Editor*** option. Click on ***OK*** after reviewing information about *Registry Editor*.

Question: What is a Group Policy and why is it important for system administrators?

Answer: The Group Policy allows system administrators to control hardware and software settings for user's profile to minimize the security risk for their systems. A system administrator can restrict the user's rights to modify any hardware or software settings using the Group Policy Object (GPO). You can restrict domain user's rights using Active Directory (AD) which is widely used to manage user's rights and limit their administrative privileges to modify hardware and software settings.

Question: Define an administrator local group policy?

Answer: The administrator local group policy settings are only applicable to those users who are member of the local administrator group.

Question: Define per-user local group policy?

Answer: Per-user local group policy is only applicable to a specific local user.

Question: What is Registry Editor?

Answer: A Registry Editor is a tool designed for administrators to manage system registry. It stores system hardware settings, Microsoft and non-Microsoft software settings, local user and remote user's preferences, and preferences of the local machine.

Question: Can I edit Windows registry?

Answer: This is user's choice, if you have knowledge to modify system registry, you should modify it, if needed. It is not recommended to delete, add, and modify system registry without any special needs. Ask your system administrator if you do not have permission to edit registry for security reasons.

Question: Can I take ownership of a registry key?

Answer: Yes, you may take ownership of the registry key, if you want to have permission to delete, modify, and add new registry key for your system.

Question: Define Event Viewer?

Answer: The Event Viewer enables administrators to collect copies of events from multiple computers and store them locally.

Chapter 6 - Microsoft Windows Vista Administrative Tools

Topics covered in this chapter:

- Remote Desktop
- Windows Remote Assistance
- User Accounts
- Local Area Network
- Shared Resources
- System Configuration Settings

Remote Desktop

Remote Desktop Connection is designed for system administrators to remotely connect to the client machine from the remote/host machine to perform administrative tasks such as downloading and installing Windows updates, and changing system configuration settings, if necessary. The Windows Vista Starter and Windows Vista Home editions are not capable of establishing a *Remote Desktop Connection.* To establish a connection to the host machine, both the host and the client machines must have Internet connectivity, *Windows Firewall* must be configured properly to allow communication through Remote Desktop port, and administrator must have a valid account to log-in remotely to the machine to perform administrative tasks. Only an administrator or member of an administrative group has privileges to change *Remote Desktop* settings.

Open Remote Desktop Connection

Click the ***Start*** button, type ***Remote Desktop Connection*** in the search bar and then press ***Enter*** from the keyboard.

In the *Remote Desktop Connection* window, click on ***Connect*** after typing a valid remote IP address or remote machine name to establish a connection between the host and the client machines. A secure port needs to be added in front of the IP address, if connecting to a secure remote system.

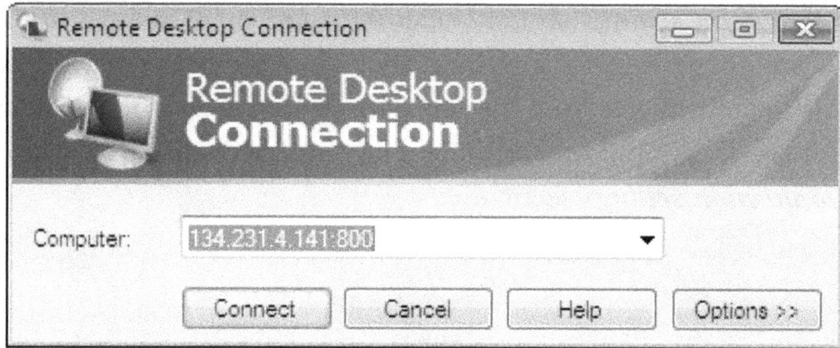

Establish Remote Desktop Connection

Open *Remote Desktop Connection* and type IP address of the remote computer in the search bar, and then click on ***Connect*** to establish a connection from the host machine to the remote machine.

If the remote computer is not running Microsoft Windows Vista operating system, you may be prompted to verify the identity of the computer that you are connecting to. Click on ***Yes*** to continue.

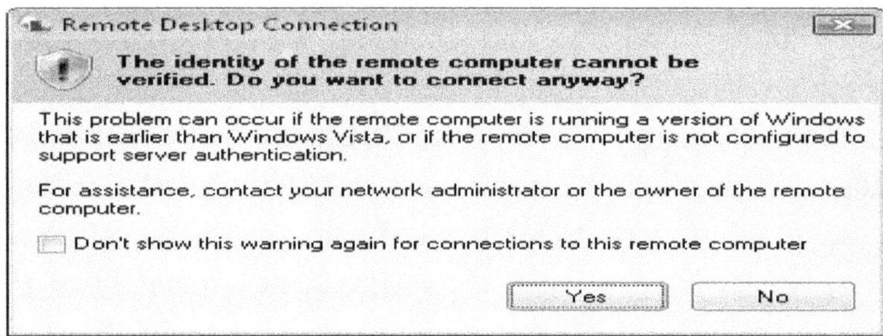

To authenticate yourself, enter the username and password of the remote computer to validate your session. If a connection is established successfully, you (as a system administrator) will have the full control over the client PC to perform maintenance, troubleshoot technical issues, copy, delete and modify user settings of the remote computer. It is highly recommended to allow only trusted users to control your system, remotely. This connection shall only be permitted to administrators who manage or perform regular maintenance on your system.

Remote Desktop Options

In the ***Remote Desktop Connection*** dialog box, click ***Options*** to adjust settings. The connection settings for *Remote Desktop Connection* are explained below.

In the ***General*** tab, under the ***logon settings*** section, enter the name or IP address of the remote computer that you are connecting to, and then click on ***Connect***. You will be asked to provide credentials to authenticate your session. The current connection settings can be saved as a RDP (Remote Desktop Protocol) file on the local hard-disk by clicking on ***Save*** button from the ***Connection settings*** section.

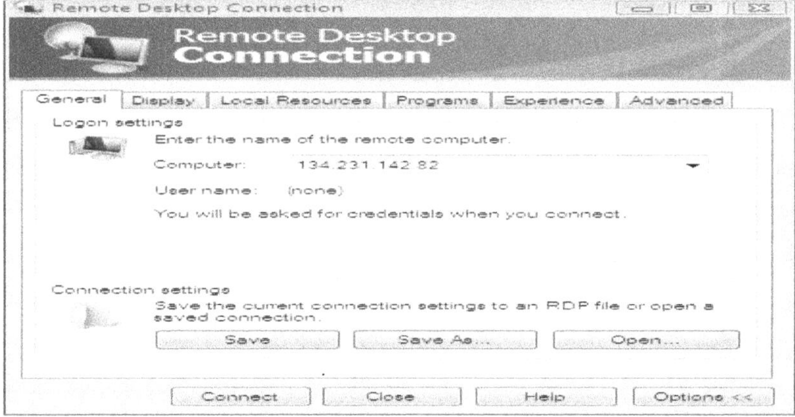

In the ***Display*** tab, remote desktop size and color scheme for *Remote Desktop Connection* can be adjusted to improve the speed of the remote connection. In the ***Remote desktop size*** section, drag the slider right or left to maximize or minimize the size of remote desktop, respectively. To set a color scheme for *Remote Desktop Connection*, choose one of the available color options under the ***Colors*** section. To display remote connection in full screen mode, check the ***Display the connection bar when in full screen mode*** option.

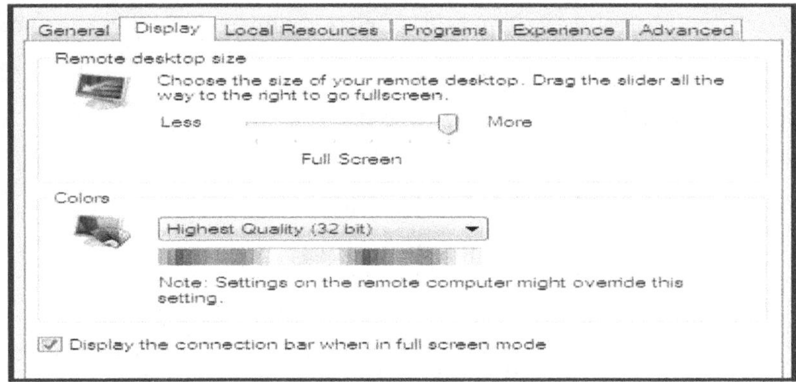

In the ***Local Resources*** tab, the remote computer sound, keyboard settings, connection to the local devices and resources can be adjusted to customize current remote session settings. To adjust remote computer sound, select one of the available options (*bring to this computer, do not play, and leave at remote computer*) from drop down menu of the ***Remote Computer Sound***. By default, keyboard is set to work in ***full screen mode only*** but it can be changed to the one of the available options (*on the local computer, on the remote computer, and in full screen mode only*), if needed.

It is best practice to manage local devices and resources for remote computer that helps an administrator to perform necessary task remotely. If remote machine needs to be configured for printing and copying documents from the remote machine to the client machine and vice versa, select the ***Printers*** option under the ***Local devices and resources*** section to print from a remote computer. Then select the ***Clipboard*** option to copy documents from the client to the remote machine or vice versa.

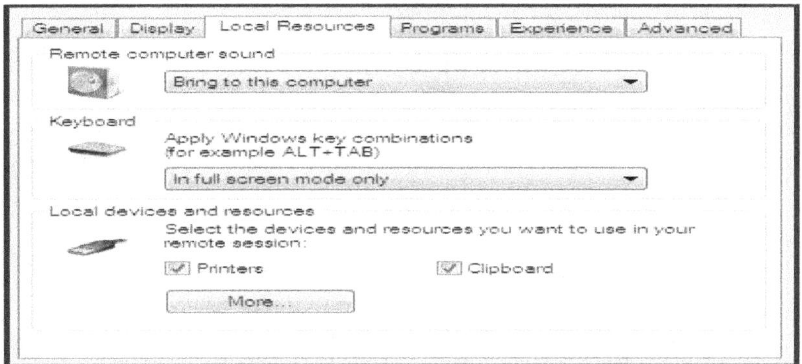

To optimize the performance of the *Remote Desktop Connection*, choose one of the available connection speeds. The connection speeds are: Modem (28.2 Kbps), Modem (56 Kbps), Broadband (128Kbps – 1.5 Mbps), and LAN (10Mbps or higher).

By default, the *Remote Desktop Connection* speed is set to be Modem (56 Kbps) to optimize connection performance. The desktop environment can be adjusted by choosing one of the following options: desktop background, font smoothing, desktop composition, show contents of window while dragging, menu and window animation, themes, and bitmap caching.

The performance of Remote Connection is associated with the connection speed and desktop environment objects which are listed below:

Connection Speed	**Desktop Environment**
Modem (28.2 Kbps)	Bitmap caching
Modem (56 Kbps)	Themes and bitmap caching
Broadband (128 Kbps -1.5 Mbps)	Desktop composition, show contents of window while dragging, menu and window animation, themes, and bitmap caching
LAN (10Mbps or higher)	Desktop background, font smoothing, desktop composition, show contents of window while dragging, menu and window animation, themes, and bitmap caching

To save *Remote Desktop Connection* settings, click the ***General*** tab, and then click on ***Save*** button to save current RDP settings.

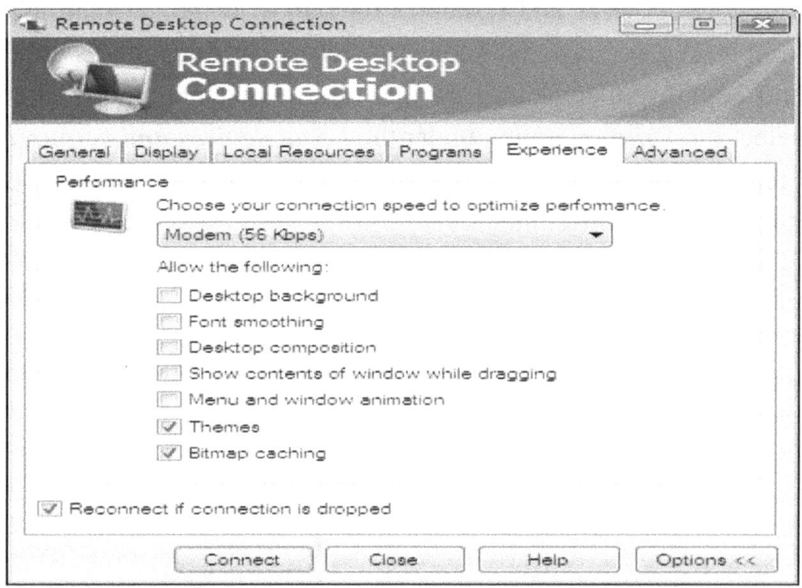

In the ***Advanced*** tab, a server authentication and Terminal Services Gateway settings must be configured if it is required to make remote connection more secure. A server authentication verifies connection to the remote computer that helps to stop establishing an unauthorized connection between the host and the client machines. Terminal Services Gateway helps to create a more secure and encrypted connection because it uses Remote Desktop Protocol (RDP), port 3389, and Hypertext Transfer Protocol over Secure Socket Layer (HTTPS), port 443, together to establish a secure connection between the client machine and the server machine. The RDP 3389 port is reserved for *Remote Desktop Connection* and it can be blocked by *Windows Firewall* to enhance network security, if needed. The HTTPS 443 port provides an extra layer of security to transmit data through a Secure Socket layer (SSL) tunnel for TS Gateway to establish a secure network environment.

The TS Gateway server authentication method is designed for authorized users to establish a secure connection to the remote computer on a corporate network, if it is configured properly. The three options are available to choose for server authentication.

- **Always connect, even if authentication fails**: If *Remote Desktop Connection* cannot verify the identity of the remote computer, it still connects to it. It is not a recommended option to choose for authentication purpose.
- **Warn me if authentication fails**: If *Remote Desktop Connection* cannot verify the identity of the remote computer, you will be notified so you can take necessary steps, if required, before connecting to the remote computer.
- **Don't connect if authentication fails**: If *Remote Desktop Connection* identity cannot verify the identity of the remote computer, the host computer will stop establishing a connection to the remote computer.

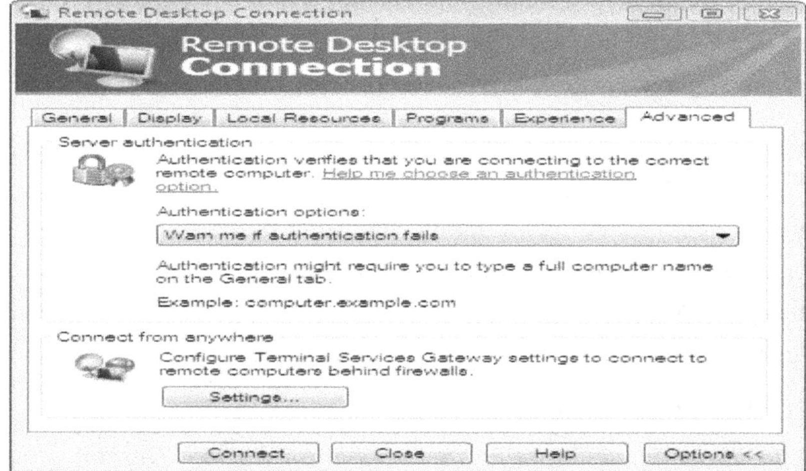

To configure *Terminal Services Gateway* server settings, click the ***Settings***, under the ***Connect from anywhere*** section. By default, the client computer is configured to detect TS Gateway settings automatically. To customize TS Gateway server settings, click the ***Use these TS Gateway server settings***, and then type server name in the ***Server name*** box. Select one of the following ***Log-on method*** from the Log-on method list as given below:

- **Allow me to select later**: At the time of connection, this option allows you to select a log-on method.
- **Ask for Password**: At the time of connection, a valid password is required to authenticate the session.
- **Smart Card:** At the time of connection, insertion of a smart card is required for authentication purpose to continue.

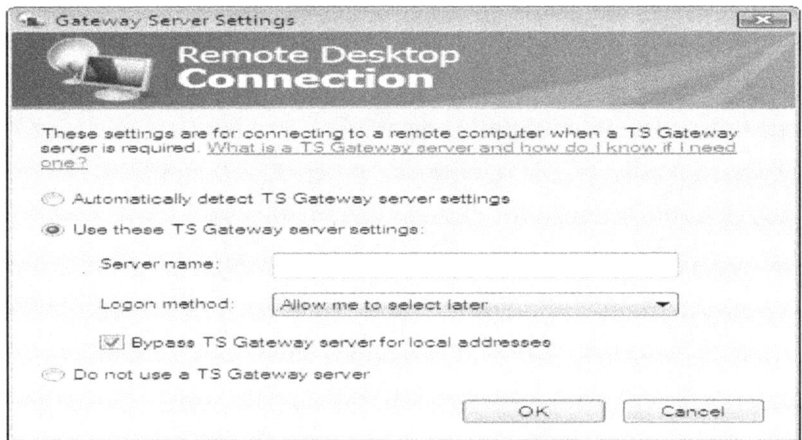

If the TS Gateway server authentication is not required to enhance network security for the client machine, disable this feature by selecting the ***Do not use a TS Gateway server*** option and then click on ***OK*** to save changes. The *Remote Desktop Connection* can be made faster by clearing off the ***Bypass TS Gateway server for local addresses*** box.

Remote Desktop Connection Settings

To adjust *Remote Desktop Connection* settings, click on the ***Start*** button, and then right-click on my computer to choose the ***Properties*** option. From the left navigation pane of the ***System*** window, click on ***Remote settings*** link. Select one of the following preferences for *Remote Desktop Connection*:

- *Don't allow connection to this computer*
- *Allow connections from computers running any version of Remote Desktop (less secure)*

- *Allow connections only from computer running Remote Desktop with Network Level Authentication (more secure)*

Select one of the above options to set *Remote Desktop Connection* preferences. Click on ***Apply*** and then click ***OK*** to save system settings.

Add Remote Desktop Local User

To add a Remote Desktop local user, from the *System Properties* window, click the ***Remote*** tab, under the ***Remote Desktop*** section; click the ***Select Users*** to add users who can connect to this computer.

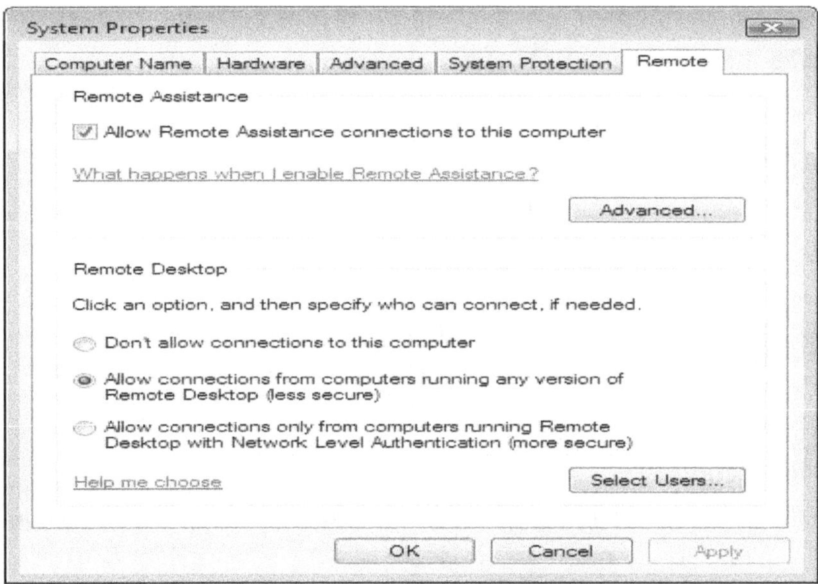

Click on ***Add*** to add a *Remote Desktop* user. An existing/active local user can only be permitted to connect to this computer.

From the ***Select Users*** window, click on ***Advanced*** button and then click on ***Find Now*** to search for the active local users. Then select the local user that needs to be added to the *Remote Desktop Group* to have permission connecting to your computer remotely and click ***OK***.

Configure Remote Desktop Connection Port

By default, a standard port 3389 is reserved for *Remote Desktop Connection*, but it can be changed to another port number that can only be known to authorize users to add an extra layer of the network security for your system. To change a listening RDC port, open *Run Command* (*Windows Key + R*), type ***regedit*** in the search bar, and then press ***Enter*** from the keyboard. To navigate registry path, click on ***KEY_LOCAL_MACHINE\System\ CurrentControlSet\Control \TerminalServer\WinStations\RDP-Tcp*** and then double-click on ***PortNumber*** registry. In the *Edit Registry* dialog box, under the ***Base*** section, click on ***Decimal***. Type the new port number, and then click ***OK*** to save listening RDC port preferences. To quit *Registry Editor*, go to the ***File*** menu, and then choose ***Exit*** option. You have finished editing listening RDC port.

Windows Remote Assistance

Windows Remote Assistance enables Vista users to ask for help remotely from other trusted users while troubleshooting or fixing computer problems. It is recommended to only seek help from trusted users. Once they are connected to your computer remotely, they have access to your files and personal information. An administrator or member of an administrative group has privileges to configure *Remote Assistance* settings.

Open Windows Remote Assistance

To open *Windows Remote Assistance*, click the ***Start*** button, type ***Windows Remote Assistance*** in search bar and then press ***Enter*** from the keyboard.

Windows Remote Assistance allows Vista users to remotely connect to your computer to offer you help to troubleshoot computer problems or you can offer help trusted users to fix their computer issues.

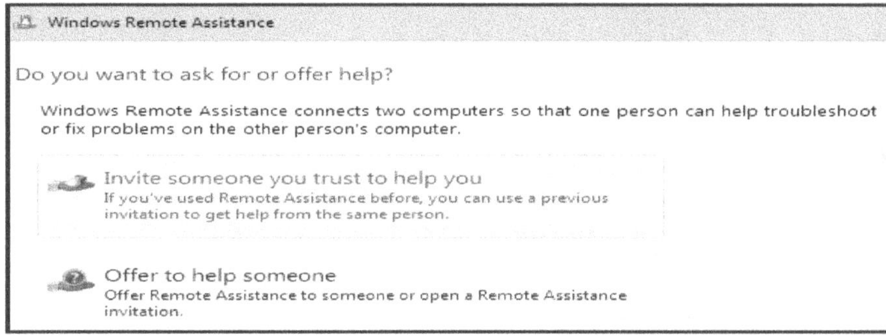

Assistance from others can be asked by sending an invitation file using Windows Mail, if it is configured properly for your system. Otherwise save an invitation file in the local hard-disk and then send it to the trusted users later as an attachment using other email vendors, e.g. Google mail, Yahoo mail, Hotmail etc.

Remote Assistance Settings

To open *Remote Assistance* setting, right-click on the ***Computer*** icon and then select the ***Properties*** option from the list. From left navigation pane of the ***System*** window, click on ***Remote settings*** link. To allow remote assistance connections to this computer, click the ***Remote*** tab. Under the ***Remote Assistance*** section, select the ***Allow Remote Assistance connections to this computer*** option in order to get remote assistance request from other users.

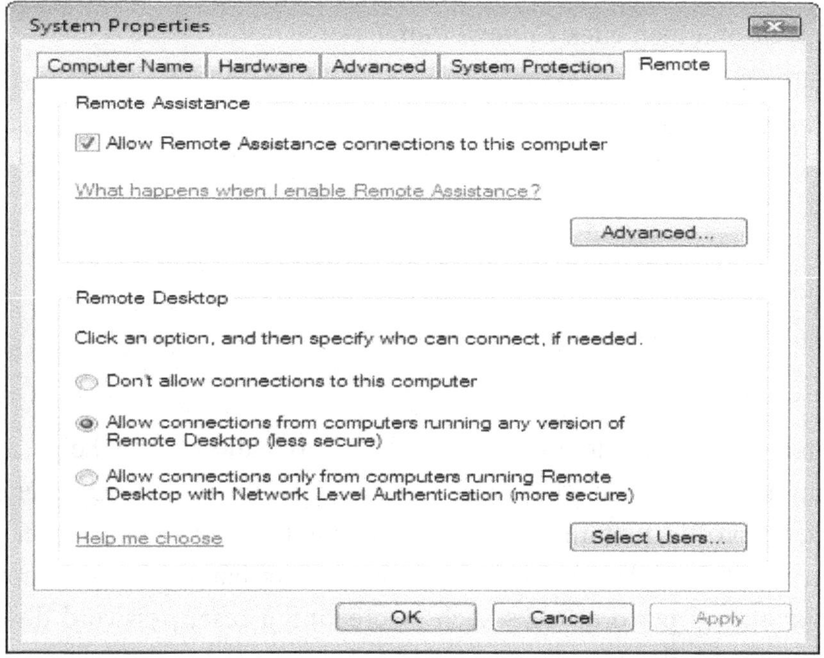

To adjust Remote Assistance advanced settings, click on ***Advanced*** button to access remote assistance settings from the ***Remote Assistance*** section. If an authorized user wants to control client computer remotely, check the ***Allow this computer to be controlled remotely*** option, under the ***Remote control*** section. To set the maximum amount of time an invitation can remain open, adjust the duration of the invitation from the ***Invitation*** section to restrict the user not to use same invitation for a long period of time. To seek assistance from Windows Vista users only, check the ***create invitations that can only be used from computers running Windows Vista or later*** option under the ***Invitations*** section and then click on ***OK*** to save changes.

User Accounts

A user account is an authentication method to get access to the local machine or the remote machine. Microsoft Windows Vista operating system allows you to either create a standard user account and/or an administrator account on local machine for users. A standard user account has limited permission to change system settings, but on the other hand, an administrator has full rights to manage user's accounts and their profile settings. They also have permission to modify local machine hardware and software profile settings. To modify, delete, and manage user's accounts, you must be an administrator or a member of the administrative group or must have administrative privileges.

Open User Accounts Window

To open *User Accounts* window:

- Click the ***Start*** button and then click ***Control Panel***
- From left navigation pane, click ***Classic View***
- Double-click ***User Accounts***

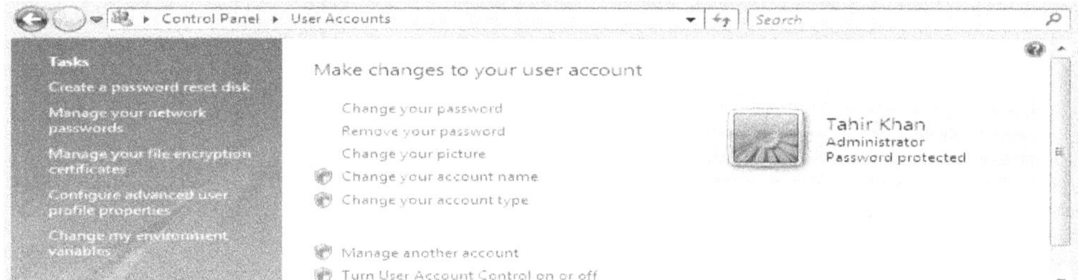

The *User Accounts* window is split into two panels, right navigation panel helps an administrator to perform tasks such as changing user's passwords, removing user's passwords, changing user's profile picture and user's account types, re-naming user's accounts, and turning on or off User Account Control. On the other hand, left navigation panel enables an administrator to perform tasks such as creating a reset password disk, managing network password, and file encryption certificates.

Setup User Accounts

Open the *User Accounts* window. From right navigation pane of the *User Accounts* window, click the ***Manage another account*** link to manage local user's accounts. A user account must be created in order to access the resources of a machine. A local user account is created for a specific machine and for a specific user.

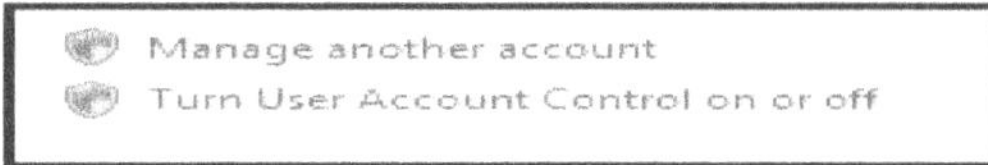

Click on ***create a new account*** link to start creating a new local user account.

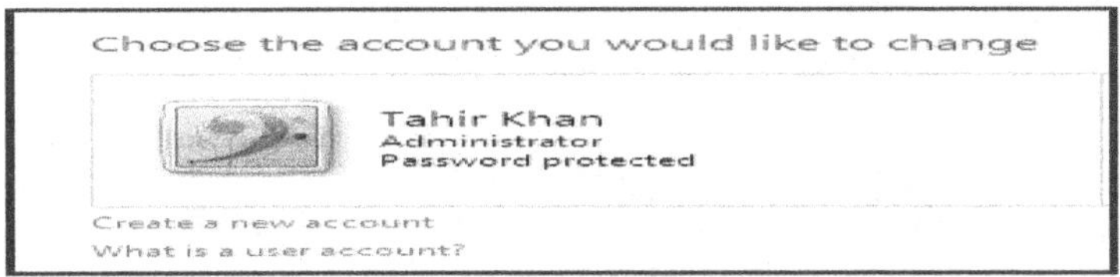

To create a new user account:

- Type a unique name for the user's account
- Select one of the available account types, either a ***standard user*** or ***administrative*** group
- Click ***Create Account*** to create a new user account

The available user accounts types are explained below to make an appropriate user account choice.

Standard Account: A standard account user has permission to run most programs but may not be able to install new programs. Standard users have limited privileges to modify hardware and software profile settings, but can change system settings that do not affect other users or security of the computer.

Administrator Account: It has privileges to perform all administrative tasks such as creating and managing local user's accounts, changing any hardware and software configuration to make the system performance better, and restricting users to modify any hardware and software profile settings to maintain the security of the system.

Change User Account Type

Open the ***Control Panel*** in classic view and then double-click the **User Accounts**. From right navigation pane of the *User Accounts* window, click the ***Change your account type*** to change the local user's account type.

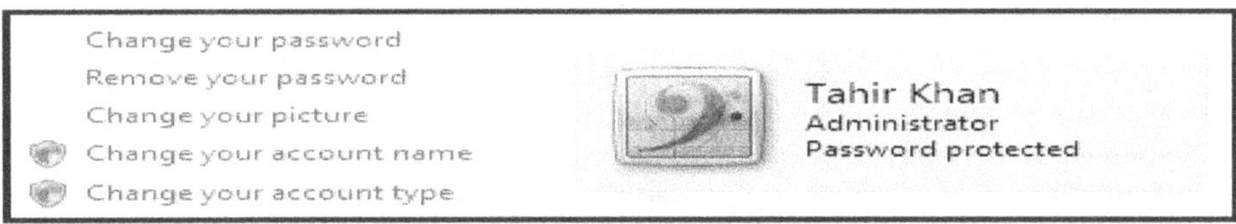

Select an account type (a *standard user or an administrator*) and then click the ***Change Account Type*** to change account type for a user.

Change User Account Password

Open the *User Accounts* window. From the right navigation pane of the *User Accounts* window, click the ***Change your password*** link to manage a local user's password. If *User*

Account Control window is prompted to you, click on ***Continue*** or provide administrative credentials to continue.

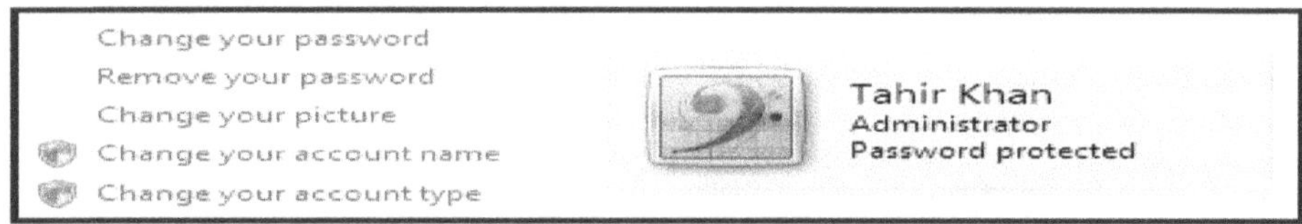

To set a new password for your account, type current password and then create a new password that you want to set for your account, and then confirm the new password. Click on ***Change password*** to reset user's account password.

Remove User Account Password

Open the *User Accounts* window. From right navigation pane of the *User Accounts* window, click the ***Remove your password*** link to remove a local user's password.

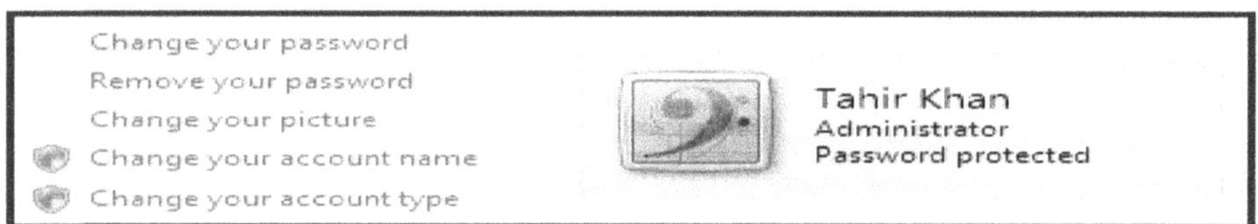

You will be asked to provide the current password and then click on ***Remove Password*** to remove current user account password.

Remove User Account

Open the *User Accounts* window. From right navigation pane of the *User Accounts* window, click the ***Manage another account*** link and then select the user account that needs to be removed.

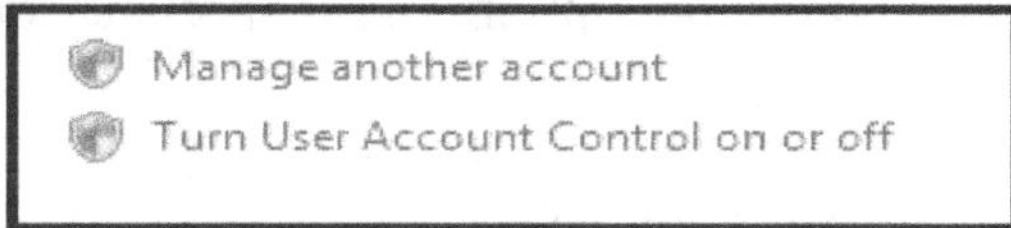

Select the ***Delete the account*** option to remove the account from your system.

System asks an administrator, what needs to be done with the user's personal files which are associated with the user's account. If you decided to keep the user's files, click on ***Keep Files***. A folder will be created on the desktop of the computer, and then all of the documents, favorites, music, pictures and video files will be moved into it. If the files are not necessary to keep, click on ***Delete Files*** to delete the user's account and user's personal data files.

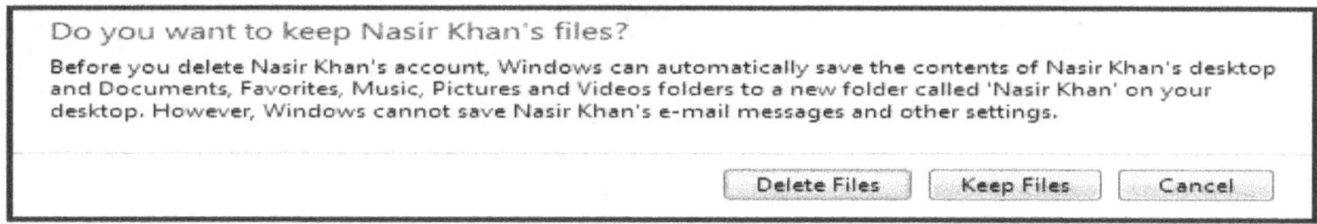

This process may take few minutes to delete desired user account.

User Account Control

A *User Account Control* (UAC) is a security feature added to Windows Vista editions of Microsoft operating system that adds an extra layer of security to minimize the risk of installing malicious codes into your system. The UAC can be turned off as needed, but it is recommended to leave it on.

To enable/disable UAC, open the *User Accounts* window. From the right navigation pane of the *User Accounts* window, click the ***Turn User Account Control on or off*** link to change local *User Account Control* settings.

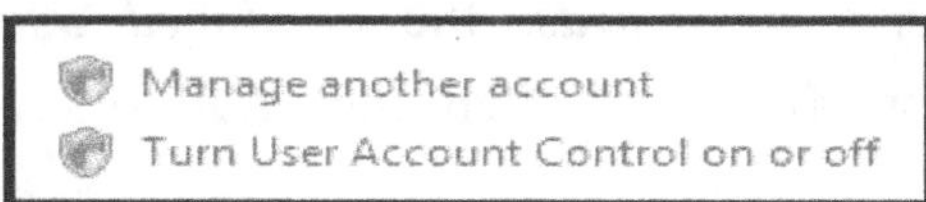

To disable User Account Control feature, clear the ***Use User Account Control (UAC) to help protect your computer*** checkbox. It is recommended to have ***User Account Control*** feature active to protect your system against installing any spywares, adware and malicious codes in your system. To enable User Account Control feature, select the ***Use User Account Control (UAC) to help protect your computer*** option and then click on ***OK*** to save changes.

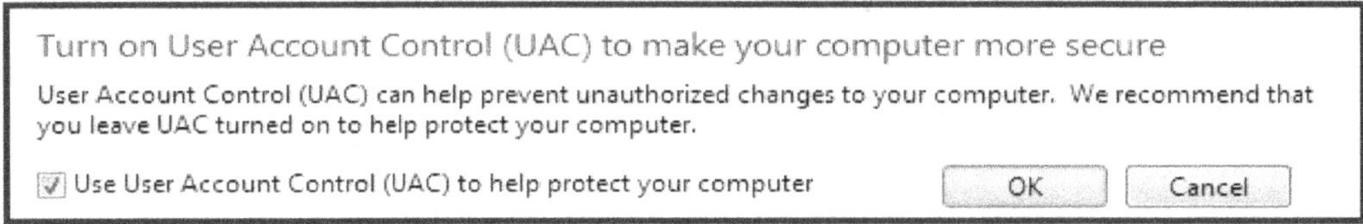

Advanced User Account Properties

The advanced user account is design for system administrators to manage user's accounts and their passwords. To access advanced user account properties, click the ***Start*** menu and type ***netplwiz OR control userpasswords2,*** in the search bar, and then press ***Enter*** on the keyboard.

An administrator can add new user accounts, remove existing user accounts and it can also reset password for any user listed under the ***Users*** tab.

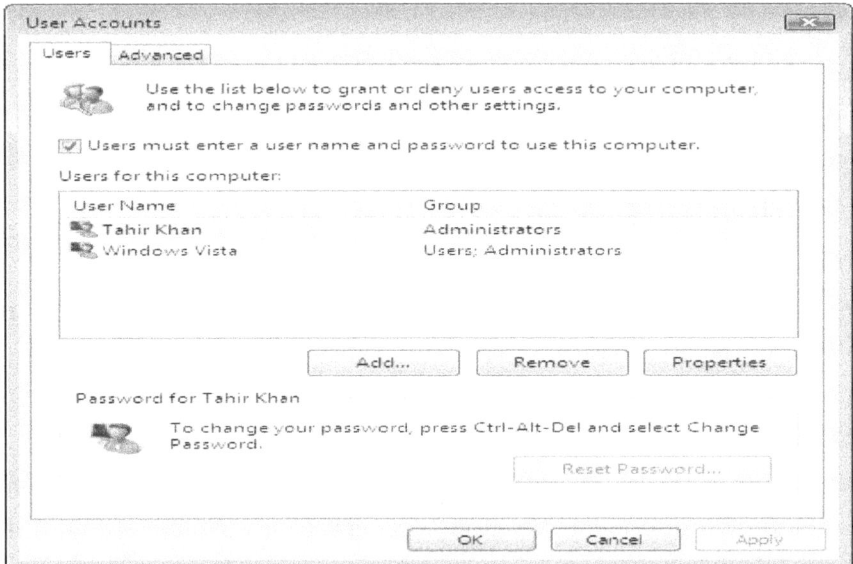

In the ***Advanced*** tab, you can manage the ***user's passwords***, the ***advanced user management***, and the ***secure logon*** types. Click on ***Apply*** and then click ***OK*** to save changes.

Local Area Network

A local area network covers a small geographical area such as your home, office, and school. The connectivity of the connection is limited to a single building or group of buildings. An administrator or member of administrative group can only modify local area network settings.

Open Network Sharing Center

To open *Network Sharing Center,* click ***Start*** button, click ***Control Panel***, and then double-click **Network *and Sharing Center***. *Network and Sharing Center* window is split into two panels, the right panel is called, ***Network and Sharing Center***, and the left panel is called as ***Tasks***. The right navigation panel helps an administrator to view and manage following network features: network connectivity, network discovery, file sharing, public folder sharing, printer sharing, password protected sharing, and media sharing options. On the other hand, left navigation panel helps an administrator to view computers and devices over the network, connecting to a network, setting up a connection or network, managing and performing diagnoses on the network connections.

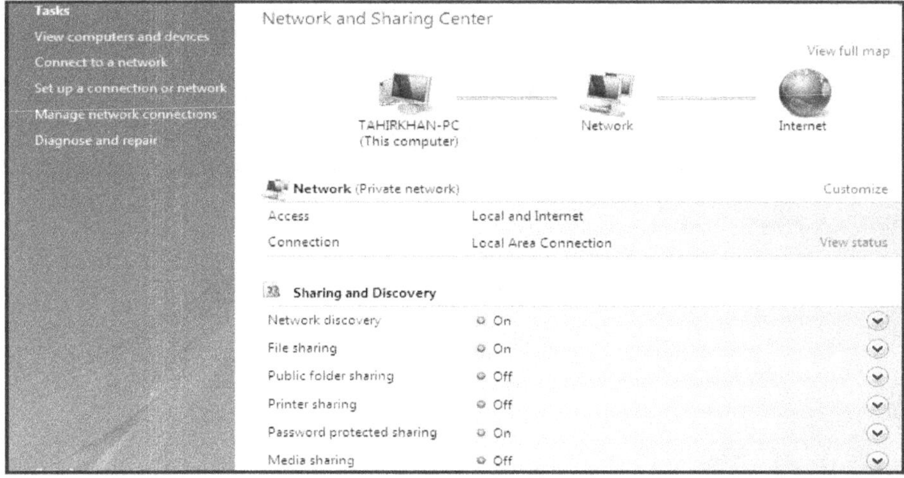

Local Area Network Status

Open *Network and Sharing Center*. From right navigation pane of the ***Network and Sharing Center***, click the ***View status*** link to see the connectivity of a local connection.

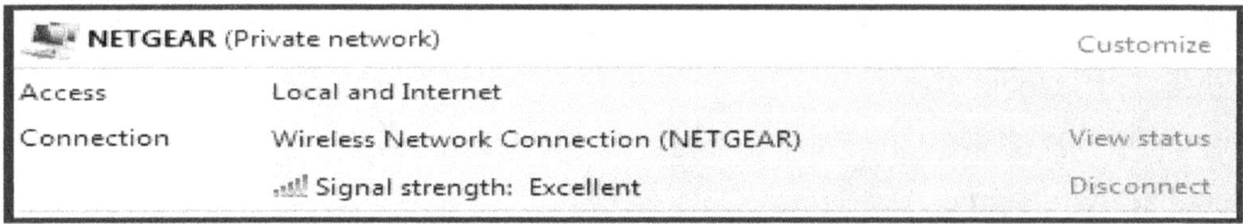

A *Local Area Connection Status* window shows: the connection speed, duration of connection time, media status, IPV4 connectivity status, IPV6 connectivity status, and data packets being sent by the router and received by the computer. Click on ***Close*** after done reviewing the local area connection status information. The network connection details can be viewed by clicking on ***Details*** button from the ***Connection*** section.

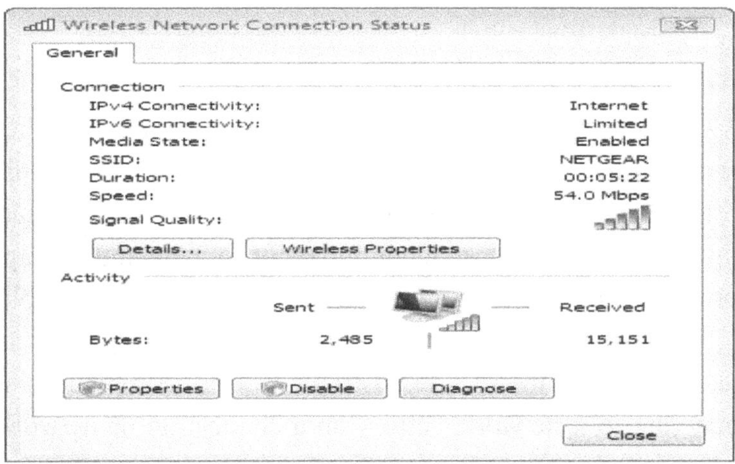

Disable Local Area Network Connection

Open *Local Area Connection Status* window. In the ***General*** tab, under the ***Activity*** section, click the ***Disable***. A *User Account Control* (UAC) window may be prompted to confirm this action, click on ***Continue***, or provide administrative credentials to continue.

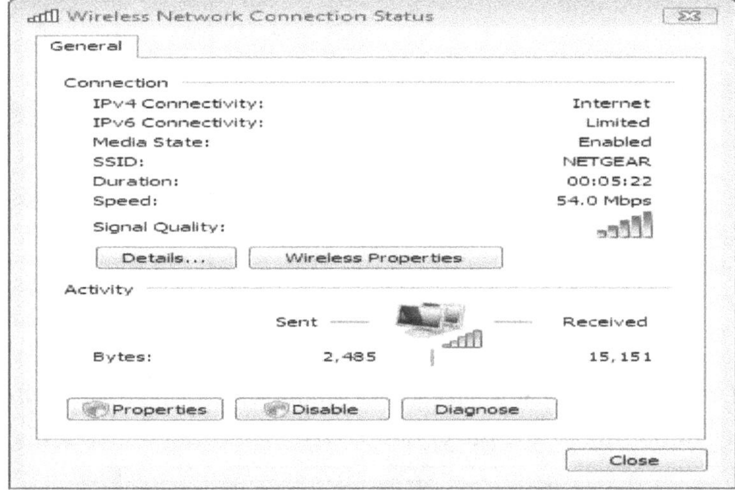

After you disable the local area network connection, a **Red Cross** will appear on the computer icon in the system tray (located at right-bottom of computer desktop) that shows no connectivity signal.

Enable Local Area Network Connection

Open Network and Sharing Center. In the ***Network and Sharing Center*** section, a *Red Cross* on a line that connects your computer to the Internet indicates no connectivity between your computer and network. There can be many possible reasons of not having connectivity between two devices but the most common reason is disabling of the network adaptor card. To enable the network card, click the ***Manage network connections*** link from the left navigation pane of the ***Network and Sharing Center***.

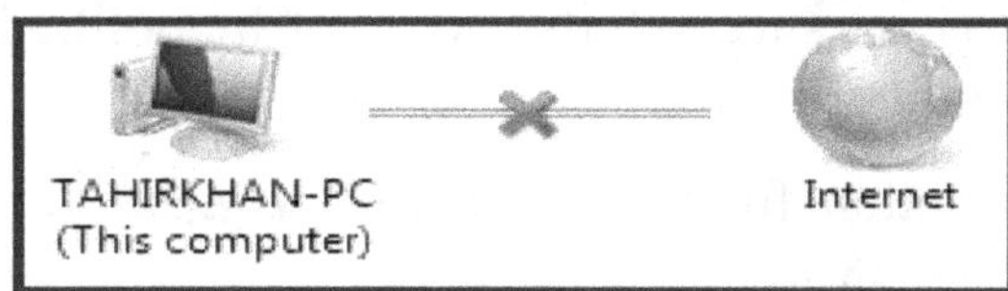

From the ***Network Connections*** window, right-click on the disabled local area network connection and then select the ***Enable*** option from the list. If the system has both wireless and wired network connections, you may see more than one local area network connection.

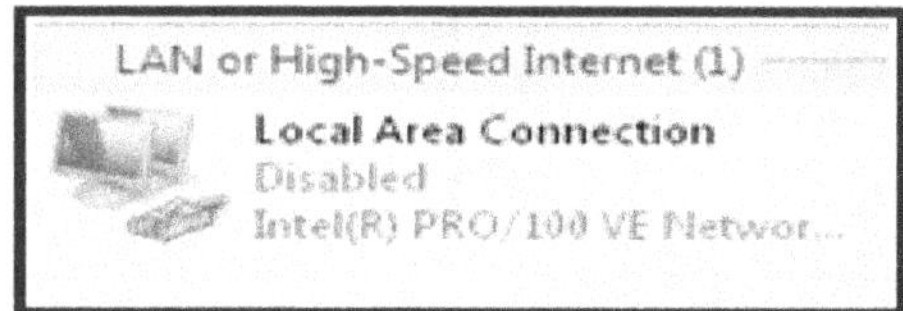

Now, the local area network is enabled and it has connectivity to it. A local area network icon will appear in notification area (located at the right-bottom of the desktop).

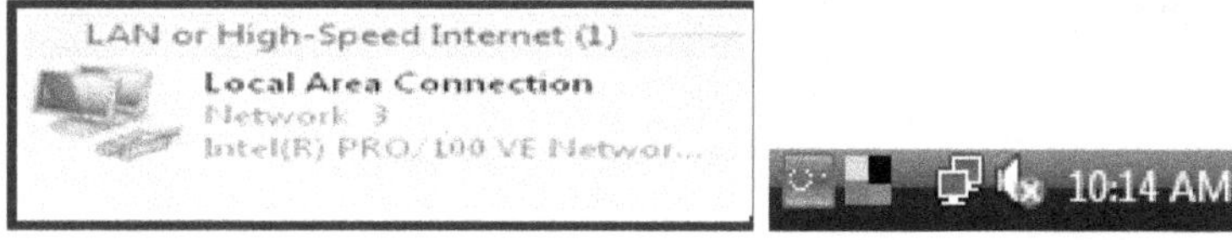

Change Network Location Type

To change network location type, click the ***Customize*** link to customize local area network settings, from the right navigation pane of the ***Network and Sharing Center*** window.

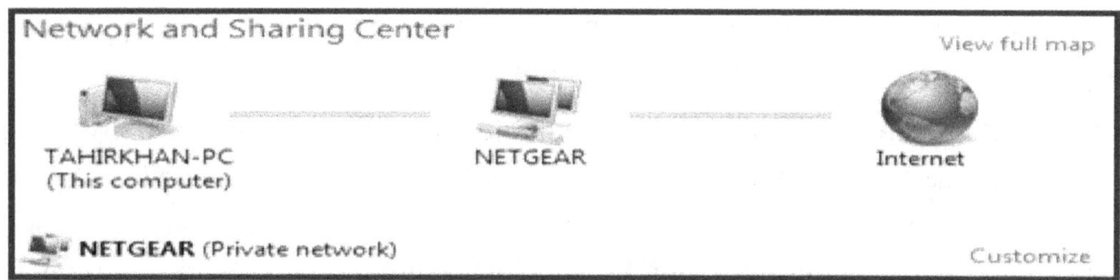

Select the preferred network location type and then click on ***Next***. There are two network location types are available to choose from, ***Public and Private***. A public network is designated to work in public area, such as an airport, coffee shop, and unsecure places where a security key is not required connecting to the Internet because it is available to public for free of charge. A private network is more secure network such as your home or office network where security is not a big concern because once the system is authenticated, it will remember the settings and will authenticate you every time you log-on to the system. If the network location type is set successfully, you will be notified. Click on ***Close*** to exit out of the window.

To change a network icon, click on ***Change*** button from the ***Network Icon*** section. Choose network icon of your choice and then click ***OK*** to save settings.

IP Address and DNS Server Configuration

IP stands for Internet protocol and it must be a unique number for every computer to stay connected with Internet to share computer resources with network users. The IP addresses, subnet mask, default gateway, and other IP parameters for a home user is assigned automatically but Dynamic Host Configuration Protocol (DHCP) server needs to be installed for domain users to get the IP address for their system which helps system administrator to manage and control IP addresses over the network.

A Dynamic Name System (DNS) translates hostnames into IP addresses to deliver that information to the network equipment that are only capable of understanding IP addresses, not hostnames. For example, www.yahoo.com is a hostname and it is only understandable by human beings but not by network equipments such as computers, servers, routers, and switches. To establish a communication between human beings and network equipments, we need to know the IP address of the hostname. The IP address of yahoo website is 69.147.76.15 and it needs to be sent to the network equipment to establish a successful communication.

To configure IP address and DNS server for your system:

- Open *Network and Sharing Center.*
- Click the ***Manage network connections*** link from the left navigation pane.
- From the ***Network Connections*** window, right-click on the local area network connection that needs to be configured manually for IP address and for DNS server, and then choose the ***Properties*** option from the list.

There are two Internet protocols available for Windows Vista users which are IPV4 and IPV6. The IPV4 are 32-bit address and IPV6 are 128-bit which is a group of 8 hexadecimal characters. To configure any of the Internet protocols, select the appropriate protocols from dialog box, and click on ***Properties*** button, and then type correct IP address and DNS server for your network device.

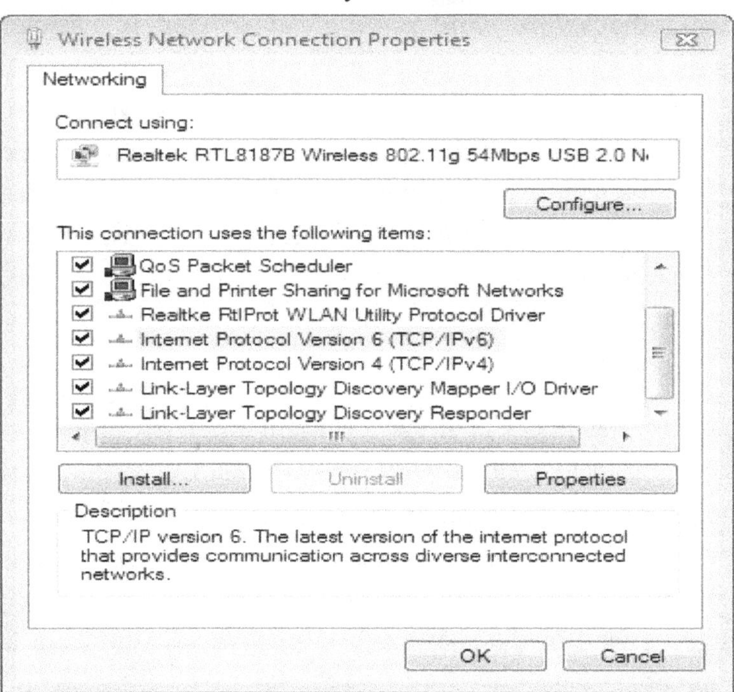

Diagnose and Repair Network Connection

Diagnose and repair utility helps a user to enable the network adapter, resolve IP conflicts, and renew IP address, subnet mask, DNS server, and DHCP server.

To perform a diagnostic on a network connection, open *Network and Sharing Center* window. In the ***Network and Sharing Center*** section, a red cross on a line that connects your computer to the Internet indicates that there is no connectivity between your router/switch and your computer. To solve this issue, you may use diagnose and repair utility. The diagnose and repair utility analyzes the network of the computer and will repair the connection, if possible. For example, if the network card is disabled, or any IP addresses conflicts over the network can be resolved by just running this utility.

To perform diagnose and repair on the local area network, click the ***Diagnose and repair*** link from the left navigation pane of the ***Network and Sharing Center*** window. Diagnose and repair utility will perform a diagnostic on the network and it will display a diagnostic report to solve the issue. For example, if your network card was disabled, you will be asked to click on ***Enable the Network Adapter Local Area Connection*** option, which will enable your network card, automatically. The diagnose and repair process may take few minutes enabling the adaptor or fixing any other issues which are related with the network adaptor card. Click on ***Close*** to exit.

Shared Resources

It is a method to share files and documents between the local and the network users. A sharing can happen between users via local area network or wide area network. A local area network covers a small geographical area such as your home, office, and schools; whereas the wide area network covers a large geographical area such as a state, a province or a country. A sharing resources can be categorized as files sharing, public folder sharing, printer sharing, and media sharing. You must have administrative privileges to modify shared resources settings.

Share Folder with a Local User

Right-click on the folder that you wish to share with local users, and then choose the ***Properties*** option from the list. To enable network file and folder sharing, click the

Sharing tab from the ***Folder Properties*** window, under the ***Network File and Folder Sharing*** section, click on ***Share***.

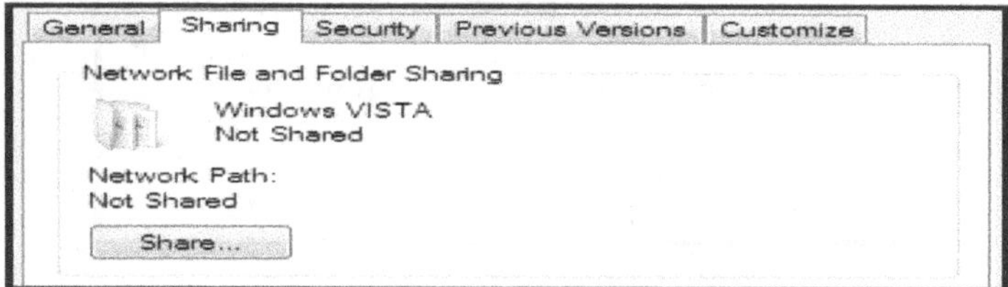

To share the folder with a local user, type the name of the user who needs permission to access shared folder over the network and then click on ***Add*** button. The local user accounts must be created in advance to share network resources.

To share the folder with the local users, click on ***Share*** to start sharing files and folder.

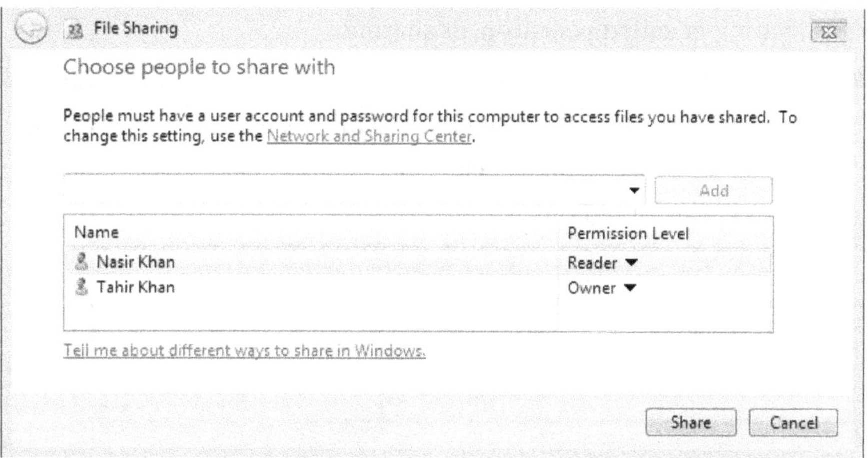

Now, the local user is permitted to have access to the shared folder and a path for the shared folder is created to share with other local users, if needed. Click on ***Done*** to finish the file sharing process.

It is simple to differentiate between a shared and an unshared folder. A shared folder must have a sharing icon (two human beings are next to each other) on the top of the shared folder.

Printer Sharing

The printer sharing is a way to share printer resources over the network. The network users must be configured properly to share printer resources. Open *Network and Sharing Center* window to configure printer sharing settings. From the ***Network and Sharing Center*** window, under the ***Sharing and Discovery*** section, click the toggle arrow to view the printer sharing on and off options. To turn on the printer sharing, click the ***Turn on printer sharing*** option, and then click ***Apply*** to save changes. Now, printer sharing is on for authorized users to have access to the printer shared resources. An authorized user must have a username and password to access shared resources

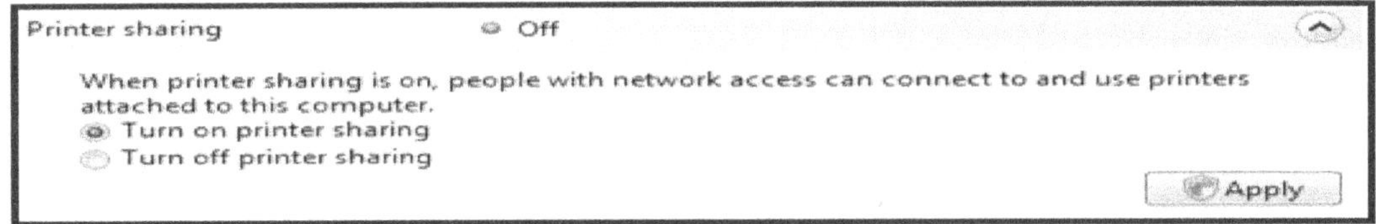

File Sharing

A file sharing happens between network users to transfer files from one system to another over the network. This method can slow down network traffic if large files are in process to download. If file sharing is happening between two network users where a files server is not involved such file sharing is called peer-to-peer sharing.

To turn on ***File Sharing*** feature, open *Network and Sharing Center*. Under the ***File Sharing*** section, click on toggle arrow and then select the ***Turn on file sharing*** option. Click on ***Apply*** to save file sharing settings. The file sharing can happen between authorized network users, once it is turned on.

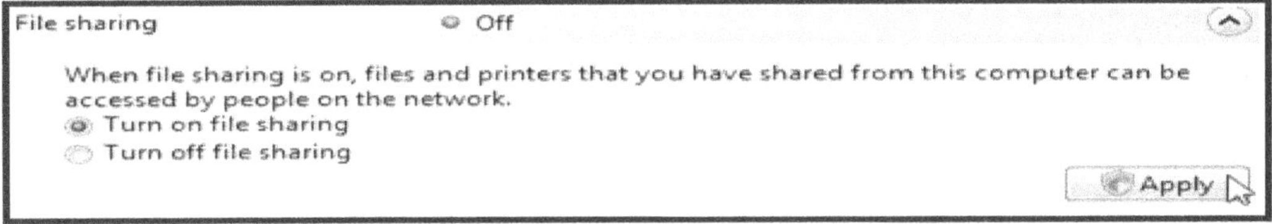

Password Protected Sharing

A password protected sharing requires you to have a valid username and password to authenticate your session to access shared folders over the network. It is recommended to have a strong password for any resources that needs to be shared over the network.

To turn on ***Password protected sharing*** feature, open the *Network and Sharing Center* and select the ***Turn on password protected sharing*** option from the ***Password protected sharing*** section. Click on ***Apply*** to save password protected sharing settings. It is recommended to have the password protected sharing feature turned on to protect sharing resources from unauthorized user access.

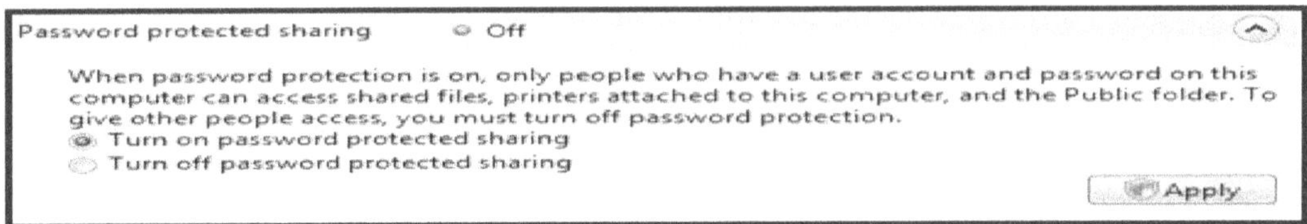

Network Discovery

A network discovery allows network users to discover other network devices over the local network. This is an easy way to establish communication between network users to share computer resources over the network.

From the ***Network and Sharing Center*** panel, if the ***Network discovery*** is turned off, network devices, such as network computers, and routers over the network are not discoverable. To enable your system to discover other network resources, the network discovery must be turned on. To turn on ***Network discovery*** feature, open the *Network and Sharing Center*. Click on toggle arrow to turn on and off options from ***Network discovery*** section. Select the ***Turn on network discovery*** option and then click on ***Apply*** to save settings. Once the network discovery is turned on, you may need user's permission to access their personal resources.

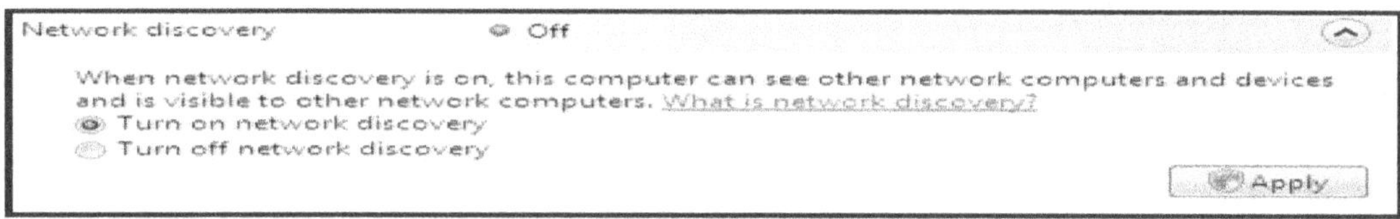

Media Sharing

A media sharing happens between two or more network users who shares media files across the network. The ***Media Sharing*** feature must be turned on to share media resources, such as shared music, pictures, and video files across the network. To start sharing media over the network, open *Network and Sharing Center*. Click on toggle arrow from the ***Media sharing*** section and then click on ***Change***.

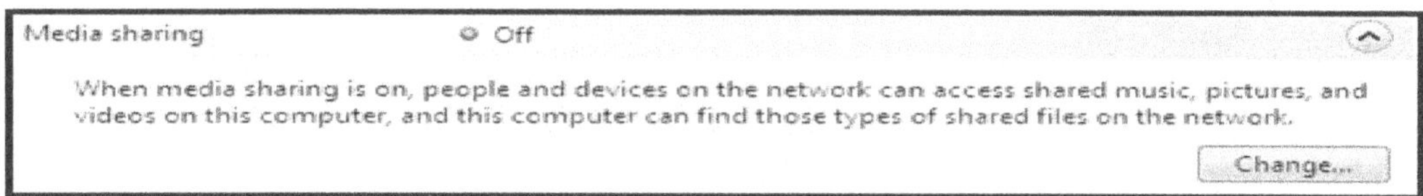

From the ***Media Sharing*** window, under the ***Sharing settings*** section, select the ***Share my media*** option and then click on ***Networking*** button to find shared media resources. You must be on a private network to share media resources over the network.

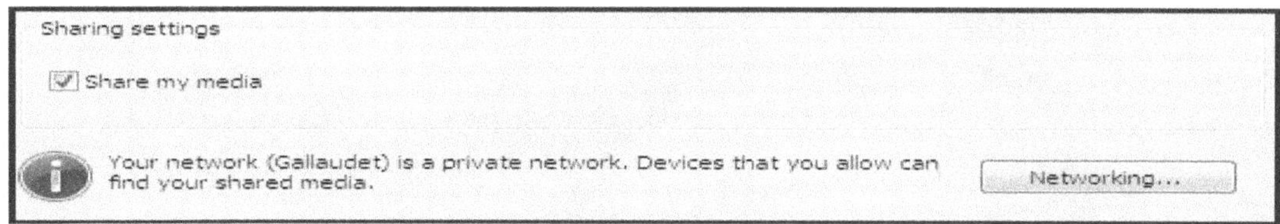

If *User Account Control* window is prompted to you, click on ***Continue*** or provide administrative credentials to continue.

Select the network PC to share media with other users, from the ***Share my media to*** section, and then click on ***Allow***, so sharing can happen between network users. Click on ***Apply*** and then click on ***OK*** to save media sharing preferences.

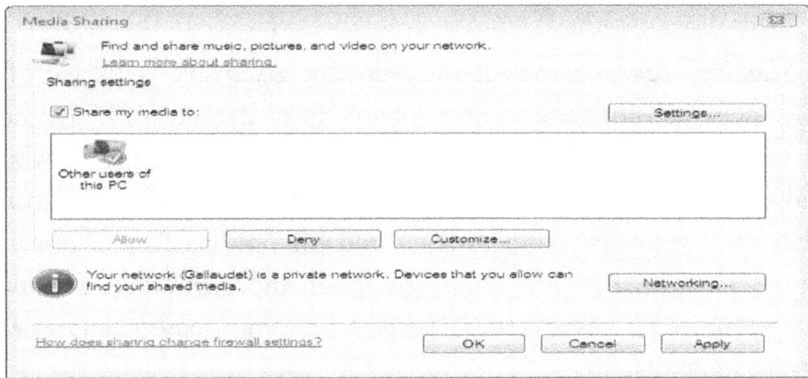

System Configuration Settings

A system configuration window is designed to allow the system administrators to make appropriate changes to startup options, application services, and startup programs to troubleshoot computer issues.

Open System Configuration Window

To open system configuration settings, run command line (*Windows Key + R*) and type ***msconfig*** in the search bar and then click ***OK***. You may be prompted to confirm this action, click on ***Continue***. If you are prompted for administrative credentials, provide credentials to continue.

The system configuration options are explained below to have a better understanding of each configuration to isolate computer issues.

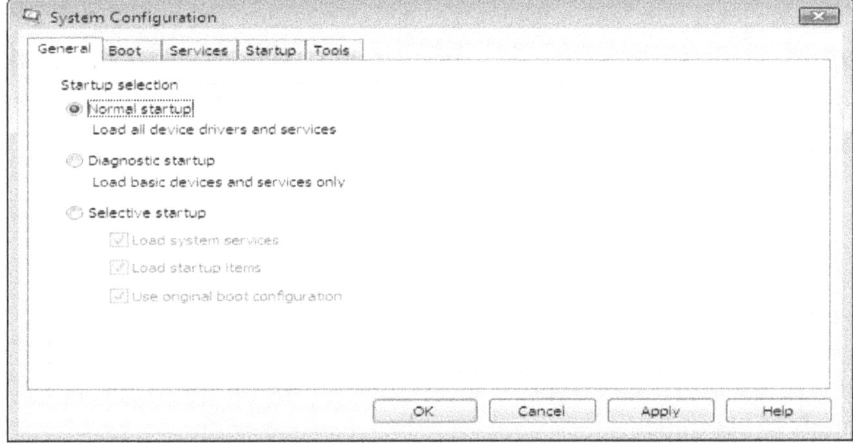

Configure Startup Options

In *General* tab, *normal startup, diagnostic startup, and selective startup*, are available options to apply to the system.

Diagnostic Startup Mode

The diagnostic mode only loads basic devices and services and checks for corrupted Windows files to isolate a program or service which may be causing issues for your system to startup.

Selective Startup Mode

The available selective startup services are:

- **Load system services**: If this option is enabled, the system will only load services that are necessary to run your system properly. To make changes to the currently running system services, click ***Services*** tab from the ***System Configuration*** dialog box and then make necessary changes, if needed.
- **Load startup items**: If this option is enabled, the system will load only startup items. This option allows selecting individual services and startup programs to isolate a program or a service that is causing problem for your system. To view the list of startup items for your system, click on ***Startup*** tab from the ***System Configuration*** dialog box.
- **Use original boot configuration**: If this option is enabled, the system startups with original boot configuration settings.

Normal Startup Mode

In normal startup, the system will start up with all device drivers and services which are part of the system. By default, the system starts in normal mode which loads all of the device drivers and application services.

Boot System Configuration settings

To boot your system in *Safe Mode*, select the ***Safe Boot*** option from the ***Boot options*** section, and then select one by one safe boot options to isolate the issues, if it is related with system startup. Then restart your system and then it will boot into the *Safe Mode* with selective services turned on.

All of the following boot system configurations play an important role to troubleshoot a computer issue.

- **Minimal**: Windows run into the *Safe Mode* with only essential system services turned on.
- **Alternate Shell**: Windows boot to the command prompt and it allows you to make changes to your system using DOS command line.
- **Active Directory Repair**: If the system is unable to load directory services, the system can be started with this option and it will restore or repair *Active Directory* services.
- **Network**: Windows boot to the safe mode with active network device tuned on that will provide you an access to Internet, if your system needs to download any device drivers.
- **No GUI boot**: If this option is disabled, your system will boot faster than normal startup. At the startup of your computer, you may see a screen with the logo of Microsoft Corporation on it. This option will eliminate that screen and will make your system to boot faster.
- **Boot log**: This option stores the device drivers that are being installed for your system in the ntbtlog.txt file.
- **Base Video**: Your system will boot with basic display drivers to solve video resolution problem or other problems that are isolated with video card of your computer.
- **OS Boot Information**: Device drivers will display on startup screen.
- **Make All Settings Permanent**: All the changes made to the boot configuration are marked permanent for all users.

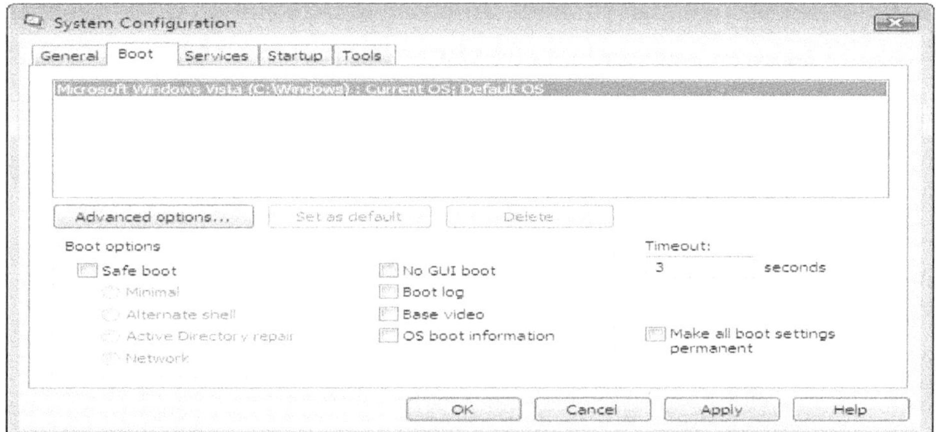

Application Services Configuration

It is recommended to disable application services which are causing significant problems for your system to run properly. To disable a service, click the ***Service*** tab from the *System Configuration* window, and then clear the ***application service*** checkbox. Click on ***Apply*** and then click on ***OK*** to save changes

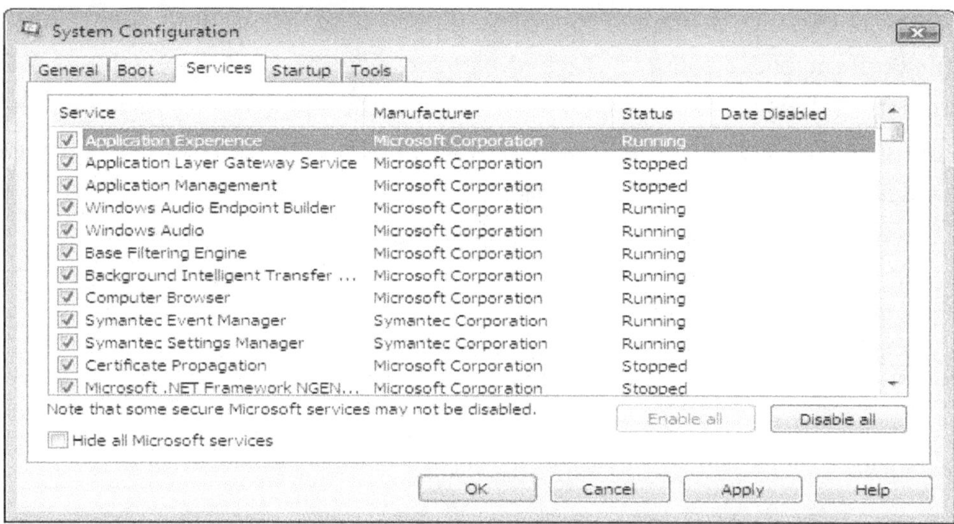

Startup Services

In the *Startup* tab, the startup items are listed with their names, their manufacture name, command line to run the program on startup of the system, location of the startup items, and date they were disabled. The startup services start automatically every time you log-on to the system. To start your system faster, disable the services that are not important to start with the system. For example, anti-virus and spyware programs are recommended to startup with your system but all other services may be disabled, if it is not required by an administrator to run at the startup. To disable a startup item, clear the appropriate application checkbox and then click on ***Apply*** and click on ***OK*** to save changes.

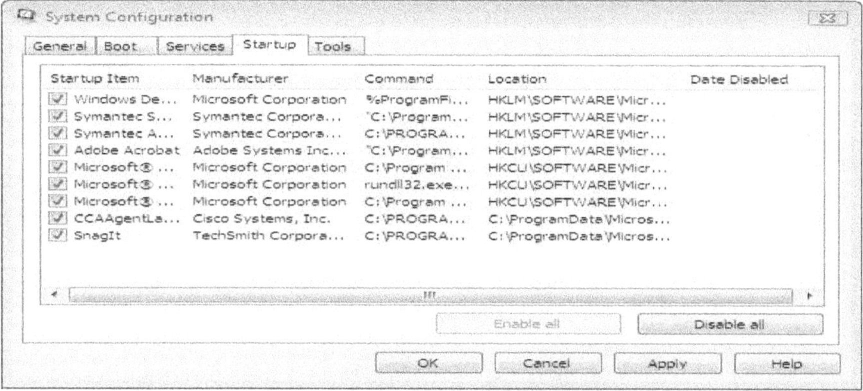

System Tools

In the *Tools* tab, a list of computer management tool is complied for administrators to launch an application by using system configuration window. The tools which are accessible from the *System Configuration* window are: About Windows, System Information, Remote Assistance, System Restore, Computer Management, Event Viewer, Programs, Security Center, System Properties, Internet Options, Internet Protocol Configuration, Performance Monitor, Task Manager, Disable UAC, Enable UAC, Command Prompt, and Registry Editor. To launch any of the above listed computer management tools, select the application that you want to open and then click on ***Launch***. Click on ***Apply*** and then click ***OK*** to save changes.

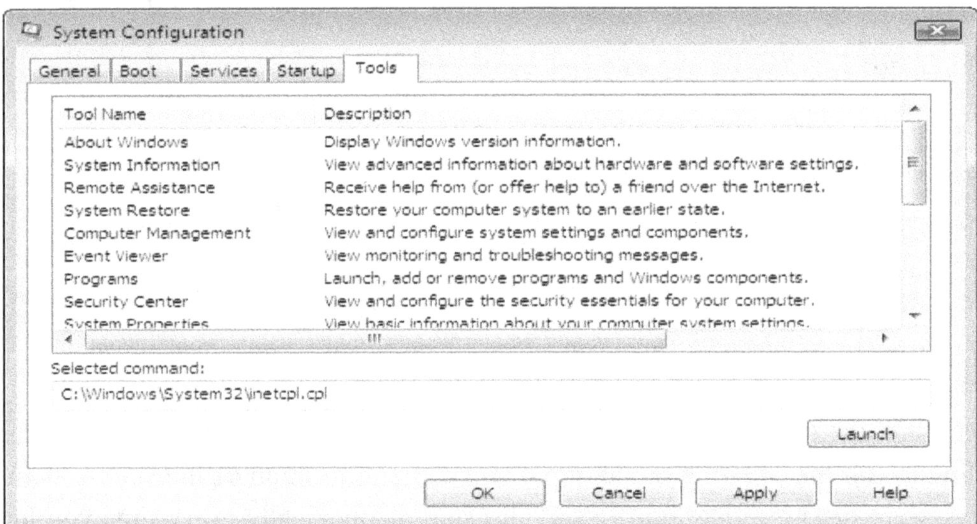

Question: What RDC stands for?

Answer: RDS stands for Remote Desktop Connection.

Question: What is RDC and why we need it?

Answer: RDC allows you to connect a client computer to a remote/host computer to perform regular maintenance. It is a smart way to access host computer resources from the client computer whenever it is needed to transfer necessary files or need to have access to a specific programs that are installed on the host machine but not on the client machine.

Question: Does all Windows Vista editions are capable of establishing a Remote Desktop connection?

Answer: No, the Windows Vista Starter and Windows Vista Home editions are not capable of establishing a Remote Desktop connection.

Question: How do I install Remote Desktop Connection?

Answer: The RDC is pre-installed program for Windows Vista operating systems.

Question: Can I customize Remote Desktop Connection settings? **Answer**:

Yes, you may if you log-on to the machine as an administrator. **Question**:

Why am I unable to change Remote Desktop Connection settings?

Answer: Your system administrator may have set special permissions using Group Policy Object (GPO) to restrict anyone to change RDC settings.

Question: Can I copy text from remote computer to my computer and vice versa?

Answer: Yes, if Remote Desktop Connection is configured correctly.

Question: What is Terminal Services Gateway and why is it important to me?

Answer: The TS Gateway server authentication method is designed for authorized users to establish a secure connection to the remote computer on a corporate network. If your company wants to have a secure connection from a client computer to the remote computer, then you must use this authentication to establish a secure connection.

Question: What is a server authentication?

Answer: A server authentication verifies connection to the correct remote computer that helps to stop establishing an unauthorized connection between the host and the client machine.

Question: Why is it necessary to configure Terminal Services Gateway server settings to create a secure connection between your machine and the remote machine?

Answer: Terminal Services Gateway helps to create a more secure and encrypted connection because it uses Remote Desktop Protocol (RDP), port 3389, and Hypertext Transfer Protocol over Secure Socket Layer (HTTPS), port 443, together to establish a secure connection between the client machine and the server machine. The RDP 3389 port is reserved for remote desktop connection and it can be blocked by *Windows Firewall* to enhance network security and HTTPS 443 ports that provides an extra layer of security to transmit data through a Secure Socket layer (SSL) tunnel for TS Gateway to establish a secure network environment.

Question: Does Windows Vista support multiple monitor for Remote Desktop Connection?

Answer: Yes, as long as both monitors have same resolution and aligned side by side.

Question: Which command line to use to adjust remote computer's desktop span multiple monitors?

Answer: Run command prompt (*Windows Key + R*), type ***mstsc /span*** in the search bar, then click **OK**.

Question: What is listening port for Remote Desktop Connection?

Answer: By default, a standard port 3389 is reserved for RDC, but it can be changed to another port number that is only known to you to add an extra security layer for your organization. You need administrative privileges to run and modify RDC registry.

Question: Why I cannot connect to the remote computer?

Answer: Possible following reasons:

- Remote computer is in sleep mode or turned off.
- Remote computer's power option is not configured correctly.

- Firewall is blocking you to connect to the remote computer.
- Remote computer is not connected with network.
- Not enough memory to connect to the remote computer. Try closing any open programs and then try again.
- Remote connection is not enabled on the remote computer.
- Remote computer does not have a password for user account. You must have a username and password for an account to be connected, remotely.
- Remote computer is busy and not accepting any more connections at this time.
- You may not be an authorized user to connect to a remote computer. Ask your administrator to add you to the remote desktop users group.
- You may have an invalid username and password for the remote computer.

Question: What is Windows Remote Assistance?

Answer: Windows Remote Assistance is a tool that allows you to invite someone to help you remotely to troubleshoot or fix computer problems. It is recommended to only seek help from trusted users, once they are connected to your computer remotely, they have access to your files, folders, and personal information.

Question: What is a local user account?

Answer: A local user account is created for a specific machine and for a specific user. A user account needs to be created to have access to the local machine resources.

Question: Define different types of user accounts?

Answer: There are three types of user accounts named as Administrator, Standard, and Guest. A standard user can perform general tasks that do not affect other users or security of the computer. An administrator has full privileges to make any changes to the computer. A guest account has limited access to the computer resources and does not have any privileges to make changes to the computer settings.

Question: What is a built-in administrator account?

Answer: By default, a built-in administrator account is created by the system itself. It has administrator privileges to perform all administrative tasks such as creating and managing local user's accounts, changing hardware and software configurations to make the system performance better, and restricting user's not to modify any hardware and software profile settings to maintain the security of the system.

Question: What is a Guest account?

Answer: By default, Microsoft Windows operating system creates a Guest account by itself for guest users, who will have limited access to the computer resources.

Question: Can I change user account type?

Answer: Yes, you may consider changing the user's account type to restrict their privileges or allow them to have more rights to maintain the computer services. You must be an administrator or a member of an administrator group to change user account types.

Question: Can I rename user accounts?

Answer: Yes, but you must be an administrator or must have administrative privileges to re-name a user account.

Question: What is a User Account Control?

Answer: A User Account Control is a security feature added to Windows Vista version of Microsoft operating systems that makes your computer more secure and adds an extra layer of security to minimize the risk of installing malicious codes in your system without your consent.

Question: Can I turn off the UAC?

Answer: Yes, the UAC can be turned off as needed, but it is recommended to leave it on.

Question: Is it recommended to turn off UAC?

Answer: No, it is not recommended to turn off UAC anytime.

Question: What happens when UAC feature is enabled by an administrator?

Answer: If a standard user attempts to perform a task that needs administrative privileges, he will be prompted to enter administrative credentials.

Question: What is a local area network?

Answer: A local area network covers a small geographical area such as your home, office, and school. The connectivity of this connection is limited within a single building or group of buildings.

Question: What is a wide area network?

Answer: The wide area network covers a large geographical area such as a state, a province or a country.

Question: What are designated location types for a local network?

Answer: The designated location types are ***Public*** and ***Private***.

Question: What is an IP address?

Answer: IP stands for Internet Protocol and it is unique for every computer to stay connected with Internet and able to share computer resources with network users.

Question: What is an IPsec?

Answer: An IPsec is an Internet Protocol Security which provides authentication, encryption and it also filters network traffic.

Question: Can I renew my IP address?

Answer: Yes, you may renew your network IP address by typing ***ipconfig /renew*** in DOS command prompt. To open DOS command prompt, run command line (*Windows Key + R*) and type ***cmd*** in the search bar, and then click ***OK***.

Question: What is TCP?

Answer: TCP stands for Transmission Control Protocol. It provides a reliable way of communication between a web server and a web client.

Question: Can I change network type?

Answer: Yes, you may need administrative privileges.

Question: Can I enable/disable a network adaptor card?

Answer: Yes, an administrator has permission to enable or disable a network adaptor card.

Question: What is an APIPA?

Answer: An APIPA stands for Automatic Private IP Addressing and it uses IP address ranges from 169.254.0.0 to 169.254.255.255 with a subnet mark of 255.255.0.0.

Question: Does APIPA assign default Gateway address?

Answer: APIPA only assigns IP address and Subnet mask, but not default Gateway.

Question: What are IPV4 and IPV6 connectivity protocols?

Answer: IPV4 and IPV6 are Internet Protocols (IP). IPV4 are 32-bit address whereas IPV6 protocol is a group of 8 hexadecimal characters and consists of 128 bits.

Question: What are the types of unicast IPV6 addresses?

Answer: There are four types of unicast IPV6 addresses named as site-local address, link-local address, global address, and unique local address.

Question:What does DHCP stand for?

Answer: The DHCP stands for Dynamic Host Configuration Protocol.

Question: What is DHCP server?

Answer: The purpose of DHCP server is to assign IP addresses, subnet masks, default gateway, and other IP parameters for the domain computers.

Question: Who uses DHCP server and why?

Answer: The standard Windows Vista users do not need DHCP server, but domain users do. If you are a domain user, the more chances to get the IP address and subnet mask for your system is by DHCP server which helps system administrator to manage and control IP addresses.

Question: What does DNS stand for?

Answer: The DNS stands for Domain Name System.

Question: What is DNS?

Answer: The DNS translates hostnames into IP addresses to deliver that information to the network devices that are only capable of understanding IP addresses but not hostnames. For example, www.yahoo.com is a hostname and it is only understandable by human beings but not by network equipments such as computers, servers, routers, and switches. To establish a communication between human beings and network equipments, we need to know the IP address of the hostname. The IP address of yahoo website is

69.147.76.15 and it needs to be sent to the network to establish a successful communication between human beings and network devices.

Question: What is loopback adaptor?

Answer: A loopback adaptor performs a self-test on your network adaptor card to check the functionality of network card. It is recommended by Microsoft to use loopback utility to resolve IP conflicts over a network adapter. There are two kinds of loopback adaptors, IPV4 loopback and IPV6 loopback. The IPV6 is the newer version of the loopback and used with latest operating systems like Microsoft Windows Vista and IPV4 is used with older operating systems like Microsoft Windows XP.
To perform a self-test for the network adaptor, run command line (*Windows Key + R*) and type ***cmd*** in the search bar, and then click ***OK***. To ping the network, type "ping 127.0.0.1" or "ping 0: 0: 0: 0: 0: 0: 0:1" without quotation marks in DOS window and wait for few seconds to view the ping statistics. Ping statistics report shows the number of data packets sent to the network card and number of data packets received by the network card. If the number of sending data packets and receiving data packets by a network card are equal, that shows your network card is functioning properly.

Question: What is IPV4 loopback address?

Answer: The loopback address of IPV4 is 127.0.0.1.

Question: What is IPV6 loopback address?

Answer: The loopback address of IPV6 is 0: 0: 0: 0: 0: 0: 0:1.

Question: What is a public network?

Answer: A public network is designated to work in public area, such as an airport, coffee shop, and unsecure places where a security key is not required to connect to the Internet.

Question: What features of public network are not available as you connect to it?

Answer: The following features of public network are not available:

- Discovery of other devices is restricted
- You may not able to connect with other computers
- Other computers are restricted to not discover your computer over the network

Question: What is a private network?

Answer: A private network is more secure network such as your home or office network.

Question: What is a Gateway?

Answer: A piece of hardware that ties two networks together that use different protocols.

Question: What is a Point-to-Point protocol?

Answer: A Point-to-Point(PPP) protocol facilitates a TCP/IP connection over the long distance connection.

Question: Define an application log?

Answer: An application log keeps track of error and warning events that can be useful for system administrator to correct the application errors.

Question: Define security log?

Answer: A security log keeps track of all events which are related to your successful and failed logon attempts.

Question: What is a network discovery?

Answer: A network discovery allows network users to discover each other network devices over the local network.

Question: What is a password protected sharing?

Answer: A password protected sharing requires a username and password to authenticate your session to have access to sharing folder over the network.

Question: Is password protected sharing recommended?

Answer: Yes, it is recommended to have a strong password for any resources that needs to be shared over the network.

Question: What is a file sharing?

Answer: A file sharing happens between network users to transfer files from one system to another one over the network. This method can slow down network traffic if large files are in process to download. If file sharing is happening between two network users where a files server is not involved such file sharing is called peer-to-peer sharing.

Question: What is a printer sharing?

Answer: The printer sharing is a way to share printer resources over the network. The network users must be configured properly to share printer resources.

Question: What is a media sharing?

Answer: A media sharing happens between two or more network users who share media files across the network.

Chapter 7 – Keyboard Shortcuts

Topics covered in this chapter:

- General Windows Logo Key Shortcuts
- Control Key, Alternative Key, Shift key, and Function Key Shortcuts
- Windows General Microsoft Office Shortcuts
- Control Panel Shortcuts
- Command Prompt
- System File Utility

General Windows Logo Key Shortcuts

A standard keyboard is designed to open some of the Windows applications with holding down the Windows logo key, the ALT key, the CTRL key, or the Shift key with the combination of another key to lunch an application which is listed below in table.

Application Name	Keyboard Shortcuts
Display Windows Help	Windows logo Key + F1
Display Windows Sidebar	Windows logo Key + Spacebar
Ease of Access Center	Windows logo Key + U
Lock and/or log-off the System	Windows logo Key + L
Maximize all open Applications	Windows logo Key + Shift + M
Minimize all open Applications	Windows logo Key + M
Quick Access Toolbar Shortcuts	Windows logo Key + 1, 2, 3, 4……
Run Dialog Box	Windows logo Key + R
Search Computer	Ctrl + Windows Logo Key + F
Search Files and Folder	Windows logo Key + F
Show Desktop	Windows logo Key + D
Systems Properties Window	Windows logo Key + Pause/Break Key
Windows Explorer	Windows logo Key + E
Windows Media Center (If supported)	Alt + Windows logo Key + Enter
Windows Mobility Center (If supported)	Windows logo Key + X
3D-Flip	Windows logo Key + Tab
3D-Flip (Persistent)	Ctrl + Windows logo Key + Tab

Control Key (CTRL), Alternative Key (ALT), Shift key, and Function Key Shortcuts

Application Name	Application Shortcuts
Bypass Recycle Bin for Deleted Items	Shift + Delete
Close Active Window	Alt + F4
Display Selected Folder Properties	Alt + Double-click
Find Files and Folder	F3
Minimize and Maximize Active Window	F11
Move Through the Items	Tab
Refresh Active Window	F5
Rename a Selected Item	F2
Start Menu	Ctrl + Esc
Switch Between Open Applications	Alt + Tab
Windows Help and Support	F1
Windows Media Center (If supported)	Alt + Windows logo Key + Enter
Windows Task Manager	Ctrl + Shift + Esc

Windows General Microsoft Office Shortcuts

Application Name	Application Shortcuts
Close the Document	Alt + F4
Close the Document	Ctrl + W
Cut Selected Text	Ctrl + X
Copy Selected Text	Ctrl + C
Cursor Beginning of the Next Word	Ctrl + Right Arrow
Cursor Beginning of the Previous Word	Ctrl + Left Arrow
Cursor Beginning of the Previous Paragraph	Ctrl + Up Arrow
Cursor Beginning of the Next Paragraph	Ctrl + Down Arrow
Cursor Top of the Document	Ctrl + Home
Cursor Bottom of the Document	Ctrl + End
Double Line Spacing	Ctrl + 2
Make Text Bold	Ctrl + B
Make Text Italic	Ctrl + I
Make Text Underline	Ctrl + U
Microsoft Office Help	F1
Open Existing Document	Ctrl + O
Open New Document	Ctrl + N
Print the Document	Ctrl + P
Past Copied Text	Ctrl + V
Redo an Action	Ctrl + Y

Application Name	Application Shortcuts
Save the Document	Ctrl + S
Save as	F12
Select all Text	Ctrl + A
Single Line Spacing	Ctrl + 1
Spelling Checker	F7
Thesaurus	Shift + F7
Undo an Action	Ctrl + Z

Control Panel Shortcuts

Windows applications can be launched by typing a command line in the search filed (*Windows logo key* + *R*). To open an application, type the desired command line of the application in run dialog box and then click on ***OK*** to launch the application.

Application Name	Application Shortcuts
Add Hardware Wizard	Hdwwiz.cpl
Add/Remove Programs	Appwiz.cpl
Administrative Tools List	Control Admintools
Appearance Settings	Control Color
Application Services	Services.msc
Application Data Folder	%Appdata%
Calculator	Calc
Certificate Manager	Certmgr.msc
Character Map	Charmap
Check Disk Utility	Chkdsk
Command Prompt (DOS-Window)	CMD
Component Services	Dcomcnfg
Computer Management Console	Compmgmt.msc
Control Panel	Control Panel
Date and Time	Timedate.cpl
Direct X Diagnostic Tool	Dxdiag
Device Manager	Devmgmt.msc
Disk Cleanup Options	Cleanmgr

Disk Management	Diskmgmt.msc
Disk Partition Manager	Diskpart
Display/Monitor Settings	Desk.cpl
Driver Verifier Manager	Verifier
Event Viewer	Eventvwr.msc
Firefox Browser (If available)	Firefox
Folders Properties	Control Folders
Group Policy Editor (If supported)	Gpedit.msc
Home Directory	%Homepath%
Home Directory Drive	%Homedrive%
IExpress Wizard	Iexpress
Internet Explorer Browser	Iexplore
Internet Properties	Inetcpl.cpl
Keyboard Properties	Control Keyboard
Local Security Settings	Secpol.msc
Local Users and Groups (If Supported)	Lusrmgr.msc
Log-off the System	Logoff
Microsoft Excel Document	Excel
Microsoft Malicious Software Removal Tool	Mrt
Microsoft Movie Maker	Moviemk
Microsoft Outlook	Outlook

Application Name	Application Shortcuts
Microsoft Paint	Mspaint
Microsoft Paint	Pbrush
Microsoft PowerPoint	Powerpnt
Microsoft Synchronization Tool	Mobsync
Microsoft Word Document	Winword
Mouse Properties	Control Mouse
Network Connections	Control Netconnections
Notepad	Notepad
On-screen Keyboard	Osk
Performance Monitor	Perfmon
Phone and Modem Options	Telephon.cpl
Power Options	Powercfg.cpl
Printers and Faxes	Control Printers
Program Files and Folder	%Programfiles%
Regional and Language Options	Intl.cpl
Registry Editor	Regedit
Remote Desktop Connection	Mstsc
Restart the System	Shutdown –r
Shared Folders	Fsmgmt.msc
Shared Home Directory	%Homeshare%
Shutdown the System	Shutdown

Sounds and Audio Properties	Mmsys.cpl
SQL Server Client Configuration	Cliconfg
System Configuration Editor	Sysedit
System Configuration Utility	Msconfig
System Information	Msinfo32
System Properties	Sysdm.cpl
Task Manager	Taskmgr
Task Scheduler	Control Schedtasks
Temporary Folder	%Temp%
Windows Account Security	Syskey
Windows Address Book	Wab
Windows Address Book Import Utility	Wabmig
Windows Directory	%Windir%
Windows Easy Transfer Tool	Migwiz
Windows Firewall	Firewall.cpl
Windows Magnifier	Magnify
Windows Media Player	Wmplayer
Windows Narrator	Narrator
Windows Root Directory	%Windir%
Windows Root Drive	%Systemdrive%
Windows Security Center	Wscui.cpl
Windows Version	Winver

Command Prompt

Command prompt (DOS-Window) is a command based interface to configure Internet Protocol (IP) addresses if needed. System administrators often use command prompt window to resolve network issues by typing one of the following suggested command lines. To open the command prompt window, open ***Run*** dialog box (*Windows logo key + R*) and type ***CMD*** in the search bar and then click on ***OK***.

Application Name	**Application Command**
Address Resolution Protocol Cache Table	Arp –a
Display DNS Cache	Ipconfig/displaydns
Display Connection Configuration	Ipconfig/all
Domain Name Server	Nslookup
Flush DNS Cache	Ipconfig/flushdns
Path Ping (IP Trace Utility)	Pathping [IP address of the host computer]
Ping the Client/Server Machine	Ping [IP address of the host/server]
Release all Network Connections	Ipconfig/release
Renew all Network Connections	Ipconfig/renew
TCP/IP Networking Statistics	Netstat
Windows IP Configuration	Ipconfig
End Currently Running Application	Ctrl +C

System File Utility

System file checker utility can be run in command prompt (DOS-Window) to fix suspected problem with Windows Vista system files. If the system files have been modify or deleted by a third-party and changes needs to be reverted, open ***Run*** dialog box, and type ***CMD*** in search bar and then click on ***OK*** to open command prompt. In the command prompt, type one of the following scan command lines to run the scan to repair the system files.

Application Name	Application Command
Scan Immediately	Sfc/scannow
Scan on Next Boot	Sfc/scanonce
Scan on Every Boot	Sfc/scanboot
Cancel Pending Scans	sfc/cancel
Default System Settings	Sfc/revert
Purge File Cache	Sfc/purgecache
Set Cache Size	Sfc/cachesize = X (X represents any number)
Scans System Files	Sfc/verifyonly
Check Disk	Chkdsk
Locate and Recover Bad Sectors of Hard Drive	Chkdsk/r
Close Command Prompt	Exit
Stop Currently Running Process	Ctrl + C

A
Account Lockout Counter, P230
Account Lockout Threshold, P230
Account Types, P108, P258, P259
Active Directory, P58, P274
Active Directory Repair, P274
Add Registry Key, P242
Additional Clocks, P217
Add-ons, P144, P147, P148, P149, P150
Administrator Account, P258, P259
Allow & Block Specific Programs,P76, P78
Allowed Sites, P145
Alternate Shell, P274
Alternative Input Language, P214
APIPA, P281, P 282
Application Log, P284
Application Services, P272, P273, P275
Approved Websites, P151, P152
Audio Devices, P188
Audit, P231-234, P238-239
Auto Complete, P154
Automatic Updating, P36, P42, P206-207
B
Backup Files, P99—100, P102, P104
Balanced Power Plan, P105-106
Base Score, P75-76, P129
Base Score Range, P129
Base Video, P274
BCD, P66
Binary Data, P245
BIOS, P86, P130
BitLocker Drive Encryption, P21, P86, P87, P130
Block or Allow Specific Games, P77-78
Blocked Sender List, P119
Bluetooth Printer, P191
Boot Configuration, P66, P273-274
B
Boot Log, P274
Boot System Configuration, P273
Broadband, P224, P252
Browser History, P144
Browser Homepage, P136
Built-in Administrator Account, P279
Burn DVD, P187
C
Calendar Details, P185
Classic Start Menu, P178, P222
Clicklock, P202, P223
Clipboard, P251
CMD, P291
COM, P192
Command Prompt, P295
Compatibility Wizard, P210
Complete PC Backup, P103
Computer Theme, P199
Computer Themes, P199
Content Advisor, P150, P158
Content Level Rating, P150
Content Ratings, P151, P158
Cookies, P137, P157
Currently Running Programs, P84
Custom (advanced), P33, P69
Custom Scan, P81
D
Daylight Savings Time, P216
Delete Partition, P49
Delete Volume, P49
Desktop Background, P197
Device Driver, P165, P220
Device Manager, P163, P220
DHCP, P266, P282
Diagnose and Repair, P268
Diagnostic Startup Mode, P273

Directory Services, P108, P274
Disapproved Websites, P152
DNS Server, P266-268
Domain, P21, P58, P71-72
DOS Window, P161, P179, P283
Dot Net Framework 3.0, P66, P93
Download Images, P115
DPI, P200-201, P223
DVD playback, P187
E
Ease of Access Center, P218-219, P162
EFS, P66
E-mail Accounts, P108-109
Encoding List, P120
Event Viewer, P233, P247, P276, P292
Existing Solutions, P125
Extend Hard Drive Partition, P48
F
FAT, P52, P92, P132
Feed Contents, P155-159
File Sharing, P263, P270, P279, P284-285
Filter Level, P154-146, P157
Firewall, P133-134, P206-209, P223-224
First-party cookies, P140-141, P157
Full Scan, P44, P81
G
Gadgets, P89-91, P131
Game Ratings, P77-78
Gateway, P191, P253-254, P266, P277-278
Generic Network Card, P193
GPO, P226, P247, P277
Guest Account, P279-280
GUI boot, P274
H
Hard Disk Partition, P47-49
Hard Drive Driver, P46
Hardware and Sound Applet,
P188, P191, P195, P197-198, P201-209
Hibernation Mode, P67
Hidden Windows Features, P93, P132
High Performance Power plan, P103
HKCC, P236
HKCR, P235
HKCU, P235
HKLM, P235
HKU, P236
HTTPS, P253
Hypertext Transfer Protocol over, P253
Secure Socket Layer, P253
I
ICRA3, P150, P158
IIS, P68
IMAP, P108, P116
Incoming Mail Server, P108
Internet Browser, P136
Internet Explorer, P136
Internet Explorer Add-ons, P159
Internet Explorer Browser, P 136
Internet Explorer Privacy, P140
Internet Information Server, P68
Internet Time Server, P217
IP Address, P266, P281
IPsec, P281
IPV4, P282
IPV6, P282
J
Junk Mail, P118
K
Key Name, P243
Key Value Data, P245
Keyboard Configuration, P203, P219
Keyboard Mode, P172, P221
L
LAN, P252
Language Pack, P138
Legacy Hardware, P167

Local Area Network, P58, P267-268, P280
Local Intranet, P140, P143
Local Network Types, P265-266
Local Printer, P191-192, P222
Local Resources, P251
Local Security Policy, P226
Local User Account, P202, P223, P227,P258-259,P261,P269
Loopback Adaptor, P283
LPT, P192, P222
M
Magnifier, P218, P294
Mail Message Rules, P117
Maintain Printer, P197
Malware Protection, P206
Managed Websites, P142-143
Maximum Password Age, P226-227
Media Sharing, P263, P268, P271-272
Memory Diagnostics Tool, P98
Message Threads, P116
Microsfot Vista Home Edition, P71, P249
Microsoft SpyNet Membership, P71, P81
Microsoft Vista Premium Edition, P72
Minimum Password Length, P226, P228
Modem, P188, P191, P224, P252, P293
Mouse Configuration, P 201
Mouse Cursor Visibility, P203
Msconfig, P272, P294
N
N version, P69
Narrator, P218, P219, P224, P294
Network Adapters, P164
Network Discovery, P263, P271, P284
Network Location Type, p265-266
Network Sharing, P263
Network Type, P281
New Appointment, P181
New Meeting, P96
New Solutions, P124
New Task, P182
Newsgroup, P117
Newsgroup Message Rule, P117
Normal Startup Mode, P273
NTFS, P66, P103
O
On-Screen Keyboard, P219
OS Boot Information, P274
Outgoing E-mail Server, P110
Outlook Express, P108
Ownership Effective Permissions, P241
P
Parental Controls, P76, P129
Password Complexity Requirements, P227
Password Protected Sharing, P270
People Near Me, P95, P134
Per Site Privacy, P142
Perfmon /Report, P99
Phishing, P160
Phishing Filter, P36, P120, P146
Phone and Modem, P191
Plug-and-Play, P167, P221
Pointer Configuration, P202
Point-to-Point Protocol, P284
POP3, P108
Pop-up Blocker, P145
Power Button, P106
Power Saver, P105
Power Management, P105
Power Saver, P105
Print Appointments, P183
Print Registry Key, P243
Printer Ports, P195
Printer Sharing, P269
Private Network, P266, P281
Problem Reports and Solutions Tool, P123

Protected Mode, P160
Public Network, P37, P43, P266, P283
Publish Calendar, P184

Q

Quick Scan, P81

R

RDC, P256, P277-278
RDP, P224, P250, P253, P278
Reading Messages, P112
Ready Boost, P92-93, P132
Real-Time Monitoring Report, P98-99
Real-Time Protection, P82-83
Recurrence, P181
Regional and Language Options, P213
Registry Editor, P234, P247, P293
Registry Key Owner, P240
Reliability and Performance, P99
Reminder, P180, P182
Remote Desktop, P21, P224, P249-256, P277-279, P293
Remote Desktop Connection Port, P256
Remote Desktop Size, P251
Requesting Read Receipts, P113
Restore Files, P101-103
Restricted Sites, P115, P140, P143, P157
Returning Read Receipts, P113
Reversible Encryption, P226, P227, P229
Roll Back Driver, P167
RSS, P155, P157-159
RSS Feed Contents, P159
Run Command, P179-180, P222

S

Safe Senders List, P118, P119
Scanners and Cameras, P204
Screen Rate, P198
Screen Resolution, P198
Screen Saver, P200, P223
Search Registry Key, P242
Secure Mail, P115
Security Center, P206
Security Identifer, P67
Security Log, P284
Selective Startup Mode, P273
Send /Receive Messages, P111
Server Authentication, P253
Shared Resources, P268
Sharing Desktop, P97
Sharing Programs, P97
SID, P67
Signature, P122
Sleep Mode, P67
Smart Card, P254
SMTP, P110
Snipping Tool, P127
Sound Scheme, P190
Sound Volume, P188
Span Multiple Monitors, P278
SRT, P67
SSL, P253
Standard User Account, P258
Standard User Rights,P67
Standby Mode, P66
Start Menu, P19
Starter Version, P69
Start-up Items, P91
Start-up Options, P91
Start-up Programs, P84
Startup Services, P275
Supervisor Password, P150, P152
Synchronize Internet Time, P217
Syndicated Content, P158
System Configuration, P272
System File Utility, P296
System Tools, P276
System Wakeup Password, P107

T
Table PC Input Panel, P221
Task Manager, P174,P222, P288, P294
Taskbar, P174, P222
TCP, P281, P295
TCP/IP Port, P192
Temporary Internet Files, P137, P161
Terminal Services Gateway, P253, P277
Third-party Cookies, P140, P157
Time and Date, P215-216
Top-level Domains, P108, P120
TPM, P86, P130
Trusted Sites, P140, P143
TS Gateway, P253, P277
Two CPU Support, P72
U
UAC, P261, P280
Upgrade Advisor, P27-31, P40, P68
User Account Control, P226, P261, P280
User Account Password, P259-260
User Account Types, P280
User Accounts, P258
User Permission, P236-237
User State Migration Tool, P65
Userpasswords2, P262
USMT, P65
V
Virus Protection, P115
Visited Pages History, P138
W
WDDM, P22-23, P63-64, P128
Web Site Fonts, P139
Website Contents Permission, P153
W
Welcome Center, P74
Windows Aero, P63, P128
Windows Calendar, P180, P220
Windows Contacts, P122-123
Windows Defender, P79
Windows Defender Updates, P80
Windows DVD Maker, P186, P222
Windows Easy Transfer, P64
Windows Easy Transfer cable, P65
Windows Experience Improvement, P127
Windows Experience Index (WEI), P75
Windows Explorer, P20, P64
Windows Logo key, P287
Windows Mail, P108
Windows Meeting Space, P94, P133
Windows Product Activation, P72
Windows Remote Assistance, P256, P279
Windows Sidebar, P89-92, P130
Windows Sidebar Startup, P91
Windows Start Menu, P19, P176, P222
Windows Starter, P134
Windows Update Options, P35, P42
Windows Updates, P40, P206-207, P210
Windows Vista Capable PC, P22, P63
Windows Vista Capable PC hardware, P22
Windows Vista Clean Installation, P49
Windows Vista Premium Ready PC, P63
Windows Vista Upgrade, P27, P39, P68
WPA, P72

www.ingramcontent.com/pod-product-compliance
Lightning Source LLC
Chambersburg PA
CBHW080355060326
40689CB00019B/4025
* 9 7 8 1 4 3 9 2 1 9 1 2 6 *